BEST
NEBRASKA
TEEN
WRITING

2025

BEST
NEBRASKA
TEEN
WRITING

2025

 Hastings College Press | Hastings, Nebraska

ISBN: 978-1-942885-95-5

Contents

flash fiction

short story

novel writing

poetry

dramatic script

critical essay

personal essay & memoir

humor

journalism

senior portfolio

INTRODUCTION

As an Affiliate Partner of the Alliance for Young Artists & Writers, Hastings College is honored to celebrate the winners of the 2025 Nebraska Scholastic Writing Awards. We invited students age 13 and above from all 93 counties within the state of Nebraska to submit their writing in one of ten categories, such as Critical Essay, Poetry, and Short Story. Graduating seniors also had the option of submitting a Writing Portfolio, a collection of works that demonstrate the writer's technical versatility. All of this year's 162 submissions were read and scored by a jury of Hastings College faculty, staff, and students. The original work featured in this publication showcases the creativity of our Gold Key, Silver Key, and Honorable Mention award recipients.

The Scholastic Art & Writing Awards program, established in 1923 by Maurice R. Robinson, the founder of Scholastic Inc., identifies teenagers with exceptional artistic and literary talent and brings their remarkable work to a national audience. All works are blindly adjudicated based on originality, technical skill, and the emergence of personal vision or voice, first on a regional level by more than 100 local affiliates of the Alliance, and then nationally by an impressive panel of industry experts. Students at the regional level are awarded an Honorable Mention, Silver Key, or Gold Key distinction. Gold Key work then advances to national adjudication to receive Gold Medals or Silver Medals. Each region also nominates works for American Voices & Visions Medals, the highest regional honor.

Annually, the Alliance partners with individuals, foundations, and corporations to offer scholarship opportunities for students in certain categories or addressing particular themes. National Medalists' works are published in national publications and on the Alliance's website, artandwriting.org. Select writing is published in *The Best Teen Writing* annual anthology. The Alliance strives to teach young students to develop a strong creative capacity along with celebrating the role of art and literature in society.

Dr. Pedro Vizoso
Hastings College
Hastings, NE

SCIENCE FICTION & FANTASY

THE EMERALD DAGGER

EMMA BALDEH

Grade 11, Dundy County Stratton High School, Benkelman, NE.
Emily Cameron, Educator.

It had been 32 years since anyone had visited the Witch's Hut.

To most, the Hut was nothing more than a myth, a cautionary tale mothers told their children to keep them in bed at night. They spoke of crumbling stone walls deep within the mountains, of twisted trees, and of the woman who had been sent to live there in exile.

But Rhyene knew the hut was real. Her mind was set. There was no turning back now, not after what she had decided to do.

The witch's lair was hidden deep within the woods, far beyond the borders of the kingdom where no one dared to venture. It was said that her magic was corrupt, untamed.

But that was exactly what Rhyene needed.

She stopped in front of a small hut, sunken into the Earth. Vines wound tightly around the walls, choking the structure, and the roof sagged beneath its own weight. The door hung askew, wood swollen from years of damp. She hesitated, one hand brushing the hilt of the dagger she carried—a thin, pathetic thing, the kind noblewomen were given for ceremony rather than combat.

A creak broke the silence as she pushed the door open. The air inside was dense with the scent of dried herbs—rosemary, perhaps, or sage—and something metallic, sharp enough to bite the back of her throat.

A woman sat by the hearth, back to Rhyene. Her voice came before her face. "I knew you would come."

The witch slowly turned around. She was old, skin stretched tight over sharp bones. She smiled, showing teeth far too white and sharp for someone so seemingly ancient.

Rhyene lingered in the doorway. The witch's smile grew into something pointed. "Come inside, girl. You are the first visitor I've had in a long time." Her voice drew Rhyene forward like a hook embedded in her chest.

Rhyene nodded slightly as she stepped inside.

"What is it you seek?" the witch asked, not unkindly.

Rhyene bit the inside of her cheek. "There is—someone I want to be rid of. Someone I want gone."

The witch cocked a brow. "Rid of *who*, girl?"

"Gedeon." Rhyene spoke the name no louder than a whisper. Even the air stilled as if it were leaning close for an answer.

"Who is this *Gedeon* you speak of?"

"You must know. The firstborn child and only son of King Dolion and Queen Lirianne. My brother."

"You want what he has—what you think he doesn't deserve?"

"What I want is for him to be *dead*," she said, voice hardening.

The witch stood up from her seat and shuffled to a cabinet swaying along the wall—every surface was cluttered with strange objects: beads threaded with strands of hair, dried feathers woven into brittle cords, and cracked beakers with faded powders. She flung open the doors and fiddled through the contents until she turned, pleased. In her hand rested a small vial. "Here. Only a drop in your brother's drink and he will be gone before—"

"No."

The witch's lips quirked. "You are refusing my gift?"

"I want to *feel* it. I want to see the life leave him." Rhyene straightened her back, lifted her chin. "I want a weapon. Though I fear I may not have the strength to—"

The witch's laughter echoed through the dark hut. With a flick of her wrist, she conjured a gleaming emerald dagger—a weapon with an ornate hilt and a blade that glimmered green. Rhyene reached for it, the blade feeling impossibly light.

"Of course, that is no ordinary dagger. The blade will find its mark only when you see the truth," the witch continued. "You must know that every bargain has its price—"

"I'll pay it. Whatever it is, I'll pay." Rhyene reached for the coin bag in her cloak.

The witch stilled a moment. "I want your eyes."

Rhyene blinked. "My-my eyes?"

"I wish to see what you see. You will be my window into the world beyond this cursed forest. While I remain in exile, you will be my eyes in the kingdom."

"You want to see *through* me?"

The witch nodded slyly. "You will walk the halls of the castle, sit at the throne, look upon the kingdom, and all the while, I will see it too. I will be with you, always. And in return, I will help you—*dispose* of your brother."

Rhyene swallowed hard. "Fine. You may have my eyes."

The witch moved swiftly, bony fingers gripping Rhyene's jaw, breath hot against her skin. "Then it is done."

Rhyene's vision blurred for a moment, a searing pain shooting through her skull. She gasped, stumbling backward, hands clutching her head as the world around her twisted and darkened. When her vision cleared, everything looked unnatural.

The witch stepped back, satisfied. "Now, go to your brother. Let me see what you see."

◇◇◇◇◇◇◇◇◇◇◇◇◇◇◇◇◇◇◇◇◇◇◇◇◇◇

The castle loomed on the horizon, towers clawing at the gray sky like skeletal fingers. The walls were as familiar to her as her own reflection, yet now, they felt different, distorted. Colors were too vibrant, edges too sharp, as though the world had been polished to an unbearable gleam. She entered the castle, moving swiftly through the corridors.

A voice cut through the air.

"Have you seen Rhyene? She was supposed to be at the banquet now, but I was hoping to speak with her before—"

Her brother's voice.

The *banquet*. She had forgotten.

"—she does not know what's coming. She never does—"

Rhyene stood frozen. The witch's voice entered her mind.

He doesn't see you, does he? Not as you are. Rhyene clenched her jaw, pushing the voice aside as she turned toward her chambers. When she was dressed, she turned toward the mirror. The gown clung to her frame, the color bringing out the subtle gleam of her eyes. They had turned green after her deal with the witch.

And she liked them. She liked them a lot. The way they seemed to shimmer and sparkle, glowing with every beat of her heart—they quite suited her.

Rhyene took a deep breath, striding to the door. When she reached the banquet hall, two guards pushed them open, revealing the scene inside. The room was filled with nobles gathered around long tables with food and drink.

Gedeon sat at the far end of the room, smiling as he spoke. His easy laughter reached Rhyene's ears, and she felt her blood boil. She took her place at the table, sitting across from Gedeon. He barely glanced at her.

You could do it now, the witch's voice whispered. *Slide the dagger into his side.* No one would even notice, not until it was too late.

Her mother's voice drowned out the witch. "Rhyene, Lord Keres was just asking if you've had the chance to see the new stables."

Rhyene swallowed, forcing herself to focus. Lord Keres was watching her intently, waiting for a response. She gave a tight smile. "No, I haven't yet."

"Ah, you must!" Lord Keres said, his voice too eager. "I've always thought a true noble ought to appreciate the art of fine equine care."

"Art, yes," Rhyene replied, her tone flat. "But a horse is a horse, my lord."

He blinked, caught off guard, and she could see the moment he regained his composure. "A pragmatic view. But I assure you, each horse has its own story, its own spirit. I would be honored to show you."

"I imagine they're lovely," she said, glancing to where Gedeon was deep in conversation. He hadn't acknowledged her once since the banquet began.

The hall fell silent, and her father stood, raising his glass. "I have an announcement."

Rhyene glimpsed at Gedeon, who finally met her gaze with a knowing look in his. When was the last time he'd made the effort to speak with her? How long had it been since he'd looked at her—*really* looked at her?

"We are pleased to announce the betrothal of my daughter, Rhyene, to Lord Keres of Delmore," her father declared.

Rhyene didn't look away from Gedeon. He only pursed his lips.

He *knew*. Of course, he knew. Yet here he was, at ease. As if her life being sealed away in some distant marriage was nothing to him.

She remembered the witch's words—the blade would only strike true when she saw the truth. And what truth was there? That he had what she never could?

Finally, Gedeon pushed back his chair and rose from his seat. He moved with a grace that always unnerved her.

She stood quickly and began following him. No one seemed to notice—they never did—as she slipped out of the banquet hall. She caught sight of Gedeon's figure as he disappeared down a corridor.

This is it, Rhyene. Do not hesitate.

Ahead, Gedeon pushed open a door leading out into the courtyard. He walked with a deliberate pace, as though he knew she would follow.

The door closed behind her, and they were alone in the cool night air. Gedeon paused by a fountain, staring down into the rippling water.

"I know you're there, Rhyene." Gedeon's voice broke through the silence, calm and unhurried. He didn't turn to her, still focusing on the water. "Why are you following me?"

Rhyene's breath hitched, but she forced herself to take a step forward. "We need to talk."

Gedeon turned slowly, and though he appeared fine, there was something in his face—tiredness, perhaps. Or maybe he had always worn that look and she had never noticed before.

"About what?" His tone was neutral, neither cold nor warm.

She swallowed, the words she had been rehearsing in her mind dissolving under his presence. "Why didn't you tell me?"

His brow furrowed, though only slightly. "Tell you what?"

"About this. The betrothal. Everything. You knew, didn't you?"

He didn't speak for a moment. "I did."

"And you said nothing?"

"What would you have me say?" Gedeon asked, his voice measured, careful. "This was decided long ago."

"That doesn't make it right," she spat. "This will ruin me."

"It won't."

"And how would you know? You've always been untouched by any of it."

Gedeon's expression suddenly shifted; he tilted his head. "Your eyes. They're different."

Rhyene's throat tightened. "It doesn't matter," she said quickly, taking another step toward him. "What matters is what I'm going to do."

Gedeon frowned. "What do you mean?"

Now. Do it now.

Rhyene gritted her teeth, her fingers trembling around the dagger. "You've taken everything from me, Gedeon."

His eyes widened slightly. "What are you talking about? I—"

"You did!"

"Rhyene, I never asked for any of this."

Her breath came in gasps now. The witch's voice grew louder, feeding her fury. *He's lying. He always has. End it now, Rhyene.*

She lunged at him.

But Gedeon was faster than she expected. He knocked her arm aside, the dagger clattering to the ground between them. The force of his strike sent her stumbling backward.

For a moment, neither of them moved.

Gedeon stared at her, his chest rising and falling rapidly. "Rhyene, what have you done?"

Her fury drained away as quickly as it had come. She looked down at the dagger, lying motionless on the cold stone. The witch's voice was silent now, leaving only the sound of her own breathing.

Gedeon sighed, expression softening, though not with pity—something closer to regret. "I was going to leave."

"Leave?"

"I was going to leave tonight," he continued. "I didn't want to tell you like this, but Mother and Father—they had other plans for you. They don't—"

"Don't what?"

"Rhyene." He placed a hand on his forehead. "They don't care about your future."

"What do you mean?"

Gedeon exhaled slowly. "Mother and Father—they've aligned with King Fenon. They were going to send you to Delmore under the guise of this betrothal, and once you arrived—you wouldn't return."

Rhyene's breath stilled. "They—planned to kill me?"

Gedeon's jaw tightened. "They were going to blame it on the lords of Delmore. Your death would spark the war they've been craving for years."

"And you just stood by? Knowing this?"

"I was going to take you with me today. Away from here. Away from all of them. But there wasn't time to tell you—"

"There wasn't time?" Rhyene's voice cracked. "There was *always* time, Gedeon. You just didn't care."

"Care? I've been trying to protect you. Do you think any of this has been easy?"

For the first time, she saw the strain in his face, the weariness behind his gaze. "Then why didn't you tell me the truth? Why let me think you were just—*laughing*, enjoying all of it?"

"Because I had no choice! Do you think they don't watch me too? Do you think I haven't been trapped? Every move I make, every word I say—I thought if I could find a way out for both of us, quietly, we'd be safe."

Rhyene felt her lip quiver, felt the pressure build behind her eyes. "No, they wouldn't, they *couldn't*—"

"Rhyene," Gedeon said, his voice almost pleading. "We can still run. We can leave tonight, together."

She shook her head. "Where would we go?"

"To Hirath," he answered without hesitation. "I know people who owe me favors, people who could keep us out of sight of King Fenon, of Mother and Father. We could disappear."

"We leave tonight?"

For the first time in a long while, a genuine smile tugged at his lips. "Together."

But then, something shifted. The warmth in Gedeon dimmed.

It is done.

Gedeon's smile faltered, his lips parting as if to say something, but no words came. A sharp breath escaped him instead, and his body stiffened.

"Gedeon?"

He gasped, stumbling forward. His knees buckled, and in a terrifying instant, he collapsed onto the cold stone.

"Gedeon, what's wrong? Talk to me," Rhyene cried, dropping to her knees beside him. She reached out, her hands trembling as she cradled his face.

His breaths were shallow and labored. "Rhyene," he rasped. "Run. To the coast. To Hirath."

His eyelids fluttered, struggling to focus, then fell shut. Panic surged through her as the life left her brother. "No, no, no," she whispered frantically. She looked to the ground where the emerald dagger had fallen earlier.

But it was gone.

And so was Gedeon.

The blade will only find its mark when you see the truth.

◇◇◇◇◇◇◇◇◇◇◇◇◇◇◇◇◇◇◇◇◇◇◇◇◇◇◇◇

So she ran.

She ran until the ache in her legs threatened to bring her to her knees. She ran until the world blurred around her. She ran for Gedeon, for the betrayal of the witch, for the lies of her parents. She ran until she collapsed on the coast.

Rhyene. The witch's voice slithered back into her mind, coiling around her thoughts.

"Go away!" Rhyene screamed, the wind swallowing her voice as she pressed her hands to her ears, as if that could block out the witch.

I gave you exactly what you asked for. You wanted the truth. And you wanted power. You cannot have one without the other, girl.

"Then take it back!" she demanded. "Bring him back!"

The moment you made the deal, his fate was sealed.

"No—"

It is not too late to claim what is yours.

"Claim what?" she seethed. "Everything has been taken from me. There's nothing left."

You are wrong. Let me in, the witch urged, *her voice more insistent now. I can make you whole. Together, we will take everything. All you need to do is let go of who you once were. Become something greater.*

A gust of wind whipped across the shore, salt stinging Rhyene's skin. She wanted to fight it, to run.

But there was nothing left to run to.

And with her last bit of strength, she let go, and lept into the ocean.

<hr />

The waves crashed against the jagged, weathered rocks, their relentless force pulling the girl's limp body closer and closer to the shore.

The girl should have been dead. She should have been a lot of things.

As the receding waters released their grip, the girl's body lay still. In that fragile moment, her chest began to rise and fall with short, shallow breaths, gradually lengthening into a steady rhythm. Her eyes opened.

They were green. Green, the color of trees and bright emeralds and the shallow parts of sea when the sun hits them just right.

The color of envy.

Green eyes so bright they seemed to glow; even the girl herself seemed to be radiating. And though the girl seemed young, her eyes held something old, something ancient in them.

Something *other.*

Awakening, the girl was disoriented, but she knew one thing for certain: she was now far from home.

Narrow, nondescript buildings lined the roads, their muted hues of beige, brown, and gray blending into the unremarkable landscape. The kingdom was simple, dull, and underwhelming. With each step she took, the girl fixated on the towering silhouette of a castle in the distance. So many fresh, untouched minds littering the streets.

Yes, she could get used to this.

Footprints in the Stardust

Emma Baldeh

Grade 11, Dundy County Stratton High School, Benkelman, NE. Emily Cameron, Educator. Honorable Mention.

That night, stardust fell from the heavens, which meant one thing to Ariad: escape.

She pounded through the woods, bare feet completely covered in stardust. Each droplet sparkled like a tiny, radiant gem; each cast a soft, iridescent glow as it descended from the moonlit sky. They settled on the forest floor, creating a delicate carpet of light. Leaves became frosted with silvery brilliance and blades of grass sparkled like a myriad of tiny stars.

The humans gorged themselves on stardust, so drunk on power that they didn't notice Ariad slinking away into the night.

And although it was a beautiful sight, Ariad had no time to focus on such things. She needed to get to the Eastern Border before the Nightstalkers found her—or another creature that could grant her a worse fate.

Through the glimmering rain, Ariad spotted a clearing in the distance. Ahead, a quaint building nestled between two towering Notespine Trees, whose leaves sang songs of sorrow. As the structure drew nearer, she read three letters hastily carved into the side of the building: INN. The building was small, its wooden planks covered in moss. The roof was a patchwork of wooden shingles and thatches of straw, while a lone wooden door stood as the sole entrance.

A black figure stood atop the roof.

The creature was perched there, its hauntingly brilliant eyes fixated on Ariad with a deep hunger. Ariad's wings twitched; she didn't have enough magic to fight the creature and win.

The beast's form lurked forward. It had no defined shape, but rather a form cloaked in an ebony shroud that was soft around the edges. Its eyes emitted a green glow, which cut through the glow of the stardust.

The creature lunged at her. In an instant, it vanished into the very shadows it seemed to be made of, only to reappear behind her. Its cold, bony claws extended, and with a dreadful screech, it attempted to strike her. Ariad barely managed to evade the attack, wings warming with magic under her cloak.

Once again, the creature melded into the darkness and out of Ariad's sight. She threw herself at the inn, furiously beating her fists against the door, waiting for someone—anyone to save her. The creature materialized behind her and pinned her body to the door. Ariad could see the beast's face up closer now—its mouth full of rows and rows of razor-sharp teeth, the two pits of green that seemed to freeze her in place.

No. This was not how it was supposed to end. Ariad should've made it to the border. She should've—

A blazing light broke through the core of the creature; it clawed against Ariad's cloak, clinging to its last bit of life. The flames hissed and sizzled until the creature was gone.

In the monster's place stood a gangly woman with tawny skin. The woman huffed out a breath and clapped her hands together, putting out the fire dancing between them.

The woman's gaze started from Ariad's shoeless feet and swept upward until they locked onto her cloaked head. Ariad recoiled when she remembered what a disheveled state she must be in. She tightened her cloak over her wings, pulled her sleeves over the markings on her wrists, and brushed away the stardust on her dress. Not that it mattered. The green garment she wore was tattered and dingy beyond repair.

It was an odd sensation, being able to move her arms wherever she pleased. Her wrists felt light, though they still bore the scars of chains.

"Thank you," Ariad breathed.

The woman stayed silent as she pushed the door behind Ariad open, revealing an underwhelming interior. On the walls hung Glowblossoms, each petal glowing a different shade of silver. The inside was bare, save for a wooden counter in the center of the empty inn. The woman walked behind the counter, made a sort of clucking sound with her tongue, and motioned for Ariad to come forward. *The innkeeper.*

"Well," the woman began, "what are you doing out on a night like this?"

Ariad focused her attention on the counter rather than the innkeeper's face. Her heart hammered against her chest. "I suppose I could ask you the same."

"Hm." The woman tapped her finger on the counter. "A group of men came knocking on my door a while ago, asking about a fairy of some sort. I was searching the area to take the fairy for myself."

All of the air left Ariad's lungs.

"And did you find the fairy?"

The innkeeper scoffed. "Look around you, girl. What business would a fairy have running around these parts?"

"What did you tell them—the group of men, I mean?"

"I hadn't seen any type of fairy—besides my own in-house ones, of course. I told them they'd find their little runaway soon. Even if a fairy did escape, they wouldn't be on the run very long; hardly any Glowblossoms grow in this area," she explained to Ariad as if she were a small child. "No Glowblossoms, no magic. They'd be caught before the next stardust."

Ariad could feel the heat rise to her cheeks, the magic flowing through her wings. "You are aware of how rare it is to find Glowblossoms, yet you have several put up as decoration." Ariad gestured toward the flowers on the wall. It disgusted her. Glowblossoms were a sacred plant, only used to power fairies' wing magic, not to be picked and pinned as some gaudy lighting.

The innkeeper tilted her head and narrowed her eyes, suddenly analyzing Ariad's demeanor. "They're for my fairies. I only channel wing magic; collecting stardust takes far too long."

Fairies. As in she had more than one fairy slave. One fairy could provide enough magic for the entire lifetime of a human. Multiple fairies created tyrants, dictators, rulers.

A young fairy with long locs emerged from behind the counter and changed a dim Glowblossom with a newly lit one. The fairy's wings were covered with Nullweave fabric, something invented to suppress wing magic. Ariad studied her, searching for the mark on her shackled wrists that would identify what kind of magic her wings held.

Her own slender wrists were adorned with white lines curving and coiling up to her shoulders. She was what the humans called Water Wings—powerful fairies who could manipulate water.

"I don't wish to speak of such things," Ariad said, eyes flitting to the fairy. To stay here would be a death sentence. This woman seemed to be a very powerful fairy holder; Ariad needed to distract her. "I am simply seeking shelter, and perhaps a warm meal if you have one to spare."

The innkeeper brushed a curl away from her gaunt face. "You seem to be in a hurry, my dear. Where are you coming from?"

Ariad cringed at the sudden softness of the innkeeper's voice.

"I visited the capital but I'm traveling back to the Eastern Border, and I wish to return before the next stardust. Could you provide me with directions or a map of some sort?"

"The border?" the woman's voice trailed off, brow furrowing. Ariad gave a slight nod; her cloak concealed the quiver in her wings. "Why, that's—" She stopped herself. "I'll get you a map."

The woman bore her eyes into Ariad's for a moment too long, and Ariad let the innkeeper break eye contact first. The woman chuckled, a low, unsettling sound, and retreated into a door behind the counter.

Ariad nearly leaped to the fairy the second the woman left, startling her with the sudden movement.

She spoke in a hushed tone. "I'm traveling back to the Homeland. I have a bit of wing magic left to guide us down the river to the Eastern Border. If you allow me to free you, I would like you to join me." The fairy stared at Ariad, confusion swimming in her eyes. "Hurry, we must leave this place. I'm a fairy, you see."

The young fairy gasped; she could not be older than 10. "You're a fairy? Oh no, miss, you must stay! The lady will be very pleased to hear this news, indeed."

Ariad's heart sank further as a thump sounded from behind the counter. Their time to flee was slipping away. "No, please listen—"

"What a wondrous day this is! The Gods have graced us with a fairy!" The fairy leaned in to hug Ariad.

Ariad pushed the girl off of her and grasped her thin shoulders. "We have but moments left—"

Something behind the counter creaked.

Ariad pulled the girl close and whispered a prayer in her ear.

The door behind the counter opened, and Ariad disappeared into the night once again.

<hr />

Reia knew that girl was a fairy the moment she stepped into her inn.

The young fairy would be a fine addition to their little refuge—no, it was more than a refuge—it was a *home*. A family.

Reia returned to the counter, a bowl of hot stew in hand, steam rising from the broth. She smiled to herself, the warmth of the inn settling into her bones. But very quickly, her gaze fell upon the empty space the fairy had stood just moments ago. The stew slipped from her hands and clattered onto the counter, the warmth in her chest turning to a cold dread.

Reia's eyes landed on Lilah, the young fairy, standing alone, eyes wide and trembling. Lilah opened her quivering lips. "She-she said she was a fairy too, but I didn't know, I—"

"No. No," Reia muttered to herself, voice barely louder than a whisper. Her heart pounded as she scanned the room. She dashed outside, feet moving faster than her thoughts.

But all that was left of the fairy was a trail of footprints in the stardust.

Everything Lives On

Eve Bishop

Grade 11, UNL Independent Study High School, Lincoln, NE. Honorable Mention.

Flowers ripple beneath the breeze, pliant against dewy sunlight, and the grass is cool beneath him. He feels his mother hum as gentle fingers run through his hair. She is kind as she holds him close the way she did when he was no taller than the grass surrounding them, and he feels memories flare up like old wounds, like forgotten scars.

(He must be dreaming again.)

He keeps his eyes closed and lets his mother sing her hymns of a long-forgotten past. She laughs, and he lets her bask in the warmth of the sun fluttering down from the unreachable heavens. The sun of his dreams is the real sun, for everything lives on when remembered. Everything lives on when one, naive and forgetful, is caught unaware. Everything lives on, even the sun, the *real* sun.

Her voice soothes the pain along his ribs, and when she rises, he cannot stop her. He stands to join her, but he is no taller than the grass surrounding him. Sharp blades of green cut into him, and the earth's roots wrap their tendrils around his limbs. He cries out as he is pulled down to his knees. After all, what is a boy worth when weighed against the world? His mother continues to sing her songs, *those damned hymns*, walking away. She never turns back. The sun bleeds out into the sky, drowning the world in crimson. Shadows run down his throat, and he chokes on the air that once gave him life. Fire runs across the field like a river cut free. A blazing winter arrives in the form of ash that falls from the embers of the sun. Everything lives on when remembered.

(Is this where he dies?)

Dirt begins filling his throat, and a startling jolt runs up his spine. He stares at the ceiling, trying to catch his breath. In his chest, his heart hammers away. His brows furrow as he sits up with a groan, his rib cage aching dully. The cold air digs into his skin when he stands and pulls on his uniform. On his way out the door, he does not bother looking in the mirror. He knows what he will find: dark hair, blue eyes, a mole on his cheekbone. His mother's inheritance.

She was selfish. What mother abandons her son, leaves him to die, for no fathomable reason?

He curses her memory.

(He misses her.)

It is spring when he steps into the field of flowers. It is always spring. The overseers see to it. Such is the decree of Her Majesty. A lavender-scented air trickles out from a vent somewhere, but if he closes his eyes long enough, he can convince himself that it is real. He cannot quite recall how the air smelled before the sun was born. He traces the sapphire sky with his eyes until it ends at the horizon. The sunlight from above is warm the way sunlight should be, and the people, naive and forgetful, accept it as such.

The ground's hum reverberates throughout his bones, and he stares at the tower that spirals up towards the sky like a serpent longing for wings. The clanging of bells sends a hush over the flowers. No doubt, at the precipice of the tower, the overseers gather before Her Majesty. They say she is benevolent and divine, wrathful and loving, but no one knows who sits at the throne. He thinks she is nothing but a mirage, but he does not mention it aloud when he makes his way to his assigned post.

Soldiers should not think. You are the sword and shield of Her Majesty, the sacrifice. You cannot protect us and think at the same time.

A cruel order, but an order nonetheless. Soldiers follow orders, guarding their posts and protecting the empire by laying down their lives. Soldiers should not think. Soldiers should not reminisce about days before the sun was born. Soldiers should feel neither resentment nor longing when they recall their mothers.

Yet he does. He stands at the ready, just out of arm's reach of the sky, and he thinks of his mother. He wonders if she likes spring and the scent of lavender and gentle breezes, wonders what makes her laugh and why she left. He wonders why she was selfish and if she loved him the way a mother should.

(He wonders if he loved her the way a son should.)

His grip tightens, and he grits his teeth. Pain burns along his ribs. His heavy breaths tighten the ache, and he suppresses the urge to scream. Bile froths at the back of his throat like a bitter friend crawling back to him. Yet he remains in place and focuses on his duty: to protect, without thinking, because *soldiers should not think.*

Yet he cannot help himself from feeling both resentment and longing.

He will go through the rest of the day thinking and feeling the way a soldier should not, even when sleep comes for him. Night will slither to him, wrapping around his throat and covering his eyes. Even then, he will see his mother.

He sighs and curses her memory.

(He misses her.)

When his eyes flutter open, he is greeted by the sight of countless flowers bending to the breeze's will. Soft grass tickles his cheek to usher him towards the dawn. Sunlight pours down, and peace settles over him like a quilt, easing his aching bones.

(He must be dreaming again.)

He hears his mother sing, and he hums along. Her footfalls echo through the earth. A smile spreads across his lips.

She is coming home.

He laughs the way a son would, and his heart is overwhelmed when he hears her own laughter. She laughs the way he thought she would. She laughs like a mother.

Standing to greet her, he reaches out his hands, but she is gone. A shadow runs over the field, rushing to envelop the gold. A weapon thrusts past his rib cage. He collapses to his knees, grasping the cold metal, and a gaping wound is left in his chest. Blood spills out of him, and a frenzied dizziness sinks behind his eyes. The sun bleeds crimson, and shadows tighten around his throat. He clutches the wound with red hands, and his mother sits before him. She has dark hair, blue eyes, a mole on her cheekbone.

She is beautiful.

His vision blackens like fading candlelight as his rib cage curves inward, and he can't breathe. She sings to soothe his pain, her hands cool as they hold his face. Her thumb strokes the scar on his cheek: an apology. Her hymns rise and fall with each breath, but there's a gaping hole in her chest. He watches her heart shiver, and there's so much red. He needs to help her, to stop the bleeding, to be the son he should be. He reaches out his hands, but he can't breathe, he can't breathe, *he can't breathe*.

(Is this where he dies?)

His mother smiles the way he thinks she would, *knows she would*, and she removes her hands from his face. Cold sweat drips down his neck as he chokes.

Her fingers, lithe and callused, dig into her chest and tear out her heart. The arteries tug away from her raw flesh with a creaking snap. Her heart, pulsing and shuddering, bleeds and bleeds. She tenderly pushes her heart into his chest, the way a mother would. Her life for his.

Blood sputters past her lips, but she is still smiling, teeth stained scarlet. She is still singing her songs, *those damned hymns*. Breath evades him, even with her heart beating in place of his own, and he cries out as she collapses into his arms. He is no taller than the smoldering grass surrounding him. The earth swallows them, and he can do nothing to stop it. After all, what is a boy worth when weighed against the world?

Roots claw down his throat, and he can't breathe. He can't breathe. He can't breathe. *He can't—*

He gasps hard. His room is cold, and, hacking on his spit, he chases the feeling of air in his lungs. Drenched in sweat, he wildly brings a hand up to his chest to feel around for a wound. There is none, only the frantic beating of his heart, *his own heart*.

Lying back down, he closes his eyes and curses his mother's memory.

(He misses her.)

The end of an era begins as soon as it is born. It weeps crimson as it falls to its knees, its ivory spine collapsing. Soldiers are pitted against one another to devour each other piece by piece, left to bleed out into a field of flowers. Celestial bodies commit murder against themselves, for all stars must die. The end of this era began when the sun was born.

It is spring when the people gather below the tower at the sounds of the bells to hear these words of a forbidden hymn, and he is among them. A woman stands in the middle of the crowd. Her voice is raw, as if she has never sung before, but no one seems to mind. They watch. They wait.

The hymn ends with the woman panting for breath. Her gaze flits to the serpentine tower. With clenched fists and a taut voice, she says her name is unimportant. He wants to laugh. When has anyone's name ever been considered *important*? She holds an air of stubborn self-righteousness, and under other circumstances, he might have thought she was beautiful.

(She looks like his mother.)

But soldiers don't think, and he knows he should arrest her for civil unrest. His eyes dart about the crowd. Others in uniform stand among the people, their eyes fixed upon the woman and their hands tightly gripping their weapons. When she begins to speak again in a voice from the old world, no one moves. As if she holds the air captive from their lungs, they watch.

She says we drink the sacrifice of our forefathers, and the sky, which is no sky at all, is gnawing itself away. We must grieve, she says, for soon the sun will die and we will be reminded that we are nothing more than sand in the hand of our ruler. She says our blood pulses with a heartbeat not our own. She says they immortalized the earth and that we must take up arms. We must tear down the high-strung stars from their place in the vast, empty sky. We must see the world for what it is. They will say we are ungrateful, but we must fight for our forefathers and our children alike. We must see the real sun, the sun before that abomination was born.

He thinks it odd how worked up everyone gets over her words. Even odder that he feels compelled to join in their rage. He wonders how many of them remember it, the days before the sun was born. How many, naive and forgetful, had accepted this sun?

She cries out once more that they took our past, our hymns, our mothers. *They took our mothers.* Her lips quiver as she passes judgment on the overseers, on Her Majesty.

The woman storms past the crowd with determination burning her gaze, and they follow her. Like a wildfire sparked alive, the blazing winter arrives with the coming of the nameless woman. She marches to the field's end and digs a weapon into the sky. An alarm goes off in a blaring panic, one resembling the beating of a heart. Sparks fly as the metal screeches and ruptures, and the people join her. The sky groans. Flickering and trembling, the sun goes out, and they break out of their cage.

Like old wounds, like forgotten scars, memories flare up again. Once more, he is no taller than the grass surrounding him. Pain ignites along his rib cage as his breath catches. Before him is a sun hung low in the gray sky, and it weeps crimson. Ashes surround the people crawling out. The earth shakes.

They will say we are ungrateful.

And they will be right. He is cold when he falls to his knees. The woman runs ahead of the crowd, searching for whatever she thought she might find.

He knows she does not when she screams at the sky and bitterly weeps. But how could she find it? It is dead.

But our hymns, she whispers. Our mothers. The shouts of the people overlap and rise into the heavens, whatever is left of it. He watches as the people begin to tear away at each other's throats.

The end of an era collapses into itself. It is spring.

Breath caught between his lips, sitting in silence, he wonders which sun is the real sun. Which one did his mother abandon him under? Everything lives on when remembered, when caught unaware. Everything lives on, and thus even the sun must live on. It must.

His fingers curl inward to crinkle the paper. The little black words stand proud on the page, marching with all the self-righteousness the margins can afford them. Arrogant, pedantic words. The truth, he supposes, or the closest thing to it. The overseers say that one cannot perceive divine things in the same light as mortal objects. The truth and Her Majesty are divine. Is the sun as well?

The overseers' truth, Her Majesty's truth, feels fragile between his fingertips. He holds his breath and reads it again, searching for answers between the vague prose. It is a hymn of the new world. Perhaps it is divine.

It says our forefathers' sacrifice molded the sky, so we mustn't grieve for the old world. It says our sun shan't perish for as long as breath fills our lungs. Beneath our rib cages are hearts belong not to us, for they weep when we tear down the era they fought for. Our mothers offered themselves to end an era, to give birth to another. Had they not torn their hearts from their chests, their young would've been slaughtered. High-strung stars, divine and infallible, stay their course, lest the world halt and give into the respite of death. See the world and its sun for what they are, it says, for the end of an era begins as soon as it is born.

Emptiness fills him, writhing in the core of his body, seeping into his limbs. The breath in his throat sours. The way rot takes hold of new fronds branching into the soft greenery of the young summer months, a burn takes hold of him. He turmoils and churns in a feeling he cannot place his finger on. He knew it once, but perhaps it died a long time ago. He has forgotten what it was like. Things only live on when remembered. A cruel truth, but a truth nonetheless.

He closes his eyes and lies down. The overseers undid the ugly gash the people left along the sky, but a silver seam runs down the sapphire. The only scar of the incident. He has not seen the woman from that day, the one who wept. He doubts he will again. His heart hopes to catch a glimpse of her, if only to know she still lives. If he could, he would ask her to sing.

The pain along his rib cage is unrelenting. His eyes drowsily open to blink away the pain, and the sun glows above him. He pushes himself upright from the indulgent grass. A saccharine breeze brushes against his torso, dancing and twisting through pale flowers. The world ripples around him in pulses as if he is the heart keeping the sun from falling down.

(He must be dreaming again.)

He searches for his mother, and when he cannot find her, a bitter smile stretches across his lips. How could he find her? She died with the sun and its hymns, with the love only a mother could hold for her son. She is dead, and he knows this. *He knows.*

And yet, reaching out his hand into the sky, he can feel her. She is the dulcet lavender in the grass's embrace, the whispered breeze, the marrow of the roots nurturing the earth. She is the sun, and she loves him the way a mother does.

He falls back with a childlike laugh, letting it ring out towards the heavens. Light dances across his body, and he sings the songs of his mother, *those damned hymns*. The pain of his ribs subsides and in its place is left the kind inheritance of his mother. Her life for his. The old world for the new.

When the sky begins to fall away, he clings to the dream. A distance worms between him and his mother. It tugs at him, unfurling the tension in his hands and dragging him away. His mother is being taken from him, and he cries out.

(Is this where he dies?)

Soft-spoken hymns trace along his cheek in reassurance, and his eyes sting. A gentle weight rests on his ribs, and it tells him to breathe. How long had it been since he last breathed?

A gasp flutters across his lips, and the ceiling watches him. He stares back at it and laughs. He lifts his hand and places it on his breast. Beneath his palm beats a heart, and each pulse is a kindness he cannot repay.

It is still spring when he treks beneath the sun to the edge of the field, where the sky ends. He hums when no one watches. His lungs embrace the lavender-scented air, and he can breathe.

Everything lives on when remembered. Thus a son holds his mother close, just beneath his rib cage, the way any son would.

He cherishes her memory.

(He loves her.)

A Dreadful First Night

Emma Bowery

Grade 10, Fort Calhoun Junior/Senior High School, Fort Calhoun, NE. Sara Gross, Educator.

On a blistering hot summer day in June of 1984, Carl Wright and his daughter, Dawn, sat on the porch of their dinky cabin right outside Pineville, Kentucky, waiting for their guest to arrive. According to her father, Amelia Wright was a rebellious seventeen-year-old girl who needed the strong hand of a sheriff to help keep her in line. Carl hadn't seen his niece in almost nine years, long before he adopted Dawn, who hadn't a clue about her cousin until just yesterday when Carl's brother, Joseph Wright, called for the first time in eight years, desperate for help. So they waited on the porch for any sign of Amelia.

"Carl, is she gonna be here soon?" groaned Dawn, looking up at him from her spot in the shade provided by the porch. "It's like 100 degrees out here and you said we could go to the pool today!"

Carl sighed at her antics and continued reading his newspaper, though he was also getting antsy. How would the first meeting between his daughter and niece go? He wouldn't tolerate disrespect towards Dawn; at the first sign, he would phone his brother and send Amelia packing.

"It's not 100 degrees out, and I told you that before my brother called," Carl huffed, pushing up his round glasses, accustomed to her complaints and criticisms. "We can go another time. It'll be much hotter next weekend, and maybe we can bring Amelia," Carl considered aloud. "It'd probably be good for her to meet some other town folk."

Joe didn't give up much information about what exactly he needed help with, only expressing to Carl her school troubles and run-ins with the law. Carl dreaded how that might transfer over to Pineville as well, but he held out hope that his brother was hyperbolizing his daughter like he did most other things.

At that thought, Carl and Dawn's ears perked up at the sound of a roaring engine that disturbed the serenity of the forest.

"Remember," Carl started, a spiel about safety on the tip of his tongue before being interrupted by Dawn.

"I know, I know," she pouted, "don't answer the door or any calls, do my homework, and be careful if I walk around the forest," she huffed, crossing her arms. "I already know all the rules, Carl. Why are you reminding me?" Carl stroked his mustache, chuckling. Before he could answer, however, a grey AMC Hornet pulled up to their cabin. He stood and waited for Amelia to step out of the car. When she didn't, he made his way over to the driver's side window and saw her sitting there, and he didn't even recognize her. Her hair was blonde, cut unevenly, unlike the long dark hair she used to sport, and a scowl replaced her easy smile. She climbed out of the car and her clothes were different as well. She had dark shorts on and a dingy sky-blue t-shirt with a pair of old, beat-up tennis shoes.

Amelia examined the small cabin and then her eyes met Carl's. He could practically feel the frustration and distrust that radiated from her.

"Hey, Mel," said Carl with a smile, the nickname sounding awkward and unused. Amelia's nose scrunched in distaste but she nodded anyway.

"Hey, Uncle Carl." She gave a toothy, fake smile. Amelia walked around the car to get to the passenger's side, where she pulled a duffel bag out and approached the porch, seeing Dawn for the first time. Her brows furrowed, and Dawn gave her a timid wave.

"I'm Dawn," she said sitting up and smiling shyly at Amelia. Amelia's face lost its hostility, but her confusion was still evident.

"Mel," she responded, tilting her head at Dawn with a small smile. Dawn stood up and reached out for her hand, saying that she wanted to show Amelia her room, passing the shotgun that leaned by the door.

Carl sighed and rubbed his growing headache at the situation that he got himself into.

A few hours later, Amelia's lackluster amount of things were settled in the guest room, and in the living room, she sat in a faded reclining chair watching cartoons with Dawn. Carl approached the two of them and Amelia's attention snapped to him, though Dawn's eyes stayed glued to the television.

"I'm working late tonight. Dawn, you know the number to the station in case anything happens, right?" he asked, buttoning his uniform, his badge shining off the dim kitchen lights. Dawn nodded without looking at him.

"Yeah, Carl, I remember. And I told Mel the rules." Carl chuckled and ruffled her short hair, glad he didn't need to waste time explaining them to his estranged niece. He turned to Amelia and met her piercing eyes, his hands on his hips.

"Behave," he said pointing at her, "and keep an eye on Dawn." Amelia rolled her eyes at him, giving him a mock salute before turning back to the TV. Carl sighed and opened the front door, before turning back to the teenagers. "I'll be home around eleven o'clock. Don't answer the door."

After he left, Dawn and Amelia continued to watch cartoons, before Amelia finally broke the silence.

"Why do you call him Carl? I thought you were his daughter," she inquired and Dawn finally looked away from the TV.

"He adopted me a couple years ago," she answered, "but I still see him as my dad. I'm just used to calling him Carl." Dawn turned back to the TV. Amelia's attention on the show dwindled as she thought about her situation. How could her father just send her away? What would her mother say if she were still around? Thoughts swirled around her head before Dawn's sudden voice interrupted them.

"Why are you here?" she asked. "I mean, why did your dad send you to live with us?"

Amelia's brain stuttered, but before she could answer there was a loud bang against the front door, as if someone threw themself at it, startling both girls.

Amelia shot up from her seat, cursing having to be here already, but thankful Dawn wasn't dealing with this alone. She stepped towards the door to see who was there, but Dawn grasped her arm and shook her head. At Amelia's confused face, she mimicked calling someone, and Amelia knew what she meant. They needed to call Carl. Amelia ushered her toward the kitchen, where she'd seen a phone hanging on the wall hours earlier. While Dawn went to call him, Amelia stayed by the door, periodically jumping at the loud crashes against it. She noticed the shotgun standing near the door that she ignored earlier in favor of moping to her room. She grasped it and hoped it was loaded before racking it and pointing it towards the door, just in case. She could hear Dawn talking to Carl.

Before Amelia realized it, the loud crashing paused, and she glanced at the window closest to the door, covered by a curtain. She reached out to peek behind it. The seconds felt like hours as she slowly grabbed it, feeling that whatever might be behind it was better to stay a question. A crash followed by an ear-splitting scream coming from the kitchen broke her fixation. She raced towards the sound, clutching the shotgun and jumping over the sofa in her haste.

What she saw in the kitchen made her pause, her mouth agape. The thing that had crashed through the window was an ugly, hairless monster, with beady eyes and a mouth full of gangly teeth. It was gaunt and the same red as that of a brick, and all of its bones were poking through its skin. The creature was hunched over Dawn, who cowered near the fridge, and out of the thing's spine protruded brick-colored spikes. After what felt like an eternity but couldn't have been more than 10 seconds, the thing turned to Amelia and let out a beastly screech, barreling toward her.

Before she could even think, she raised the gun and pulled the trigger, the kickback causing her to tumble back as the creature let out a cry of pain as she had shot it point blank. Her ears ringing, Amelia knew that that wouldn't stop the creature for long. Dropping the gun, she scrambled forward, grasped Dawn's arm, and yanked her up, ignoring the putrid smell of the monster's blood that covered her and Dawn both.

She raced past the creature that still screeched in pain, and out the back door with Dawn at her heel. Around the house, they went straight for the grey Hornet. Amelia fumbled for her keys that were clipped to her waistband. She unlocked the door, practically throwing Dawn into the back seat before hopping in after her. She climbed into the driver's seat and started the car. As the engine roared to life, the monster slammed against the hood of the Hornet, both Dawn and Amelia let out a scream and at the same time the creature screeched. Amelia threw the gearshift into reverse and slammed on the gas, sending the monster careening off the hood and onto the ground.

"Get buckled!" Amelia shrieked. Dawn did as she was told, as the car shot backward, away from the cabin and the monster that had just broken into it.

"We need to go to the station," Dawn stressed. "I called Carl, but I barely got a word in before that"—her voice shook—"that *Neerar* got in. He's probably really worried."

Amelia put the car in drive when they were far enough away and pressed the gas to the floor, sending them hurtling out of the forest. When her brain finally caught up with her, she realized what Dawn said.

"Wait, what do you mean *Neerar*?" interrogated Amelia. At Dawn's hesitance she continued. "How do you know what that thing is? What the hell is going on?"

Dawn looked away from Amelia and hugged herself tightly, her eyes filled with tears that didn't fall.

"Mel, you have to promise not to freak out." At Amelia's nod, Dawn continued. "They're, they're from some kind of meteorite that crashed on earth, that hatched the *Neerar*."

Amelia considered this, thoughts of how this could even be possible swirling through her head, but she decided to freak out about this later, not in front of Dawn.

"Okay, okay, let's just get to the station," she sighed, running her hand through her hair. It was quiet on the car ride, the only noise being Dawn directing Amelia to the station, and as the flickering lights of the precinct came into view, Amelia knew that she would have an interesting visit for the foreseeable future.

Rat, Raven, Dog, and Snake

SAMANTHA LADWIG

Grade 12, Fort Calhoun Junior/Senior High School, Fort Calhoun, NE. Sara Gross, Educator. Honorable Mention.

After the human race joined the International Galactic Confederation (IGC) in 2789, the other species were initially excited. The council now has 783,681 members, but there is still a lot of space to explore. It has been a long while since another species was deemed sentient enough to join, but the human species did not live up to their foretold standards. For all the great things they could've accomplished, they "failed." They were weaker, had no history of great wars, and all of the ambassadors were mousy and weak-minded. The only thing they had going for them was that humans are hard to kill. Humans are so small compared to the rest of the species on the council. However, humans are still included in the council but are cast off to the side and often ignored.

One hundred years later the beginning of a war is being waged, the Muscles attacking; they wanted to be the supreme leader of the galaxy. It was easy to forget about the humans. The humans prefer this, as they are very secretive about their languages and customs. Humans are prideful as they hold on to their traditions. Humans are known as great storytellers; everyone in the galaxy knows the story of "Rat, Raven, Dog, and Snake." "Rat, Raven, Dog, and Snake" was originally a children's story, one that all human children took to heart. Rats are dirty creatures; they are filthy and often treated like trash but they are often ignored and forgotten about. Ravens are creatures that collect and trade things; they have a melodic voice that rings out beautifully. Dogs are protectors; they bark and warn others of danger. Snakes betray their own kind; they draw attention to themselves with their rattles, and you don't want to be a Snake. The most important part of the story, the part that the children never forget, was if you are a Rat, a Raven, or a Dog, all of these animals have a pack or flock that they can depend on. No human is ever truly alone. This is the part that other species don't understand.

Rat, Raven, Dog, and *Snake* are all symbols of the only four things a human can be in a time of war. Together they form a secret organization known as the Liberation. Each "department" of the Liberation has its inner workings and secrets but all of them are connected on one level or another. Rat is a slave, snitch, or servant, maybe all three at once. Only Rats, being the smallest, can get in between the pipes and crawl around the vents to fix broken parts of the ship. Rats are dirty and often overlooked. No one notices a Rat on the corner of a street in New York. Rats are the most common type of human. Raven is a smuggler, thief, or merchant. A Raven could get you to trade your soul before you've realized what you agreed to. Their voice is sweet and melodic like a raven. Their hands are swift like their wings and collect shiny objects that seem to serve no purpose. But be careful of a Raven because its flock is never far behind. Dogs are fighters, soldiers, or guards. Dogs will do almost anything necessary to survive. The way Dogs cling to life, like mold on bread. They fight with teeth sharp like a canine and hunt in packs. You push a Dog down and it gets blood in its mouth and the Dog spits it out in your eye; they are seriously loyal and protective. A Dog will always bite. Snake is a betrayer, traitor, liar. You don't want to be a Snake. A Snake betrays their kind, mixes and mingles with the other species, thinks of the leaders on the council, their eyes sharp but scales weak, and be careful of a Snake's rattle.

Rat

Charlie Evans did not want to be a Rat; however, he is small enough, fast enough, and just smart enough to be one. The life of the Rat is something no one wants, the tasks, the solidarity, the abuse from the "masters," and the absurdly tight places. Charlie has always hated tight places. The life of a Rat is necessary, the Rats run the subway, an underground connection route where information travels from planet to planet. If something is going on, the Rats are the first to know about it. All of the registered ships that are a part of the IGC have a Rat aboard them; the only one that does not is the *Deathmonger*. Their Captain Hela refuses; she sees Rats as what they are, slaves. Captain Hela refuses to have a slave Rat on her ship. The captain's ship is the missing link in the connection of the perfectly oiled machine that is the subway.

Charlie remembers the day he got his assignment. A dark cloudy day, as if Mother Nature was promising the sorrow about to come. He can picture the letter sitting plainly on his dad's kitchen counter, he can feel his name imprinted on the stamp. Charlie remembers the noises his father made as he wept because they both knew that Rats don't last long. He especially remembered the ink was smudged, blurring the name of Ambassador Sangra, the woman who sent him to his death.

Charlie snuck onto the *Deathmonger* with ease. He learned the ins and outs of the ship, the wiring and inner workings of the monstrous ship that is *Deathmonger* in just under a week. The inhabitants of the ship took two weeks to find their stowaway. Their reactions varied, some like Commander Joelle and Lt. Elijah, who were shocked that a Rat stayed hidden for so long on their ship. Captain Hela and many other members of her crew were horrified. It seemed after fighting so long to not have a ship Rat, she finally had one.

Five Earth-Months Later
Charlie for the first time in a while is nervous. He got over his fear of tight spaces and the dark a little after two months. Charlie is nervous because this is the first time that he is going to be planetside. This will be his first introduction to the subway. One that he cannot mess up. Charlie has spent months hiding in vents, sneaking onto computers, and eavesdropping on conversations, collecting all of the information to report back to the liberation. He is the final missing link in the ever-running chain of the subway; Charlie cannot fail. The whole outcome of human secrecy depends on how well Charlie can relay the information. He cannot be the one who exposes them all. As soon as *Deathmonger*'s wheels touch down on Planet A-93-Y Charlie is off, crawling through the bustling crowd. He bumps into the Black Cloak, a feared Raven. Charlie very carefully slips the files and all of the smuggled information into her pocket while walking away. He scurries back to the ship; only once *Deathmonger* is leaving Planet A-93-Y's orbit does Charlie breathe a sigh of relief and finally slip into a restless sleep.

He wakes to the blaring sound of the alarms going off. The *Deathmonger* is under attack. Charlie moves through the hull to the control room to see where the most damage is. Charlie climbs his way through the vent to the damaged area. The smell of smoking wires and melting metal brings tears to his eyes. The metal vents are starting to burn his skin. As Charlie traverses further into the vent the harder it gets to breathe; smoke almost fills the entire vent way. He is about to turn around when another blast hits the ship, causing the vent to collapse. Charlie feels the vent squeeze him, the hot metal searing his skin; he can smell his flesh frying. Charlie knows that he is going to die. He can hear the rest of the ship being hit, blast after blast shaking everything. Charlie knows that no one will look for him, as he was designed to be forgotten. As he sits there, he thinks about his mother and how he left her. He thinks about his father and the impersonal letter that he will get sent signifying his death. But he mostly thinks about how much he hates small, enclosed spaces. Charlie's body was burnt to a crisp.

Raven

Saige Thussle had everything a human could ever want—money, stable housing, and a loving family—but still it was not enough. Saige craved action and adventure even from a young age. She could spend days in the little forests that surrounded her village, making friends with all the birds and woodland creatures. Saige could tell stories that entertained her parents for hours. Saige realized she could lie like there was no tomorrow. The more that Saige learned about the world, the more things she craved—power, fame, and the need to be feared—which is how she became the Black Cloak, the biggest information broker east of the IGC. If you needed information, dirt, or leverage, the Black Cloak is who you went to. She made deals with all types of species, always coming out on top. "Beware the Black Cloak," they would whisper, "a devil in human skin." Over time she became the crosspath on the subway, and Saige could spread the information within minutes.

Saige was waiting in the middle of the market square on Planet A-93-Y. She had been waiting for over an Earth hour and was beginning to get frustrated. Time is money and the little Rat who is delivering the package is taking longer than expected. Someone knocks into her back and almost pushes her over. She feels the package slip into her pocket and quickly rights herself. Before she can utter a word to the little Rat, he is scurrying off into the rest of the crowd, already forgotten as he disappears. Saige walks leisurely through the streets of planet A-93-Y passing shopkeeps but paying them no mind. She is the Black Cloak and no one would dare to cross her. Saige approaches one of her many safe houses, where she finds a man waiting for her. He has scars running all over his body. They wrap around his exposed arms, showing off his fine-tuned muscles. Saige looks at his face and barely holds off a reaction. He has a terrible scar running from his forehead to his lip exposing his left canine, but somehow it misses his eye. Saige instantly knows that this man is a Dog.

"What is a mutt like you doing on Planet A-93-Y?" Saige ponders.

"I heard that the Black Cloak needs protection," he grumbles.

"So what if I do?" Saige replies.

"I am that protection," he says.

"What is your name?" Saige asks.

"Atlas," he grumbles.

"The man with the world on his shoulders?" Sagie mocks.

"Well my father was a pretentious man, among other things," Atlas says with a hint of a smile.

Saige leads Atlas into her safe house. It has various knick-knacks scattered around the building. She has a meeting with the Ambassador later this week and the Black Cloak has made some enemies in the IGC. These files are very important and she can't risk them falling into the wrong hands. She and Atlas discuss the details of their alliance and shake hands. They head deeper into the safehouse to get ready for the long journey in the IGC's compound.

Dog

Atlas Grant never liked violence. Although he was bred from it, one can't break the cycle so easily. He was strong. His father made sure of that. Grueling days of the sun beating down, the sun making him sweat, his hands slick, causing him to drop his weapon. "Again," his dad would scream, every mistake taken and pulled apart. Atlas had to be perfect, so he was. When he was younger he did not quite understand. His father made sure that he would understand. His body bears many mistakes of his youth. He knew the taste of leather, rather than the feeling of his father's love. Atlas's father was not a good man, but he made Atlas a good Dog.

Atlas laughed as he ran away. It bubbled out of him a beautiful full sound. He can't remember the last time that he laughed. Covered in his father's blood, he stumbles to their little airship. His father cannot hurt or control him anymore. He takes off and for the first time in his life, he has no idea what he is going to do next.

He lands on the bustling planet A-93-Y; he heard through the Libration's grapevine that they needed protection. He stalks and watches the Black Cloak for many days before he approaches her. He waits outside her safehouse for an hour waiting on her return. As the Black Cloak walks up, he can see her judging and stereotyping him as he waits there. After a short conversion, she leads Atlas into her safe house.

"My name is Saige, and many people want me dead," she leads.

"I figured that's why you wanted protection," he responds.

She smirks. "A deal then. You give me protection, and I will give you almost anything you want."

He sticks out his hand for a shake to seal the deal, and Saige's smirk grows wider. Atlas looks at the smile and can't help but think he made a deal with a devil. Whether he sold his soul or sacrificed some part of himself is yet to be seen. Her smile makes his stomach turn.

They make a stop on Planet Yune; Saige has some unfinished business here. To watch the Black Cloak work in person is a terrifying thing. The way she can twist words just right, make one thing seem like the other, to get deals just the way she wants them. Saige is the devil.

The alien that just got scammed out of half a million credits moves to strangle Saige. She barely moves when Atlas intercepts the alien's arms, snapping the left like it's nothing, twisting the arm behind the alien while shoving its body to the ground. It screams in agony an ear-piercing sound, but Atlas doesn't even flinch. The alien gives them the credits and they head to their ship.

Atlas wonders when others see him, fighting or protecting, do they see him as a monster? Do they fear him like they fear the Black Cloak? A part of him is afraid of that—that the others will fear him. A different part, a part he keeps hidden deep, is excited by it. Others should fear him and what he can do, the lengths he is willing to go to protect those he is loyal to.

Snake

No one wants to be a Snake, least of all Ambassador Sangra. She took this job because she had to. It's a job that everyone "takes" with a heavy heart. No one wants to be a Snake lying in the grass waiting for the perfect opportunity to strike. To be a Snake is to be cut off from the rest of humanity. In case something drastic happens, Snakes need to depend on no one. Ambassador Sangra learned how to turn her fangs into placid smiles, and how to twist her venom into her words. Ambassador Sangra was most likely pulling the strings if something was going on in the Liberation.

Ambassador Sangra moves through the hallway of the Confederacy building. The council just got done with another meeting; the Muscles bombed and purged a planet full of women and children civilians. The council is in shock since they have never seen this level of violence produced by a war. Some are weeping while others are pounding angrily on their desks. Sangra is thinking, *"Where is the best area to deploy my soldiers but remain unaffected by the council?"*

Ambassador Sangra was not surprised, she even expected this; war brings out the monsters hiding in everyone. In Sangra's mind there are no winners in war, only bodies and survivors. The Ambassador walked to her office calmly since she needed to get a message out to the Liberation. An update on the war and where the next human troops need to be placed. The other species on the IGC mustn't know of human violence, of their capability of war, of the monsters lurking beneath our skin. She opens her office door to find the Black Cloak and Atlas waiting in there for her.

"Ambassador Sangra Evans," the Black Cloak announces.

"Atlas, I haven't seen you in forever. How is your dad?" she questions.

"Dead," he grumbles.

"Your files," the Black Cloak interrupts.

The Black Cloak slams the files on the table. This is just the information Sangra needed. The whole plan is coming together; by the end of the week, the Muscles should be no more. The Liberation troops are going to bomb the Muscles' home planet, while attacking all stationed ships, effectively ending the whole population of Muscles. The Black Cloak leaves but not before taking her payment, dragging Atlas behind her.

One Earth-Week Later

There is a new file on her desk. She opens it and gasps, the only noise in her other than the silent office. The *Deathmonger* was destroyed; there were no survivors. Sangra does not cry. She is the Ambassador before she is human, and she is a Snake before she is a mother. She sent her son to his death. She feels everything. She feels nothing. The Ambassador takes her communicator and presses the command key, letting the release go for the bombs to drop. Far away Muscles are screaming, crying, and dying. The humans are monsters, beasts lurking beneath their skin. But, no one will know because of the skills of a Rat, the cunning of a Raven, the protection of a Dog, and the sacrifice of a Snake.

THE CURSED

SAMANTHA LADWIG

Grade 12, Fort Calhoun Junior/Senior High School, Fort Calhoun, NE. Sara Gross, Educator. Honorable Mention.

The Blessed were not always feared. Humans who were chosen by the gods were given gifts and powers beyond imagination. The Blessed are only favored and praised when the royal bloods are chosen. When a commoner or peasant is chosen they are no longer Blessed but rather cursed. When the number of Blessed commoners outweighed the number of Blessed royals, the Blessed were hunted down with dogs and swords. The knights looked ready for war. Aceldama was very young when the hunting first started, but she remembers how neighbors turned on neighbors. She remembers the little children slaughtered in the street for being "special." Aceldama remembers how some fought back, killing tens of the royal soldiers at once. She remembers how the Blessed and the knight's blood all bleed the same color and how the red covered entire streets. How the Blessed went from something that everyone loved to something that everyone feared, something that everyone hated.

Aceldama wakes to the sound of her mother screaming. Her sounds shake the whole house. Aceldama rushes up to her parents' room, her mother is drenched in sweat and her father is clutching her mother's hand. Aceldama's little sibling is coming sooner than expected. Aceldama runs down the stairs to grab towels from the kitchen and a water pail to clean off her mother's forehead and her new siblings'. Aceldama stumbles up the stairs to the sight of her mother and father smiling holding her new sibling.

"Do you want to meet your new baby brother?" her mom asks.

Aceldama nods excitedly as she bounds over to the bedside. Her dad very carefully passes over his newborn son. Aceldama stares down at him, very carefully using the rags to clean him off.

"What is his name?" Aceldama mumbles.

"Isaac," their mother mutters softly.

Aceldama removes the wet rag from his forehead and gasps. Under his soft brown curls is a marking of the Blessed. He has been chosen by the gods. Aceldama's eyes start to water as she hands her baby brother back to her father. Her father and mother take one look at the mark and start to sob. At twelve years old Aceldama understands that being blessed is nothing but a curse. Aceldama cries silently while her parents mourn the life that Isaac could have had.

Six Years Later

The clouds are heavy and stormy as if the gods are upset. The knights are searching the streets with vigor Aceldama has never seen in the town. She moved Isaac and her to the countryside in hopes of keeping him safe. Thunder sounds in the distance and Aceldama takes a deep breath. A pit begins to form in her stomach. She feels something thrumming in her blood, begging her to do something, warning her that something is wrong. She rushes to the front of her cottage where Isaac is out playing and prays to the gods that she can save him. The knights march forward at a crushing pace, their footsteps marching to the pounding of Aceldama's heart. They are marching too fast and they reach him before Aceldama even has a chance. Aceldama can do nothing as they search for her little brother. The gods' mark branded into his forehead. The head knight brandishes his knife and slashes it across Isaac's throat. His bright red blood runs over his tiny hands as he tries to stop the bleeding. Isaac may not have understood his curse but in this moment he understands what death is. Aceldama looks at the head knight, the one who killed her little brother. He has a twisted smile on his face. She cannot bear to glance at her brother's small body. The knights throw his lifeless body to the ground; the cursed do not get a proper burial. The knights march away at the same pace they came in at like, Aceldama can almost imagine, they are going on an afternoon stroll. She races to Isaac's body. Her tears cloud her vision causing her to stumble and trip. As she reaches his body, Aceldama breaks down into ugly sobs that rack her body. She gently cradles Isaac's small frame, and she sets her hand down on his forehead closing his dead eyes. Aceldama hates the townspeople who hate Isaac. She hates the Knights who killed Isaac, she hates the King who condemned Isaac, and she hates the gods that made Isaac Blessed cursed. Because people fear hate what they do not understand, they killed Isaac because of how the gods made him.

Cleo's Travelling Circus

CALIANA MCBRIDE

Grade 12, Lincoln Southwest High School, Lincoln, NE. Honorable Mention.

Black and white stripes twist from the ground, and golden poles with flickering flames of every color light the tent up.

"Come one, come all!" a woman calls, gesturing to the tent with her hat dramatically. "Step into Cleo's traveling circus!"

"Witch!" a woman retorts from the crowd, spitting at the woman's feet, which she ignores.

"Let's try it," Nisha whispers to me, nudging us forward to the ticket seller.

"What—no way—your father will be so mad!" I whisper-yell back as she shuffles us forward. "You know what they call the workers here—witches! And I bet there are some fae too!"

"So?"

"So unlike you, I would like to not be completely cast out from town!" Nisha rolls her eyes and continues walking forward, causing the ticket seller to look straight at us. Or into us is more like it. Her eyes were a piercing yellow-amber color, like a hawk's. Her lips curl up into a cat-like smile as Nisha continues to approach.

"Well hello there, ladies—are you braving the circus today?" she purrs, placing her hat back on her ebony hair.

"Yes—how much do tickets cost?" Nisha questions, placing a hand over my mouth.

"Just a silver each. Of course, you can also get a *premium* experience for an additional five coppers each," she explains, pulling out four tickets, two shining silver in the light and two pure black with silver chromatic writing. I give Nisha a look, who tilts her head. *Don't you dare.*

"We'll take two premium tickets," she responds, fishing out three silvers from her purse and pressing them into the woman's awaiting hand.

"Very well then, ladies—these tickets will get you into any attraction, right away. Now step right in and enjoy the circus," she tells us, giving the black tickets to Nisha before ushering her in. As I pass, the woman glances over me again, her smile curling up into a smirk before she glances back out at the waiting crowd.

"Come on, Cori, don't be a wimp," Nisha encourages, all but dragging me into the tent. The second we stepped inside, it was like we were in a different world. The sky was the same black and white striping as it had been outside, but small vermilion and violet tents peppered the ground, while trapeze artists did tricks above everyone. To my right a woman in a skintight red dress juggles fire while to the left a man is holding an emerald snake that's double the size of him.

"This is amazing," she sighs, tugging me through the crowd and stopping in front of a slightly bigger violet tent. "Hall of Mirrors—that sounds fun, right?"

"Absolutely not."

"What—why?"

"I don't know, maybe because every single horror story we hear involves a mirror in some form," I point out. She rolls her eyes and lets go of my hand, stepping into the entrance.

"Well, to stop me you'll have to catch me first," Nisha taunts.

"No—don't you dare—" I hiss, stepping forward, right as she dashes into the hall, laughing. *I am locking her out of the house tonight.* I think unhappily as I follow. Mirrors coat the ceiling and make up the wall, creating a dizzying path. I see a flash of Nisha's blue dress and start to follow, then promptly run into a mirror.

"Ow ..." I glance around, but all I see is myself mirrored back at me. Each one with the same dark brown hair resting in a braid on my shoulder, each rust-colored dress the same and every pair of green eyes staring back at me. Until one in front of me winks. I jolt back, stumbling into another mirror, hand flying to my eye.

"Gods, gods, gods—" I mutter, glancing back at the mirror. All I see is myself staring back, wide eyed and shaking. *I've officially gone mad.* I shake my head as I continue down the hall, occasionally running into the other mirrors. *It's just your imagination, just your imagination*—I halt as I see two of my reflections leaned over, one whispering in the other's ear through the mirror. They both pause, turning to look at me, right as I start running. I hear my own footsteps and breaths echo, and as I run past more and more mirrors, I see more of me stopping, staring or laughing. When I collide into another mirror in front of me, I see another reflection move forward, as if to grab me. I step back and hit another mirror, before turning and sprinting to the left. The mirrors pass in a blur before I see a painted 'exit' sign. Panting, I run out, running straight into Nisha, who is still laughing.

"I can't believe you caught me—wasn't that so much fun?" she asks, dragging me back into the center of the circus.

"Nisha—the mirrors were coming alive—" She stares at me like I'm crazy, which I suppose isn't too far off.

"I think it was just a trick of the light," she replies slowly. "How about we get some food and then check out some of the stalls?"

"I—sure," I sigh, defeated. She leads us to a cart where a short, blonde woman with a cobra mask is an array of shining, jewel-colored sweets.

"Hello—I'd like to purchase some candied popped corn," Nisha tells her, beginning to take her coins out of her purse.

"Alright—no need to pay. Your ticket covers it," the woman instructs her, handing over a bag of the multicolored treat. "Enjoy!" Nisha takes it gratefully and grins at me, handing me my own ticket.

"Alright, what do you want?"

"I think I'm fine," I respond. The woman glances over, smile never leaving her face.

"You sure? We have candied fruits, caramelized nuts, pastries—even some mini cakes." She gestures to the stacks of sweets.

"I'm fine," I repeat, averting my eyes to glance back at Nisha, who shrugs and leads us back down the path. As we walk away, I feel the heat of a glare on the back of my neck. But when I glance back, the woman is re-organizing her displays. *Calm down.*

"Want to head to the fire juggler's show next?" Nisha questions.

"Can we please leave?"

"Come on, just fifteen more minutes," she pleads, grabbing my hands. "Don't you want to see the shops, the magician and the acrobats?" *Not quite.*

"Sure," I sigh. She smiles ear to ear and drags me further down the seemingly never-ending path, into the smaller cluster of scarlet tents. The shops are stunning, ranging from dresses to mirrors, embroidery to tiaras and necklaces that look like they'd cost a minimum of 20 gold each. Nisha stops outside of a mask stall, eyes widening.

"Oh, wow, look at that—" She points to an emerald mask with roses winding up the left, and a scarlet veil that cascades down from the highest one.

"It's stunning."

"And half-off," a cheerful voice interrupts from behind, causing both of us to shriek. A tall man—or really boy—is standing right behind us, an onyx mask on his face with a golden snake slithering around the edges.

"Oh—sorry—" Nisha apologizes to the man. "I didn't hear you come up behind me."

"It's my fault entirely," he responds, leaning down and grabbing the tickets we both dropped. "Oh? You can get that mask for free, you know—the tickets are all inclusive."

"It is stunning … but it'd clash with my dress." She shakes her head.

"That's such a shame," he sighs, moving some of the blonde hair out of his eyes. "Oh—pardon my manners, this is so rude of me. Most people call me 'Adder' because of my mask right now, and because it's not really safe for us to give our names because of all those annoying guards. Oh I got off track again— may I have your name, my lady?"

"Nisha," she laughs, shaking his outstretched hand.

"Well Nisha, Laurel. That dressmaker down there has the most stunning gowns—now that isn't included but rather than 6 silvers, it'll only be one with your tickets," he explains, grabbing the rose mask and setting it on Nisha's face. "But as you see it's really not that much more—and this rose mask looks divine on you. But see, she's just that stall right now there—enjoy—" He shuffles her to the outside of the tent, and without even looking back she walks down to the dress maker. Adder turns back to me, smiling ear to ear.

"What about you, my lady? Any of these masks catch your eye?"

"Sorry I wasn't really looking—just trying to follow my friend," I explain, inching back to the exit.

"Then allow me to help you," he replies, either not picking up on the fact that I was trying to leave or completely ignoring it. "Hm—I definitely don't think you're the rabbit or housecat—most likely not the sun—ah the fox." He picks up the intricate russet fox mask, before walking over and tying it on me.

"Did you make all of these yourself?" *Nevermind the fact that I did not agree to buy this.*

"Oh no, I'm just filling in for the usual shopkeeper today since he got a cold—ah I forgot to ask again, how rude of me: may I have your name?" I open my mouth to respond, then pause, eyeing him again. He smiles back innocently, but as he moves to resituate the masks, I notice the tip of his ears. *Fae.*

He's fae. Goddess—I feel my heart start pumping inhumanly fast as I back up a bit.

"Sorry, you can just call me, Cori—excuse me, I need to go find my friend." I quickly turn to leave, but he's already in front of me.

"Are you ok? You're looking a little ill," he asks, conveniently blocking the exit.

"Yes—I think I just had too much of those sweets on an empty stomach," I lie, trying to squeeze past him.

"Funny. I didn't see you eating anything on your walk over." We stare at each other for a second before I make a run for it, pushing past him and dashing to Nisha in the dress stall that she's just now walking out of, now in a deep emerald dress with scarlet roses embroidered along it. I don't waste time trying to explain it to her, simply opting to grab her hand and pull her along with me. She doesn't protest as I lead us out to what I hope is the exit—in fact, she doesn't make a sound. Until we come to the exit gate, where she yanks her arm out of my grip.

"What are you doing?" I demand, grabbing her arm and pulling her towards the exit. "Ni, we have to go—there are fae—"

"I want to stay here," she responds, uncaring.

"Nisha—there are real *fae*—"

"I'm staying here," she responds again, pulling away. As I look over her face, I finally note the difference. Her eyes aren't supposed to be green. *She gave her name to that fae—she's enchanted.*

"Ok, we don't go," I respond, holding my hands up. "But can you wait in this spot for me?" She nods and I slowly walk over to the edges of the circus, trying to look inconspicuous. *The mask should hide who I am right—the seller won't remember me?*

"Leaving so soon?" *Of course she would notice—of course—fae can tell lies. So I just have to tell half-truths—ok, well that would be easier if I had a good excuse—*

"Oh, yes—I got a little overwhelmed from how big the crowd is, so I'm stepping out now. Can I get back in, or will I have to buy another ticket?"

"Oh, it's no worry, just show me your ticket from tonight," she explains. "I understand—I work out here because I hate how claustrophobic it can get in the tents." I smile back as I walk away, my heart beating out of my chest. *Guards, I need guards—there!*

"Sir—sir!" I jog over to the guard, taking off the mask. "I need help."

"With what?" he sighs, bored.

"There are fae—in the circus—my friend got enchanted and she won't come out but there are real—" He holds up a hand and I stop, waiting anxiously as he glares down.

"How did you find this out?"

"What?"

"Did you talk with a fae?"

"Yes but—" I yelp as his hand clamps down around my arm.

"I hate this stupid circus—infecting every citizen," the guard grumbles, dragging me back to the town.

"What are you doing?!"

"You talked with the fae—you're as infected with that magic as your friend. Lucky for you, you got out so you have time to get it drained."

"Drained—what do you mean—my friend is stuck inside. We can't waste time doing whatever this is. We have to go help her—"

"Your friend signed her own death decree when she entered," he responds, fingers tightening as I thrash, trying to get back to the circus. "Keep that up and we'll have you on the pyre."

"She could be dying!"

"You will too if you don't shut up." He yanks open the door leading to the jail, and I use that brief distraction to pull away. I manage to get back near the circus before white hot pain erupts from the back of my head, causing me to fall to the ground. Groaning in pain, I move to crawl away but am stopped by a foot on my back.

"Pyre it is then," the guard mutters, increasing the pressure.

"I don't think so," a voice replies cheerily, before the pressure on my back completely disappears. Adder leans down, offering a hand. "Well this was very annoying—I'd be careful about getting up. You did get hit on the head." I back up and he sighs.

"Really, there's no point in that. One, I could just use my magic to drag you back with me. And two, although I do not have your name, you accepted a gift from me. And thus, you are in my debt. Now you can either take my hand and have help walking back to the circus, or I can use my magic to drag you with me." I slowly take the hand and he pulls me up, then catches me as I fall.

"Ah my bad—anyways you may want to close your eyes."

"Why?" He doesn't offer an explanation and instead puts a hand over my eyes. When he takes it off, we're both inside a scarlet tent, with a woman sitting behind the desk. Her dark blue eyes flick over me as Adder shuffles me to a seat.

"Before you start asking questions, I'm Cleo, the Ringmaster and owner of the circus. No, we are not going to kill you or your friend. Yes, your friend is safe," she explains. "We are slightly annoyed that you did pick up on things, but that is Adder's fault for playing around with the mirrors when you went through." She levels a look at the fae who shrugs innocently.

"So what are you going to do to me then? I doubt I'm going to be allowed to return to the village."

"Well, part of that is for your safety," Adder responds, leaning on my chair. "You confessed to seeing a fae, which to them means you are a witch. Well, usually it's a witch or victim, but since you're not acting insane, you're a witch."

"You get two options," Cleo continues. "You can either give Adder your name and be dropped off ... somewhere, and have a debt we'll call in at some time, or you can give him your name right now and work here in the circus. But no matter what, he's taking your name."

"Both sound like bad options."

"It's not much, but if you work here, you'll have room and food provided for you," Cleo responds.

"Can I say goodbye to my friend?"

"She's already left." I glance back at Adder, who is still smiling like all of this is a normal experience. *I suppose it is for them.*

"I can't do acrobatic tricks or magic."

"I figured as much—I'll have you working with him since he'll have your name. You won't do anything that makes you uncomfortable," she states. I sigh and Adder stretches out his hand.

"So, may I have your name?" I slowly take the hand.

"Corinne." Once I say it, I feel a little shock from his hand, and he smiles brighter.

"Lovely—I'll set you up with your own tent," he explains, moving to the exit. "Oh and keep your mask. I have an idea for our act."

Three months later, underneath a large violet tent, a magician with a golden and black snake mask is performing some type of transformation trick.

"And 3, 2, 1!" He taps the golden box and where there had once been a human assistant was now a fox. As the crowd claps, the man glances mischievously at the fox, who gives him an annoyed look back.

"I told you the fox mask would fit."

DEATH HUNT

KAEDA PARDE

*Grade 12, Boys Town High School, Boys Town, NE. Anne Tompsett, Educator.
Honorable Mention.*

One rainy night, a family of twelve was celebrating their good fortune in their house. There was a knock on the door. A little boy asks to come in from the rain, with nothing to shield him from it. However, the little boy was not drenched by the rain.

"Aunt Vera, who is it?" one of the kids asks running to the door. Vera knew the little boy as her little brother. She has not seen him in years, and starts crying, with happiness.

"Adair, this is your uncle Juniper," Vera says.

"Then why do you cry so much, from seeing him, mom?" Another kid arrives, this time it is one of her own.

"Well, because I have not seen Juniper in years. That is why I am crying, Nadia," Vera says to her.

Juniper walks in. He knows all the people in the house. He gives Vera a hug and introduces himself to her husband Obi. After that Juniper starts walking to meet his younger brother Henry, who notices him walking over and Henry gets up so fast the chair he was sitting on falls over. He walks over to Juniper and sits him down with a plate of food, near the fireplace to warm him. Then Henry's wife comes over with their two other kids, Lucas and Zara. "Tell us a story, Uncle Juniper, please," the little boy, Lucas, pleads.

Softly whacking Lucas on the head, Zara says, "No, Lucas, you should let him eat and settle in first. He just arrived. Be respectful."

"No, it's fine. What kind of story would you like to hear, Lucas?" Juniper asks kindly.

"A gruesome one. It's almost Halloween after all!" Lucas replies, his face lighting up with joy.

"Ok. Once upon a time there was a mother who was full of hate and anger towards her own son, because she thought that her husband left her because she gave birth to a boy. What she did not know was that her husband had caught her cheating on him, and he was so full of grief and sadness that he killed himself." At this point all the kids have gathered around the fireplace to hear Juniper tell this story. "The mother was so furious about having to take care of two kids on her own that when the older sibling went off to get more education, the mother decided it was time to start fresh. She lured the son into the basement, and then into a small room off in the back of the basement storage room. She had asked him to clean it up, since the previous owners had left it a mess. As he is cleaning the little boy hears the door close and lock behind him. Knowing that there is no one else in the house, he starts pleading with his mother to let him out; he promises that he will be a good kid, even though he never made a mess or threw a fit. Days go by and the mother does not come back for him. He believes that leaving is a lost cause, so he finds what he can in that room only barely big enough to lie down in. For weeks he had to rely on eating the dead rats in the room with a small fire only big enough to last a brief time before he must relight it again, and only drinks the water from the ceiling that lands in a bucket on the floor. People say that little boy is still in the basement, waiting to be let out." When the story ends the kids are asleep. Then there is a knock at the door. Helen, the Grandma, goes to answer the door, only finding a letter. She brings it to the table and gives it to Vera, who reads it aloud. The letter reads:

In a quiet village, shadows deep,
A little boy was laid to sleep.
His mother, with a heart of stone,
Left him beneath the earth alone.

That is all the letter reads, but on the back of the letter there is a smaller note. That reads:

In a place that you call home I've hidden treasures for the soul. Here is your first riddle:
    I take you places near and far,
    with laces tied.
What am I?
    Where you rest your head at night,
    look beneath the bed for sights so bright.
Where am I?

"Do you think it's a shoe?" Obi says. "It would make sense, though. There are tied laces, and you tie your shoes, as well as walk places."

"Well, the second section would have to be a bed. Why don't we look in every bedroom for these shoes," Vera says, heading towards the main bedroom. Obi heads to the first kid's room down the hall. Henry heads to the second kid's room, while his wife Eleanor heads to the third kid's room.

When three of them come back and they say they did not find anything, Eleanor says she found a small pair of red kid's shoes that were not on the boot tray, which came to be very odd. When they search the shoes, they find in the shoes another note. The left shoe had another part of the poem to it, that said:

My mother, she took my life away,
In the dark of night, where shadows play.
I longed to live, to laugh, to be,
to run through fields, so wild and free.

The right shoe held another item, riddle and clue, reading:

I hang around your neck with grace,
a sparkling charm in a special place.
What am I?
Where you keep your clothes so fine,
a shiny treasure you will find.
Where am I?

They debate again and produce the idea that they are looking for a necklace in the laundry room. The laundry room is in the dark, damp, cold basement. They look for what seems like forever, and when they finally find the necklace, it's behind the washer, towards the back of the room. Under the necklace there's another note. The note reads the poem first, then on the back of the note another riddle and clue, which reads:

I dreamed of days beneath the sun,
of games and friends, of joy and fun.
But fate was cruel, and so was she,
who ended all my dreams for me.

Here's another riddle and clue for you:
    I grow with light and water too,
    my leaves are green, my flowers few.
What am I?
    Where sunlight streams and nature thrive,
    find a plant that's alive.
Where am I?

They knew that the plants that got the most sun were in the living room. The living room had a fireplace on one of the walls, but it was quite small. When they got to the living room the kids were still there sleeping so peacefully. They knew that this might be a problem because there were about twenty-five plants in all sizes, varieties, and colors. There was one plant that was the closest to the window by just a few inches. It was a type of tree, a tall tree. The green tree was nice and beautiful. Under the very heavy plant pot was another note reading:

    Now I rest beneath this tree,
    My spirit bound, yet longing free.
    I speak of wrongs, of pain and strife,
    Of a stolen, precious, innocent life.
    Now you have found three of seven,
    Next let's see it be even.
    Round and shiny,
    I hold tunes galore, in a player,
    I make you dance more.
What am I?
    Where music plays and sounds delight,
    find a disc that is out of sight.
Where am I?

It's almost dinner now, and the group is getting antsy. When they finally find the CD, it's titled "Mother." In the CD compartment there's a note, for yet another riddle and clue:

    Oh, how I wished to see the dawn,
    to feel the dew upon the lawn.

To grow and learn, to love and share,
to live a life beyond despair.
Here's your clue and riddle:
Sweet and juicy, a healthy treat,
in a bowl, I'm ready to eat.
What am I?
Where healthy snacks are kept in sight,
find a fruit that's just right.
Where am I?

In the kitchen they find fruit, but what fruit is it? Vera finds a small note under the white bowl holding red juicy apples.

But here I lie, my tale now told,
In whispers through the branches bold.
Remember me, and let it be,
A lesson learned for all to see.
Now you're almost there to find the one who is dead and were he lies his head. Before that you have another riddle and clue, just for you:
I'm soft and small, I wipe away tears,
in a pocket or purse, I've been for years.
What am I?
Where you keep your accessories neat,
find a cloth that's always a treat.
Where am I?

They find a black handkerchief, in Vera's room and a white one in Henry's room, each with a note stapled to it. Vera's handkerchief reads a poem:

For every child deserves to live,
to know the joy that life can give.
To be normal, to be free,
to grow beneath the juniper tree.
If you want to know the person dead, look for
captured moments, smiles so wide,
in a frame, our love resides.

What am I?

> Where memories are framed and smiles are bright,
> find a picture that's just right.

By this time Helen is the only one who stopped looking. She stopped maybe because she was scared, but the others persisted and found an image of Juniper, on a swing that was near the basement of the old house. When they turned it over, they found another note this time with a full poem, and a note:

> In a quiet village, shadows deep,
> A little boy was laid to sleep.
> His mother, with a heart of stone,
> Left him beneath the earth alone.
> My mother, she took my life away,
> In the dark of night, where shadows play.
> I longed to live, to laugh, to be,
> to run through fields, so wild and free.
> I dreamed of days beneath the sun,
> Of games and friends, of joy and fun.
> But fate was cruel, and so was she,
> who ended all my dreams for me.
> Now I rest beneath this tree,
> My spirit bound, yet longing free.
> I speak of wrongs, of pain and strife,
> Of a stolen, precious, innocent life.
> Oh, how I wished to see the dawn,
> to feel the dew upon the lawn.
> To grow and learn, to love and share,
> to live a life beyond despair.
> But here I lie, my tale now told,
> In whispers through the branches bold.
> Remember me, and let it be,
> A lesson learned for all to see.
> For every child deserves to live
> to know the joy that life can give.

To be normal, to be free,
  to grow beneath the juniper tree.
                              —Juniper

You see all things, but what you don't see are the things behind closed doors or in the basement. I spent my life in that basement. I heard Henry grow up, I heard Vera come back, but when you left that house, I was left in that basement. I died there the day you left that house.

THE SHADOW'S LIGHT

DELLOYD ROBERTSON

*Grade 12, Fort Calhoun Junior/Senior High School, Fort
Calhoun, NE. Sara Gross and Dustin Humphrey, Educators.*

I knew from the moment I got the call that today would be long—really, really
long. It was supposed to be my day off. Now I have to come in because they
needed someone "younger to connect with the subject." I get that, but why did
it have to be me? The weirdest part is that they're keeping me in the dark on the
specifics. All I know is that she tried to break into the compound. At least the
case seems interesting; that's the only silver lining I could find on my way to the
interrogation room.

In the hall leading up to the room, I can hear the telltale orientation video,
meaning she's new to the system ... That's not surprising—most people are.
But who the hell would break into our compound without even knowing
what's here? I take a minute to listen to the orientation while I think things
through.

*Most people say monsters aren't real. They get the luxury of saying that because of
people like us. I know this is confusing—trust me, we were all once in your position: new
and scared by something your science just can't explain. Maybe you lost a loved one, or
maybe you were hurt yourself. Maybe you just saw something you can't unsee. Now that
you know the supernatural is real, we in the Arcanum Society are here to show you that
the supernatural is more than natural. Kno—*

The cheery voice cuts off as I make my entrance.

The woman—no, it's more accurate to call her a girl—is cuffed to the table,
scowling at me. She's a sight to see, to say the least. She has a pastel pink under-
cut with wavy and curly hair on top. She has a complexion leaning toward
golden brown. That, with her almond-shaped eyes, makes me think she might
maybe be of Polynesian descent. She's still a few shades lighter than me but
it's clear that she isn't just tan. Then there are her clothes. She's wearing a pair
of grey sweatpants and a pastel green hoodie. And then the thing that stands
out the most. More than the acne that hasn't had a chance to go away with age
quite yet, more than her golden-brown eyes, more than her short pink hair. The
thing that stands out the most is the choker around her neck with what looks

like stylized waves. Overall, she seems ... interesting. Maybe this will be simple for once. But then the look on her face goes from simmering anger to exploding fury the moment I sit down across from her.

"Who the hell are you?! I asked for an elder. You could at least humor me and let me talk to a hunter instead of some nobody trainee," she spits with venom.

There was a lot to unpack there. For starters, this isn't the first time I've been judged on my age. I'm at the younger end of being a full-fledged hunter—it's only been two years since my 18th birthday and my True Hunt. I've made a name for myself since then, even though people still like to give me shit. I've shown my merit through my skill and advanced through the ranks quickly. I'm a force to be reckoned with, and everybody knows it. It's slightly infuriating that somebody disregards all of my achievements just because of my age. Second, there's some more troubling news: she somehow knows about the elders. I try not to worry. She's probably just some kid who's read one too many fantasy books and got lucky with the right position of power. Sometimes I forget how cliché we are.

"I don't think you understand how much trouble you're in, young lady. I can't tell if you truly know where you are right now, but—"

She interrupts me with so much strangling frustration that even I have to show a little bit of respect.

"Look, I have important news about the Aureum Principis. And before you ask, no, I can't tell you. That's why I need to talk to an elder."

I sit there, truly dumbfounded. She knows about the Aureum Principis! Although her uncanny knowledge catches me off guard, I do my best to recover and play it cool.

"Hey, how about you calm down a bit and we can talk like adults? That's the only way you're going to get anywhere. I'll give my name to a fae before I let you see an elder. My name is Aspen Cree. I'd say it's a pleasure to meet you, but given the circumstances, well, let's just say my mom always taught me not to lie."

I try to show some friendliness with a joke, but it clearly falls on deaf ears given her grimace.

"What's your name?"

"Nixi. Just Nixi," she says.

"Well, Nixi, let's continue with the questions, shall we? Where are you from? How did you find this place? It's not exactly obvious with the veil enchantments.

And the most important question of all: how do you know about the Aureum Principis?"

"I really can't tell you. I don't know how much you know, but not everybody in your little organization can be trusted. They are listening. I know this sounds crazy, but it's true. I can't say more. If I do, you'll be in just as much danger as I am. You don't seem like a horrible person, so just stop asking questions unless you want to end up on this side of the table or worse."

"What the hell do you mean? You need to stop being so goddamn cryptic. What are you, part sphinx?"

"No, actually I'm part Mo'o, but nice try," she says.

Okay, I pride myself on knowing most mythological species. This, though, is an exception. What the hell is a Mo'o? Apparently, my confusion is evident.

"Look, it's simple. My mother was a Mo'o, which is a type of Hawaiian water spirit, and my dad was a horny human. One thing led to another, and now I'm here with some of the powers of the Mo'o and all of the anxiety of a human," she explains in her usual tone.

"So a Mo'o is what? And what power did you inherit?" This could be bad. She seems nice enough, but magic can be incredibly dangerous. Just in case, I start to move my hand to my mask, my assigned magical conduit. I want to be able to reach for it on my belt in case I need to put it on to channel my magic. If she decides to try anything, that would be my best bet. I could try for my coil sword, but it would probably be too slow. Even though it's nice how discreet it is, that creative bit of magic and engineering takes a second to uncoil from around my waist. It's not normally a problem, but here, those precious seconds could count. I try to look calm, but yet again she sees right through my facade.

"Look, you can calm down. I don't have any combat magic. Or at least, any combat magic that I can use here. I have Natural water-based elemental magic. I also have Natural humanoid-based shifting magic. And before you ask, no, I will not 'show you' how I shift. Mainly because I don't want to, but also because I didn't exactly disclose what I am to the guards."

Her demeanor seems to soften. She suddenly appears ... solemn. What is she thinking?

"Depending on their allegiance, I might still end up here. But if they're less than loyal to the Arcanum Society, I would end up in a random ditch. They don't like that I can sense what they're doing to the flowers. I can feel the poison. They're trying to kill them—all of them. Mo'o has a connection with the Aureum Principis. It's a long story, but the species known as Aureum Principis is a mutated Hau flower. Its true origin is unknown, but my people have been taking care of it long before your people stole it."

Okay ... that's ... I honestly don't know where to start with that. I came here expecting a strange case, yes, but this has completely flown off the rails. Those are some bold accusations, and if what she's saying is true, we have some huge issues. If our supply of Aureum Principis flowers is destroyed, we will have no way to channel magic. We will have no way of defending the world and keeping order. In short, we're screwed. And if the enemies doing this are within the organization, we have no idea how deep the corruption goes. And if they have access to the flowers, it most likely goes high. I need to know everything she does and I need to know it now. I attempt to figure out what questions to ask to get the most information out in the shortest time possible, but before I get started, three guards crash in, weapons raised. I think they finally figured out what she is, and I think she was telling the truth.

"What are you doing?! I'm in the middle of questioning! By what authority are you barging in? I don't know who you are, but—"

The highest-ranking guard interrupts me in the middle of my threat. "On the authority of the Elders. Now you sit down, kid. Let the adults handle this." He signals over his two cronies. "Grab her. We're taking her to the Chamber."

As disrespectful as they were, I'm not dumb enough to go against the Elders' orders. Even if they're lying, the consequences if they were being truthful are too great. Luckily, if they are telling the truth, Nixi gets exactly what she wants. She'll get a chance to talk to the Elders. If they're not telling the truth, she might get exactly what she fears. She might be taken by the enemy. I can't let that happen, so let's skew the odds a bit. I walk over to them and lower my voice, trying to seem friendly.

"Fine, but she's still my responsibility, and unless you can give me another order from an Outer for a damn good reason, I'm coming with you. Plus, if it's a direct order from the Elders, she must really want to talk to her, and I wouldn't exactly call you great security for someone who's apparently such a VIP. Oh yeah, and don't call me *kid*."

That should be enough to tip the scale. And they can't argue with my logic, even if I wasn't exactly cordial with my delivery. I outrank all of them. Not by too much, but it's enough—especially since I ranked up due to merit and not time. So even if they wanted to take her by force, they wouldn't exactly have the best odds. It's clear they really don't know what to do. Whether it's stubbornness and incompetence or it's treachery is not clear. Maybe they realize this is not an argument they're going to win.

"Whatever, *kid*. Just don't get in the way or the Elders won't be happy."

That's when they try to drag Nixi out of her chair. She isn't exactly cooperating either. She must have been telling the truth about not having access to any combat magic right now. If she did, somebody would be leaving this room in a body bag. It doesn't stop her from kicking, punching, and screaming.

"What are you doing?! Let go of me! Aspen, what are you doing just standing there? Are you just going to let them take me? I told you! I trusted you! I thought—"

"Calm down. They're giving you what you want. They're going to take you to the Elders. I'm going to make sure you get there unharmed."

That seems to calm her down at least a bit. I still wouldn't say she's cooperating, but she did stop with the screaming and violence. Now it's more of dragging her feet and glaring, but I kept my word. The walk there was relatively uneventful. It got a little dicey here and there. The guards kept glancing at each other and then at me, but someone would always shake their head or clear their throat. It's obvious to me that I made the right choice not trusting them. Luckily, they're not idiots, and know they would lose this fight.

The strange thing is that we are heading to the Chamber. Maybe there was a hint of truth in their lies. Well, I guess we're getting ready to find out because we've arrived at the grand doors. We are ushered in, but the guards are forced to wait outside.

"Ah, they've arrived. We've been waiting for you, Nixi and Aspen. We've heard this troublemaker has some news."

That was the head Elder, Houston Briley. Well, kind of. More accurately, it's an arcane projection of the man. That is how they all are here, except for one. Zhen Karatsu is here in the flesh. Elder Briley will do most of the talking here. Either way, it doesn't matter much who does the talking. This is a big deal. Normal members of the Arcanum Society don't meet with the Elders unless they've done something very good or very bad. Since a criminal is here, I am assuming it's the latter. I'm hoping my last rites are in order.

"There will be no beating around the bush. Nixi, you're here about the Aureum Principis, yes? We figured out that you're a Mo'o, so it's only logical you can sense they're being damaged and you wanted to tell us—or so we assume. Isn't that right, Aspen?"

Panic flashes across my face. It occurred to me that the recording equipment was never turned off. It's been a very long time since I felt like such an idiot. Luckily, it seems like that's a blessing in disguise. It looks like the Elders are on our side, unsurprisingly. At least Elder Briley is.

"Now we have a proposition for you both. We need someone to hunt these traitors down. They call themselves Umbrae Lux. They state they have the 'righteous goal' of spreading the knowledge of magic to the public. In reality, they want to destroy this foundation and disrupt the natural order of the human world."

At the specificity of the word "human," Nixi flinched.

"It is unknown why they are destroying the flowers as their first overt act, but most likely it is to weaken us. We believe you two are in a unique position to hunt them down. Nixi, your connection to the Aureum Principis will be useful, along with your apparent skill in tracking. After all, you found this very base. And then you, Aspen. You have quickly proven yourself within this organization. Normally it takes years of dedication after one's own True Hunt, but we think maybe it's time we make an exception to the rule. We want you to help and train Nixi. We know you might have some resistance, bu—"

At this point, I can't help but interrupt.

"Sorry, I've tried to keep a level head, but what do you mean I might have resistance? You need me to babysit this ... this kid? I know I could get thrown out of the organization by speaking to you like this, but this could get somebody killed. She's untrained and unfit. Yes, she's shown some skill, but there are people within our organization ten times as skilled as either of us. It must be us?"

"Aspen, I understand your concerns, but this is not a request. This is an order. It is now your mission to hunt the Umbrae Lux and use your newly recruited apprentice to help you. Remember, this mission is under wraps. That's why we chose you two in the first place. And don't call her a kid. You're both still kids, and she's only 2 years younger than you. Now we have other matters to discuss, believe it or not. Turns out time doesn't stop just because the Arcanum Society is in danger."

I take the cue to leave, grabbing Nixi.

"Look, Nixi, I'm sure you're not too pleased with this whole arrangement. You're part of this whether you like it or not, so I need to see what you can do. We're going to the training grounds. On the way there, you can explain to me how the hell you found this place."

As I led my new recruit through the hallways of the facility toward the training room, I start to think about how long the day really was. The minute I heard it was an interrogation, I knew today would be rough. If I had known to what extent, I never would have come in. Not only did I get more paperwork now, I have this apprentice, a new mission, and a splitting headache.

THE BURDEN OF BLOOD (PT. 1)

JUPITER STURM

Grade 11, Boys Town High School, Boys Town, NE. Beth Sulley, Educator. Honorable Mention.

The afternoon sunlight filtered through the treetops, landing in a bespeckled manner on the forest floor and sending threads of light reflecting off her golden skin. Her scales undulated, sending ripples throughout her skin like drops of water falling into a pond. Her blue eyes rose to meet his, and in turn his met the ground. In their countless decades of survival based solely on mutual trust, he still could not meet her in the eyes. She never blamed him, but many could say he was not cut out for fatherhood. The soft sprigs of fresh grass tickled his palms as he ran his hand over the surface, feeling the old bricks of a long past town push back against his hand. In this very wood, the two of them first met. On that snowy night, he opened the door of the overturned caravan, truthfully just looking to loot the rich folks for all they were worth. As he rifled through the late mother's coat, his hands pushed into a smaller form. He lifted her tiny pink body up, looking for the misty white puff of breath in the stagnant winter air. The firelight of the downed vehicle sent an orange glow flickering across her face, but her chest was still, as was the air where her breath should have been. When he had given up hope of her waking, or coming to, just as he was about to place her back into her late mother's coat, her little body convulsed violently. She opened her mouth and heaved a breath of air, letting it out in a thin wail. He carried her in his coat, pressed up against the fuzzy lining of his cloak. When they arrived at the tent he'd until then called "home," her little shoulders rose and fell with each sleepy breath, the night's turmoil forgotten in an instant. She couldn't have been more than a week old, and yet she'd lost everything.

As she grew, he learned that she was like him. A monster, prosecuted for simply being. A vile creature of slimy descent, with a long history of thievery and infiltration of the crown. A being who could walk into a crowd and wear the faces of anyone they touched, step into their skin like a wetsuit and leave them confused, sometimes irate, but otherwise unharmed. She was a shapeshifter.

They say a shapeshifter's biggest flaw is the imminent degradation of their sanity, as they change so many times throughout their life that they eventually forget who they were when they started. He had long since left behind whatever his identity may have been and adopted many names. But she knew him by one name, as he did of her. His name was Akuji, and he named her Morana, after the goddess of death and winter.

They'd been through many heists and break-ins together. He taught her how to pick locks, how to sweet talk her way into and out of everything, and most importantly, how to control her shapeshifting ability. They had been to a midland city and were now on a seldom used trail to a nearby village, hoping more so to rest than steal. They strolled through the ruins of a long-ago village, the large stones that made up the watchtowers now reduced to steps and growing full heads of moss. The night was peaceful, though the daylight had long since passed, but their cool evening peace was stricken by an unusual swarm of flies buzzing lazily over something, concealed by a ruined wall.

"Probably just a dead animal," he said in a rush, his voice laced with alarm. He heard the shifting of her skin and glanced over to see her body take on a greener tone, blending her form into the rest of the forest. His stuttering steps brought them both closer and closer to the flies, and closer still to the rancid smell emanating from the area. He climbed up the edge of the wall using the indents in the stones and being wary to keep his tread light.

As he peeked over the wall, he was greeted by the sight of what was at some point a body. He'd seen plenty of blood, plenty of death, and carnage, but never a body in a state like this. The skin had decayed and begun to peel away, revealing the stringy tendons and muscles beneath. The body was curled in on itself, locked in the fetal position and cupping its hands loosely over its face. The flesh had become bloated and burst, now sagging on its skeleton like a deflated balloon. He stepped backward, catching himself on the way down and barely had his feet touched the ground when he started dry heaving, his body trying to rid itself of nothing, as empty as the body in the thicket. He ejected a pint of bile onto the ground before the heaving stopped, and he wiped the back of his arm against his face. Morana patted his back as one would a distraught child, and he straightened, breathing hard.

"We need to keep moving. Keep an eye out for whoever might have done ... that," he said shakily. She nodded, and they'd taken maybe ten steps when the echoing sound of hooves and marching feet met their ears. He paused, knowing that running would cause them more harm than good, and waited as the past city's guard patrol marched into the clearing on foot or white horses, all wearing the gold accents that marked them as being under the local king.

"Halt! State your business," the one in lead bellowed. Akuji stood up straighter, gripping the strap of his satchel.

"We're just passing through. We mean no disrespect," he spoke clearly. The wind shifted directions, blowing from behind them. One of the guards gagged as the smell of decay wafted toward them. The head guard pointed with his spear, and one of them on foot marched over to the building, getting slower and slower with each step. The flies scattered as his feet disrupted them. He stepped cautiously around the stone wall, and at once sprung backward, a sharp shout leaving his lips. He turned to face us, skin pale as the full moon and screamed, "Murderers! They're murderers! God save us all; they've slaughtered the prince!" He ran to the head guard, who covered his look of concern with authority.

"What is it, boy? What evidence do you have to be spitting out such accusations?" The guard on foot beckoned for the general to come closer, so with a heavy sigh, he slid off his horse, and leaned in. The general's eyes widened, and he slid his sword from its sheath, pointing it at them.

"You! You both are under arrest for the murder of the Heir to the Throne of Althiir! You must attend a court hearing at the coastline city, where you will be hanged for your crime!" he cried. Akuji stepped backward, locking eyes with Morana, who nodded at him. She closed her eyes in focus, and her skin glowed as it expanded and contracted, a band of light rushing out in a shockwave around her as her skin turned to ashes, and vast fiery wings took the place of her arms, a deafening roar erupting from her great maw. As an elite phoenix, she could cause enough distraction and chaos for the both of them to flee. She let forth a tirade of fire, and the guards' horses screeched, rearing up on their hind legs and knocking the guards from their backs as they turned and ran. The general was shouting some kind of orders, either at Akuji and Morana, or his cowardly guards as they fled the scene. Regardless, it couldn't be said that that was a main worry in Akuji's mind as Morana transformed back into a person, the fire on her back fizzling out with a hiss, but not before leaving her with a few significant burns. She winced, but they both bolted in the opposite direction, headed for the village and covered by the smoke screen, thick enough to choke the breath from their lungs.

Their feet carried them all the way to the village entrance that night, and only as dawn light filtered through the tree line, did they dare to look behind them. They hadn't been followed, but now the exhaustion was taking its toll on them, especially Morana. Though he'd trained her in the art of shifting, she hadn't been alive for more than two centuries, so her stamina quickly grew weak. Her eyes were glazed over with exhaustion, and her knees shook, then buckled beneath her. Akuji caught her under the arms and hoisted her onto his back as one would a small child. He staggered to the local inn and shouldered the door open. He approached the innkeeper, who was leaning against a wooden support, her arms crossed.

"Please, miss; are there any rooms available? We've traveled long, through much difficulty, and we're in great need of a place to lay our heads," he said, a note of desperation creeping into his voice. The innkeeper eyed him, then Morana, her blond braids shifting over her shoulders as she turned her head. She let out a long sigh.

"We got an attic room. It ain't pretty, but it's all we gots left. 'Course that all depends on y'all. You ain't gon' make a ruckus, is you?" she questioned in a thick southern accent. He shook his head.

"No ma'am. We'll be out of your hair in a few days' time," he responded.

"I'll have y'all moved down to our real rooms, then. Once the freeloaders take their leave, that is," she drawled. A drunken man, possibly a soldier, staggered over to them. He took a swig from his bottle, missing his mouth for the most part. As the ale ran down the front of his ragged shirt, he stepped closer to Akuji.

"You! Y'all two's here to do it! Mhm, yessir they'll do you in for sure. You'll get what you came for!" he slurred, wavering between Akuji and the innkeeper, before weaving his way back to the table he rose from, collapsing on the chair in a drunken stupor. The innkeeper scoffed.

"Don't mind him. Just a local drunk with too much coin and not enough sense," she sneered.

After a beat of silence, she jerked her thumb in the direction of a flight of stairs, and Akuji approached them. As he reached the top step, he peered around the room. The low ceiling gave a chilling sensation of being trapped, and the beds were just three hay mattresses, with the fourth being stuffed with feathers and bird down. There were three oil lamps, placed at the foot of the beds with the previously known fourth shattered on the ground, spilling its flammable contents over the wood flooring. He heaved Morana and himself up the stairs, and placed her on the feather down bed, which was on the far end of the row. He took the bed on the opposite side, which had the broken lamp at its foot, and was closest to the stairs. After checking on Morana more times than he'd like to count, Akuji let his head hit the pillow, and succumbed to sleep.

In the morning, or more so afternoon, he awoke to the sun slanting nearly vertical through the window. He turned over in the scratchy hay bed, and saw Morana, lying on her back the same way he had left her the night before. He got out of bed, and surveyed the room, now illuminated by the sun. There was a small bathroom, one you had to squat to get through the door, and upon further inspection, the running water was (surprisingly) clean, and the shower ran, which he utilized immediately. He showered, glad to get the smells of forest and that dead body from his skin, and down the drain. Just as he was preparing to visit the town and see what there was, Morana woke. She sat up quickly, looking around briskly before her eyes landed on Akuji.

"We're in the attic of the local inn. Everything went fine. We were not followed. I'm about to look around town and see what it has. You also need ointment for those burns before they get infected," he explained, answering her questions before she could ask them. She twisted to see her burns; how severe they were. He himself had not had the chance to check them or treat them, so he leaned in as well, nervous to what they might find. The burn went from the nape of her neck to the base of her back. The skin was a charred ombre, lighter red on the outside, and a deep angry red closer to the middle of her back. She winced and reached into his satchel for a spare shirt. She rolled the shirt over her torso, wincing as the rough fabric rubbed against her raw skin.

"I'll come too. I need the fresh air," she said, struggling to stand. He put a firm hand on her shoulder and gently pushed her back down. "If you need air, there are windows. You are in no state to be walking around with a wound like that," he instructed. She scowled at him, but she did not get back up. Once he was sure she would not follow him, he walked lightly down the stairs and entered the lobby of the inn. The innkeeper was now replaced with the barkeep, an older man with a bushy gray beard and a bulbous nose poking out from above his mustache. He had a matching pair of bushy eyebrows that drooped down over his eyes. The hair on his head had thinned to a few struggling whisps, let loose to move about like blades of grass. Akuji nodded to him, and opened the door, hearing the bell ding on his way out. The central road of the village was dirt, beaten down by hundreds of feet passing over the loose soil until it was stomped into place. Small cottages lined the sides of the road, which opened out to a dirt roundabout, surrounded by little shops. Akuji spotted the Traveler's shop, which would hopefully have all he needed. He entered the building, surveying the goods when his eyes landed on the hunched figure of an imp. The shopkeeper smiled wryly at him, revealing a row of pointed yellow teeth.

"How can I help you, sir?" it rasped. He shook his head.

"I'll find everything well by myself, thanks." He walked down the aisle with bandages and grabbed a couple rolls. He thumped them down on the counter, startling the dozing imp.

"That'll be all, sir?" it wheezed. Akuji nodded and placed four gold coins on the counter. The imp wormed a bony hand across the table, and slid the coins into its lap, not taking its swollen yellow eyes off him.

Akuji shoved the bandages into his satchel, and left the shop, feeling chills down his spine as the gaze of the shopkeeper lingered. "Sir? Sir, any coins to spare?" a hoarse voice called.

Akuji's head swiveled around, landing on the hunched shape of a homeless man, covered in rags and holding his grimy hands out. Akuji reached into his pocket, and pulled out two coins, placing them in the man's outstretched hands. The man's eyes widened.

"Oh, thank you, sir! Bless you, bless your kind soul unto eternity," he wheezed, getting up on his knees and grasping at Akuji's hands, blessing him over and over in a most foreboding way. Akuji managed to get away politely, and walked briskly back down the road, opening the door to the inn and rushing up the steps. He opened the door to Morana's expectant face. He held up the bandage in response.

"What about the burns?" she queried.

"For that we'll have to use some old magic."

"I thought you didn't do magic anymore?" she responded.

He rubbed his hands together, feeling the healing power flow from his veins as a warm glow emanated from his hands. She gingerly lifted the back of her shirt, and he lowered his hands over the burn. The power transferred from his hands to her back in green threadlike tendrils. The points of contact sent glowing green ripples throughout her skin, and the burns seemed to lift off of her back, revealing new pink skin beneath. Akuji lowered his hands, and she rolled her shirt back down. The green glow faded from the room, and Morana felt around her back carefully, expecting pain where her burns were. Her eyebrows raised in shock as she felt over the healed skin. "It's like it never even happened!" she said in awe.

"I'll teach you, sometime. Do you feel up for travel, because I have a feeling, we've overstayed our welcome." He gathered their small haberdashery of belongings into his satchel and slung it over his shoulder. Morana stood up, and slid her feet into her boots, lacing them with nimble fingers. She straightened up and nodded to him. With that, they stepped carefully down the stairs, nodding to the innkeeper on their way out.

They stepped through the town, patches of gravel crunching beneath their feet as they went. The cool morning air brushed Akuji's face like the cold hand of death, and he shuddered. They had barely stepped over the threshold of the village, when they heard the telltale sound of hooves clopping over the packed dirt.

He grabbed Morana's arm and pulled her into the bushes that flanked the woodland path. Akuji's ears shifted to that of an animal, and he leaned in to hear what was said.

"... They've killed the ... The prince, sir."

THE BURDEN OF BLOOD (PT. 2)

JUPITER STURM

Grade 11, Boys Town High School, Boys Town, NE. Beth Sulley, Educator.

"Good heavens, no!"

"Yes, I'm afraid."

"Dear god! Well, I believe they just passed through town!"

"Thank you, we'll be on our way now." The voices faded as Akuji's ears turned to human flesh again.

"What? What is it?" Morana urged, her fingers fidgeting aimlessly with anticipation.

"We need to go. The capitol, Althiir, it's nearby, no?"

"Yes, but going there is suicide! We're sentenced to death in Althiir, we'll be hanged!" She peeked out of the bushes, and Akuji looked from behind her head.

"They're gone. For now. They'll be back, and we can't be here when they arrive. They'll burn the village down," Akuji said grimly.

Morana gaped. "They said they'd be on their way. Why would they set fire to the village? They did nothing wrong!"

"Morana, the search for our kind has been happening eons before us, and they will continue for eons after we're gone. They're trying to flush us out, so we need to relocate." Akuji rose from the bushes, brushing leaves from his trousers. He offered a hand to Morana, helping her to her feet. They turned their backs on the village and followed the beaten path.

By morning they'd walked until their feet burned with blisters, and their eyelids weighed heavily on their face. The seaside city of Althiir peeked out from behind the tree line, glittering in the harsh sunlight. Akuji and Morana dragged their weary feet down the slight incline, stopping at the city gate for interrogation by the guard.

"What brings you to the capitol city?" he inquired.

"We are weary travelers in search of a place to rest. Please sir, we'll be gone in a fortnight," Akuji said tiredly. The guard looked from Akuji to Morana, then back to Akuji.

"You best not cause trouble here, or I'll have you both hanged, myself." The guard pulled a lever, and the great gates creaked open, the wooden bottoms of the doors scraping against the stone-paved ground.

The two weary travelers trudged through the gates and made their way to the nearest inn. Akuji had barely glanced at the innkeeper as he slapped the handful of coins down on the desk. He could have sworn the innkeeper's eyes flashed with recognition, then fear, but he couldn't trust what his weary eyes perceived. The innkeeper slid the room key across the counter and flinched when Akuji reached to grab it. Now he knew something was wrong. From the nervous fidgeting of the man across the counter, to the way his coworker paled at the sight of them, Akuji knew now that something was amiss. He followed Morana up the stairs, stepping quietly down the dark hallway and sliding the key into the lock of their room. The room was nicely furnished, with two twin beds, sharing a wide nightstand between them, and a woven rug softening their steps on the floor. Morana slipped out of her boots and crawled into bed, squirming under the covers. Akuji sat on the opposite bed, closest to the door, and stared at it for a long time. He felt increasingly uneasy with each passing second, fearing the coming of dawn more than he had feared anything before. He'd tried to sleep, though without much luck despite being on night two of sleeplessness. When the pink tendrils of sunlight had just begun climbing up the horizon and you could taste dawn in the air, there was the sound of a single pair of boots echoing against the stark silence surrounding them. The door to the inn opened and closed. Akuji felt the hairs on his arm stand on end, and a chill went down his spine. The realization of danger dawned on him, and he bolted out of bed, shaking Morana awake. She'd just opened her sleepy eyes when the sound of boots, many pairs of them, thumped up the stairs. Akuji spun around to face the door just as the shiny black boots of the royal guard splintered the aged wood. The guard drew his sword, while someone behind him blew a handful of powder into the room, certainly magical. This man had a distinctive look about him, his face obscured by the hood of his dark robe, bejeweled with rubies and amber. The head guard, the one holding the sword, reared back and swung the blade at Akuji. He instinctively shifted his skin to that of a crocodile, raising his arm to absorb the impact. Exactly three things happened then, as he would later remember in startling detail.

One: His shapeshifting abilities failed.

Two: The blade sliced deep into his flesh.

Three: The remaining guards flooded the room.

The blade wedged itself into his arm, going deeper than he cared to think about. A shriek tore from his throat, and he fell to his knees. The other guards swarmed Morana, tying her hands behind her back, her arms to her sides, and bound her ankles together while the first guard wrestled his sword from Akuji's arm. It swung free with a sickening squelch as the guard sheathed it and quickly dove on Akuji, binding his wrists and ankles. That was when the pain, the blood loss, and the exhaustion all came crashing down, and he fell unconscious.

When Morana awoke, she was affronted by a pulsating pain that made her ears ring. She'd been hit in the head after attempting to bite one of the guards. She glanced from side to side quickly. She was in a dim, stone room, sitting upright on a ledge next to Akuji's motionless form. With great difficulty, she leaned over, bumping his shoulder with hers.

"Hey, 'Kuji. Akuji!" she whispered. His head bolted up from his chest, and his pained expression showed that he immediately regretted it.

The wound on his arm wasn't bandaged or cleaned. Simply stitched together rather crudely with a burlap twine, the fibers of the thin rope scraping his raw skin. The wound was already an angry red, obviously harboring a deep infection. Who knew how long it's been festering there. A guard walked briskly into the room, halting in front of them. An executioner meandered his way into the room after him.

"Yakob and Morren, of the village of Rivulram and Mirfel, respectively," the guard began. Morana saw Akuji bristle at the names, those they'd been given generations before this time. The guard continued. "You've been tried and found guilty of the murder of the Heir to the throne of Althiir, Prince Pythius. You're sentenced to beheading for your crimes at the time of your awakening. You both will be marched aboveground and beheaded in the town square on this day," the guard said. Morana lunged at him, but the shackles on her wrists were chained to the wall, and the movement jarred her concussed head, making her sink to her knees. The executioner approached, using a key to release the chains from the walls, first Akuji, then Morana. Akuji had fallen back to unconsciousness, so he slumped to the ground upon his release. The guard hauled him up by his underarms and dragged him to the door where several other guards took him. The head guard came back for Morana, gripping a fistful of her hair and dragging her from the room. She twisted and writhed on the ground, the stone rubbing her skin raw. The guard dropped her in the doorway, a fistful of her hair falling out as her head bounced against the floor, jarring her brain. The throng of guards parted as she fell, a few of them gripping her under the arms and hoisting her upright. For once, she was glad they were holding her so tightly, because they were the only thing keeping her from meeting the floor again. Once they were sure she and Akuji were secured, they marched up a long, curving flight of stone stairs. They went down another long hallway, opening out to the town square. There was a large wooden platform with three steps to the level of it. In the center was a stone block with a circular indent carved on one side of it, likely for the chin of the tried to sit. The executioner sauntered up the steps and took his place by the block while the head guard made his way to the podium. Only then did the severity of their situation dawn on Morana. The panic made her breath come in short gasps. The guard was saying something, and the crowd responding, but she couldn't comprehend what they were saying. Only one thought crossed her mind, bouncing around in her head over and over again. She didn't want to die, and she didn't think she deserved to die. Akuji stirred, his eyes scrunching together as the pain of consciousness crashed down on him. He opened his eyes, clouded with pain and managed a small smile. Then the guards were heaving him over to the block, and every moment came in snapshots through her intense panic, her chest heaving breath after desperate breath. Akuji kneeled, and bent over, his front half lying on the stone. The executioner walked to the block, taking each step slowly, savoring the panic and fear. Akuji had his eyes closed, maybe praying, maybe saying his final goodbyes or maybe thinking of a way to escape.

Regardless, he wouldn't have had time to finish his thought. The executioner heaved the axe over his head, the dawn light glinting off the sharp blade, a moment frozen in time. The blade came down with a thud that turned Morana's stomach. She vomited, the fear and disgust and exhaustion all gathering, coming to a head in one final thought: Akuji is dead.

They kicked his lifeless body off the block, his fresh blood staining the stone and dripping down the side of the block, seeping into the wooden platform. She was leaned over the block. The blade of the axe kissed the back of her neck and lifted high. She waited for death to whisper in her ear, for the axe to separate her head from her body. Nothing. She risked a glance up and saw the axe resting by the executioner's side. There was a deep rumble that shook her to her core, her very bones. A great roar, followed by a gust of wind that could have toppled buildings. A dragon. The ground trembled, and she felt the burn of flames shoot over her head. She stood up in a crouch and barreled into the executioner, knocking both him and his axe over. She rubbed her bound wrists against the blade until the ropes released. Then she swung her legs around and rubbed the axe head against the rope binding her ankles. She stood up and looked around. The dragon had set fire to the seaside capitol city of Althiir, and soon she would, too. She closed her eyes, channeling every ounce of power she had left in her. She felt her bones stretch, stringing out her muscles and tendons as her skin turned scaly and rough. Her body sprouted new bones, wings extending from her back, a thin sheet of flesh stretched between the joint bones, horns sprouting from her forehead, her skull elongating to form a snout.

She beat her great wings, lifting off the ground and climbing through the air. She soared high above the city until the forest was beneath her and the air smelled of sweet flora and sea salt. The bitterness and grief had not yet come crashing down on her, but she could feel it lurking at the corners of her mind. She traveled for the entirety of the waking day until the exertion caught up with her. She searched for a village, stopping at the first one she saw. She coasted to the ground, shifting back into her human form. Her whole body ached, and she could feel her concussion echoing the screech of metal-on-metal inside her mind. She stumbled into the village, collapsing on the ground. She couldn't muster the strength to heave her tired bones off the ground, and lay in the dirt, waiting to succumb to death. The world came to her in hazy flashes, double vision, the pounding pain in her head her only anchor to consciousness.

The cold mud on her face, the hot blood pulsing through her veins, the contrast of light and dark, life and death blurring before her eyes. Two callused hands gripped her by the underarms and heaved her up. The deep, rumbling voice uttered a sentence, but she couldn't comprehend it, the exhaustion making her delirious. She felt herself being carried slowly, heard a door open, and shut. The heat of a fire warmed the side of her face as she was placed on warm stones, finally succumbing to sleep.

She spent the next several weeks fighting for her life, a ravenous fever making her muscles turn to jelly in her limbs and her brain electrified with pain. There was no differentiation between night and day, they were all the same to her.

Sleep, wake, eat, pain, sleep. On the night her fever finally broke, the people caring for her shared a first fearful glance with each other. Then a second. Her skin was a sickly pale, her flesh clinging to her bones, and her thin arms trembling. They laid a damp cloth on her forehead and sat next to her bedside. Her breath came in short gasps, her whole body aching for the sweet release of unconsciousness, or death. Then a sheen of sweat broke out over her forehead.

They removed the damp cloth, now quite warm, and placed a bowl of soup in front of her. She could barely lift the spoon to her lips, feeling the warm liquid slosh down her throat and fill her aching belly. Then her body heaved, and the soup reappeared all over the floor. She was better, but not yet well. She flopped back into the bed and closed her eyes, falling asleep once more.

On the day she found her footing, and was able to take a few steps, they brought her out to the town square. The summer had turned to fall quite fast, the freezing wind biting her exposed skin. She sat on a nearby bench to catch her breath, and the couple who were caring for her walked away. She'd been nothing but grateful for them saving her, and healing her, but now the bitterness of her survival was a throbbing orb of hatred beaming inside her head. The unfairness of Akuji's demise, the unfairness of her survival.

Then and there, she would have been perfectly content to die with her oldest friend. He'd taught her everything she knew, been her guide for nearly a century. How was she supposed to continue without him? He'd seldom spoke of his father, only mentioning that he, too, was a shapeshifter, and he, too, was dead. She wondered if Akuji was with his father now. She could have screamed, the rage bubbling inside her, burning its way up her throat, but she just sat.

The couple returned, and took her hand, helping her to her feet. She thought they were going back inside, but they took her to the center of the town square. In it, there was a deep hole dug in the ground. Panic flashed in her mind. The man put his hand firmly on her back and shoved her into the pit. She fell hard, her concussion throbbing as she slammed her head on the hard packed dirt. She stood up, jumping and gripping the edges of the dirt pit. Bits of earth crumbled off in her hands, but she got a grip and pulled. Just when her head made it over the edge, explosive pain shot through her fingers, and she cried out, falling back down. The man had brought his steel toed boots down on her fingers, and she was sure they were broken. She could tell by the way they took on a purple hue, the swelling turning them into puffy gloves. She looked back up, desperate for any sign of mercy. She was met with a clump of dirt to the face. More and more shovelfuls of dirt rained down on her, rising like the tide, hugging her tightly in its moist grip. The pit was filled in up to her shoulders when the dirt slowed, then stopped. She opened her eyes, and saw a crowd had gathered, looking at her with a glint of malice in their eyes. Piles of rocks sat all around the town square, tumbling over each other as everyone grasped handfuls of stones. The first one hit her in the temple, and she felt hot blood welling on the wound. The second hit her in the nose, jerking her head backward as blood streamed from her nose. The rocks continued to pummel her head and shoulders, each stone like a nail hammering into her coffin. She and Akuji had survived so much and enjoyed so little. They talked often about their plans for the day when society would accept them, when they could step out of the shadows and live their lives. Akuji would never get to see that day, and neither would Morana. They'd escaped from big cities and little towns. Fully armed guards, and barehanded heathens.

And now she would meet her end in the center of a tiny village, stoned to death by townspeople who had no qualms with her other than who she was when she was born. And Akuji, he only met his end from false accusations by a startled teen who'd never seen a dead body before. That, or he was an easy target. But Morana would never get to finish this thought, as two rocks pummeled her temple in quick succession, effectively caving in her skull and ending her agony.

A Letter to the Plastic Soldiers

Grade 11, Kearney High School, Kearney, NE. Charlotte Dvorak, Educator.

SILVER

(Each character will be associated with a different number, so things don't get confusing.)

_We_ were soldiers. _They_ made us soldiers. All of our early memories of the world were where we were inside of our capsules being given food and water via the tube connected to our chests. We had masks on so we could breathe. We could not open our eyes, but we could think.

Some time later, our batch would be released from our capsules, only to have barcodes tattooed to the back of our necks and forced through military training. At some point in the past the people decided to _use_ artificial people instead of _real_ people. They don't care how _we_ feel about it. To them, we are disposable. _We_ are their plastic soldiers.

∞∞∞∞∞∞∞∞∞∞∞∞∞∞∞∞∞∞∞∞∞∞

Day one: How do I (1) write this? How can some authors make it so their stories are written like a diary? Or maybe a story that goes, day one, day two, day three, day four, etc.? Do they even do that, or am I (1) the first one? Anyway, I (1) think it is best to write this story going from day to day, it is my real story, after all.

Let's start over. I (1) have a story unlike any other. One that you probably won't believe is true after all. Whether you believe it or not, I (1) don't care, because I (1) know that it happened.

∞∞∞∞∞∞∞∞∞∞∞∞∞∞∞∞∞∞∞∞∞∞

It was the day after my brother's track meet. I (1) was sitting in my room listening to music on my phone (the same phone I am using to write this story) when suddenly I (1) saw myself (2) leaning against the door, wearing a suit that definitely wasn't from the twenty-first century. I (2) stared at myself (1) for a few seconds, both me and me not saying a word, before I (2) decided to get on with my mission. I (2) stepped away from the door and lunged at my (1) arm, which was dangling off the side of the bed, and strapped a time band to it. I (1) didn't have a second to think before I (1) felt my body leave the bed and was whisked off to the future, 100 years from now.

※※※※※※※※※※※※※※※※※

I (2) was told that my (2) mission was to bring myself (1) to the future and then stay in the past and pretend to be myself (1) until I (1) could be returned to the past. As I (1) disappeared from the bed I (2) began to make my (2) way to the living room of the house, but I (2) was greeted by an unexpected face, a face that told me that the future will be different than I remember.

※※※※※※※※※※※※※※※※※

Day two: I (1) woke up in a dark room. A dark room with glowing capsules inside of it. Each capsule had a person inside of it (human batteries maybe?). At the end of the room I saw myself (3) sitting at a desk with an old-fashioned computer on it, but what appeared on the computer screen was anything but old-fashioned.

As I (1) approached the desk, I (1) started to hear myself (3) talking under my (3) breath. I (1) swear I (1) heard myself (3) saying "the batteries are almost out of juice, so they should be replaced." And then I (3) pressed a button on my (3) keyboard, and in an instant, the people inside of the capsules were vaporized and replaced by the people that came through the back door. When they were being hooked up to the machine, they fought back for a moment, but their bodies quickly went limp.

I (1) was so focused on myself (3) sitting at the desk, that I didn't even notice what was going on with the capsules. As I (1) got closer to the desk I (3) turned my chair around to see a confused me (1) asking where he was and why I (3) looked almost exactly like him. But our conversation was cut short when I (1) began to feel dizzy and lightheaded before fainting.

Luckily, I (3) just had a few minutes left in my shift, so when it ended I picked up my unconscious self (1) and took myself (1), not to a hospital, but back to my house. And when we arrived I quickly took myself (1) to the guest bedroom and set myself (1) down on the bed and then went downstairs to make myself (3) a sandwich.

※※※※※※※※※※※※※※※※※

Day three: The next time I (1) woke up, I wasn't in any laboratory or anything, but instead I was in a very nice-looking bedroom. I still felt a little dizzy, so when I tried moving around I just kept bumping into things and kept knocking things down. Someone must have heard me, because I heard someone yelling "stay in that room please! I will be up there in a minute!" Whoever was yelling must have forgotten that they locked the door because when I tried leaving the door wouldn't budge.

About five minutes later someone who looked almost exactly like me came into the room holding a plateful of pancakes. "I thought you would be pretty hungry after traveling through time and sleeping for a day," I (3) said. "I mean, I know I would be. I have never traveled through time before, but I was in a capsule for a few months, and I got hungry quickly then." It's true, I was hungry, but I was also curious about my current situation, so as I sat down to eat my pancakes, I began to ask questions.

Question one: "What am I doing here?" I asked. It seemed to take myself (3) a while to come up with an answer, but when I did get an answer, all I got was, "That will remain a secret until later." I was left with more questions than answers.

Question two: "Why do you look like me?" This was the question that I was the most curious about. Why did he look like me? "Well, you know how I said that I was in a capsule for a few months?" I (3) said. "That was because I am a *clone* of you, we all are. Our creators used *your* DNA to create us. We all were born in capsules." The words, "clone" and "we all are," sent a shiver down my spine.

Question three: "why were all of you created?" Yet again, it seemed to take myself (3) a long time to answer, but then I (3) took a deep breath and said, "for war."

"What, why war?" I (1) asked. I (3) took another deep breath and said, "One day the government decided the *valuable* lives of the people are being wasted when they join the military. So they created us. We replaced them."

Yeah, I'm done with that question.

Question four: "Why did they use my DNA?" I (1) asked. "Out of all the bodies that they considered using, they thought your DNA was the best for the job," I (3) said. "Although, if you ask me, I would have gone with someone else."

Question five: "Those people that I saw in the capsules in the lab, they didn't look like me, so what purpose do they serve?" I wish I hadn't asked this, because I (3) responded with, "the non clones. After the US used us to take over the world, we finally decided that *they* will no longer have control over us. They were too *powerless* to stop us, we were their army after all. After we conquered them we discovered that the human body actually makes a really good energy source, and we figured that they should be punished for the way they treated us. So half of them became a part of the energy plants, and the other half were sold into *slavery*." At this point I was done asking questions. It took me the whole rest of the day to process what I (1) had heard. And I was left alone in a room that was *mine* in a world that was *mine*.

◇◇◇◇◇◇◇◇◇◇◇◇◇◇◇◇◇◇◇◇◇◇◇◇◇◇◇◇◇

Day four: I finally had enough bravery to leave the room. The rest of the house was nice as well, and when I went downstairs I heard a voice behind me say, "and the rising prince has arisen!" I turned around to see myself (3) sitting on a couch looking back my way with a paused TV on the wall. The TV seemed to have been playing the news, and the anchor looked like me as well. "You want something to eat?" I (3) said. I (1) turned around to see a counter with a plate with some eggs and bacon on it. "I made it for ya."

After I was done eating, I decided that today I was going to go walk around town to see how things are. I asked myself (3) if it was okay. He said that it was okay, as long as I took a phone with me. After I grabbed the phone, I headed for the door and went out into a beautiful dystopia.

After I stepped out the door, I noticed that a neighbor's family was having a barbecue and the entire family, including the children, looked like clones of me. I continued walking downtown and began to notice more and more people, people who were me. As I kept on walking, I walked past a school, and the school looked relatively normal (except for all the child me's), until I looked through a window and saw that the teachers didn't look like me, but they were chained to a pole inside of the classrooms.

I noticed a billboard that advertised an event that they call the "festival of the original." By "original" do they mean me? And what is going to happen during this festival? As I got a closer look at the billboard I noticed the date of the festival. It was tomorrow. And ... it also said that ... this year the original will be the one to bring death to the chosen slave.

I got back "home" later that evening, and I decided that I should ask myself (3) what his job was. And he said that he was a "slave manager" and that his job was to monitor the slaves' thoughts and make sure that the slaves never thought anything negative about the society. With that info I began to wonder why the slaves were chained up. Maybe it was just a failsafe?

After I asked him about his job, I asked him what the "festival of the original" was. He said that it was an annual celebration celebrating the clones' victory over the non-clones. Each year there is a lot of dancing, singing and food. And they end it all off with the death of a chosen slave. Every year one person from the crowd is chosen to come on stage. On the stage there will be two guns, one loaded and one not loaded. The crowd will know which one is which, but the slave won't. Both guns will be used and it is against the law to choose the loaded gun first. The non-loaded gun is used for psychological effect. And this year, instead of the murderer being chosen at random, it will be me. And there is no way that I can escape it.

◇◇◇◇◇◇◇◇◇◇◇◇◇◇◇◇◇◇◇◇◇◇◇◇◇◇◇◇◇◇◇◇

Final day: I (3) dressed myself (1) up in a tuxedo for the festival. I (3) was in tux as well. We then proceeded to get into my (3) car. On our way there I noticed that I (1) looked nervous, so I looked at myself and said, "Don't worry about it, you'll do just fine!" After I (1) was told that, I took a deep breath and put on a fake smile, which he seemed to believe.

Once I arrived at the festival, I (1) was greeted by a lot of paparazzi. The lights nearly blinded me. All of the flashes quickly ended when a person went on stage. When I (4) stepped on stage, my nerves felt like they were about to explode. But when I stepped up to the microphone I yelled "death to the non-clones!" The crowd erupted in cheers but was quickly silenced. I (4) continued to yell, "Welcome one and all, to this wonderful festival!" "This year, like every year, we shall be celebrating the defeat of our enemies, of our creators!" "The day that we declared our independence from them all!" "They are not human! We are the only true humans! The *master* race!"

The event was more like a high school prom than a festival. There was a lot of dancing in the middle and a lot of food and drinks on the outer parts. And, to top it all off, several bands played their songs, all of which are about how "perfect" their world was, and how the non-clones are evil.

As I (4) walked off stage, the first band began to play their song. Several songs are supposed to be played throughout the festival, these songs are:

"Our World"

"Science and Cells"

"Used"

"When Can We Be Free?"

"Perfect"

"Creation"

"Dominance"

"A Clone World"(Our international anthem)

After the final song was finished, I (1) was quickly ushered up onto the stage. They had just put the table with the two guns as well as the tied-up slave on stage. When I was brought on stage I began to reach for the first gun, and then the crowd began chanting "life!" "life!" "life!" I picked up the gun. "Life!" I checked for ammo. "Life!" I aimed it. "Life!" And I fired. "Life!" Nothing came out. "Life is so much more than stone!" As I began to reach for the other gun, the crowd began chanting "death!" "death!" "death!" I checked for ammo. "Death!" I aimed it. "Death!" And I fired. "Death!" The body went limp. "Death is a cursed blessing that never ends!" I was escorted off stage and the festival was brought to an end.

<><><><><><><><><><><><><><><><><><><>

Before I was sent back to my time, I was given a time band so then I could come back whenever I want. But I (3) explained that there are some events that are "time locked," which means that I can't stop them from happening, like the creation of the clones. And after he explained that, we waved each other good-bye, and I felt my body being whisked off to the past.

The other me that sent me to the future was nowhere to be seen when I got back, and so I got to work. I got out a piece of paper and a pencil and began to write a poem.

THE PLASTIC SOLDIERS

By _____

Born of science and cells

Born all the same

The barcodes are our scars

Forced through training

Do what you are told

All the people we killed

They saw them too
I wanted to hate the viewers
But I didn't
I turned to them and said
"Do you want peace?"

Once I was finished with the poem, I folded the piece of paper and put it into an envelope. I gave the envelope to someone (I won't say who) and told him to put it in my coffin when I die.

A few days later, I was listening to music on my bed again when I saw myself (2) leaning on the door. But instead of forcing me to the future, he extended his hand and said, "Do you want to come with me?" I put my phone in my pocket and took his hand and felt my body being taken to the future.

When we landed in the future, we seemed to land on the stage from the festival, and I saw myself (2) walk off stage and take a seat at a nearby table with myself (3) and a me I did not recognize. I looked forward and saw the announcer from the festival looking back at me. I (4) turned around and announced to the crowd, "The original has arrived!" "It is now finally time to celebrate the peace we made!" "Humans and clones, celebrating together!" I looked over my (4) shoulders and saw that the crowd was not just made up of clones, but half of them did not look like me. I (4) walked off stage and took a seat at a table with my friends. I saw the announcer walk off stage and take a seat at a table with I (2) and I (3) and the me I did not recognize.

I looked to the left and saw a non-me walking onto the stage, and when he reached me, he extended his hand. The crowd began chanting "take the hand!" "take the hand!" "take the hand!" And so I placed my hand in his and then the crowd yelled "*Peace!*"

I took a seat with the other versions of me I knew because of my five days in the future, as well as the me I did not know. I (3) leaned over and whispered, "We don't know how, but we still remember, and our creators liked your poem." And he winked at me. And so I took out my phone and we all agreed that this was a story worth telling. We all played a role in the making of the story. The name of the story? Well, we decided to call it *A Letter to the Plastic Soldiers*.

WHAT I AM, WHAT AM I?

GAGE TOWNSEND

Grade 11, Kearney High School, Kearney, NE. Charlotte Dvorak, Educator.
Honorable Mention.

Your development is going quite well. You started out as just a blob of gelatin (a bunch of cells and tissue). But soon your body began to form inside the incubator (basically a giant glass and metal tube). You are not a normal human.

You see, you are at the center of a revolutionary project. They are trying to combine an AI with a human body. They are trying to break the line between human and AI. And it is going quite well.

When your blob form was created, all it took was a small zap from a machine to insert what would eventually become your digital consciousness. It had taken a full decade for you to be ready to leave the capsule. And when you opened your eyes for the first time on day 300, it was truly something to celebrate. Your eyes were filled with warmth, curiosity and kindness. And you looking around the futuristic lab, taking it all in, was a priceless moment.

You weren't left out of the celebration, though. Before you woke up they had to manually connect the feeding tube to your mouth. And during the celebration one scientist named Dr. Mitchell, the kindest of us all, decided to give you a taste of chocolate cake, as well as some water. (They always gave you water during feeding time.)

Since you were awake then, you willingly grabbed the tube and connected it to your mouth. They were luckily able to use a chemical to remove all the bad stuff from the cake while still retaining its flavor. (Why don't they sell the stuff? They could make a fortune!) Your eyes closed as your mouth received the chocolate cake goop. You were clearly enjoying it as you cupped your hands around the tube. And when there was no more cake, you opened your eyes again, satisfied.

From that day on you just watched them do their work. You were such a curious little bunch. And we usually didn't have to tell you when it was feeding time. You learned that all by yourself. You were usually fed by your favorite person, Dr. Mitchell. You were always so excited to see her. And although you liked the special food mix that was made specifically for you, chocolate cake was your favorite.

After feeding time was testing time. During testing time they would test your brain development by playing games. One of the games you played was where they would show a color and a series of objects. In order to win the game, you had to point to the object with the same color. If you were to win every game, you would be rewarded with the chocolate cake goop for dessert at the next feeding time.

At around the age of five they decided to test your audio and mobile abilities. They would test your mobile abilities by anchoring you to the bottom of the tube and watching you try to walk. They tested your audio abilities by activating the tube's audio system, allowing you to hear them and them to hear you. The goal of that test was to see if you could copy the words and letters they are saying.

Both of those tests ended with huge milestones! After a few months of practicing every day, you were eventually able to take your first steps inside the capsule and say your first word. Your first word was "out." (You had once asked them how you were able to do things such as cry, talk, hear and breathe while in the liquid filled tube. But they never really gave you a clear answer. But, hey, at least no one wants to know how you went to the bathroom!) Both of these milestones ended with parties and a lot of chocolate cake goop. They decided to keep the audio system on 24/7 from that point on. But the night after the first word party, there was an unexpected test.

You see, these scientists live here in the lab and reside in different apartment-like places. And one night they woke up at midnight to you wailing at the top of your lungs. Dr. Mitchell rushed over to see what was happening, only to find you with tears streaming down your face. "What's wrong?" Dr. Mitchell asked. (She had always been kind to children ever since her son died ten years ago. Her son's death gave her a new perspective, which is why she is so nice and values every life.) "Out, want out," you said while sobbing. "Out, please." Until this point the scientists had never thought what you thought about all this. You had never asked to be made. But they knew you couldn't go out of your capsule yet. Your body wasn't ready. You had to stay in there for a few more years. And so, Dr. Mitchell tried to calm you down in the way she thought was best. She sang lullabies. And she did not leave your side that night.

The next morning they used the events of the previous night as an opportunity. They began emotion-based tests.

Anger: they would pretend to give you chocolate cake goop only for there to be none.

Fear: they would bang on the capsule.

Joy: they gave you chocolate cake goop.

Frustration: they would give you a task they knew you would fail.

Sadness (perhaps the most cruel test yet): they would pretend to abandon you and leave you crying in the building for several minutes. (That test is a cruel thing to do to a five year old!)

But after every negative emotion test, Dr. Mitchell would rush to your side and try to calm you down by saying that everything will be alright. Heck, you should see her after every sadness test. She *sprints* back into the building because she can't stand to hear you crying. She was once a mother, after all.

Even though the emotion tests were cruel, Dr. Mitchell did her best to give you a good childhood. She took over as the person who ran the game-based tests after feeding time. She always made those games fun. And when you wanted her to, she would find a picture book to read to you. She was the mother you needed.

Even though she was a mother figure to you, she did not make the game-based tests any easier. In fact, she made them harder! You started playing things like memory games and spelling games.

Shortly after she took over the game-based testing, she introduced you to something extraordinary, music. And I'm not talking about the lullabies she sings to you. I'm talking about real music. She managed to hook up her phone to the audio system and play "what does the fox say" for you. It was both entertaining and educational. And soon you found yourself moving to the music. She would have it play in the background of every game-based test.

Combine that with the fact that she is the only person who treats you nicely, it would make sense that you would only feel comfortable practicing speech in front of her. You had five, fifteen-minute-long practice sessions every day. With her as your teacher it wasn't surprising that it didn't take you long to get good.

After you started to get good at talking, she started teaching you other things. She somehow found time to teach you things like math and English. It was funny how she had to press books to the glass so then you could read them by yourself.

By the age of six you were able to form full sentences, understand addition and subtraction and read picture books by yourself. With your ability to talk, you did your best to describe what it is like to live in the capsule. "It's very lonely" and "I want hugs and kisses" you would say, usually with tears forming in your eyes. Tears would form in Dr. Mitchell's eyes as well, knowing that she can't give you hugs and kisses yet.

Another thing you loved to do back then was call the other scientists "big meanies." Often they would respond with something like, "Oh come on, you're not even fully human. You're an experiment. So it doesn't matter what we do to you." Those words felt like a punch to the gut to you. You are human, aren't you?

One time after one of the scientists said that it didn't matter what they did to you, Dr. Mitchell finally snapped. She marched over to him and threatened to go all mom mode on him if "you don't stop saying those hurtful words to my son!" You didn't know how to react to hearing those words, as you were only six years old. You had never been anyone's child before. But you smiled anyway. And after the man left, you spoke. "Can I call you mommy?" you said. Tears began to form in her eyes. It had been years since someone had called her that. She thought back to all the fun times she had with her biological son before he died. All the picnics, parks, and genuine fun. She turned back to you, eyes red from tears, and said, "Yes, you can, my child."

And so, that's what you started calling her. Whenever you needed something, you would yell "Mommy!" and she would come over and ask you what you needed. Usually it was something like "I'm thirsty," and she would fill up the feeding tube with some water and let you have at it.

But around the age of seven, you began to express ... different desires. You wanted entertainment. You wanted something to play with. "Mommy!" you had called out. And as usual, Dr. Mitchell would come rushing and ask what you needed. Her eyes widened when you said, "I want a toy."

How could she have been so stupid? Of course a child would want something to play with! So she became a woman on a mission. You had wanted a toy, and she was going to get you one. But it wasn't easy. She had to find a toy that would be fit for the conditions of your tube.

And oh how you loved that metal choo-choo train! You would play with it on the floor, walls and even ceiling of your capsule. And Dr. Mitchell loved to see you having fun with her gift. And perhaps the most important thing it did was it and Dr. Mitchell helped you through one of the most cruel tests of all. The pain test.

The pain test ... I honestly can't believe that they would do something like that. I like to call it "the boiling." They would ... begin to heat the liquid of the capsule. Your screams of pain were music to their ears. But they were like claws to a chalkboard to Dr. Mitchell. She begged for them to stop, but to no avail. Burn, scream, burn more, scream more. It seemed almost endless. You couldn't help but think, "Why ... what did I do to deserve this?" You looked at the scientists. You saw nothing but red in their eyes.

8 ... 9 ... 10, the years seemed to go on forever. Until it came time for you to come out. The glass of the capsule came down like a sliding panel. The liquid briefly hugged the feet of the scientists as it came spilling out. You couldn't help it. You collapsed onto the floor. Dr. Mitchell rushed to help you up, but you motioned for her to stop. You got back up on your own, and walked over to the scientists, to me, and looked at us in the eyes. I can still remember seeing the faint hint of red in your eyes.

TO HAVE A LITTLE FUN

GAGE TOWNSEND

Grade 11, Kearney High School, Kearney, NE. Charlotte Dvorak, Educator.
Honorable Mention.

Pain shot up through my arm as the man with the glowing eyes bit into my arm with his sharp teeth. I tried to scream but his hand was covering my mouth. After he released his teeth from my arm he said, "Don't worry, you will be one of us in just a moment," and a few seconds later the pain subsided and he said, "Your teeth are sharp, just like mine. Now it's time to have some fun." He lifted his hand off my face and I felt my teeth with my tongue. They were sharp now. I looked at the man and saw that his eyes weren't glowing anymore. He noticed my confused expression and said, "Don't worry, they're still glowing. It's just you're one of us now, and we can't see each other's glowing eyes." And then I felt adrenaline rush through my body and I realized that my next course of action should be to make others join in on the fun of being one of us.

Once I made that realization, my brain became flooded with information. Information about what is happening. About what this is. About what will happen when the sun rises again. As well as what will happen when it sets. And most of this information is incomprehensible to a normal human mind. But not to the mind of someone like us.

"How did you know that I wasn't like you?" I said. He just shrugged and said, "I don't know, honestly. We can't really tell the difference physically, unless your mouth is open. But when we are near a person who is not like us, we get the urge to bite them. No one really knows how our brains know. They just do." And with that I began to feel the feeling that he said would happen. My parents haven't joined us yet, but I just shook my head and said, "Can't do it." The man looked at me with confusion. "Why not?" he asked. I waited a few seconds for his brain to start working properly. "Oh ..." he realized. He looked at me again, this time his eyes filled with understanding. "And to be honest, even though this all sounds fun, I wish you had given me more of a choice. But there's nothing we can do about it now." I turned to the door and said, "I've resisted strong urges before, and believe me this is nothing!" (sigh) "And even though I do want my parents to be with me, I am going to give them a choice."

Martin nodded and said, "I'll be waiting here. And, dude, look, I'm sorry that I got you roped into all this without your permission. It's just that in my life I was never given a choice to do anything. It was always do this and do that, and if I didn't, I would be severely punished. And tonight I was given the opportunity to take my own frustration out on someone else. And that person was you, and I guess I never really thought it through. But now I see that you are right, and I will keep that in mind for the future."

As soon as we all left the house, we were greeted by a lot of cheering coming from the people who were waiting outside to see if the other guy would be able to invite a whole family to the party. These people also had sharp teeth, some of which are bloodstained. That party is being one of us, of course. Oh how I love being one of us. It truly is a party.

In the middle of all of the cheering, the other guy introduced himself as Martin. "Alright, let's see that arm," Martin said. I didn't understand why he would want to see my arm. But I showed it to him anyway, and then I saw it. The bite wound had completely healed. There wasn't even a scar. "Rapid regeneration, cool!" I said. "Isn't it?" said Martin. "When you're one of us, the amount of time it takes for an injury to heal depends on how much you want it to heal, although we still have weak spots. An injury to the head or the heart can still lead to death. And you can also use it to heal others, although you have to have harmed them in some way. We also don't have to sleep!"

"Check this out," Martin said. "Hey! I am going to need two people from the crowd to please come up here for a demonstration!" And then a man and a woman came up to him. He held out his hands and gestured for them to sit on his palms, which they did. And then, almost effortlessly, he started to juggle them. And then I came to realize that doing something like this in a normal society would be seen as weird and unusual. But yet, I wanted to do it as well. As these people were loving it. And because all of the attention was on Martin, I was able to get a good look at the audience. It was filled with men, women, and children of different colors, shapes and sizes. "Weird," I thought. "You usually don't see this kind of stuff."

After the little show, Martin was approached by a small group of men and women. One of them was wearing a backpack. "Hey, Martin," one of the men said, "we are getting a little hungry and we thought we might as well get a midnight snack, not a normal, boring one, but a more fun one at the nearby farm. Do you want to join us?" "Sure," Martin said, "as long as I can bring my new friend with me." "Yeah, he can come. We don't discriminate against teenagers," the man said. I looked at my parents and they nodded. "It's more fun that way," they said. And I smiled.

We arrived at the farm half an hour later. It almost looked deserted because of how the animals were all in their pens and cages, sleeping. "A'right." Martin pointed at me. "You spread the fun to the farmer and we will get our snack ready." I pointed at him and said, "but only if he wants me to."

When I arrived at the house part of the farm, I heard no noise from inside the building, which makes sense because it isn't even one o'clock yet. And as I slipped through the front door into the kitchen, I saw something very unexpected. Blood was covering the floor, and in the middle of the floor was the farmer. His mouth was open. He had sharp teeth too, and a knife wound in his heart. I couldn't breathe. I tried to walk backwards, but I slipped. Now my hands are covered in blood. I looked at the knife and saw that it had a bloody handprint on the handle. Slowly, I got up and made for the door.

Once I left the building, I noticed that the others had already built a fire, and that there were several cows in the field. I joined them and sat down next to the fire. And I noticed that they were eating the raw flesh off the cows' legs, which were ripped off, although none of the cows were in pain. And so, noticing how hungry I was, I did the same. And when I placed my right hand on a cow, my hand started to glow. About one second later, the cow was no longer in pain. Raw meat actually tastes good when you are one of us, although it makes me wonder what the fire is for.

"Where's the farmer?" Martin asked. "When I found him in the kitchen, he was dead. He got a knife to the heart," I said. They all gasped and said, "Who would dare to disrespect us? We did nothing to them!" Then Martin said, "Those who give no respect, get no respect!" And we all yelled in agreement.

The man with the backpack took his backpack off. He opened the backpack and pulled out a teddy bear. "You know, I thought that I would always have to keep this guy a secret, because I don't want to be seen as weak just because a teddy bear gives me comfort. But I know that I don't have to keep him a secret when I am around people like me. Right?" We all nodded. He then pointed at the bear and said, "I call him Ted. And now I realize that when you're one of us, you don't have to hide who you truly are. Because we're all unusual here. And unlike society, we don't care what gender you are, what race you are, nor your religion. We just want to have fun, and we want to do it together."

We spent a few hours doing a variety of things around the campfire. We sang songs, we danced, we also told scary stories. And just as we started to leave, we heard an ear-shattering scream coming from the nearby forest. Instinctively, we checked it out. And after a few minutes of searching, we found multiple dead bodies in a river, a few of which were children. Each body had sharp teeth and a stab wound where their heart should be. And the river water was dyed dark red.

Before any of us could say anything, I felt something whisk past my head. I looked back and saw, not a bullet, but a knife, embedded in the tree behind me. We couldn't tell where the knife came from, as it was shot from an area that was so far out that not even our eyes illuminated it. We all ran back to where we came from. Once we got back to the fire, we had to pull knives out of each other. We all debated on what we should do next. And then suddenly we all paused and stared at each other. And simultaneously, we all said, "lunar manor."

Lunar manor is actually an abandoned building located near the end of town. The building once belonged to a company called S.O.L.A.R (save our lives and rights) and was dedicated towards making the world a better place. But the whole company went bankrupt a year ago, and they have yet to demolish the building.

Once we reached the building, we all got the urge, telling us that someone is inside who is not one of us. In a way, the urge sort of acts like a radar. The stronger the urge, the closer you are. And with that, we were able to determine that there are at least two locations in the building that have people in them. They sent me to the closest location by myself. I tried to argue, but it was a majority vote. Once I reached the location, however, I was met with a gun to my head.

The room had four people in it. There was an older male and female and two young boys. They must be a family. One of the boys must have been injured, as there was a lot of blood coming from his arm. There was also a mysterious contraption in the corner of the room. The older male had a gun pointed at me, and he told me that if I take one more step that he will shoot. "Can I sit at least?" I said. The man looked at me intently and then said, "Yes, you may sit down."

In the man's left hand was a knife, a knife with a lot of blood on it, as if he used it to kill someone. "Look, we're not who you—" I started to say, but I was interrupted by the man. "I know exactly what you are! You are a monster! a zombie! wanting to eat us in order to satisfy your hunger!" he said. "What?" I said after gasping. "I am not a monster! I am human, like you! I'm just different, that's all!" The man looked at me. "If you really are human, then why do you have those sharp, bloodstained teeth?" he asked. "The blood is from animal meat! and I healed the poor thing!" I said. "And the eyes?" the man argued. I couldn't come up with a good response, so I just said, "Okay, I don't know about the eyes! That is just one of the things that happens when you become one of us!" I yelled. The man continued to argue: "One of us! That is definitely not something that a monster would say!" And right after he said that the injured boy fainted.

I immediately stood back up, but the man yelled at me. "Sit back down!" he said. The woman was now crying while hugging the child. A window in the room began to glow, as the sun was beginning to rise. I felt my powers begin to weaken. "I can save him. You just have to let me help!" I yelled. "Now why would I want to get help from—" he began to say, but the woman took the gun and the knife and covered his mouth. "Please, do whatever you need to do in order to save my son!" she pleaded. And so I got to work. But right as I released him from my jaw, my teeth became dull. And now we can only hope that there is still enough time.

I met up with my friends again once it fully became morning. They had turned back as well. Although where were the other people that they detected in the building? Did they escape? "We gave them a choice," Martin said.

We all decided to go back to our own homes. I spent the whole day remembering the past night's events. And when midnight came yet again, my room was illuminated despite the fact that no lights were on.

A smile crept across my face.

A Talk Between Aliens and People Who Once Thought They Were Alone

Annah Vogelpohl

Grade 8, Elkhorn Ridge Middle School, Omaha, NE. Honorable Mention.

Getting Ready Before the World Ends

Shirley always wore saturated orange-beige. It went along nicely with her dirty blonde hair on the brink of being brown. It went along nicely with her tan skin. Today was a special occasion, though. Today Shirley Darlene put on ancient blue earrings. A vibrant blue. Radioactive perhaps. They clipped onto her ears with minimal ease. An older model. The new ones she didn't even have to try to put on; they just knew that she wanted them. The action was merely nostalgic, something that would be a recurrent feeling this night. She heard Rodney calling for her, but she didn't care.

11:37 PM and Shirley was putting on vibrant blue earrings before the world split into nothing but the world it used to be. It was a statement. A pop out of her ordinary colors. It would be a little secret between her and the world. A pop to the old life she lived currently but wouldn't in mere minutes. To the friends she made. To the friends she lost. To Rodney who wore blue and called her name outside her old room. To the people on this ideal earth that would not be able to say their goodbyes. Their odes. Even to the world itself. For it would not make it out of this mess alive. Its history—oh—*its history*. The people that were in the ground, the flowers above them, both of which would not see another person again. All of that. Just debris. In nothing but mere minutes.

Rodney had given up waiting for her; he burst into the room, his blue outfit contradicting Shirley in almost every way. He startled her and caused her jacket to appear on her, glitching with the chair. This outfit was going to have to be enough. She sighed as Rodney walked to her, telling her that they had to go. Shirley and Rodney walked out of their empty home arm in arm. The boxes had been evacuated weeks ago. There was no point even being in the house besides sadness.

There were advertisements in the sky. They barely looked alive. Everyone had already packed up and left. It was almost poetic. How even in this ideal world they lived in, there were still imperfections. Like there had always been.

It felt humane. *Perfect* even. Shirley placed her holographic letter right above her house. It looked like a barrier. A way of saying that they meant no harm. That they never did. She had written it a couple of days before; it was her final goodbye to everything this world had to offer.

All Shirley Darlene could do was stare at the stars and the moon. 11:49 PM. Any minute now. Any minute at all. The stars would be there, but not this one. When she looked with Amare, their star would not be among the others in many years. Someday not one soul would remember earth. Someday not one soul would remember the star that would be gone in any minute now. Perhaps it already had. It was too soon. Too—too very soon.

"Shirley? Are you OK?" Rodney brought Shirley back to reality. She was sitting at the wheel of the ship.

"Yeah. Yeah, I'm alright." She put the keys in it and powered on the engine. "Did Lollipop—did he get the reservation down?"

Rodney nodded. "I, uh, thought we talked about this."

"We did." She started to drive. This world was as beautiful as ever.

On the Floor in an Outer-Space Bubble

Lollipop was not the one who had gotten down the reservation. In the end, Amare was the one who had called in and got them the last bubble in the group. Lollipop was like what Shirley and Rodney would call a dog. He looked almost like a smeared dog, not exactly whole. On his neck he wore a red bandana. Amare, on the other hand, had two heads. One of them carried their eyes and the other was made for their mouth. They were green, and their heads stuck together with a neck on what was supposed to be ears. All in all, Amare's body looked mostly humanoid, other than their extra arms sticking from the elbows. Their eyes were a lovely shade of navy blue.

Shirley and Rodney walked into the bubble arm-in-arm just as they had left. Lollipop and Amare were giggling like little kids, talking about something that humans would never truly understand. They both turned towards them smiling. Shirley took her place next to Amare while Rodney sat in the middle of the group.

There was not a noise in that bubble for many moments. Not a peep. Not a whisper. And absolutely not a tap. Shirley suddenly covered her mouth. The others took a good look at her. "Jon's out there," she whispered. Her blue earrings swayed with every movement she dared to make.

Amare put their hand on her shoulder. "Oh, Shirley. I'm sorry." Their voice was rather clear for someone who knew the feeling well.

Jon was Shirley's uncle. He had been a "test drive" for the new rocket ships that the makers claimed could bring humans anywhere. For Jon, however, it only brought him to his grave. A little pod floating around earth as if it was an asteroid. They said he must've lost oxygen or some other excuse. The truth is they most likely gave him a faulty ship. He was not the only guinea pig who didn't make it.

"Well, let's hope he's warm!" Lollipop laughed. He did not know the feeling well; in fact, they were strangers to each other.

They all glared at him. Shirley, though, chuckled through whatever tears she had conjured up. "What—do you think he'll hear the explosion?"

"A nice thought, but he's not been, well, alive for a while," Rodney offered. "Not to mention that isn't how sound works."

Shirley shrugged. "Well, of course."

Lollipop shook his head. "What would an explosion of a star even sound like?"

Amare smiled. "Why don't you figure that out yourself when yours does?"

"Or you can just get a front row seat right next to Jon himself and let us know!" Rodney popped in.

"Ugh. *Jon*. He's so overrated." Lollipop rolled his eyes.

Shirley elbowed him. "Hey, now." It was so difficult to be upset when people like them existed. Lollipop snickered in any retaliation he thought he had.

"Great. Now I'm jealous. Can't believe they get to see the sun explode, or whatever, right before their very eyes!" Rodney crossed his arms.

"You wouldn't even be able to see it, Rodney, considering, one, your eyes already are terrible, staring at the sun won't help. And—, uh, *two*—it's a star exploding! It's clearly going to be bright—whatever sight you savored in those useless eyes of yours would be completely gone!" Amare joked.

"I'll bet you're fun at parties," Lollipop said.

Rodney argued, "None of that means it wouldn't be amazing to see. You know, uhm, before my sight goes away."

Shirley interrupted, "I think I forgot about him completely."

Amare added after a second of silence, "Surely it wouldn't be outrageous to. It was a mess. Nobody is anticipating the end of their star and world to be so soon."

Rodney stared right back at the space they could see through the clear interior of the bubble. Nobody would be anticipating the end of their star to be so soon, nobody but the people of earth it seemed. "I mean, we did, didn't we? You and I, Shirley, always really knew that our world wouldn't make it as long as the other ones. The problem was we just got the 'how' part wrong."

Amare nodded. "You're right. You could've known that earth wouldn't live as long as other planets, but you never could've known the date. The time. How you would actually feel. What actually went wrong. Where you'd be when you found out. Never where you'd be as it happens. Of course, you always know it *will* happen, but you never *anticipate* it." That was the difference between Amare and Rodney. Amare was a nerd and Rodney was a geek.

"Come on, Amare. When you put it like that it almost sounds depressing." Rodney smiled.

"That's because it is depressing," Amare spoke, as if they were holding in a laugh. "You lost your home."

12:11 AM. They would not recognize that this world they spoke of would be gone in another 16 minutes.

Rodney remarked, "I don't think I've really thought about it like that."

"You didn't? Really?" Shirley laughed. "What did you think then? Oh—*just another day!*"

Rodney did not know what he thought it was. He didn't even think he realized what the whole situation meant now that he thought about it more. He had told himself that he had nothing to lose and, thus, believed it. "I don't even know."

It was quiet in the bubble for a little while. Quiet not in the way it was when Shirley and Rodney first sat down, quiet in the way of: 'This is happening, isn't it? No jokes or anything to doubt it.'

Shirley put her head in her arms. "Yeah. That's, uhm—fair."

Lollipop spoke: "Like Amare said, *it was surprising*."

"But like what I said: it wasn't when we heard what was happening," Rodney repeated. "The people of earth accepted that it was dead millennia ago."

Amare exclaimed, "That doesn't make it any less surprising—*just like I said*." They paused. "Let's put it like this. You have a grandparent. They're old and you know full well that they won't actually be here by the time you start your life—"

Lollipop interrupted, "Jeez, Amare, can you maybe try a different analogy?"

They continued speaking: "Yet you, uh, continue seeing them every now and then. You talk to them knowing that. 'Accept' it as you say. Why is it then that when that grandparent does eventually pass, you weep? Do you wish that they were still here? Miss them and care about them still? Why even though you said you accepted that fact years ago, you still lie there surprised?"

Rodney slowly agreed. His head nodding as if it was always what he meant. "I suppose. Earth, however, isn't a grandparent."

"Oh, for goodness sake," Amare muttered quietly and put their hand on one of their faces.

Shirley got a notification on her phone. Her hand hesitantly lifted above the screen, debating whether or not she actually wanted to open this message. Yet, even with her hesitation, Shirley opened it. 12:27 AM and Shirley, Rodney, and billions of others did not have a planet to call their own. "It's gone." In nothing but mere minutes could they try and see any remnant of that explosion.

Rodney ignored her. "I'm exhausted tonight."

They had remained in silence to wait for the explosion to hit the bubble. They hadn't kept track of the time. They all just stared in awe, solace, and even despair at the space that could be occupied by any sight of the explosion that they could possibly see. People had made the bubbles for the same reason people placed chairs outside concerts years and years ago. To see a show.

The bubbles, unlike those chairs, were more sustainable. Livelier. The inside smelt like soap while the outside would make you like that star right now. The floor still remained a nice carpet. None of the group could be bothered ordering a table or chairs, so they stayed on that nice carpet like their lives depended on it. Lollipop was practically asleep on the floor; Amare wasn't paying their full attention outside; but Shirley and Rodney glared at that space hoping to see the beauty that it was. It'd be years before they saw the complete picture, but for now any little piece of evidence would be their dream.

Lollipop opened his eyes. "Did I miss it?" His voice was rather lethargic.

12:47 AM. Shirley looked over at him. "No," she said. "There was nothing to miss."

He yawned while he spoke: "That's not a very good answer, is it now?"

They all sat on that carpet, that nice carpet, and waited. Perhaps they were doubting their judgment. Maybe there wouldn't even be evidence to see. It was a Sunday now. They waited patiently for something that maybe wouldn't even come.

Shirley took off her blue earrings, stuffing them back in her pocket, and lay on the floor. She had seen a flicker. That was enough evidence for her. There was no use for any little secret between her and the world if that world didn't live. If that world wasn't where she woke up in the morning, then there was no secret. If that world wasn't where she went to school and worked on her degree, there wasn't a secret—possibly there wasn't even one to begin with.

If that world was always meant to die, was it even her world; or was it in the hands of destiny?

"Where am I going to live?" Shirley sighed. It seemed more of a statement than the question it was meant to be.

Amare lay down between her and Lollipop. "You two can stay with me for a while."

Shirley didn't move, yet she took a breath. She couldn't be bothered to think of something to say. There were so many items. So many little things that filled up the full picture even with most destroyed.

Rodney finally acknowledged everything. "It'll be okay, Shirley."

Neither believed the claim, but still they tried to back it up. She responded, "I guess it will. At some point, that is."

Lollipop muttered, "There's always a tomorrow."

Heading to Bed After the World Ends

It was 1:32 AM and the group decided that the flickering they saw was enough. It was enough closure to fill the void of a world for years to come. Years before it would become apparent on what the actual aftermath decided to look like. What shape had that star took in its final breath? What was the final noise that earth made? Was it a bird chirping? A dog barking? Was it maybe a single notification on a phone? Perhaps it was the same one Shirley got. The same one marking the end of it all, in different locations entirely.

Amare had gotten smoothies for all of them to end the night. A smoothie, that is, to end everything. Shirley had booked a hotel room shortly after she saw the first flicker. It was no use trying to cower in someone else's home for days trying to think of a plan. This would be her final plan for a while.

Rodney decided to stay with Lollipop for a couple of days and then regroup later.

Shirley walked to her ship and waved back at everyone. It was a weird feeling. Waving when she knew that her home for generations was nothing. Smiling when she knew that some people couldn't afford to leave. She plopped herself in the ship. No use. It was over anyway. She was doing this because she could—not because she wanted to. Shirley kept her hands over the ignition. It was never going to be good, but perhaps it would be enough.

1:45 AM. She turned on the engine; the music on her phone connected to the car. She hadn't a clue when she put it on. 1:45 AM and Shirley Darlene might've accepted her fate for the final time.

FLASH FICTION

If Life Is a Highway

REBEKAH DAILY

Grade 11, Home School. Honorable Mention.

I tugged on the wheel, urging my choking car to the side of the road before it coughed out its last greasy breath and died. Leaning against the side of the U-Haul, I sighed. "Saves you time, work, and money!" it cried. "Yeah, right," I replied.

The Crossword

Magnolia Moriarty

Grade 11, Millard South High School, Omaha, NE. Tessa Adams, Educator. Honorable Mention.

"Harvey, I haven't seen you eat anything all week."

Laurance was leaning over the stove, stirring some kind of sauce, but all Harvey could smell was something like onions. He had been cooking since before Laurance and he had even moved in. He assumed that it was a sort of therapy for him.

"I've been busy, Laurance, you know that," he muttered into this week's copy of *The New Yorker*—his favorite newspaper, even though Renton is nowhere near New York.

It wasn't a lie. His life has been full between press interviews for his company's new spring line, to getting ready for the upcoming summer lines. Studying the latest trends, flying to New York for fashion shows, and staying up late watching the newest fashion documentaries and drama podcasts, all to stay ahead of his competition.

Laurance knew the spring line was beautiful. Everyone did. The pastels mixed with bright reds and beiges, the designer silks, the wristwatches, handbags, belt buckles, and rings, all plated in fine silver and 18-karat gold. He would pass by Harvey's office every night on his way to bed, and he would see the warm yellow light seeping through around the door, hear the mechanical thuds of the sewing machine, calls with Harvey's contractors, editors, and marketing team. He knew Harvey was proud of himself, too, but he wouldn't show it. Spring turned to summer too quickly, and Laurance knew that the warm light seeping from the door was now lighting swimsuits, button-up shirts, fine linens, and Egyptian cotton—all colored in whites, golds, beetroot pinks, and sky blue. However, Laurance also knew of Harvey's poor eating habits, especially when he is under stress.

He finally cleared his throat. "Well listen, Harv, how about this?" The red sauce came to a boil, and he pulled out a strainer. "I've invited Arden over for dinner tonight, and some of your friends from work called earlier today while you were at the chiropractor. They wanted to stop over sometime and see your models. I don't know why I'm telling you this. I'm sure you're already well aware. Anyways, though, I told them they could come over for dinner tonight, make it a party, and you know how they get when they hear you're not eating. Lectures and checkups and time management, and bla-bla-bla-bla-bla." Laurance presses his thumb against his four other fingers, opening and closing to look like a mouth. "Bla-bla-bla."

Without looking up from the crossword, Harvey stretches his shoulders along the back of the couch, feeling what could only be the sense of his spine playing tug of war with itself, before grunting and muttering, "You could have told them I'd call them back."

"I wanted to do you a favor, Harv. I know how busy you've been." And he grinned into the sink.

Stuck on the last clue, he looked up and rolled his eyes. "Whatever, man."

"You know I care about you," he said almost sarcastically, but Harvey knew it was an endearment.

He removed the strainer from the sink and began to rinse his hands roughly. His hands were stained with a dark amber hidden underneath a dark crimson, and the color began to wash down the drain in wet clots.

"You know I care about you," he repeated.

INCREDIBLY MINISCULE, BUT ALIVE

L. M. NELSON

Grade 12, Logan View Junior/Senior High School, Hooper, NE.
Emily Saylor, Educator.

The morning sunlight cascaded into the bedroom through the open window, landing on the pillow where your head lay. The curtains flowed and danced in the faint breeze. The book in my hands had fallen to the ground during the night. I had fallen asleep after you, your slow breathing like a lullaby. I was still in my jeans, sitting against the headboard of your bed. My dreams were quickly becoming nothing, wiped from my memory, as I let it all sink in. Let myself feel everything. Your bedroom was lived in, an endearing clutter. Your bed was usually messy, used, and you never cared to fix it until you changed the sheets again. Your life was splayed out in photographs along the walls. I always wished I'd known you my whole life, known and kept every secret. Known and kept every souvenir, every gift. But I was grateful for the chance to be in your life now, even though I had to catch up on all the years.

You stirred in your sleep, drawing my eyes back from studying the bedroom I wish we shared. Turning onto your back, you started to snore lightly. I didn't mind it, though. It filled the silence of the early morning. And it was you. I could never hate anything that came from you, not even the aggressive words you used when you disliked something about me. I always sat and took it and you detested that. You still like a good argument.

I felt the sun rise a little higher into the sky, bleeding out onto my arms. It felt like being loved. A beautiful warmth that I wanted to drown in. I wanted to freeze time and be with you forever, in any way I could be. I wanted it to be just us. Just us and only us. I wanted to be yours.

And then you woke up, sleepily blinking and shifting in bed again.

And my feelings didn't change at all.

"Hey," your groggy voice cut through to my bones. It's always been more than a craving to be the one you love.

"Hi."

I almost cringed at the sound of my own voice. I sounded like a kid, small and insecure, unsure of myself. You lazily smiled up at me, though, turning onto your side to face me. You moved a little closer and I felt my heart stutter. Your arm pressed against the outside of one of my thighs as you held yourself up on your elbows and you laughed a little. A small, still slightly drowsy noise. I felt the warmth of your skin, even through the denim.

"You slept in jeans? You could've asked for some shorts or something." Your voice was laced with laughter, but soft, gentle, like you knew I was too embarrassed to do so. And I was. I felt my cheeks heat up, ashamed for some reason.

"Uh, yeah. It's fine, though. I didn't need—" I cut myself off, shaking my head. I didn't want to make a fool of myself, even though I knew I already was. I weakly smiled, softly saying, "I slept okay still."

You just laughed again and I let myself adore you. The sharp noises ricocheted off my skin, but I almost wanted them to sink in. I had your laugh memorized, but I wanted it to be a part of me. I still do. I love your laugh and the smile that comes along with it. I love your eyes as you look at me, like you love me just how much I love you. I found it extremely easy to adore you, to love you, to want you. It always has been.

We rotted the day away, lying in your bed and on the living room sofa. I don't even remember the titles to the movies we watched. But that doesn't matter, does it? I just cared about being with you. The world was falling away from us, becoming nothing as you became everything. It was beautiful. More than beautiful, even though we left no imprint on the universe. We were incredibly miniscule, but alive.

THE BIRTHDAY CAKE

GAGE TOWNSEND

Grade 11, Kearney High School, Kearney, NE. Charlotte Dvorak, Educator.

My family hates me. Everyone in my family has hated me ever since they found out that I have autism. I don't understand why they hate me. What did I do to them?

Because of my autism I found it hard to make friends. I did have a friend before. But that only lasted a few years. And now, I am living on my own. And I feel very lonely.

Today is my birthday. I am turning twenty-five. In the morning I bought myself a chocolate birthday cake. Chocolate is my favorite flavor of cake.

I was planning on celebrating my birthday by myself, like I do every year. But then something came over me. I got out a large piece of cardboard and wrote something on it. "I am autistic. I have no family and no friends. Today is my birthday. All I want to do is share my birthday cake with someone."

I took my cake, still in its case, and headed outside. I sat outside holding my sign with my cake right next to me. If today didn't go well, then I don't know what I will do with the rest of my lonely life. Maybe I should just give up.

I sat there for what seemed like hours. I went back inside, defeated, when the sun began to set. I got out a trash can and dumped my beautiful birthday cake inside. I am going to give up on life.

I spent the next few hours contemplating whether I should do it. But as I grabbed the rope, I heard my doorbell ring. I opened it to find my neighbor holding a much bigger chocolate cake than the one I had. He told me that he saw my sign and thought that I deserved much more than a small cake. The cake had twenty-five candles on it.

I felt a tear run down my face.

THE POWERFUL POWERLESS

GAGE TOWNSEND

*Grade 11, Kearney High School, Kearney, NE. Charlotte Dvorak, Educator.
Honorable Mention.*

One day, something extraordinary (I think not) happened. That morning almost everyone woke up possessing some sort of superpower. However, I and the other people with autism found ourselves excluded from this bunch. We had no powers.

At first the people sympathized with us. But soon society became reformed around powers, and we autistic found ourselves competing for scraps of food. Even our own families forgot we exist. We had nowhere to go, no job to get, and no home to sleep in. Then one day I found myself confronting a villain that was trying to harm a little boy. I will never forget that feeling of importance. The feeling that the little lost boy was relying on me for survival.

Usually small saves like that don't get much attention, but since I was a powerless autistic, that was all anyone could talk about. Soon other autistic people from all over the world followed suit. We found ourselves making our own little teams that would patrol the city and stop lesser villains in exchange for food and shelter. It may not be much, but it's enough for now. We autistic people are no longer referred to as weak. We are referred to as the *powerful powerless*.

SHORT
STORY

AND SO WE STOOD THERE

DARBIE DEFREESE

Grade 9, Holdrege High School, Holdrege, NE.

SILVER

I stand at the top of a cliff, holding a book and wondering the same thing you wonder now. Why am I standing here? Why am I holding a book? I can't remember how I got here, and I certainly don't remember this book. Closing my eyes, I try to picture how I got here. Nothing. How peculiar. Something important must be here; otherwise, why would you be here?

Am I here to admire the view? No, there's not much to admire. The sorrowful clouds block out all the stars, leaving the night empty and dull. There's no moon to swoon over either. It hides sheepishly, too timid to face the Earth until another week has passed. The only thing visible is the edge of the cliff: a faint greenish-gray line in a sea of similar shapes and blobs.

Am I here to die? No, there is no one around to commit the act, and, at least right now, I am quite content with myself. Is someone lurking in the trees? I squint towards the woods nearby, trying to discern a shape amongst the darkness. I can't make anything out. Though, I suppose that would be the point if I'm going to die.

Maybe I am here to help the gods in some mortal way? To cry out their message? To receive a blessing? No, no, I highly doubt that. I've got no message to give with only the knowledge of a minute life filling my head. And, while I hate to be so cynical, it's safe to say I'm not the kind of person who would be gifted a blessing. Any gods around would find me too doubtful and curious for pure, blind faith. If such faith exists.

Perhaps I am here to connect? To gain a friend or a different view? But of course, no one is here except me. The only voice I've heard speak is a faint echo bouncing up from far below the cliff. Though, I suppose you're here. We can't talk to each other, but perhaps we could get to know each other, just through our actions. Still, try as both of us will, reaching beyond our dimensions like that can only get so far. I don't mean to be cruel, but I honestly wouldn't have come all this way just for you. And you certainly aren't here for me. You're here because something important is happening, but what?

Well, since simply pondering won't answer my question, maybe this book will. I open it up and begin to read the first page.

I stand at the top of a cliff, holding a book and wondering the same thing you wonder now. Why am I standing here? Why am I holding a book?

I blink. Now, I know I don't have the greatest memory, but doesn't that seem familiar? Sure enough, at the bottom of the page I see words appearing. These words actually. This book is the story you're reading now, also known as my story. But why do I have it?

And if I'm currently the reader, aren't I ... you? But that can't be true as I still don't know why I'm here, and you must know why I'm here. But I am the reader, and since you are the reader, I must be you. And since you, who is also me, are reading this, then I, who is also you, must know why I'm here. But since I, who is you, don't know why I'm here, then you, who is me, also cannot know. So perhaps you, as well as I, both do and do not know why I am here. Meaning that I, as well as you, must somehow know why I am here.

I close the book. This is getting to be a bit confusing. I sigh and sit down on the edge of the cliff, dangling my feet over the abyss. Swinging my legs, alternating back and forth, I hit the side of the cliff with my heel. I swing harder, my heels digging a gash into the dirt. A few stray rocks are pulled loose, tumbling down the cliff. I wonder, if I kept going like this, would the ground below eventually become weak enough to collapse? And would that be so bad? To fall down there, into the abyss? I've found no reason as to why I'm here, so why should I stay?

But you're here. Why are you here? What are you getting out of this? This story of me standing around wondering is nothing to you. But here you are reading, and here I am wondering. How pointless.

Squeezing my eyes shut, I once again try to remember how I got here. I have a family. That I know for sure. I can picture them, lying in bed, sleeping soundlessly. Their dreams, built from the day's thoughts, would surround them in pleasantries. Perhaps they haven't even noticed my absence. Maybe they dismissed the gap in the table at dinner as only a figment of their imagination. I can't blame them; it's much easier that way.

But no, they notice. I can hear it from here, as clearly as you read it. My mother lies awake, counting the lies she's been told in the ceiling tiles. My father's snores are longer and louder than usual, his illness contracted from his own father. My sister dreams a nightmare in which her closest friends, who have all turned on her over trivial things, hunt her down. And my brother stands by the window, having never gone to bed, and watches the horizon, waiting to see if it will fall.

They all ask one question. I can hear it so distinctly. Their voices raise and call out the question. They do not want me, nor you, to answer it, just to hear it.

Why?

I collapse on the grass. I think if you were beside me, you would too. I don't understand. I don't understand anything. Couldn't whoever put me here—myself, my family, God, you—have left a sign explaining why I'm here? Even a crude drawing in the dirt would be fine. At least it's something.

Looking up at the sky, I watch the clouds drift. It's peaceful here. The breeze brushes over my face, bringing with it a misty coolness. The cold embraces me. It's the nice kind of cold, though, like the chill of a window on a snowy day. The grass below me is a soft blanket, each blade bent in just the right way to make room for me. The sky darkens, as if a lamp has been blown out. The world, for a moment, allows us to rest. So we do.

◇◇◇◇◇◇◇◇◇◇◇◇◇◇◇◇◇◇◇◇◇◇◇◇◇◇◇◇◇◇

When we wake, the stars greet us. Twinkling orbs shine down, strong enough to pierce through the sky's black hide. But the sky does not die. Instead, it welcomes the light, spreading the glow across itself. The stars, having come so far and shone so bright, now rest.

Their glow, I notice, is warm. I can feel it from here. Reaching out, I pretend to touch the star above me. Its light is so content. These stars could sit here forever and still be warm. To them, it doesn't matter.

I sit up. I am not alone here, am I? They've all been here: my mother, my father, my sister, my brother. They've all stood here at the edge of this cliff. I remember now, so clearly. There would be days, weeks, even months or years sometimes where they would disappear. They would come here. I once even saw my mother here, hanging a book precariously over the abyss below the cliff. How could I have forgotten that?

And you. You've been here too, haven't you? Yes, you're here now, but you've been here before, wondering and dangling and resting just as I have. You've stared into that abyss, and your thoughts have consumed you. You've screamed at the moon, cursed your family's name, and, in some cases, torn your book to shreds. I can see you now, crumpled on the ground, staring up at the stars just as I was. You've forgotten why you came here in the first place. All you can think is ...

Why?

Why am I here?

Perhaps it is enough to be here. Perhaps we could be like the stars: warm, content, glowing.

I crouch down and pick up the book, which I had long ago abandoned. Clutching it close to my chest, I can hear the sound of pen on paper. My story's still being written, I suppose. How wonderful. I hope you never return here, but I know you will. We always do eventually. I have no answers, but stay with me a moment longer.

And so we stood there, and that was enough.

Snowfall

AUTUMN HALL

SILVER

Grade 12, Daniel J Gross Catholic High School, Bellevue, NE.

Loretta's blood is still racing, boiling and bubbling to the surface that is her deep mahogany skin. Her face is hot and the world is teetering.

No, she's teetering.

Ah yes, this must be the after effects of the drink, the one that'd been so foolishly laced with poison. As if the princess, who has been a target her whole life, wouldn't notice the added tartness to her wine. She remembers fainting on the dining hall floor and countless knights rushing to her aid. She also recalls being whisked away by a familiar stature, the stature that would belong to her personal guard, Sawyer. The one that has only recently been appointed to her.

Now here Loretta stands in the unfamiliar foyer of her uncle's winter home, bracing herself against a lush chair in front of the mantle. She'd been taken here immediately, along with her most trusted guard, who stands here with a furrowed brow, seemingly unsure of how he's expected to help the crown princess.

The manor is humble, quaint and along the Eastern border of their kingdom. It's in the middle of nowhere, quite frankly. Tucked between the river and a thick forest. Sawyer has kindled a fire, ushering Loretta to a nearby chair, easing her down to sit with a glass of tea.

"This isn't poisoned too, is it?" she teases, a light tug pulling on the corner of her lips. She gestures toward the steaming cup outstretched toward her.

Sawyer looks at her, mouth agape, his face stolen of all its color. "No, of course not, Your Highness." He looks offended, as if she's crazy to even suggest such an outlandish thing.

"Calm yourself, Sawyer. I am only teasing." She takes the cup, sipping tentatively. She commands her shaking hands to still themselves, determined not to spill anything on her designer gown.

Sawyer watches her so carefully. As if every movement she makes might cause her to shatter. He's dedicated so much time to knowing her, protecting her, that he's grown to fancy not only her company but everything about her. Her laugh, her eagerness to make light of every situation, like this one.

In this short time, he's grown so fond of her. So eager to see her smile, to see her stand strong. Viewing her as this wobbling, fragile princess, is so foreign to him. He cannot begin to fathom how this unassailable woman could so easily be brought to her knees by just a little bit of tonic sprinkled in her wine.

He's grown to admire her, love her even. Although, he could never admit that to her, not after everything he's done. He can't hold her with the same hands that are so densely stained with blood. He has far too dark of a past. In it he was someone else entirely.

But here, with her, he is reborn.

"Fetch me my paint, won't you, Sawyer? If I am to be held here against my will by my Father then I suppose I shall at least enjoy it." She pinches the bridge of her nose, attempting to self-soothe the aching that has crept its way across her temples and forehead.

Sawyer nods, standing to go find all of her supplies. But before he slips out of the doorway she calls out, "How long do you anticipate we'll be here?"

Sawyer contemplates a moment, "In all honesty, Your Highness, it could be quite some time. I'm not sure if they'll catch the man who did this."

Loretta nods, seemingly disappointed by his answer. It is odd that the woman who usually has all the answers is asking him for advice. "Days you suppose? Weeks?"

All Sawyer can do is shrug. He feels like a fool.

"Perhaps weeks. Although I cannot predict the future, M'lady."

"Well, if we are to be stuck together for such an extended amount of time, I suppose you can call me Loretta." She smiles, her dark braids nestling behind her ear. His ears curve to cup the sound of her voice, reaching to let it echo in his mind for eternity. He'd sell his soul to hear it for the first time, to catch the first ever moment she'd referred to him by name.

He's been her knight for only a few months now. But love knows no bounds, and love does not hold itself to the confinements of rules and expectations. Love is urgent and unavoidable. He's become quite familiar with that concept. His love for her took over him with a wave of intensity.

He didn't choose to love her and he couldn't choose the opposite either. To love is to lack control. One day it abducted him, took him by surprise, and he realized that he never had any decision in the matter.

He's memorized every curve of her face and each freckle on her nose. He knows the difference between her rehearsed diplomatic laugh and the hearty and rich one she'll let loose in the privacy of his company and her chambers. He couldn't possibly imagine how anyone could have the urge to kill her.

Loretta smooths the thick fabrics of her dress, flattening the deep emerald velvet to lay obediently across her legs. She fiddles with the ornate gold trimmings, crocheted across the top of her bodice and along the wrists of her sleeves. Her hair, she decides to pull up, wrapping the pearl-adorned braids into a low bun at the base of her head. She's grown anxious and awkward, desperate to fix every hair out of place.

She waits.

Sawyer watches her intently, eyes flitting over her skin and her hands. She looks up at him, acknowledging his striking gaze.

"My paints, Sawyer?" she asks, surprised that she's had to repeat herself. Although patience is a virtue, she is tainted with the vice of restlessness. This impatience stirred with worry, as he's always been quick to be at her command. Not once faltering or hesitant.

"Right, yes, of course!" He jumps away, heading for the stairs. He returns with her canvas, oils, and easel, placing each of them down neatly before her, precisely so she may sit comfortably while she paints.

She assumes that this has come as a surprise to him as well, being attacked and ushered to a manor in the middle of nowhere. Tucked away for heaven knows how long.

The sun has set now, nestling itself below the earth, curling into a slumber and only to be roused awake in the morning. The moon has taken its shift, like a changing of the guard. Swapping places with the sun, ready to take watch.

"Do you suppose life would've been different, if I weren't destined to be a princess?" Loretta asks, portioning her paint onto her palette. She dips her brush into the oils, and begins preparing the canvas.

"How so?" Sawyer asks, finding a seat near the fire.

"Do you think that I could've lived a life free of living in constant danger? Been a painter?" She stares at her canvas, contemplating carefully each brush stroke. "Fallen in love?" She looks up at him, peering through her lashes. Timidly awaiting his reaction.

He opens his mouth to respond but no words come out.

Once again, a fool.

"I'm sure love will find you, M'lady," he offers. "The truest of all kinds."

Seemingly disappointed at the lack of use of her name, she smiles and looks away from him, although this smile is a husk, empty of all sincerity.

"I was close to dying tonight, Sawyer." She furrows her brows, following her brush across the white backdrop. "Yet my supposed last moments weren't filled with my mother or father. Instead I was replaying each moment I had spent with you." Loretta still does not glance up.

"I had thought of each night we wandered the gardens and played hide and seek in the castle corridors. Those nights we snuck up to the rooftops and you pointed out every star you knew the name of. You've given me a glimpse of life, true and unadulterated life. For that I thank you."

"You, M'lady, have reminded me that there's more to living than just my career. For that, I thank *you*."

"What made you choose to be a knight, Sawyer?" She takes a sip of her tea, peering at him over the rim of the glass.

Sawyer is asked that question constantly, yet he still hasn't curated a proper answer.

To put it simply, he didn't choose to become anything.

He'd been tossed into this position, forced to become what was needed of him by his older brother. Even though he would not have come to this conclusion willingly, he wouldn't take it back for anything. He'd never deny himself the privilege it has been to know and love Loretta.

"To help fund my brother Simon's business," he says, cleaning the dirt from under his nails. "And what of you? What possessed you to take up painting?"

This makes her break out into a smile. "This is not my first time being held here against my will for my safety. The first time, the only options for entertaining myself were this or staring at a wall. I opted for the canvas. It has been my passion ever since."

In all this time of knowing her, he's never seen the product of her work. She always orders him to stand on the other side of the room, not permitted to see the other side of the canvas. She's always clear about this rule, exceptionally so. Going as far as never leaving a painting unattended, glued to its side and never leaving Sawyer and it alone together. This being so, he couldn't say for sure if she was actually talented, although, even if she weren't, he'd think anything she created to be absent of any flaws.

<hr>

They remain there for days. Captive in the small house until they will be brought home by the Royal Guard. Until her mother and father deem it safe for her to return. She sleeps, eats, and enjoys the normality of a secluded life away from the court. These few days were her glimpse into what life would've been like had she not gained the misfortune of being princess.

Snow begins to fall. The army of winter at their borders, ready to take the land by force. The ground succumbs to ice and the skies surrender to gloom.

Wind punches the outer structure of the manor and the stone absorbs the chill. The air, achingly cold, causes Loretta to wring her hands, hoping to bring some range of motion to her stiffening fingers.

"I always forget the violence of winter," Loretta says, coming down the stairs and donning her cloak. She ties it sturdily around her neck and shoulders. "Being cooped up in a castle causes you to take warmth for granted."

Sawyer wished he could agree. But his body's so used to the cold that it no longer has any effect on him. In fact, there were countless nights that he couldn't feel his toes even while wrapped in a blanket and held fiercely by his mother. "The servants will be decorating for Yule soon, yes?" he says, tucking another log in the flames. They were running low and he'd need to fetch some more from the cellar soon. "It's my favorite time of year."

"For me as well." Her grin, seemingly uncontrollable, slides across her face as she becomes lost in thought. "It's a shame we won't be home in time to attend the Yule ball. You would've loved it." She glides over to her easel, unveiling the art she'd covered in an effort to hide it from her present company.

"Since I am your Knight, M'lady, I would've been stuck by the wall," he says, standing to find more logs to burn.

She laughs.

His heart skips a beat.

"Do you think I'd allow you to watch from there? I'd drag you onto the dance floor, if necessary!"

"Truly?" he asks, eyes sparkling at the thought.

"Most definitely." She nods, brushing her paint across the canvas. She stares at it, a finger itching to curl around her chin. "Say, I do believe it's finished."

He pauses, neck craning to look back at her. "Is that so?" he asks, hand paused on the trim of the door.

"Yes. Tell you what, you return fast enough and perhaps I will allow you to see." Her face, at the thought, claims a light shade of pink, as if lightly brushed by the very instrument in her hand. Albeit the shade being fair, didn't mean it went unnoticed by the knight.

"I shall return quickly then." In an effort to exit the room swiftly, he bumps into his satchel he'd placed on the table. It goes unnoticed by him, so he continues to descend the stairs into the cellar.

Loretta walks carefully over to the pile of items, gathering them and beginning to place them neatly back inside. She lifts the last paper off the floorboards, beginning to fold it back into its original shape.

She freezes.

Her name, she notices, has been mentioned halfway down the note.

Sawyer,

Four of the five tasks have been completed. The next move is yours, please remind yourself we have until the ball to complete the list and finish the job we were hired for.

Your Brother, Simon

As her eyes gloss over each of the "tasks," bile claws up her throat. She recognizes each of them, all royalty from neighboring kingdoms.

The entirety of them, recently assassinated.

All but one.

Her.

~~Friedrick Sanliar~~

~~Anastasia Beaumont~~

~~Charlotte Farewell~~

~~Erick Avington~~

Loretta Montgomery

Loretta stumbles back, her body clamoring into the wall and knocking over her easel. She can't breathe and her skin is on fire. She drops the letter and races for the door. With the world spinning, she struggles to unlatch it.

All of this time the one who had sworn to protect her, has been awaiting the perfect opportunity to kill her. After all of the trust she's given him, all of the nights she'd wished he'd kiss her. In reality, she was falling for a killer. Had he been the one to poison her drink those few days ago?

She throws open the door, a blizzard stabbing her face as she runs out into the cold. Snow reaches her ankles but that doesn't stop her, nor does the constricting lacing of her bodice. She runs, until she can no longer see the manor, until she comes across a road and a nearing carriage. She screams, waving her hands in the air for her to be noticed on the side of the road, begging for help.

The coachman jumps down from his seat, grabs her by the arms, confused. "You must listen to me; you must ring for the knights. I am Princess Loretta, and I am about to be killed."

His eyes widen as recognition overcomes him. She throws herself into his arms, desperate for comfort and security. So quickly she's experienced both horror and heartbreak.

"All is sound now, Princess." Chastely he wraps his arms around her as well, while tears drench his coat as she buries her head in his shoulder.

"What's your name?" she asks, sniffling and pulling herself away. She can barely see him in the dead of night.

"Simon."

Her tears come to an end and before she can pull away, she's struck motionless.

A dagger, right through her bodice. Warmth melts across her abdomen, even in the freezing temperature.

Blood.

Sawyer emerges from the cellar smiling to himself, eager to finally see the talents of the princess. But when he returns to the foyer, he finds the whole room in disarray. The door has been left ajar. He notes a letter on the floor, and he picks up the canvas near his feet.

Captured in paint is himself, holding Loretta in a tight embrace. Noses touching intimately. It's beautiful. Snow engulfs them, swirling around as if by magic.

He reaches for the paper and when he reads what she must've, he connects everything. With both the painting and letter in hand, he races out the door.

He follows her footprints, running for what feels like miles. The cold stings his lungs, he tastes copper when he breathes. Eventually he finds her, sprawled out in the snow like an angel. Blood spills onto the white ground, pooling around her, staining her clothes and her hair.

He's too late. He never had the chance to back out, to tell Simon he was never going to uphold his end of the deal.

Sawyer falls to his knees, sobbing over her. He cannot bear to touch her, even with the urge to smooth her hair. Her eyes begin to freeze, but he cannot bring himself to close her lids.

He glances over at the knife beside her.

He doesn't even think as he grabs the dagger. He doesn't scream in pain as he plunges it deep in his chest. Even as blood fountains out of him and coats his hands, he doesn't make a sound. Tears freeze to his face and finally, he embraces her. With blood coating his finger tips and clinging to his nails, he holds her.

He falls asleep to the sound of screams and his brother calling his name, but attempts to enjoy the view. The moon peeks between the spruce trees and snowflakes dance toward him, turning the sky into a ballroom floor.

With one last motion he caresses the canvas, red painting the fine piece, smearing across their fictional bodies.

He was never an artist.

But tonight, his hands are the brush, she his muse, and his blood the paint.

THE ANTICS OF

AJ KIRSCH

Grade 10, Westside High School, Omaha, NE. Honorable Mention.

A cigarette hangs loosely from her lips, smoke curling in streaks of white licks from the glow of the orange burning ember. Her red painted lips print in smudges on the foot of the stick, smears of many pulls. She glances down at the hand she grips fairly tight. Her tongue reaches forward to the edge and tilts up the cigarette into her mouth. Her lips purse and she takes a long drag. As she exhales, a cloud of smoke puffs from her mouth in a veil of swirls and billowing flurries. She looks up from the old oak table.

Across from her, Tracy sits, looking down at his hand, grinning. A few seats down from her sits Rupert, hand covering his two cards, and staring off at the back warm brown, half wood-paneled wall, the other half a dark emerald green wallpaper with a faint design. The only show on his face is the slight crease between his brow in deep thought. The other players have folded and now sit quietly, taking sips of their brandy and fiddling with their ties and button-downs.

She checks her cards again, running her finger along the once smooth and glossy finish, now creased and worn with age. She traces the crimson red hearts printed on each of the cards. Biting her lip, she looks back at Tracy. He is more composed now, but his smug smile still lingers on his face. He doesn't think she has anything good. The quiet music drifting through the room from the record player sitting on the brown short bookcase against the wall, now other-wise filled with booze, crackles as the diamond runs along the curves and divots of the old and scratched vinyl.

But maybe his hand is better than hers. No, she has trust in her deal.

With a soft sigh, Rupert sets his cards face down and slides them forward.

"I fold," he says, his mouth slightly pressing together as he leans back in his chair.

Her lips squeeze together in an even, straight line, and she looks back at Tracy, real inscrutable, that guy. He lifts his head abruptly and looks at her, squinting his eyes faintly. He looks back down at his cards, and then back up at her. Then he takes a bill from the nicely sized pile next to him and drops it into the heap of cash in the middle of the table.

"I'm in," he declares, studying her through the dark brown bangs hanging over his coffee brown eyes.

She holds his gaze a moment more before she takes two folded bills from her pile and drops them in the middle.

"Alright," he says questioningly, his eyebrows slightly raised and his lips slowly curving upwards.

Jumping up from his chair, he slams his cards down on the table, revealing a five of clubs and a five of diamonds. "Full house, baby!"

She can't help but smile. Taking a leisurely breath, she drops her cards and they fall flat before her, displaying a five and six of hearts.

"Read 'em and weep, sucker," she smirks.

The room is silent as they all stare down at her cards, some of their eyes wide in disbelief.

"*Godammit*, Joan!" Tracy shouts, pushing back in his chair hard and running his hands roughly through his hickory-colored hair.

"Holy s—"

"A straight flush!"

"Man, I've never seen that."

She reaches her arms out towards the middle of the table and wraps them around the ruffled and wrinkled bills, pulling the large mound of money towards her.

Tracy's nostrils flare slightly as he watches her, his lips firmly pressed together in a thin line, trying to stifle his smile. But his attempts are in vain as a laugh bursts from his lips.

"Jeez, Joan," he says, shaking his head. "Gangbusters."

<hr/>

About 10 minutes later, the old creaky brown door to the backyard swings open and slams against the wall next to it. A leg, clothed in fine, tailored, and slightly worn grey slacks pushes through the doorway, the brown Oxfords stepping in on the old carpeted floor to meet the door as it falls back closed. Coming through, his shoulder pushing back the door open again, walks in Jude, his arms wrapped around two big brown paper grocery bags, various items peeking above the edge of the sacks. His mousy brown hair slightly askew and ruffled, he steps into the room, that toothy grin front on his face.

"How's it going, dipwads?" he says, smiling smugly. He wears a dark red sweater vest, the school emblem embroidered in a neat dark blue on the right of his chest. His clean white collared shirt is buttoned in the wrong holes and peeks over the top of his vest, his black tie slacken and wrapped loosely around his neck.

"Razz my berries, it's Jude," Tracy announces, getting up from the table and sauntering over to him.

"Ah, Tracy, mommy's allowance got taken again, didn't it?" Jude asks, grinning.

"Ay, you really know how to rattle a cage, don't chu?" he says with a smirk.

Tracy throws his arm back, and in a slow-motion imitation, he brings it forward in a fake punch, putting his whole body into it as he slowly turns and brings his fist towards Jude's face, making the sound with his mouth. Jude turns his head back slowly as the fist comes to meet him, contorting his expression into one of false agony as his full arms spread apart, and he pretends to fall backward, an imitated grunt of pain sounding from his lips. Tracy then squats down and plants another one to his stomach, where Jude leans his chest forward and pushes his lower body back in mimic of a real blow.

He stands back up and Jude and Tracy laugh and elbow each other.

As they start to move in the room, some of the other boys get up from the table and stretch from the long deals.

"Say, what'cha got in there?" Wilfred asks, rising from his chair and trying to peek in the bag.

"Hey. Nothin' to concern you," Jude responds, backing away and lifting up the bags so he can't see in them.

"Probably something to bribe Mr. Sandoval," Tracy suggests.

"Yeah, he's a real pain." Wilfred shakes his head knowingly. "How is he anyway?"

"A delight as always," Jude remarks, rolling his eyes.

As the others recall their experiences of staying after class in detention with Mr. Sandoval, Jude looks around the room, until his eyes find Joan, and a smile pleads for his lips, but he can't help it shining through his eyes instead. She grins at him.

"He really likes to flip his lid," Tracy says, taking a black comb from his shirt pocket and dragging it through his hair, slicking it back.

"Gee, Tracy, are you a greaser or what?" Wilfred quips.

"Hardeeharhar," Tracy says sarcastically, glowering at Wilfred.

"Aw come ere," he says, springing towards Tracy, wrapping his arm around his neck and pulling him down as he ruffles his head with his fist, disheveling his neatly combed hair.

Tracy squirms and hits him. "Aw, cut it out," he shouts, trying to spring free of his grip.

But Wilfred doesn't relent. The other boys rush forward and join the tomfoolery, picking sides. Some try to pull Wilfred off Tracy, while others pull them off Wilfred. As the antics go on, Jude walks around them, dodging the flying elbows and pushes of the ensuing scuffle, and heads towards the creaking stairs. Joan stubs the end of her cigarettes in the ashtray on the table and follows him up the stairs.

In the kitchen he sets the grocery bags on the gray brown island in the middle of the floor. He looks at Joan standing on the other side. His eyes run over her face. Her several small brown dots of birthmarks. Her sharp cheeks. Her flashing eyes. Her short, chin-length, light blonde hair. He notices how pale her skin is. The dark bags under her eyes. Her bruised lips hiding under the bright red lipstick.

"Hey," he says softly.

"Hey," she responds.

He starts to empty the contents of the brown paper bags, putting them away in the umber-colored cabinets and drawers.

"Are you going to the bash tonight?" he asks her.

"I don't know—" she hesitates.

"You should come," he says, turning to face her. His eyes drift over her loose maroon sweater, her tight collared shirt, her dark tie, her light gray linen trousers, her worn oxford shoes. He gazes back to her face. To her scarlet-painted lip. Strands of hair loosely pinned back from her face. Her almost silver-colored eyes. He studies them. The streaks and dots of colors swirling in her irises. Mesmerizing. He could get lost in those eyes. Or maybe her smell of sandalwood, lilacs, and late night coffees.

She watches him. His cutting jaw. His freshly shaved cheeks. Those full lips. The sharpness of his nose. His long lashes. Those striking eyes she could drown in. His hair curls in a perfect manner around his face, many pieces tucked behind his hair. That musky smell of pine, books, and ink. She could close her eyes and almost see him in the old library, sitting right next to the open window, a gentle breeze drifting in as he hunches over the old and yellowed pages of a long book resting on the table before him.

Jude looks at her a long second more before he speaks.

"So are you in?"

She takes a deep breath.

"Why not."

<hr>

That year, the year of 1951, seemed to be one that would be hard to forget. It was a time of summers full of bathtub gin and passion pits; falls of brewing beer in buckets under the stairs and drag races on the long cement roads a mile in the country; winters with spiked eggnog and sock hops; and springs of brandy, red wine, and playing games in Jude's basement, the windows pulled open, and music playing from the collection of old vinyls that sat in a large shelf on the wall. Those days cruising the main street, looking for trouble or a good time, or hours at the diner right off that street, cramming for exams and plotting their next project.

They find themselves often reminiscing that year, and time and time again it seems to come back. That night haunts her like a sweet night's dream, too troubling to remember, but too dear to forget.

<hr>

The sun is now hidden behind the horizon, and the street lamps start to come on as the sky grows darker in its changing shades of blue. They left the pad 8 minutes ago and now amble steadily through the neighborhood street to the party a couple of miles away. The trees and bushes bloom in green, purple, and white blossoms as new leaves are formed. The brown of the trunks and outstretching branches deepens. Moss grows in their bark's divots and detailed texture. The grass grows longer, and weeds and flowers sprout from the lawns and cracks in the sidewalk, reaching taller by the second. The fragrant smell of spring fills their noses. The light of stars start to pierce through the evening sky, and the moon shines brightly overhead. Jude has his hands dug in his pockets, his head slightly tilted down watching his feet walk along, deep in thought. Joan picks at the beds of her fingers, clawing at the loose skin and peeling it off until blood is drawn to the surface and she has to put it in her mouth or wrap it in her shirt to make it stop. They walk side by side on the edge of the road, and nothing is said for a while. They listen as the wind rustles the leaves on the trees and twirls the ringing wind chimes that hang from some porches. They listen to the scuffle of their feet on the cement, the frequent hum of the bugs in the grass or the chirp and caw of the birds in the trees, and their sniffs or coughs every so often.

"Something's been on your mind lately, hasn't it?" Jude asks, breaking the silence.

Joan doesn't say anything.

"You know I can see it," he continues. "Don't take this the wrong way, but you don't look like yourself. Something's not right, is it?"

Still she says nothing.

He glances over at her, and though she tries to keep her face blank, he can still see the slight flare in her nostrils, the subtle knit between her eyebrows, and the small quiver of her lips as the emotion seeps onto her face.

"Hey," he says softly, turning towards her. "You don't have to hide. What's been going on?"

"No," she forces out, and after a few seconds of silence, she follows up with, "I'm not okay."

They keep walking.

"I know," he whispers. "Is it getting worse?"

"Yes."

"For how long?"

"For a while."

A cricket chirps somewhere.

"I'm losing control. I don't know what to do anymore," she grimaces.

"You're stuck in your head."

"I know, but I can't get out." She shakes her head. "I just want to be okay again."

"I'm here," he tells her, wrapping his arms around her shoulders and pulling her in. She rests her head on his shoulder, and embraces him, bringing her arms around his back. For a moment they remain so, but another moment passes, and they pull apart from each other. As their arms release, she sniffs and wipes her nose, and he looks at her and smiles.

They continue on together through the neighborhood. A block further, Jude turns to look behind him.

"Are you coming, Stan?" he asks, smiling.

"Yeah, give me a second," I say, jogging to catch up with them.

BEHIND CLOSED DOORS

LORELAI KLOSNER

*Grade 12, Boys Town High School, Boys Town, NE. Beth Sulley,
Educator.*

Trigger Warning: Bullying and offensive language

2006

"I told you he wasn't going to answer."

I was all too familiar with this room. Dusty air and frozen butterscotch—the smell of the principal's office. She was lanky and pasty, greasy blond hair falling at the sides of her face. She lightly slammed the phone down on her desk.

"Well, I have to send you home. You've gone too far this time, Bret." She flung her hands up in the air. "We don't tolerate bullying in this school."

Ironic.

"Johnathen is sitting with a concussion, waiting for his parents to pick him up." She sighed and did that thing that adults did when they are mad. She squeezed that area between her eyebrows.

"Well, we can't keep you. Is there anyone else we can contact?"

I continued to furrow and stare out the window, tracing the branches with my eyes.

"Bret?"

Then I reluctantly shook my head. I hated Mrs. Torres, but I think it's because she was good friends with my mom. She knew I was vulnerable, and that's what I hated most about her. Not her disgusting office, not this dreadful middle school, not her far-spread eyes and perked up nose—it was that she knew who I was two years ago. Before I lost my mother. She knew my weak spot. She thinks I'm confused and hurt. But nothing can hurt me anymore. Not since Mom died.

"Bret, look at me. Why him? He's such a sweet boy. You two used to be swell friends."

I snapped my head at her and squinted my eyes. "That 'sweet boy' is a trick! He doesn't leave *me* alone!"

"Oh, Bret, please. He doesn't do anything to you."

"Yes, he does!"

"Like what?"

My cheeks burned and my words flustered. I couldn't tell her why. Not because I didn't know, but because I'd be destroyed even further with her if she found out.

"Well, here's what I think," she said. "I think that you feel like you need to destroy his kindness to get rid of anything that reminds you of your mom."

"Shut up," I muttered. Before she could squeak out any sort of retort, I left. My bag weighed me down. It needed organized badly, but I flew out of those doors like nothing was dragging my feet. Stomping to the exit, I stared forward and ignored Johnny's call for attention, holding an icebag to his head.

I didn't know where to go. I certainly couldn't go home. The door was probably locked too, and we had lost the key long ago. It was around one, but I wasn't going to be the face he saw when he awoke from his drunken slumber. I went to the truck stop instead, sitting in the rest area. I pulled out the letter he had written me.

Dear B,

I couldn't continue past that. My eyes hovered the page, but I rejected the words.

I met Johnny around a month ago. He was much different from myself. Blonde, glasses, skinny, rich ... married parents. I envied him at first, always analyzing his every move. He sat by himself most of the time, nose deep in a book. He was my type to pick on, but I didn't. My buddies did, but I just stood on the side when they pushed him around.

You're my dearest friend.

We were assigned to do a partner discussion in English, and we had been assigned to each other. He spoke to me, surprisingly. Asking something completely unexpected, something I'll never forget.

"What do you do for fun?"

Not "Why do you hate me?" or "Why are you friends with jerks?" What did I do for fun? I shrugged at him. I hadn't done much for fun since Mom died. Now I just pass my time by working to blend in with the older boys. Being in middle school sucked, but it became easier when others couldn't push you around. It was the same thing every day. You use Mom's old makeup to cover your bruises. You skip first period with your "friends" and throw rocks at parking lot cars. You go to school and spit on that one girl. You write on that one classmate's locker to kill themselves because your friends told you to.

You play it off.

They continue to pressure.

You resist and try to get them to move on.

They hit you.

You do it, trying not to cry because they hit the same area that was still swollen from last night.

They act like nothing happened.

And so do you.

Because that's just what you do.

Being in the wolf's pack doesn't mean you're safe from their bite. It just makes the bark personal. I did nothing "for fun"; it was all for survival. But he asked me anyway. I shrugged, but he continued to ask about who I was. Eventually I snarked at him and asked why he was talking to me. I tried to give him the hint that I didn't want to be friendly, but instead he answered, "Because I don't think you're as bad as your friends."

And so, he invited me to his house after school. I went because I couldn't go home. I went because I needed a warm home-cooked dinner. I went because ... I needed ... I needed a friend.

We had fun. We played his Nintendo and played outside with his Nerf guns. We watched cartoons and ate dinner together. His house became my home for that next month, and I never wanted to leave. But when the streetlights came on, I told them I didn't live far so they would let me walk. In truth, I didn't want them to see where I lived. The dump it'd become. Our mailbox stuffed with bills we were clearly behind on and our unkempt lawn. Worst of all, my father.

The biggest shame I bore. My drunken father. Heavy-handed and always with a temper. Before Mom died, he used to beat on her. I didn't understand what he was doing until after she died. He needed a new person to push around. He only looked for me when he sobered up. When he drank, I just had to remain invisible, and I was safe. Or I thought I was safe. The only safety I felt was with Johnny. At his house. At home.

School became the biggest barrier. I couldn't talk to him like I knew him because of my friends. He was shy, he was tired, but he was still kind to me despite the number of times I had just watched them stick gum in his hair, dangle his glasses above his head, rip up his homework ... terrorize him. I was frozen. I don't know why I didn't say anything. I could've done something. Anything.

Two weeks ago, we swam in his pool over the weekend. My makeup came off, revealing the swollen bruises over my cheeks and jaw. To be honest, they didn't hide so well under the makeup, but it covered the darkening colors of my cream-colored skin. I was splashing around, forgetting completely where I was and where my dark secrets so brightly shone. He had just stared, and I became embarrassed. He told me it was going to be fine. I said it wasn't. I begged him to not tell. I cried and yelled. He shushed me and rushed me inside, a towel over my head. He took me to his mother's restroom and caked my face.

He took me to his room, and we dried off. I told him everything. The nasty truth: Mom's death, my disgusting father, my burdening friends.

I always knew you weren't who you tried to be.

He hugged me. Hugged me the way my mother did those nights I would ask where daddy went. Then he told me everything was going to be okay. I stayed the night that night. Then everything between us changed forever.

I had never told anybody what my life looked like behind the doors of my house. I had never admitted to not having a mother anymore. He was the first one that made me feel safe enough to truly admit how weak I was. How empty I had felt. How lonely things had gotten.

I will never judge you.

We spent that Sunday playing games the way we normally did. I thought everything was going to be normal. Everything was going to be the way it was. Like best friends did on the weekends. We had an off day from school the following Monday, so I stayed again that night. After getting ready for bed, we stayed up in his room to talk. We sat on the bed and only the lamp was on. He told me how his daddy wasn't his real daddy. His mom had remarried when he was younger because his dad was having an affair. I thought his family was perfect.

I'm glad we understand each other.

There was a long pause between us, and I never would've expected what was to happen next. Johnny drew in close to me and grabbed my face. He kissed me. Genuinely kissed me. I had never kissed anyone before, and it didn't even occur to me in that moment that what we were doing was wrong. I pushed him away in shock.

"I-I'm sorry," he stuttered. "I don't know what came over me."

"I thought only high schoolers did that," I said, staring down at my feet. "I thought ... only girls ..."

"Me too," he whispered, embarrassed.

All these feelings. That single moment explained everything. I always wanted to be with him. I only wanted to talk to him. My stomach swirled when

I thought about him. The way he held me. The way he made me laugh. The sort of happiness I was feeling I thought died long ago with my mother. But this happiness was different.

I kissed him back, surprising him.

And we lay, holding each other until our slumber overtook us.

You make me feel safe.

I stopped hanging out with my friends, started showing up to school on time. I left the house early anyway to avoid my dad, so going to school wasn't hard. I used to hang out here at this truck stop until it was time for us to meet up. But things were different now. I was free.

I only spoke to Johnny, and he only spoke to me. There was a day when my friends tried to drag Johnny to the bathroom, probably to give him a swirly like we did so many times in the past. I kicked the leader in his groin, and we both ran away from them until our lungs hurt. After we caught our breath, we just laughed. We laughed and laughed.

I didn't go to his house that weekend. I couldn't tell you why. He didn't invite me, he just stopped talking to me. He was disengaged, uninterested. I became invisible. The same draining feeling I had when Mom died ... I cried only in my bed when she died. And now I cried whenever I saw him. Distant. Gone.

Dad had this unusual thing he did when the anniversary of Mom's death came around. He started to tidy things up. He spoke to me quietly and sad. Almost guilty. He didn't drink. He showered and wore clean clothes. He treated me the way he did before she died—but he constantly choked on melancholy. I skipped school on her anniversary. I stayed in bed and didn't eat. Around three o'clock, I heard the doorbell go off. No one ever came to the house. Not since Mom died. I heard my dad talk and the door close.

My bedroom door opened, and Johnny stepped in.

I will always be here for you.

"Go away ..." My voice was foreign. It was groggy and vulnerable.

He walked over to my bed and sat next to my buried body. "I'm sorry ... my parents said you're not allowed at my house anymore."

My eyes widened and I could feel my heart pump in my throat. "Why?"

"I told them I liked you, and they told me it was wrong to be a 'homo.' I don't even know what a homo is, but it's enough to tell me I was grounded."

Gay. They meant gay. Pansies is what we were to them.

"You shouldn't be here. You're going to get in trouble."

"I don't care, Bret. You're the only thing I care about."

I stared at his face.

He stared at mine.

"I think this—" He paused and took a deep breath. "I think I love you."

I love you.

He grabbed my hand and held it, so I held it back.

"Goodbye, Bret."

"Johnny ..."

He got up and left, leaving me absolutely lost without him, missing in my own mind.

The next morning, I found a note in my locker, the very letter I am holding in my hands right now ...

Dear B,

I always knew you weren't who you tried to be. I knew under your tough façade that there was a boy who so desperately needed some kindness. I'm so glad I got to know you. You're my dearest friend. Even though you forgot how to be long ago, you're nice and fun and I love being around you. I'm glad we understand each other. Sometimes, I feel like it's just you and me in this school that know what it's like to be different. My new dad never really liked me. He ignores me and only deals with me so he can be with my mom. I felt lonely before we moved here, but now I feel like I found my place. You make me feel safe. Accepted. You didn't judge me when your friends did, and I will never judge you. I want to be best friends until we die. We're only 13, but I really believe my heart. I think I love you.

No. I love you. I know I love you. I don't care that it's wrong.

Please understand,

J

"Oh my God!" the leader cackled, spitting in my face. He ripped the letter from my hands and pushed me to the ground. I looked at the circle laughing at me, stunned. I used to be the predator, but now I was the prey.

"Bret, who's this from?" he taunted. I didn't say anything. I thought I was going to pee my pants.

He persisted to read the letter aloud. I tried to fight him and take it back. I only wanted him to shut his face, but he hit me back harder every time I got up. The same way my dad hit me over the head. He slapped my temple so hard that I had to fight back vomiting while my vision spun. The crowd only laughed harder with every sentence read. They taunted me and pointed fingers.

He reached the last sentence ...

"Please understand," he mocked in a high-pitched voice. "J." He had to take a second look at the paper. "Hold on! J? I thought a *girl actually* liked you. It was funny at first, but now it's *hilarious!*

"This can only be from"—he gasped dramatically teasing the crowd of middle schoolers—"Johnathen!"

My heart felt like it stopped. My gut spun, threatening to vomit empty content. I quickly spotted Johnny behind a girl with brown hair.

"Bret's a faggot!"

Stop. Stop!

"Shut up!" I screamed. I stood up, stiff upper lip.

"I'm not gay."

He got close to my face, his breath attacking my nose. It smelt the way Dad's did. "Prove it." Like alcohol ...

I snatched the letter back and stomped over to Johnny and pushed him.

"What are you doing?" He shook.

"I'm not gay! I'm not like you!" I yelled at him, "You're the fag! Not me!"

He scrambled to his feet, pleaded with me to think. My hands came down on him. My best friend. The boy I loved.

I hit him over and over until his nose bled. The students shouted "fight" repetitively. I picked him up and threw him headfirst into the lockers. The teachers grabbed me and then I was in the principal's office faster than I could blink.

That was two hours ago ...

Now I was here ... more broken than before. Continuously falling apart, that's what I did. Self-destructing. Hurt others. Just like my dad.

A hand rubbed my shoulder, and I jumped. Behind me was Johnathen. My first kiss. My first love. His eye swollen shut and glasses bent. Because of me ...

"Figured I'd find you here." He smiled.

A Coffee, a Creek & a Memory

MARCUS LUEVANO

Grade 11, Northwest High School, Grand Island, NE. Honorable Mention.

Yesterday I was walking down to Tommy's Cafe to get my regular cup of coffee. The dismal weather turned the morning into the afternoon and the clouds released drops of rain, creating puddles everywhere. As I continued to walk, the gusts of wind became stronger, and the raindrops fell more rapidly. When I finally reached Tommy's, I opened the door, took off my jacket, and walked to my regular table. I saw all of my friends sitting at their regular spots as well. Gus was at the counter reading the newspaper, Linda was sitting in the corner reading a book called *Life as a Daydreamer*, and Daryl sat in the booth nearest to the window talking to Tommy about the weather.

Shortly after sitting down, Johnny came by and asked, "Hey, Walt, how are you doing? What can I get for you today?"

I responded by simply saying, "Oh, Johnny, I'm doing swell this morning. I'm doing a lot better than the weather. I'll just have my regular today."

When Johnny turned around, I became confused as I couldn't remember if I had ordered yet or not, so I said, "Hey, Johnny, have I ordered yet?"

He looked at me with eyes full of sorrow as if something was wrong. However, he smiled at me, made his way over to my table and said, "I'm sorry, Walt, what can I get for you today?"

With a cheery grin on my face, I happily said, "I'll just have my regular today, Johnny."

Before turning around and starting for the counter he said, "I'll get that out for you shortly, Walt."

After Johnny walked away, the cafe returned to its regularly scheduled silence. As I went to grab the newspaper lying in front of me, my eyes were caught by a painting that was hanging on the wall. The painting intrigued me because I never remembered it being there before.

Interrupting Tommy's conversation with Daryl, I asked, "Hey, Tommy, when did you get that painting?"

With the same expression as Johnny, he looked at me with a grin and said, "You know what, Walt, I just hung it up this morning."

Even after hearing what Tommy told me, I couldn't take my gaze off of the painting. The painting puzzled me because it looked so familiar, but I couldn't remember why. The painting was of a long and winding creek with the sun rising in the distance. There was a bare tree in the corner that looked like it had been around for centuries. Surrounding the creek were fallen leaves of different colors and minute patches of green grass placed sporadically on the ground. Looking at the painting, I felt a sense of belonging. I could tell that whoever painted it put their heart and soul into every single stroke of paint. As I continued to look at the painting, I became more and more puzzled, not being able to remember why it looked so familiar.

I finally removed my eyes from the painting when Johnny came back to my table, and said, "There you go, Walt," as he put the steaming cup of coffee in front of me.

After letting the coffee cool for a moment, I took a sip and grabbed the newspaper. I briefly glanced over the headlines, which never had anything interesting, and skipped to the sports section, which talked about how the Huskers were preparing for a comeback season even though they would do the same as they did last year. Then my reading was interrupted by the chime of the door being opened. Caught off guard and wondering who would have entered the cafe, I looked up from the newspaper. However, I didn't see a new customer, and no one was looking around as I was. Subsequently, I returned to the newspaper and looked at the funnies. Then my reading was interrupted by a still, small voice that said, "Hey, Walt, it's been a while." Upon hearing the voice, I immediately put the newspaper down and looked behind me. That's when I saw a man with long black hair and a five o'clock shadow wearing a black leather jacket sitting two tables behind me. I couldn't stop looking at him as he was also reading the newspaper. He looked so much like an old friend. I wanted so badly to get up to ask, "Sean, is that really you?" However, I couldn't bring myself to get up and actually do it. The longer I looked at the man, the deeper my mind went into the past. Looking at that man took me back to the good ol' days.

It was two days before graduation, and I was at the diner getting something to eat with my best friend, Sean. As usual we each ordered a hamburger, fries, and a Coke to keep us busy while we talked about each other's day. Sean was the kindest and coolest guy that you could come across. He was always willing to lend a helping hand to someone in need. However, there was another side of Sean that was always looking for a way to have fun or create mischief.

Although Sean and I had our differences in looks, we pretty much lived the same lives. Both of us came from homes that were beleaguered by broken families that constantly argued with each other. The two of us knew—and accepted—the fact that our parents didn't care about us at all. The irrefutable truth was, believe it or not, that we wanted our parents to argue all day because it gave us more time to run through the alleys and hang out in the woods. We were best friends. Oftentimes, when we were little, we would be the only ones to show up to each other's birthday parties, which was fine because we didn't need any other friends around to have a good time because the two of us had everything that was needed to have a good time. Sean and I never had any other friends because we never saw a need to. I guess we always figured that other people wouldn't ever understand things how Sean and I did. The two of us were closer than brothers until the day everything changed.

Lunch had finally arrived, I was eager to be done with school and I wanted to do something fun, so I walked over to Sean and said, "Hey, Sean, what's up? Want to go over to the station and grab a soda?"

Quickly looking up at me in an impatient manner Sean said, "Sorry, Walt, I'm a little busy right now."

I nudged him on the shoulder and sarcastically said, "What are you busy with? You're never worried about getting anything done ... Come on, let's go."

Sounding more agitated and annoyed, Sean, with a more serious tone, said, "Walt, I said I'm busy."

Nudging him on the shoulder once more I said, "Come on, Sean, knock it off. Let's go."

Suddenly Sean got up, looked me right in the eyes with a look I'd never seen before and yelled, "Didn't you understand what I said, you idiot?! I said I'm busy! Can't you see I'm trying to figure everything out?!"

Filled with trepidation and confusion I asked, "Figure what out?"

Losing all self-control Sean, in his thunderous voice, shouted, "You know what, I'm so sick of seeing your face and being around you! Go find someone else to talk to! Better yet, why don't you just shut up, and go home and quit being a pest?!"

After Sean yelled at me, he immediately sat down and continued doing what he was doing. As for me, I just stood there in complete shock for two seconds, which felt like eternity. With the entire cafeteria looking at me, I walked out and listened to what Sean told me to do. The whole way home I cried trying to figure out what I did wrong. I couldn't believe that this was the end of the road for Sean and me. We had been friends our entire lives and I never thought that would change. The Sean I saw that day wasn't the Sean that I was friends with. The Sean that I knew was slow to anger and fun-loving. It made absolutely no sense for him to suddenly explode like how he did earlier.

Maybe friendships aren't meant to be kept. Maybe you can only hold onto them for as long as you can. As I was walking home the sky became gray and rain began to fall. The rest of the way home my tears mixed with the rain as my mind became empty.

When I finally arrived home, I walked onto the porch and knocked on the door. However, I quickly turned around and walked back into the rain after hearing the sound of my parents arguing. By now the night had settled in and the rain, along with my tears, had finally stopped falling. With nowhere else to go I walked down to the old creek, where Sean and I used to go when we were little. The whole way there the only source of light came from the old street lights until I reached a path in the woods that led to the creek.

After I navigated my way through the woods, approaching the creek, I noticed that someone was sitting at the creek. Then I realized that it was Sean. Instead of ignoring him and heading back home, I sat right beside him. In that moment our words were few, yet somehow I could tell that neither of us were upset with the other. We didn't even bother looking at each other.

As we sat there, the silence was only interrupted by the sounds of chirping crickets, flowing water, and the occasional cool breeze rustling through the leaves, which leisurely made their way downstream to the great unknown.

With a voice as calm as the water itself, Sean said, "Do you think the trees ever wish they could move?"

In the same tone of voice, I replied, "Do you ever wonder if the crickets get cold, or if the rocks get tired of drowning?"

Totally ignoring my question, Sean, not looking at me, said, "Have you ever realized how similar we are to the trees, Walt? I mean, think about it, we were born and raised here and haven't ever been anywhere else. The farthest we've ever gone is the beginning of this creek ... It just makes me wonder what lies beyond this town and where we'll end up ... Where do you think you'll end up, Walt?"

Caught off guard I said, "Well, I don't know. I guess I've never really thought about that. How about you Sean?"

Looking into the night, Sean responded, "You know, Walt, I don't know either."

As the night drew on the breeze became brisk, and neither of us said a word to each other. Occasionally, I would look over at Sean as he just stared into the night. I could tell that something was different. Something in his eyes told me that we were thinking the same thing. That we both knew that times were changing, doors were closing, and that the most important things that night were the silence, the sporadic sound of chirping crickets, and the creek.

It was getting late, the night was wearing thin, and I wanted to go home and get some sleep. I was beginning to wonder if we were ever going to leave. We never stayed at the creek this long. However, I couldn't stand to just leave Sean here alone. While I continued to sit in the still silence and look into the night sky, I became tired and my eyes closed for what seemed the length of a memory.

Then Sean gently slapped his knees, got up, looked at me with a smile, and said, "Well, see you around, Walt. You've been a good friend," and handed me an envelope before starting downstream.

Perplexed and still partially asleep, I asked, "Sean, where are you going?"

Not looking back, he said, "I don't know, Walt, but I'm going to find out."

As he continued down the creek, the sun began to rise and all its heavenly hues of yellow and orange illuminated the sky and glistened off the sparkling water. This was the first time we had ever seen the sunrise at the creek. As he continued walking, he became smaller and smaller until he disappeared into the bright yellow fluorescence of the rising sun. I knew this would be the last time I would see Sean and the last time we would be kids, so I didn't bother to go after him. Instead, I sat there reminiscing about all of the good times we had together laughing and wrestling in the woods. I remembered all the times we sat at this creek, climbed the trees, and skipped rocks. Then I got up and started home, but I stopped and lifted my eyes from the envelope that was so thin yet so heavy laden with changes and uncertainties. I took one last look at the creek, running my fingers over the words United States Selective Service System on the envelope. The creek was so different that morning. The grass was greener, and the water was crystal clear. Then I looked at the trees that were bare with occasional leaves falling to the ground. Just then a golden leaf fell from the sky and landed on the water. Then, under my breath, I said, "Yeah, see you around." I never went back to the creek after that day, but I knew that, like the trees, a new season of life was beginning, a new day was on the horizon, and things would not be the same.

Ding-dong!

Upon hearing the chime of the door being opened, I returned to reality, realized my coffee had become cold, and found that the man, who looked so much like Sean, had just gotten up to leave. Then I quickly got up to catch up to the man. I was right behind him.

Then he opened the door, looked back with a sly smile on his face, and said, "It was nice seeing you, Walt."

At that moment I was drawn back to the painting that hung on the wall. Then everything came back to me. Having finally realized why the painting looked so familiar, I stopped for a moment and took in every detail of the painting one last time. Once again, I reminisced of all the wonderful times Sean and I had together.

Then with a bittersweet and sorrowful sigh, I said, "Yeah, Sean, it was nice seeing you, too."

After saying those words I grabbed my coat, and placed my hand on the door handle. As I turned the knob to open the door I couldn't find any reason why I had to catch up to that man, so I took my hand off the knob, returned to my table, and spent the rest of the day sitting at the cafe trying to reclaim memories that time had taken from me, trying to hold onto memories before they faded once more.

Sand Through the Hourglass

Alexander Schuler

Grade 12, Fort Calhoun Junior/Senior High School, Fort Calhoun, NE. Sara Gross, Educator.

It was a crisp Saturday morning in the middle of autumn, days before my 16th birthday. I was casually sliding through the ever-browning grass in the field behind my house. As I walked, I let my mind wander, per usual. I never knew what ideas were to be found roaming around up there. Sometimes, I would begin to almost slip away from my world and into a vast, ever-growing sea. I don't know what it was about the thought, but it always seemed to pull me in. Everyone has times when they are so relaxed they almost drift out of their being. On that cool Saturday morning, I saw more than just my thoughts. I saw my future but with less color. I heard my voice but not my words. I felt the autumn air, but it did not send the same chills down my back, as it always had.

I watched and waited. I took a deep breath and slowly opened my eyes. Soon, I began to fade back into my reality when I felt a tug like I was being pulled back into a world that was not my own, to myself, whom I did not recognize. Suddenly, I had a clear view of the man on the other side of the pull. He had a curvy plastered nose and wavy brown hair just like me, but there was something different about him ... something haunting. It was his eyes. When I stared into them, I saw a lonely, empty world, a life I had never lived.

Seconds later ... gone. All of it is gone. Me or him, the presence was gone ...

◇◇◇◇◇◇◇◇◇◇◇◇◇◇◇◇◇◇◇◇◇◇◇◇◇

I sit up and release a relaxing sigh. A gust of wind blows through the open window near my dresser. I feel the autumn breeze that I always look forward to waking up to. I slip my legs from under the sheet and drape my feet onto the floor. I get up and walk over to the window. I lean under the blinds and peer across the gentle plain of grass and flora. The rustle of the leaves draws my eyes. The branches subtly rock on the cherry blossoms, 80 feet from the window where I stand. I take a deep breath in, tasting the dry, warm air.... Warm? It startles me for a moment. My mind expects a cool sensation but it is not receiving it. I shake it from my mind and turn to leave my room.

I slowly lope across the hall to my bathroom vanity, as I do at the beginning of every new day. I reach to my left and flick on the light. I tilt my head towards the mirror and see myself with a large nose and ears. My hair is streaked with highlights of gray. My face is covered with glaring wrinkles up and down. I slowly shake my head. Five minutes later, I stand next to the door, my shoes on, and grab my coat from the closet. I step outside and taste the morning air before starting on my walk down the street. I take the same route every day just like the retired 70-something-year-old man I am. I walk, one slow step after another, bare and alone.

The bell quietly jiggles as I open the door to the coffee shop. I shuffle over to the counter and pick up my coffee. It's the same spot, every morning. Same order, dark roast with a sugar cube, every day for 10 years. I take a seat solitarily by the window. As I sit, slowly sipping my coffee, I see a young couple walk by; visions of when I was their age begin to run through my mind. I recall my first girlfriend, my first kiss, and Friday nights after the football games. Moreover, I remember walking down this same street each morning before school with my best friend. He could be sitting right next to me, coffee in his hand, shooting the breeze. But he isn't, he is gone, forever. My gaze shifts back to the sidewalk, and again, I feel a pain in my chest. Another couple, almost 60, laughing and smiling, his hand in hers as they walk. That could have been my life if it wasn't for that night.

I tip my coffee into the trash and hang my head as I proceed to leave. I swing the door open and turn, bumping into a man. He has his head down, just as I do. He can only muster a couple of mumbled words as he shuffles out of the way. I watch for a moment as he sits down against the side of the building, tossing his rucksack beside him. He is homeless. I wait another moment until finally, he looks up at me. I start to notice the crevices on his face that are caked with dirt. He wears a black hood over his head. His features mirror my age. It is Paul. Paul was once one of the most outgoing people that I ever knew. Back in high school, he truly made a name for himself. I remember he walked as if he were an idol, one that no one would ever forget. He had big dreams and an even bigger smile. He would tell everyone who he was and who he would become. Not many people could see in him what I could; I noticed that even through the spotlight, there were times when his path seemed to become unclear even to himself. There were times when he would lose sight of his dreams. Who knows, maybe he just finally came to a sense of reality. I remember the day when a shadow slowly began to cover his spotlight. With the spotlight went his persona, but even more disconsolately, his desire. Plenty of people contributed to the weight that dragged him down, and I would be lying if I said I wasn't one of them.

Paul's story was yet another item to add to my list of regrets. I realize that no benefit comes from worrying about these regrets; however, they continue to burden me to this day. There are nights that I pray that I can spare myself. I yearn for the chance to rewrite my story, just one more time. With this thought comes a short spurt of motivation. I bring my eyes to where Paul is sitting and I begin speaking, but there's no one there—just a pile of dirt and scraps in his place. A single tear slowly rolls down my cheek. I make my way to a bench not far from the shop door. There I collapse into the cold metal. A hollowing shiver runs down the length of my spine.

I begin to recall a cool autumn morning from when I was a child. I remember the placid walk I took through the field behind my home. This is just a fragment of a memory, but it was a memory of a childhood where my future, and all of its possibilities, still stood ahead of me. The long-lost dream begins to fade away once again. I sit there alone on the bench taking in every missed opportunity, knowing that with every passing moment, my hourglass comes one grain closer to its last.

My hourglass, it's something I remember my father talking about in his final days on the hospital bed. The room was bleak and gray. Standing in that room made me feel like time was cascading down around me. On the east wall, was a large window with a clear view of the pale sky. Through it, I saw a snowflake gently glide past. It seemed as if that crystal of ice had frozen that moment in my mind forever. That was the scene that lay in front of me, but a different stage was set in my mind. What I saw was his face, and what I heard was his voice. I remember each one of his faint words perfectly. He spoke to me and said, "Son, I am almost to my last grain of sand. You have your hourglass, and it lies within your grasp right now. Each grain of sand in that glass signifies a moment in your life. As you watch each piece file down, you are presented with a choice. The sand can only fall two ways. It either falls vacuously into a scattered pile at the bottom of the pitcher or lands perfectly, solidified, helping to build a tower that will become your life."

I slowly responded, "Dad, I don't think I understand."

He clarified by saying, "I know exactly what my tower looks like. It is standing right here in this room with me. Built strong, held up with love that surrounds it. The choice is up to you now. How will you choose to build your tower?" Those were the last words he said to me, not just that night, but forever.

I drift passively through my dream-like state as I think. "Is this it? Will I waste those last few grains of sand here, alone?" The answer is yes. I have watched so many moments in my life slip away. Every day that I woke up, I took it for granted. I wasn't thankful for those days. The whole time, I witlessly made my way through school and work while doing nothing but staring at the clock. Instead of counting the moments I should cherish, I counted the minutes until I could return to where I started just to do it all again. Sitting here now, I finally know what I would tell myself that cool Saturday morning before my 16th birthday. I would tell myself not to skip the family reunion because I was "too busy"; to not blow off my best friend's cry for help; to not walk out on *her*, two months before our wedding day. But most importantly, I would tell myself to stop my father from getting in the car that day. The day that he ended up in that hospital room ... the day his hourglass ran out.

I wake to the sound of a car horn. I look up and see that the sun is absent. I am still on the bench where I had ended up that morning after my time at the coffee shop. The day has gone in a flash. I sit up and rub my eyes. Then, standing, I begin the prolonged walk back home. Carefully, I notice that this walk is unlike the first at dawn. The moon shines a different light on things around me. As I walk, I am tormented with memories. Though little is different, this time I take a chance. I decide to receive these memories with a joyful heart. I begin to remember the good things that I have forgotten. I even pursue those memories that were cast with regret. I look up to see the moon and the stars above me, and with a clearer mind, I connect all of these good memories. It is now that I realize, for the first time, that each one of these memories ends the same. They finish with me standing by the window, just as I had each morning. I think of how my gaze floats over the landscape. It is almost as if my present lay just 80 feet in front of me, and at night, my future lay millions of miles above. A different path resides in each one of those stars; I once had the choice between any one of them.

I make my way into the house and to my bed. I dream of what worlds lay in each one of those stars. In one of my dreams, I see myself on a cool autumn morning. I am young and casually sliding through the ever-browning grass in the field behind my house. I am deep in thought, eyes closed, head tilted towards the sky. As I dream, I try to reach out to the young boy before me, hoping to clutch my youth. I tug at him with all my might. I try to shout to him, but he can't hear me. So instead, I just watch as he stands in serenity. For a moment I feel as if I were standing beside him. I watch him slowly open his eyes and turn to start home. The farther away he gets, the weaker our connection becomes. Just as I nearly lose sight of him, he slows his pace and begins to turn around. He is half around his rotation when my eyes catch his. He is facing me now, his eyes locked with mine. His gaze draws deep into my soul. I wonder what it is he sees. I reach out to grab his hand but before my fingers close around his, he is gone ... all of it ... gone.

∞∞∞∞∞∞∞∞∞∞∞∞∞∞∞∞∞∞∞∞∞∞∞

I turn around and start heading back towards the house, startled at what I think I saw. *I must just be imagining things*, I tell myself. The man with the large nose and wavy hair is gone from my sight. I shiver as I feel the cold breeze slide up my neck. I have been thinking about life a lot recently. It's almost as if this experience has painted a new sense of importance in my mind. I don't know where it came from or who the old man was but he seemed familiar, almost like I know him.

By the time I get home, the notion has all but slipped my mind. I open the door, glad to get out of the nipping wind. I remove my shoes and walk down the hallway to see my Dad getting ready for work. I walk over to him and I ask, "Dad, instead of driving to work today, how about you just take the day off? When you're finished, maybe we can play catch. After all, it is a beautiful autumn day!"

Epilogue

I am 86 years old now, and I am almost at my last grain of sand. But this time, instead of being alone with my thoughts, I am comfortable in my bed. Family surrounds me and numerous friends stand by my side. Paul is here fulfilled in his dreams, and my beautiful wife sits next to me holding my hand. I can hear my grandkids playing eagerly in another room. I am satisfied with my view as the last grain of sand falls. I became the keystone to so many others' castles. I was given a second chance by fate to topple my regret and choose a different path forward. I rest now on my path of love, hope, and healing. I will never give up what I have built, just as they will never give up on me.

THE GREAT AUK

JIHYE SEO

Grade 11, Lincoln East High School, Lincoln, NE.

SILVER

The Great Auk's eyes flicker open and closed, sleep creeping upon his feathers. The harsh wind of the North Sea crashes onto the island's charcoal-black cliffs, fabricating a lullaby with earthen rumbles. The Great Auk runs his beak through his glossy feathers, the drops of saltwater lazily slipping away from the vane. The bird trembles in reminder of the frigid cold of the water and the tightening nervousness of an approaching predator wading in the deep. The memory awakes him but the comfort of land seems to be stronger. The lullaby of the cliffs soon eases his mind back to sleep. A ship floating alone, faraway, with white sails and three featherless passengers, is the last grasp of reality the Great Auk has before falling into a dream.

He feels familiar feathers rubbing against his own. The rising and falling of the chest, the swiping of the feathers, and the rhythmic brushing of a beak startles him. He opens his eyes. The glossy feathers stare back at him. This is mom. His mom. "Mom?" he whistles out, hearing nothing but a quick chirp, chiding him to be quiet. So he does as he is told. He closes his eyes yet keeps his ears open in curiosity. But this curiosity betrays him. Silenced squawks of fury and pain echo into the walls of the damp cave, flooding his ears with distant fear. A protective wing wraps around him as if to shield him further from the sounds. The continuous beating of his mom's heart no longer sounds comforting but more like the looming laps of water of an approaching orca. Each beat washes over him, sparking innate fear, his wings shaking in terror. Then, his mother cries out, shoving him away. "Run!" she yells, pushing him even further. His eyes open in panic—the Great Auk jolts awake. The nightmare fades before his eyes.

The Great Auk heaves in confusion. He does not remember what happened that day, his brain unable to rack any souvenirs. His mom disappeared without a trace. He buries his head back in between his wings, perhaps unaware of the three no-feathers sulking their way towards him. One cautiously puts a finger to his lips, warning the others to stay quiet. His feet graze the charcoal cliff sides slowly. A rope held in one hand with determination in the other, the no-feather extends his hand and grasps.

The Great Auk squawks in shock. His life flashes before his eyes, confusion shaking him to the core. Something has gotten him! The lump of flesh on his neck closes in harder, and it's not long before a scratchy rope grabs ahold of his torso. His wings strain under the rope but to his dismay, his legs meet the same fate. His voice goes hoarse as he cries harder, hoping some bird can hear him. Whatever comes back is not the voice of his equal. Only the voice of seabirds, those who only screech mockery. Flashes of pale skin, scruffy brown fabric, and coarse hair fill his vision. The Great Auk is powerless. The frightening calls of fellow seabirds and mischievous shrieks of gulls confuse him tenfold as he calls out with them.

A disarray of wings, legs, hair, sky, rain, sea, shrieks, calls, and ... humans make the bird tremble harder. The sky thunders. Something is coming. The Great Auk squawks out, the heat rising in his pulses, his vision blotches in panic, nothing is believable. These captors, they drag him by the vile rope they tied his feet with, jabbering in unknown calls, ignoring his protesting cries. Someone, anyone, any mystical happening, none desire to save the bird from these arrogant fools. What do they plan to do with him?

The sailors throw the screaming bird in a shack, slamming the door behind them. Deafening cries continue to escape through the cracks of the windows. "That damn bird!" a sailor exclaims angrily, throwing his cigar on the ground. "Well, it's priceless. It'll serve us well. Just look at those sparkling feathers," the other sailor points out, scratching the ground. A third grunts heavily as he sits down to rest. All three of their skin itches in boredom. They'll wait out this storm before sailing off to England, where the bird will be sold for a high price. The cries continue to erupt from the shack, a constant reminder of pain, and fear of the unknown scrapes the sailors' brains.

The Great Auk trembles in fear and hatred. Something has happened. He doesn't know what it is. He squawks once more. Please. Anyone. Please. Hours must've passed. Days, maybe. Perhaps it's been weeks. He has kept track of it. The elements fail to help him. The wind batters on the walls like vicious terns. Then, an abnormal chirp catches his ears. More and more of them begin to pile upon each other like rain splattering on moss. The no-feathers. They knock down the walls, their feet echoing upon the ground. A flash of pain strikes him on his head. Furious cries and yells refuse to let him settle in unconsciousness. Slams of sticks and rocks choke the life out of him. Pain spreads to all corners of his body as reality slips from his feathers.

Then ... darkness. The sailors wipe sweat from their brows. It's been three days and the storm hasn't cleared. They are beyond starving and their passage back home has disappeared. They blame the winged witch, the cursed creature, the forbidden feathers. The Great Auk has plunged them into isolation on this island. Revenge is theirs. Their sticks of justice beat the demon out of this bird. They are sure that this bird is behind the storm. "This feathered witch!" A sailor spits on the heaving carcass of the creature, shooting it a dirty glance. The remaining two agree as sunlight spills through the windows. They can go back home now.

The last Great Auk of the UK met his death in 1840 on the islet of Stac an Armin, beaten with sticks and stones by three sailors.

GUILTY IS THE HAUNTED

JUPITER STURM

Grade 11, Boys Town High School, Boys Town, NE. Beth Sulley, Educator.
Honorable Mention.

On a most tumultuous rainy night, when the wind whipped the trees back and forth, lashing their stringy branches back and forth like the hair of a madman, I paced up and down the halls of the castle, a man unhinged. My footsteps echoed against the empty halls, the pitter-patter displaced by my shoeless left foot hitting the ground. The rain lashed against the windows, begging to be let in, slamming its tortured face against the glass over and over again. The lightning illuminated the adjacent walls with veinlike patterns, there and gone in less than a blink of my weary eyes. The following thunder shook the foundation of the castle, the vibrations traveling up through the soles of my feet and sending tingles up my spine. My tousled hair poked at the edges of my eyelids, and I stumbled. My hand swung out and I caught myself on the wall, using my other hand to brush my oily locks from my forehead. My hand came away from the wall, moist with the rainwater that had seeped through the old bricks. The moisture on my hand was darker than rainwater, painting my hand red, as I saw through the halting flashes of lightning. The thunder roared in my ears like the desperate scream of a dying woman, the sound ringing in my ears and resonating through the halls. I glanced back at my hand, which was no longer coated in red, only rainwater. I shook my head, and continued my aimless pacing, leading me to the greenhouse, a humid room full of luscious plants, leafy greens, and magnificent flowers of breathtaking size. The room itself was huge, stretching out around me like the corners of a forest, but the huge leaves of the towering palms made the room feel confined, the humid air hugging my skin, leaving a watery trace of its touch on my arms. The stones were warm under my feet, both now bare, as I'd lost my shoe at the door, and my socks at the pressing demand of the humidity. The stones were uneven, having needed tending to for longer than I cared to remember. The dirt pressed its way from between the cracked bricks, letting blades of grass reach out from the ground. The dirt clung to the bottoms of my feet, and the moisture turned it to mud between my toes. In the center of the towering room, there was a fountain. The water ran peacefully over the stone, drizzling down to the awaiting pool. I sat at the edge, dipping my fingertips absently into the warm water. The leaves had fallen into the pond, turning the water opaque and transforming the tranquility of the clear water to dismay at the dingy colors. A leaf brushed my fingertips, a forewarning to the hand that gripped my forearm from the depths of the pool, splashing the murky water over the edge of the stones. The fingers dug into my skin, the grimy nails biting into my tender flesh. I screamed, planting my other hand firmly on the edge of the fountain and pushing back. The skin was decaying, sliding around on the hand like a loose glove. The skin around the palm tore, then ripped off entirely, sending the sickly limb sliding down my arm, leaving behind the palm and finger skin, and leaving a trail of old blood and infection down my arm. I rose quickly, my eyes trained on the turbid face of the water, undulating from the movement. I turned and bolted out the entryway, the door slamming against the wall behind me. My muddy feet slapped the carpet, leaving alternating sized footprints running from behind me. The walls seemed to breathe in time with my own aching lungs, expanding and contracting, threatening to squeeze against me, scour my skin with the bare stones. I skidded to a halt, catching myself on the banister. My lungs heaved each breath of the stale air, my shaky hands gripping the cut marble. On either side of me were stairs, curving down to a large dining hall, lit only by the occasional lightning strike, and the foggy light filtering through the windows from the slivered moon. My trembling feet found footing on the steps, the cold marble dragging the heat from the soles of my feet. I met the ground, glad to find that it was lightly carpeted, returning feeling to my aching feet. The long dining table was set for one, a singular plate at the end of the table, head of the table, but head to no family. The table was covered in a thin layer of dust, only the plate setting looking clean. There were arching doorways, leading to an open kitchen with fire still roaring in the woodburning ovens, and burned meat still coughing up great billows of smoke into the thin chimneys. I ventured into the kitchen, taking caution to keep in mind the location of the fires, always to my back. Out of the thick smoke appeared a figure, the outline of a woman, her arms outstretched toward me, reaching out for an embrace.

"Odette?" My voice quivered in my throat, pushing the name from my lips before I could ponder the reason, the motivation, the danger. The hands moved like to embrace me, reaching around. I closed my eyes, ready for the warm embrace of my late paramour. The hands planted firmly on my shoulders, gripping my shirt and pulling me closer, my ear near to her lips.

"You will soon fear me as I feared you," she whispered, her voice like a thousand strands of silk gliding over my ears, a hundred knives poised to strike. She pushed me backward, and I swung my hands out to catch myself, and screamed. The hot metal of the burning wood stove seared my hands, the flesh bubbling and popping like a fresh slab of meat laid to the griddle. I tore my hands away, losing the skin of my palms on the red-hot metal. The backs of my forearms were singed black, the flames having just kissed the tender skin, leaving it red and blistering. I bolted from the room, tearing down a secluded hallway, set off behind the stairs. The walls were dark and windowless, the grey bricks absorbing the light, the heat, the life from the air. My shoulders slammed against a wooden door, and I gripped the handle, wrenching it open and slamming it against the adjacent wall. My burning hands protested their use, but I was already bounding down the stairs, following the curve of the walls, disregarding how they narrowed, growing closer to my tender skin, my frantic escape. As I found the open doorway, my lungs pulled in a heaving breath of air, grateful for the openness of the room, the low light flicking on the walls from the candles that sat, melting into the tables they sat on.

"Lucius," a low voice whispered, the sound like the coming together of a thousand tortured souls waiting to be released. My skin crawled, and my blood ran cold in my veins. I could feel the air around me, moving like a living, breathing being. The cool, dingy air caressed my neck like a silken scarf, just waiting for an adequate chance to tighten abound my throat and strangle the life from my lips. "Lucius," the voice called again, its haunting tone ringing throughout the empty room. "Lucius," a different voice called. I turned around frantically, whipping my head back and forth. "Lucius!" a third voice shouted, getting increasingly angrier. I backed into a corner. "Lucius! Lucius, come here." One familiar voice hit my ears. Her warm voice twanged like a harp string and sprouted peace in my heart like a honeysuckle bush blooming in the early spring.

"Odette," I sighed, her name rolling off my tongue like an old friend. Her shadow came out of a doorway, and she opened her arms to me. I came crashing into her arms, disregarding the pain in my hands and forearms. "Odette, I've missed you so," I sighed into her shoulder. Her gentle grip on me tightened.

"Why am I gone, Lucius?" she asked, her voice lilting like a tulip in bloom. My muscles stiffened beneath my skin. "Why am I gone, Lucius?" There was no warmth in her voice now, only inquisition.

"I don't remember," I said haltingly, standing myself up so I could face her clearly. In the darkness, I could see her features faintly, all exactly how I remembered them, how they appeared to me in my dreams. All but one. "Odette, where did you get that necklace?" Her throat was wrapped in a thick, red necktie, which would have been quite fetching had it not been for the fact that Odette did not wear jewelry. Never once.

"You gave it to me, don't you remember? On the last night I saw you," she remarked wistfully.

"I don't remember," I said, a quiver creeping its way into my voice.

"Of course you do. Come, feel it. It's so soft." She beckoned me closer, and I took a staggering step forward. My hand reached out, halting in the air. She took my hand and moved it to her throat. It was silky, and fair, and wet. Wet and pulsing through my fingers, cascading down my arms and dripping off my elbows.

My fingers pressed against the gaping hole in her neck, and I screamed. She gripped my wrists so tight I swore they'd been broken.

"You did this to me. You did this to me!" she said, repeating the statement over and over again, getting louder each time she said it. I shook my head wildly back and forth, and found myself flying through the air, my head slamming against the walk with a thud the shook my brain like a maraca, the impact making me see stars. Something in my memory twinged, and I was thrust back into a situation so familiar it hurt.

A dark room, with an extravagant bed in the center. One lonely shape lay there. Her breathing was slow, and deep, the breathing of someone in deep sleep. My bare feet took silent steps toward the bed, gripping something in my hand tightly. I stood at the side of the bed, and raised my arm. The blade opened her throat like the layers of a rose, peeling back each row of petals to reveal the innermost workings. Her eyes sprang open, and she tried to draw in a breath of air. She choked, and continued to choke while I stood over her, completely frozen, watching the scene play out. Watching as she struggled less and less until she didn't struggle at all. Until the color drained from her face, the only pigment being the blood, so red, that spilled from her throat like a stream, painting the wood floors with red, red, red, red.

The memory hit me so hard, shocking me, horrifying me to my very core. I shook my head.

"No, no there's no way. I loved you; I love you! I would never do that," I shouted, my voice cracking and breaking.

"I thought so, too," she said softly. "I thought so, too." Her figure began to fade away, absorbing into the shadows behind her. I sat, curled in on myself on the cold floor.

"I would never, I would never, I would never." I rocked myself back and forth, feeling my sanity unravel like a ball of yarn, puddling on the ground.

"I would never, I would never, I would never."

THE CASTLE

AIDEN TINKHAM

Grade 10, Fort Calhoun Junior/Senior High School, Fort Calhoun, NE. Sara Gross, Educator. Honorable Mention.

Ethan and Jack, who were sixteen-year-olds walking home from a tough school day, wearing their crimson red uniform, were strolling along a dusty, filthy pathway. Deep, dense forests surrounded the pathway. Once they had reached the end of the path, they came to a sudden halt. Upon a steep, sheer, and craggy hill lay an eerie, spine-chilling castle. The windows were shattered, the door was flung open, and the turrets were crumbling along with the spires atop them. They decided to continue their journey forward, up the long, stone staircase, and through the towering, enormous wooden doors. They entered a large corridor, with gigantic stone pillars on each side of the walkway, red carpet sprawled down the middle, and a tall oak door standing after the carpet. Two spiral staircases lined the edge of the carpet. They entered through the door and halted in horror as they came across a stone staircase. Because of their curiosity, they continued down the staircase and entered what looked like a dungeon.

They walked through the narrow hallway, wooden cell doors on each side, skeletons in each of the cells, raggedy banners hung on each door, and there were mice, spiders, rats, and shrews that scurried all across the floor. At the end was a tiny, narrow door, but they were able to fit through. There was another hallway, but it was lined with torches this time. It led down to a circular chamber, with high columns that lined the walls. In the center, lay a coffin that was covered by a tarp and dust. They uncovered it, opened it, and to their horror, they found a vampire. It was nighttime, so they expected the vampire to be chasing them away. They tried to scurry out of the chamber, but all of a sudden, the vampire arose from the coffin. The vampire, being covered in cobwebs, morphed into a bat. Ethan and Jack started to run, but the bat, flying above, morphed back into a vampire right in front of them, trapping them. They dodged the vampire, and hurried up the stone staircase, through the dungeon, and up the other stone staircase. They tried to rush out the door, but it was locked, and the vampire continued to follow them up the stairs, so they sprinted up the spiral staircases.

SHORT STORY   155

Ethan ran up the staircase on the right, and Jack ran up the other one on the left.

They split apart from there. Ethan continued on the right side, and he hid himself under a bed. On the other hand, Jack continued to the left. Jack found a room with many cabinets; it was like a kitchen. Jack concealed himself in a top shelf, which the vampire couldn't reach unless he was in bat form. They were exhausted from running away from the vampire. The vampire went throughout the entire upstairs, going through each room, but he couldn't seem to find them. The vampire decided to go up the ladder to check and see if they were in the attic. In the meantime, Ethan and Jack made a sprint for it because the vampire was nowhere to be found. They met up again and ran towards the door. The door was still locked, and they couldn't go anywhere else, so they hid behind the spiral staircase on the left. From behind, came the vampire. Ethan tried to run, but the vampire snatched him, and munched down into his neck, leaving two holes. Jack tried to grab him, but it was too late. Ethan was lying unconscious on the stone-tiled floor. The vampire was approaching Jack, so he just started to run around in a circle, sprinted up the stairs, and into the attic. He found a tall mirror and decided to hide behind it.

Jack heard the clattering, crashing, and clashing the vampire was making downstairs. He felt like hiding behind the mirror was insufficient, so he concealed himself inside a massive chest behind a mound of clothes and other boxes. He suddenly stopped hearing the commotion from downstairs, but next, he heard footsteps heading up the tall, wooden ladder. Jack peeked out the chest and saw the top of the vampire's hair. Then, the tall, dark figure of the vampire stood right in front of the chest. The vampire concluded the search of the attic by looking out the tall window.

Jack saw the opportunity, so he jumped up out of the chest and hurried down the ladder. The vampire heard Jack, so he raced after him. They went down the corridor, and into a turret. Jack was being cornered by the vampire, until, out one of the windows, the sun was glaring through the limbs of the trees, which caused the vampire to back off, and go into the chamber to the right of the turret. Once Jack exited the turret, the door to the chamber opened, and in the doorway was the dark figure of the vampire. Once he saw this, Jack sprinted down the corridor, with the vampire chasing after him. Jack hurried down one of the spiral staircases, into the vestibule, and started running around in circles around the room, with the vampire continuing to chase him. He tripped on a loose tile on the floor and fell face-first into the stone. The vampire was swiftly approaching from behind him. The vampire grabbed his leg, and he was about to go in for a snack, but the sun started to beam through the window.

The vampire was blinded, so he ran in fear, down to the dungeon, and back into his coffin. Meanwhile, Jack hurried to Ethan to check up on him. He was lying unconscious on the stone floor as Jack approached him. Ethan started to speak in a low, monotone voice. Jack knew that he couldn't leave his friend behind, but Ethan wanted him to leave him behind. He decided to bring him with him, so he picked him up and propped him over his right shoulder. Jack tried to open the door and it worked this time because it was starting to become daytime. They walked out the wooden doors, down the stone staircase, and the old, dirt path, thinking never to return to the castle.

CONVERGENCE

GAGE TOWNSEND

Grade 11, Kearney High School, Kearney, NE. Charlotte Dvorak, Educator.
Honorable Mention.

The gun felt cold in my hand, the sleek metal against my fingers. And I'm sure it felt cold on the pleading man's forehead. I opened my mouth and repeated what I had said, calmly. "Just give us half of the paintings, and we will be on our way, okay?" and I knew we had to be quick. We don't want to be found by the P.C.F.

My family and I had sworn an oath to secretly be nice to people in this shattered world. We are never aggressive, even in a country where being nice is frowned upon. Almost everyone is a criminal here. And here, the good people are punished.

We were not robbing an art store or a museum. Rather, we just happened to find a family across town that loved art. And we could sell the art to pay the bills. They had six paintings, one for each of their family members. Maybe they stole it. Although I doubted that because this man was quite the crybaby.

"H-half? B-but you guys are lawful citizens! Shouldn't you want more?" he said while trying to wipe his tears. I looked at him with eyes filled with kindness and determination, and said, "We are not like the others. We do not steal because we like it. We steal because we have to. Yes, we are lawful citizens. But that doesn't mean we can't be kind."

I looked over at my father, who had a gun to the head of a teenage boy. This man's son, maybe? I turned back to the man and got on my knees. I used my shirt to wipe his tears. I put my hand on his shoulder. "Come on, man, don't cry. Everything is going to be okay. We are not going to hurt you or your family as long as you give us the paintings. I promise," I said in a very soothing voice, even though I knew I might have to do something regrettable. But only if things turned south.

I got back up, gun still on his forehead, and extended my arm. "Come on, the faster we get those paintings, the faster we will leave you guys alone." Reluctantly, he took my hand and stood back up

I turned to look at my family members. There was my father, who had his gun to the man's son. My mother, who had a gun to the man's wife. And then there was my brother, who was watching over everyone else. I said to my mother and father, "Come on, let's get moving. Dan can keep an eye on everyone else. We can't get caught by the P.C.F.," and so we got the stone rolling.

The rest of the house was pretty nice. It's exactly what you would expect from a rich man's home. Lots of large beds, master bathrooms, etc. The house was covered in shiny marble tiles. And did I smell ... lavender? "This would make a good backup house. If something were to happen to mine," my inner demons said. I shook my head. "I don't deserve a nice house. Not after all the things I've done," I opposed.

We went in three pairs to get the paintings. My dad and the man's son. My mom and the man's wife. And me with the man. I had my arm slung over his shoulder.

I sighed. "Look, man, I know that I'm a villain, sort of. But society is, well ... broken. The laws are the opposite of what they used to be. You have to make your mark if you want to make it in life." I pulled him in closer. "You need to be prepared for the unexpected." And then something caught my eye.

I rotated my body to face the most beautiful painting. *Convergence*, I said, a hint of excitement in my voice. It was just hanging there in a bedroom on my right, like the last bit of free speech in a ruined world.

I had always been a fan of Jackson Pollock. His paintings are like chaos with meaning. And *Convergence* is my favorite of his. "Free speech in a ruined world. I think I'll take this one," my fan boy side said. So I got on the bed and gently took it off the wall before heading back into the hallway, a smile plastered on my face. "I have what I want. How about we go back to the living room?"

I waited for a few minutes on the couch, clutching the painting like it was my child. My brother was leaning against the wall in the top right corner, arms crossed, a lit cigarette in his mouth. After a few minutes, I had to open a large window so he didn't fill the room with smoke. But instead of returning to the couch, I leaned out the window, using my arm as support. I was soon joined by my brother, who put his arm in the same position and offered me a cigarette. I gladly took it and he used his lighter to light it for me. Teenagers should never take a cigarette. Looking out the window, the world seemed so normal and peaceful, but I know what lies beneath. Puffing out a cloud of smoke, I said, "How could a society that looks so peaceful, be so cruel?" And he only shrugged.

When my parents returned to the living room, they found the two of us leaning out of the window. We both jumped and dropped our cigarettes when dad came up behind us and said, "Why didn't you two wait for me? I would kill for a cigarette right now!" My brother, clearly angry, looked at me and said, "The old man made me drop my smoke!" But I laughed at how much he cared about a dumb cigarette. That is, until I began to see flashes of green and blue. My brother's face went from anger to fear. "The P.C.F. are coming," he said, his voice trembling.

I slammed my fist against the windowsill. "Haven't those rebels trauma- tized enough people already? Why can't they see that a society with complete order is just as bad as this?" I looked at my brother, and his eyes were waterfalls. And it was only a few seconds before he let out an ear-piercing scream.

When a person gets sent to prison, it's not uncommon for friends and family members to try to break them out. But more often than not, the prison just gets new prisoners.

When my brother was twelve and I was ten, he got arrested for "underage drinking." I remember watching him struggle as they put him in the P.C.F. patrol car, hands forced behind his back. That was one of the only times I have ever seen him look scared, terrified even. He knew what was in store for him.

Our family had decided that it was too risky to try to rescue him. He spent three years in that prison. And last year my parents took me when we went to pick him up after he was released. Most of the windows were broken, so I decided to bring some cigarettes to surprise him. He looked so beaten that I almost cried at the sight of him. The all too visible ribs and bruises told one story. The black circles around his eyes told another. I swear I saw him tear up when I offered him the cigarette and lighter (in secret, of course!). It took him months to recover from his experiences.

"We've got to get the P.C.F out of here!" I grabbed the painting as the green and blue flashes filled the room, the blaring sirens accompanying it. And with one arm I held the painting, while with the other I took my gun out of its hol- ster. The rest of my family was quick to do the same.

We were quick to shove the paintings into the trunk of the car before closing the door. The siren was getting louder, closer. I opened the left car door and slid in next to my brother, who was already in a fighting position. He was on his knees, facing the complete opposite way, his gun drawn. I got into the same position. My gun felt cold in my hand, and then we saw them, and we began to fire, but so did they.

My father drove as fast as he could without wasting too much gas, which is quite tricky when you are running from people that are shooting at you. "Hey, at least we have our own firepower!" My brother rolled his eyes before taking another shot at the P.C.F. I copied him, managing to get the person in the passenger seat in the arm. Even though I couldn't hear her, I could tell she was in a lot of pain. Her other hand was covering the wound, her mouth agape. "And that's just a fraction of what you do to your prisoners," I thought. I looked over at my brother. His eyes were wide with panic. And I immediately knew what that meant. He was out of ammo. And I myself only had one bullet left.

Time seemed to freeze as I took aim for one final shot. This one bullet would decide whether we get to go home tonight, to not have to endure years of torture. So with those thoughts in my head and anger boiling in my blood, I took the shot. And the driver slumped as his head went missing. Smiling, I said, "I call the Xbox when we get home!"

I knelt on my bed, looking up at the beautiful painting above it, *Convergence*. "It is truly a masterpiece, isn't it?" I said to no one. Getting down from my bed, my nose was assaulted by the smell of hot dogs. My nose led me out to the porch, where my father was making the delicious wieners on the grill. And there he was, my brother, Ashton, waiting for someone to share a smoke with.

Brady Rachael's Confession

Annah Vogelpohl

SILVER

Grade 8, Elkhorn Ridge Middle School, Omaha, NE.

I don't remember the time I sneaked out of that house of mine. It all happened so quickly. It might've been four in the morning or maybe even 10 PM. I can't remember. It upsets me every time I try to remember that part.

I had a huge zit on my forehead. Right above my left eyebrow. I spent half my time getting ready that morning trying to cover it up. It wasn't like the rest of the pimples on my face. It was more noticeable. More painful. None of it worked, so I went to school with it. It drove me absolutely nuts the whole day.

But by the time 6th period came, it wasn't my main priority anymore.

Mackenzie.

She was beautiful. Everyone knew it, even her. I don't mean to sound shallow, but I'll admit it's what drew me to her. We met almost two years ago from that day. And we spent most of that time dating each other. God, she was the perfect girlfriend—but I was just—I don't know. I wasn't enough. At least that's what I had told myself. I broke up with her this summer. The whole school knew, maybe even people who didn't know us. But no one except me knew exactly why.

Maybe if I had actually done it right—you know, told her where it went wrong—maybe she wouldn't have left me a letter in my locker. The handwriting was gorgeous, just like she was. The note was written in a frilly cursive type font. She had the best handwriting in the grade. Mackenzie was perfect like that. It said something along the lines of: "Let's make up, Brady. I like you. And I know you might feel differently now—especially after summer, but I just have to let you know. Can we please give this a second shot?"

I don't know. I don't know what came over me. Something just clicked in me. Mackenzie was the perfect girl, and I was nothing but the bottom of the barrel. I couldn't just let her hurt herself like this. I couldn't just let her get her heart broken again by a monster like me. She needed to be free from a grasp like mine. She needed to be able to soar like she always was meant to. There was no use in her staying in the nest because my wings were broken.

It wasn't like it was my first thought. I swear it wasn't. I think I might've cried then. I sort of remember my friend comforting me. I don't think he knew how much that letter meant to me, or maybe he did and was thinking about it on the opposite side of the line. Maybe he thought that I was going to be back with her, but I know I sure wasn't. I think my first thought was pure emptiness. I remember reading somewhere years ago that the brain can't comprehend absolute nothingness. Like you can't just think of nothing. It's physically impossible. But I firmly believe I broke the laws of reality that day. I don't think there was anything back there, not even a black screen to catch my fall. I think I was crying because of the real life. Ugh, I don't know. Why even bother trying to explain this?

I couldn't sleep that night. I woke up my mom and asked her for sleeping medicine. She told me no. I didn't see the clock, not even the one that's an hour ahead on the microwave. I continued to lie down in my bed, staring at the ceiling.

I don't remember the time I sneaked out of that house of mine. It all happened so quickly. It might've been four in the morning or maybe even 10 PM. I can't remember. It upsets me every time I try to remember that part. Did I already say that part? Right, sorry.

This was my second thought. And sure, I had it hours later and it wasn't even relevant anymore, but it was the action that counted. I exited out of the garage. I remember grabbing the gasoline, my dad's lighter for his cigarettes, and some matches for when he didn't have his lighter on him.

The sprinklers were on in front of my house. I don't know exactly why but I stood in front of them for a while. Feeling the water soak on me and my backpack, I put my items in it before I left the garage. It was weird. I felt surreal almost. I think that was the exact moment I realized what I really was. I realized, and I accepted it. I felt calm. The water was cold. I was almost drenched. I think that was the last time I was cold for a while.

Mackenzie always told me that she was ashamed of her home. It was old. She lived in the city but like in the countryside of the city, you know? I don't think that makes sense. But it did make my job a lot easier. I had been to her house thousands of times. I hoped it was one of those days when her family was out of town. Mackenzie usually was home alone. I remember the family dinners she'd invited me to. Her family was so kind.

I poured gasoline around the outside of the house. The lighter shook in my hands. I was too far gone. I turned it on.

I must've poured some of the gasoline onto me on accident as well.

The whole house suddenly erupted.

I didn't have time to feel the side of my leg burning.

I only had time to think.

Shaking rapidly, I think I grabbed another match. And I think I threw it.

God, the smell.

The smell was horrible. There was smoke, but it didn't really matter. You couldn't see it in the dark. I started to bawl, I believe. I ran into the house. The locks melted on the door. I heard a high-pitched scream from above me.

The smell. The smell was horrible. I ran upstairs, the fire surrounding me. I didn't care. I saw her. She was there. She tried to get away it seemed. Her whole room was bright. It was hot. I felt burning. I looked down. Somewhere along the line I must've rolled in the dirt outside. My leg was no longer on fire. But the girl was. She was on fire. She was burnt. She was dead. That part was clear enough. I dropped a match on her corpse. It was so vivid. This was the burning passion she wanted, right? I think I jumped out of the window. I think I might've gotten hurt, but I didn't feel it.

I threw the rest of my items into the bonfire.

Oh, the *smell*.

RAVEN DOES NOT EXCEPT

ASHLEIGH WALLS

*Grade 12, Fort Calhoun Junior/Senior High School, Fort
Calhoun, NE. Sara Gross, Educator.*

The wind blows rapidly as Raven rides her bike down the hill to school. Running late is a normal schedule. The day is starting without her, but she is not letting this stop her. Nothing can stop her; day after day, problem after problem. No one knows or understands that nothing is a shock to Raven anymore. When someone is from a family with a mom and daughter being the only females, it is fascinating, to say the least. Adam, Cass, Eugene, Theo, Flynn, Dean, and Scott—seven brothers—and a dad. That is eight guys against two girls. With seven boys who are involved in many different sports, there is sweaty gear everywhere, so Raven does not have to imagine the smell coming from her house. She is surrounded by it.

Raven is a keep-to-herself kind of girl. She does not talk unless she has to. Since her brothers are in every sport imaginable, it is hard to not get attention; mostly, the wrong attention. Raven loves all the artistic activities: drama, art, Quiz Bowl, etc. The only so-called sport she plays is volleyball. She only plays volleyball to be with her friend Ariana. Ariana is a very beautiful and athletic girl. Everyone loves her but for some reason, she chooses Raven to be her best friend. She could not have chosen better. They have been inseparable since they met. Even so, she is never allowed at Raven's house. Everyone knows how that would turn out, *not good.*

Raven is a very oblivious girl. At home, she has learned to ignore. There are too many "weird" happenings going on to care. There is always someone who is not related to her; it is the new normal. The most common people to come over are her brothers' friends who play every sport; they are here all year round. Three people are constantly coming over from their friend group: Abe, Keith, and Deuse. Since they are with her brothers and Raven is the only girl, they always have to find a way to prank her before they leave.

When Raven gets home, she jumps in the shower like she always does. While washing her hair, she realizes that she forgot to check the soap. When she looks down at her hands, they are blue. The old classic dye in shampoo trick. She hurries to wash it out as fast as she can, but it is not coming out. When she realizes this, she grabs a towel, puts it around herself, and runs out to try and get help from her mom. As she runs out, she is met by her brothers and their friends. All are laughing. This is way too predictable for them. Raven runs past them with disappointment on her face.

Raven finally finds her mom in her room but not before she starts crying. Raven's mom tries to comfort her, but there is nothing she can do. Raven is so upset with herself that she let this happen. She never forgets to double-check anything before she uses it. Raven is off her game, and she doesn't know why. Everything is the same. There is nothing in her life that is different that she can think of. School is going well; clubs and drama are amazing. The only thing is her brothers are being more rambunctious lately and there is a new face in the house. One of her brothers got a new friend; he is over at the house every day. But this is not unusual for them; there are multiple of her brothers' friends that come over every day, making her feel out of control.

Raven knows a few of the boys that run around her house by name—Abe, Keith, and Deuse—because all of them have been friends since they were little. None of them are there today though she notices someone new as she is running out of the bathroom. Did he think of this prank? She tells her mom everything that happened after she calms down, but there is nothing her mom can do. She does not know this boy either, and she is not hurt physically by the dye.

Raven walks to her room to get ready for bed. She is done with today. As she is walking to her room she bumps into someone. Raven is looking down while walking; she does not see who is there until she looks up. When she does, she meets her brother's new friend. Having dark brown hair, bright blue eyes, and standing well over six feet tall, Raven does not recognize him. He retorts with, "Watch where you are going," in an irritated tone.

"News flash, last time I checked, you don't live here so watch where you're going, too, stupid!" Raven says out of aggravation for the situation.

He walks away with a "tsk." Raven rolls her eyes and continues to walk to her room. When she gets there, she throws on random shorts and a shirt and jumps on the bed with a plop. All she wants to do is go to bed, but there is one dilemma: she is not tired. Raven is wide awake. There is no way she can have her eyes shut; her thoughts are racing with what she can do to make this new development stop. Raven does not like how uncomfortable he made her.

It is a new day and Raven is running late to school again. When she finally makes it to school; she walks into her first class and sits down in her seat. When she looks to her side she is immediately met with dread. It is him. "What is he doing in this class? It is halfway through the year. Have I just not known he was there?" Raven thinks to herself. She is very confused about how she could not know he is in the same class as her. Raven decides to ignore it and focus on the class. The bell rings and she walks to her next class. Raven feels him walking right behind her, but she thinks, "He couldn't possibly be going to the same class again. It is just a coincidence that's all." Soon Raven finds out it is not a coincidence.

The day goes on and he is in every single one of her classes, not a class going uninterrupted with the sight of him. "Is he a new kid?" she thinks to herself. She would have to ask one of her brothers when she gets home. Unfortunately Raven has drama after school. As she walks into drama holding high hopes, this is her escape. With this, she is ready to put all of her energy into her role. Turning a corner she is met with a very familiar chest. "No, no, no, it can't be. How is he here?" Raven thinks.

Ms. Russel, the drama director, walks up and says, "Good you have already met. Remember when we did not have the lead male role filled to counter your role? Well here he is. Ray Gardener is a new student and is in the same grade as you, in fact."

Raven is in shock. How could he have gotten this role so fast? What did he do to Ms. Russel to make her make this decision? It could not have been from her mind alone. Raven calms herself and puts on a fake smile. "Well then I guess the only thing left is to see his performance," Raven says as an excuse to see how badly his attempt at acting goes.

Ray walks up to the stage going off to the side so he could make an entrance. Someone else stands in for Raven's role letting her see how he acts before beginning to work together. He starts with a booming voice calling out. He says every word with thought and emotion, taking everyone in the room by surprise. No one can stop looking at him. After he is done, Raven is blown away and knows why Ms. Russel has chosen him as the lead male. All she can think is, "No, no, no, no, no. How could I let myself do this? There is no way. I can't. Yeah, I'm just being dramatic because that was such a good performance." She shakes it off and looks at Ms. Russel. Ms. Russel ushers her to go up so that she can see the two of them together doing the scene to make sure that this will work.

When Raven walks up her heart is beating out of control. She is very nervous to try and act with him. Raven swallows roughly and then is ready to start the scene. His performance is just the same and everyone is in awe. Raven realizes that the flow of the scene is going so well that everyone just stares. No expression, just amazement. When the scene is over, Raven thinks to herself, "Not again. I can't like my brother's friend."

THE STRANGE PROMISE
OF THE TUESDAY RAINCLOUDS

DANIEL YOO

Grade 10, Southwest High School, Lincoln, NE.

"Hey, how are you? Long time no see! Good! What am I doing right now? Um, so right now, I am reading my old journal, and literally, it is so cringing. Here, I will read it to you: 'I have been many things in my life ... My life is a parabola, full of ups and downs. I am a graph of polarization, rapidly crisscrossing the axis, freely navigating the spectrum of polar opposites. I have been a leader, I have been a criminal, I have been respected, I have been shamed, I have been myself, and I have been far distant. I consist of many identities—and no values ...' Isn't that so ridiculous? I read it again that one Tuesday when I decided to go back to South Korea, and my initial reaction was, what the heck was I saying? I just slammed the notebook closed because I was so embarrassed. But at the same time, I realized that I was still feeling the same way, and at that moment, I knew I had to do something. So then, I was like, well, too bad. Now is the time to end it all. Whatever it took, *it took*. And that is how I found myself up on that hill on that Tuesday. But here is the thing. I am not saying this to be defensive, but I just did not know that the cost would be so great. I knew that I had to do something. I just did not know that all of this would leave me with this much guilt. Because, people say hard work never fails to reward, and effort is the only thing you need to succeed, but that is literally not true. When I was growing up, I used to believe it wholeheartedly, but as I became older, all I had was doubt. I have never met anyone more hardworking than my parents, but at the same time I have also never met anyone more unfortunate. Every day, they tried their very best to make it in this society, but nothing was working out for them. There was always something in the way to trip them up. People say great desire is a strong motivator for action, and that is so true. I feel it every day. All I wanted was that someday their efforts would pay off. I just felt so bad for them, toiling away and being looked down on by others at such an old age. I wanted them to enjoy retirement in a home that they can proudly call their own. My parents have believed mistakenly that I was ashamed of our family's poverty because as a teenager, I was obsessed with money. What they did not know is that I was far from being ashamed, and they still don't know that. My obsession came only from my desire to provide them with a better life ... All I wanted to do was give my parents a brand new apartment in their hometown, Seoul, in South Korea. That is literally all I wanted, and look where it got me today. Who am I? Literally, I tell you, I tried to answer this question so many times during my turbulent childhood. The only answer I ever came up with was, I don't know. How am I supposed to know? To me, I am just me. All I know is, I was pained by wanting too many things in life, and I still am. But what you have to understand is, as you know, I am not wanting super grand things. I just want a piece of property—even a tiny, crumbling building—alongside the Han River in Seoul that my parents can retire to. And most importantly, you know, I just want to be able to smile during the day and go to sleep at night without any worries in my mind. When I was growing up, I often felt like my life was slowly but steadily going downhill. There were many times in my childhood when I lay in the darkness of my room and thought the cold nights would never go away and the good times would never come. So what I resulted to was, instead of waiting for the sunshine to come to me, I forced myself in its way. Before I went away, I felt like I was sitting at the top of a very fragile tower on the lonely island that I call home, always looking over the horizons with my fraudulent and criminal past behind me. To me, it was a sanctuary full of secrets that only I can understand ... but I knew that I could not sit there forever. A building without a strong foundation is always bound to collapse upon a gush of powerful wind ... and that was the case with my fraudulent life. I mean, it could collapse under my feet anytime. It was scary. So that evening, after I read the old journal, I climbed up that small hill behind my apartment and lay down at the summit because I had a ton on my mind. I knew that it was about to rain because I could see the dark clouds were moving in and in further. But I did not care. I literally stared at them with bored eyes and dared them to downpour on my expressionless face, but I suddenly frowned because I saw the clouds forming a mouth and moving its lips. I thought I was going crazy, and maybe I really was. The rainclouds were whispering to me, 'Go back home to South Korea. You will meet me there, and you will find yourself. You will figure yourself out, and you will get far.' It was insane, I mean, a cloud telling me, *go back home to South Korea and you will meet me there? And you will find yourself?* It was only Tuesday, but that week was getting the best of me. I mean, just think about it. A cloud teaching me how to discover my personal identity? The psychological toll and the stress of that week was so great that I was seeing things that I should not see. It was too much to handle. But at the same time, the message *spoke* to me. I knew that there was nothing as bad as staying. I mean, look at me. My lonely life, my fraudulent past, my continuing dissatisfaction with the way that things are now, my *desire* to have more in life ... I hated my life, and I knew it better than anyone. So before I knew it, I resigned from my job, packed up my suitcase, and went back to South Korea. Bright and early one crisp November morning, I headed to a job interview in an elegant office building downtown. At the crowded subway station, I gaped at my reflection on the screen door. Staring back was a 27-year-old me, wearing a respectable business suit and holding an expensive briefcase on a professional journey. As I was standing there I was thinking, *huh, I look like I belong. I have made it this far*. As the subway train rolled into the station, I don't know why, but my face just went up in a large smile. And I was like, 'I can do this! I have made it this far. There is not a reason that I should not be able to go on even further ... *I will get even further ahead in life*.' So ambitiously, as usual, I straightened up my necktie, took a deep breath, and walked onto the subway train. But just then, a middle-aged woman interrupted me and crashed into me from behind, and without apologizing, she hit me furiously with her elbow to signal me to move along. I was so annoyed, so I was like, 'Geez! I was going to move along, thank you very much.' I was just so irritated that everyone in my life just seems to want to hurt me, and here in this new land, there was one more. As the image of all the people that distressed me rolled around in a panorama, under my breath I muttered, 'How come there are only people like her in my life? Aoo ... Everyone that I run into is interested only in hurting me.' I did not really want her to hear, but at the same time, I was hoping that she would realize that from the outside, you cannot really tell what a person is going through, so it is important to show kindness at all times. But I guess she did hear me, because right away she was like, 'Wow, you think you are the only one? Same goes for me too! What choice do we have, just deal with it!' At that point, I was just so out of it. I was *done*. So I said, 'Yes, *Ajumma* (middle-aged woman), I don't care. Now be quiet and mind your own business.' She was really mad and she yelled at me and said, '*AJUMMA*???? How dare you call me an *ajumma*. How old are you? You don't look much younger to *me*.'

"But as you know, six months later, this woman became my wife. She was right—I was really not much younger. After that day, we continued seeing each other every morning at the subway station. Things went straight from encounter to dialogue—we talked and shared things about our lives and our families. At the beginning, it was only the morning talks on the subway train, but later on that became pleasant afternoons at the cafe and then romantic dinners in downtown restaurants. We developed a bond, *a connection*, to each other. We did not initially meet on good terms, but we understood that without each other, our lives were not the same. We knew that we couldn't live without one another. Neither of us had much money, but it was alright. About fifteen minutes' walk from the subway station, there was a small basement apartment beneath an ancient five-story building. It had only one bedroom, and it was showing its age, but this was the only place within our budget that could be a place of our own. No matter how old it was, and how damaged it looked, it was our first apartment together, the very first step on our ambitious Seoul property ladder. Every day, we didn't stop smiling as we entered our modest apartment. We hoped that all would turn out well and we could work our way step by step to a riverview apartment. But it is so weird how fate plays out. About two months after we moved in together, we turned on the news as we were having dinner together ... it was the usual stuff about politics, stock market, et cetera, so we weren't really paying attention. But then, suddenly, the anchor announced that several neighborhoods were chosen by a city government taskforce to undergo high-density urban renewal ... and one of them was ours. When the anchor called the name of our neighborhood, we literally dropped our forks in complete shock. When we first bought our apartment, the real estate agents said that the reason that this neighborhood was so cheap was because there were conflicting interests at play that prevented redevelopment. But I guess they were wrong. I had built a pretty good reputation in the neighborhood by serving as the president of the residents' council, so they elected me to lead the redevelopment cooperative. That was the first time that people truly entrusted me to do the right thing. It meant a lot to me. The fate of their financial lives were at stake ... I mean, if everything went right, there were hefty compensations available for homeowners and the chance of owning a brand-new condominium in Seoul. But at the same time, all of us knew that urban renewal initiatives throughout the city often fall apart. And they wanted me—a 27-year-old lawyer from the United States—to guide them through this perilous journey. You see, now you know why I wanted to do my best. I wanted to *succeed*, not for me, but for everyone else in the neighborhood who placed their trust, *their economic futures*, in me.

"But leadership is not easy, especially when there is a ton of money—and we are talking millions—involved. There was only one argument, one door slam, one flick of the lighter, one fire ... It took only that long for my apartment—the symbol of our family's hard work—to go up in flames with my wife and infant child inside. I screamed as I covered my mouth and coughed. Ambulance sirens wailed in the distance, and residents gathered outside of their homes to watch the commotion. I was taken to the hospital with severe burns all over my body—as I was being transported, I could feel myself slipping out of reality into the empty abyss of nothingness. But even in the deepest of deep comas, my mind wandered all over the darkness, searching for my family, wanting to make sure they were okay. It was only after I woke up three months later that I found out the entire neighborhood had burned down that night, and that my wife and infant child had passed. I had missed their funeral and their cremation. Their ashes were now laid in a beautiful ceramic jar in a memorial park next to my late grandfather.

"Okay, here is the thing: I don't think I can go on further. I don't remember anything else, and this is just too much for me to talk about. I am so sorry. I don't think I am ready yet. Thanks, though. Thank you for understanding. Yep, bye. See ya." I hung up.

I walked right outside. I saw the quiet summer evening sunlight spreading itself throughout our neighborhood. Once again, I climbed up the hill behind the house and lay down at the top as I had done many times throughout my stressful adolescence—and as I had done that particular Tuesday afternoon over two years ago that prompted me to move back to South Korea, the ultimate decision that changed my life forever. They say you can never really understand people's actions until you actually become the person who has to make that decision ... and I guess that is ... true. Because only I would ever get to understand the choices that have led me to where I am today.

I seem to have woken up from a feverish nightmare, but the burns and scars and wounds throughout my body were concrete evidence that what I had gone through in the past two years was real. I mean, this is what I wanted. I wanted to find my identity, and I guess, at a great and painful cost, I ... found it. But I lost so many people and so many things along the way that I was not even sure if finding my identity was worth it. I would spend the rest of my life in pain, always struggling, trying to wiggle myself out to freedom from this nightmarish trauma that was imposed on me. The image of my wife and infant child, and my burning neighborhood, would forever haunt me, and I would spend the rest of my life in guilt and regret, wondering if my selfish and greedy behavior had got me this low, had got me down this path.

Here I am once again, on the hill behind my house that changed my life forever, squirming and cringing with the weight of guilt penetrating deep inside my body, not knowing what destiny held in store for me. Images of my late family flashed before my eyes once more, and I saw the fire engulfing our little basement apartment that was supposed to be our gateway to the Seoul Dream, the rope to the property ladder.

I glanced up at the sun setting behind the hill. I could see the entire suburbia stretching out before my eyes—neighborhood people getting home from work, getting ready for dinner with their families, residents laughing with their neighbors in friendly evening conversations. I heard children playing outside on the street, and far beyond the charming houses, I could even see the green trees and the shimmering lake on the other side of the neighborhood. The sun was setting on my life once again ... The sunset symbolizes the end of a day, the transition from a hardworking afternoon to a happy evening. The neighborhood is getting ready to wrap up its day and get itself ready for another tomorrow, but here I am, unable to move on, stuck in the darkness of the past. I knew I had to rise. I knew I had to get up. I knew I had to be strong. In a few hours, everyone else will be flying away to a distant land of tomorrow, but if I don't act, I will still be here, glued in the repression of today.

What kind of life do I want to build? I asked myself.

And at that exact moment, I knew what I had to do. God had given me the land and the soil here on the summit of the hill, and now it is my job to plant the flowers, trees, and bushes. My purpose here on Earth—it is to create a verdant garden where people can lie down and watch the rainclouds speak to them the messages that they need to hear. So here I am, planting a magnificent garden where dreams come true and people can find their purpose. It is 7 o'clock and the sun is radiating at its brightest, and so is my life—in the memory of my wife and my child, I am shining like the lone star in the clear winter night sky, and at that moment, I experience a feeling that I had so much desired to have during my childhood:

Happiness.

It was all because of the Strange Promise of the Tuesday Rainclouds.

NOVEL WRITING

Monster

ALIYAH ANDERSON

Grade 10, Blair High School, Blair, NE.

In this contemporary fiction, four characters struggle to find their identity in a world where it's predetermined.

Sawyer Halston has spent his life observing the manipulative figures of high society, shaped by his enigmatic father. On his father's deathbed, Sawyer must confront the man who molded him and the destructive legacy he inherits.

#005 is a famed EF soldier trained under respected veteran Chris McCoskey. After refusing to kill a rebel, he loses his reputation, ruins his mentor's career, and jeopardizes his brother's future. Determined to redeem himself, he embarks on a mission to locate the rebels and prove his worth as a soldier.

Raelynn, known as #013, has been taught that EF soldiers like her are weapons without identity. When she betrays her friend's illegal talk of freedom for EFs, she is sent to the slaughterhouse. Grieving her loss, Raelynn takes up her friend's cause, seeking the truth about the Vesuvius Military Base and the EF's history.

#082 graduates as an EF soldier in the air force and is soon mentored by Mr. Halston. After a rebel attack on the harbor, Halston reveals a mysterious third party as a new threat and hires #082 to eliminate them. As he tracks this group, #082 begins to question his role as a soldier, trying to form an alliance with the third party while secretly working to bring down Halston's operation from within.

Each must confront the cost of seeking truth and redemption in a world that tries to control their fate.

◇◇◇◇◇◇◇◇◇◇◇◇◇◇◇◇◇◇◇◇◇◇◇◇

My mother used to tell me stories about monsters. They lingered in the night for unsuspecting victims. They bared their teeth in a sneer and plucked the rugs out from underneath one's life. I am no monster. Among the underbelly of the city streets and the crowds of mingling socialites I could identify monsters. My mother would flip through picture books, refusing to read the story that was written and instead interpreting the pictures in an array of colorful narratives. I could never tear my eyes away, no matter how many times I saw the same pictures. The parties where my father brought me were the best place to observe such beasts. The main hall was often decorated in ivory walls and wine-colored banners. My father dragged me along to these events after my mother passed. Without fail, I would wander from my father's side, his pant-legs disappearing in the sea of identical pairs. No one commented about the little 11-year-old walking about. Their eyes were too busy peering down the busts of women and glaring at the competition. The room always smelled of cigar smoke and sex. The men would mingle and shake hands, making dirty jokes I never understood while flaunting their possessions. I hated them. But, I had to admit, they knew more about the world than I did. And amid all the corruption, I was the first child to find it interesting. After wandering from my father's side I eavesdropped on groups who discussed the world. But I lost interest when the talk turned to sex or personal relations. The scandal was the main appeal of the events—yet I found myself more enraptured by the less conventional topics. My favorite tidbits of information had to be about the EFF, a federation on the brink of collapse, or massive growth. Talk of the EFF was heated, and anyone who spoke of it could only mention it briefly. After listening I would return to my father and ask him questions about the conversations. He told me I shouldn't seek answers from other people. Even him. However, one night when I was fifteen or so, my father and I arrived back at the apartment. Late that night, the event's chatter still echoed in my ears as I stepped into the living room. The view over New York City offered no comfort. In the moonlight, I saw my father—a handsome man with silver hair, intense eyes, and a disciplined build. I inherited his brooding eyes, slight frown, rich voice, and once-dark hair. But I was always told I had my mother's smile. He stripped from his coat and folded it on the dining room chair. "Sawyer," he said.

"Yes, sir?"

"What have you learned going to these events?" he asked, with a certain expectation behind his grim expression. I didn't hesitate. "That I don't like them. Sir." He cracked a smile at my ignorance. "I meant the world, child."

My father is a hound in sniffing out lies and deceit. Although he may not enjoy my answer, I found it in my best interest to be honest. "The people are greedy and morally corrupt, but they see the world in ways I can't ignore. The worst seem to know the most." My father gave a small grunt. "Hm."

"Let me tell you this—" he said. "The most corrupt individuals tend to be the best at observation. As an observer myself, I know that we can be the most dangerous kind of people. If we allow ourselves to be." My brows furrowed in thought. "You want me to be a ... dangerous, sort of person?" He snarled, "You are weak if you are not. Weak and stupid."

"I'm not either of those things."

"But you are not dangerous."

The words slipped out before I could stop them. "Living among monsters doesn't mean I should bend to their rules." His amusement drained from his face, replaced by something colder, something sharper. "You use your mother's vocabulary," he noticed, his face hardening. "You've learned nothing."

That was the longest conversation I'd ever had with the man, and his words gnawed at me long after they were spoken. At the time, it made no sense. But by the time I turned seventeen, the weight of his words finally began to settle over me. By then, I recognized being a part of an attractive family provided some comfort—standing here in the center of this pig sty. Tonight's social event was at the Vesuvius Military Base, deep in the mountains. After the EFF's rise, it opened its final training base, inviting investors for the ceremony. Waiters moved through the crowd, serving warm dishes as the wealthy chatted. I stood on the fringes of conversations, nodding along while my thoughts wandered. Around me, kids my age were playing the game—striking deals, spreading gossip, chasing fleeting romances. Every move built a reputation. I stood apart, wondering if it was enough to be nothing at all. Younger kids were already climbing the ladder of influence, and I realized that by staying still, I risked fading into nothing. And Halstons are anything but nothing. The adults around us didn't take these efforts seriously. They watched these fledgling socialites with amused detachment, like owners watching their puppy chase a ball.

I sipped my wine as Mrs. Raynott's booming laugh echoed across the ballroom, turning a few heads. She was hard to miss—plump and ostentatious, with a voice that could rival an opera singer's. Her wealth, amassed through shares in space and engineering, had given her the air of someone accustomed to commanding attention. "Oh, but look there!" she exclaimed, her bejeweled hand pointing wildly toward a girl in a striking, ill-suited dress. "Good heavens, that's the Valencia girl—only sixteen! What *is* she thinking, flaunting herself like that? And *why* toward Mr. Capet of all people? That poor, miserable old man."

I murmured into my glass, dryly, "It's because he's her retirement plan."

The comment wasn't meant for her ears, but Mrs. Raynott turned to gawk at me with large saucer-eyes. Then came her laughter, loud and unchecked. "Oh, you're wicked!" she said, gripping my shoulder. "I recognize this face." She squinted. "Who are you?"

I gathered my bearings from this change in my party-routine. I gave her a reassuring smile so she wouldn't pounce on my weaknesses. "Sawyer Halston."

"Joshua's boy?" She seemed ecstatic. "I thought so! You've got his eyes." She practically shoved me into her circle of similarly boisterous companions, their presence a living thing that threatened to overtake the room. "But do tell," Mrs. Raynott continued, "what made you say such a thing?" As they turned their attention to me I decided to indulge them further. I leaned forward, keeping my voice low. "A year ago, I overheard Mr. Capet telling Mr. Valencia he'd be interested in ... an arrangement, once Sophia Valencia turned eighteen. Mr. Valencia cut ties over it, but from the looks of things"—I nodded toward the scene, where Sophia was now leaning a little too comfortably against the old man—"she seems to have made up her own mind."

The group erupted into delighted murmurs, their expressions alight with scandal. Mrs. Raynott rocked my shoulders excitedly. "You *are* Joshua's boy! You have the same type of humor!" I smiled faintly, letting their amusement wash over me. I realized quickly, maybe too quickly, that this was easier than I'd expected—fitting into their world, weaving the threads of gossip into something they could hold onto. My father's words crept unbidden into my mind. His warning about the need for danger. I wondered briefly if he was right. Perhaps I was already on my way.

The group dispersed, as they always do. Among these people, lingering too long with one crowd is an admission of weakness—an unspoken rule I was just beginning to grasp. Moving from one cluster to the next, I found myself no longer a passive observer. Adults spoke to me not out of politeness but with a certain calculation. I had become useful to them, and in their eyes, that made me worthy of their time. Their conversations, filled with gossip and veiled barbs, taught me more about this world than I'd ever learned by standing idly on its edges. I asked questions when I wanted answers, steering discussions back to my interests with a skill that felt natural. I threw jaded remarks and took in the culture, and these people had no problem talking about themselves. I learned it was normal to have a hand in a murder for personal gain. It was treated as lightly as talk of buying a new puppy. I also came to find out that anything forbidden was sought after. Such as a painting hung in a dining hall of a human slurping the guts of a lion. I talked with the artist, and they admitted getting their inspiration from real life, paying to have a lion's stomach slit open, with a woman coated in the warm crimson. He paid the woman a handsome amount, but he shook his head as he recalled the woman crying for the animal. "Her face took an ugly shape when she cried. And the lighting was all off because her shoulder's kept shaking." His friends shook their heads, agreeing that it was unfortunate the artist couldn't capture the moment perfectly. And although I gripped my wine glass tighter, I found myself shaking my head along with them.

By twenty, I've experienced much of this new life. Taking part in backstabbing and dirtying my hands in the aid of murders. Although I soiled myself in their filth, I had power. I was a Halston. Being a Halston meant government officials and crime lords alike came to me—not with commands but requests. Their sharp tongues and ruthless airs masked weaknesses so potent I pitied them. Secrets, pride, sordid histories—they carried their flaws like badges hidden beneath gilded costumes. I took amusement in uncovering their cracks, peeling back their masks with little effort. When they asked for my help—securing a deal, covering a scandal—I met them with a smile of firm refusal. What I valued wasn't their discomfort, but the balance it restored. Monsters like them rarely expect to meet judgment, but I have come to understand my role. Power, I had learned, wasn't granted by birthright or fortune. It belonged to those who understood its weight and wielded it with purpose. When I was younger, I recoiled at the filth these people wallowed in. Now, I've navigated it enough to understand it.

I stepped onto the cold tile of my father's room. The rhythmic beep of the heart monitor matched the shallow rise and fall of his chest. Tubes ran into his nostrils, and his skin sagged against his bones. I followed the trail of tubes to a multi-plug outlet. Such a pitiful sight. I had never been in my father's room. It was a forbidden place that my maids wouldn't even allow me to glance at. Now I peered openly at the decor. Most of his items had been packed in boxes and the paintings that decorated the barren walls were taken down and covered. But a lone painting remained just above the mantel of his fireplace. And I was brought to the realization that I had been there with my father the day he bid on that painting. A skinny wolf prowled toward the lamb in the blood-speck-led snow. I remember the painting striking a chord with me, just as it did with my father. I could hear the desperate crunch beneath the lamb's hooves as it wailed into the chilly air; and the wolves soft growls while it stalked its meal. There was something so ... human, about the eyes of the animals. Haunting and desperate.

My father stirred—turning his head to gaze at the painting. The coldness of his tone had never left, even as his voice wavered. "They tried to take it down ... I wouldn't let them." He must've been talking about the maids. "It's just another painting," I said matter-of-factly. "You've grown soft if you care about it that much."

He said nothing of my insult. My father let out a, "Hmm," and sunk back against his pillow. His eyes fluttered as he drifted in and out of consciousness. Such a serene expression on that stone-cold face. It worked out for me that he was so near death. I visited because I needed to discuss my inheritance ... But there was also a more *desperate* reason. I gripped my father's shoulder, shaking him awake. "Sir," I said. "Wake up. I didn't come here to watch you decay." My father twitched awake once more—his eyelids fighting to stay open. "Why are you here, then?" he whispered.

"I need you to die."

He shot me a sharp glance. "Oh? You have money, child." He took a shaky breath. "You have connections and power. I taught you how to stand on your own two feet. You don't need me for anything."

I chuckled in disbelief, my knuckles whitening as I gripped the handrails. "Ha! No, sir, I don't believe you grasp my situation. I crossed the wrong man. He's convinced the matter isn't resolved, and his resources far outweigh my own."

He questioned, "Who?" And when I refused to answer, he gave me a smile. "You're scared."

"Any man in his right mind would be."

"Not a Halston." He grinned wickedly.

I scowled. "The hell you smiling for?" My father laughed, a sound I've never heard from his lungs. It was a scary, deep laugh that echoed throughout his chamber. "I know the look of a doomed man," he cooed. "If you crossed who I think you did, I cannot help you."

I snarled, "I still don't understand what's so humorous."

"One man." My father lifted his trembling pointer finger. "One man was all it took to destroy the Halston name." His resonant laughter cracked, spiraling into a delirious wheeze so high-pitched and unnatural that it slithered down my spine like an ice-cold whisper. Something inside me snapped and I stepped away from the bed. "It's all your fault!" His voice tore through the room, thick with venom. "Everything I built—" His words fractured into violent coughs, followed by those gut-wrenching, nihilistic screams that clawed at the walls themselves. My temple pulsed with an ache that scraped at my mind, relentless, suffocating. "You've ruined us, boy!" His shriek punctured the air. My heart hammered faster, quicker than it should. I slowly sank to my knees, the cold tile biting my clammy skin. Metallic ringing wrapped itself around my skill, drawing out all rational thought. I wrapped my hand around a thicket of cords.

And then there was silence.

In the Vesuvius Military Bunker, there was held a trial for an economically important EF soldier. Its crime: Treason. The courtroom was alive with the murmur of jurors and shuffling feet on cold tiles. I lifted my gavel and smacked it upon the large U-shaped desk—its sound commanded everyone's attention. Dramatic lights beat down from above. Whispers darted around the room; the audience strained to hear every word. Before me, in the middle of the U-desk, stood an EF soldier in chains. EFs—a tool and a weapon, not a person. In this particular trial, I was supposed to address the EF's mentor, but I wanted to hear what it had to say. "EF soldier zero-zero-five, how do you plead?"

Its jaw tightened, eyes averting mine. "Not guilty," it mumbled. I scowled, recognizing the lie for what it was. "Liar. I know the look of a doomed man." The defendant jerked its head up. "How would you know anything?" I locked eyes with the soldier, a cold chill sweeping over me. In his face, I saw the pale remnants of Mr. Halston's slackened face. My voice dropped to a dangerous murmur. "Because I'm the one who dooms them."

THE ELEMENTS OF TRUST

CAMDYN PRUETT

Grade 11, Millard West High School, Omaha, NE. Honorable Mention.

Long ago, something struck the earth, causing life to flourish. Those who were closest to the impact grew to wield this source's power and were referred to as elemental masters. Throughout the ages, these powers were handed down from generation to generation. Now the elemental masters are split up, and most barely know of their ancestral identities. Five teenagers, each one having a different way of seeing the world, are sucked into a war they didn't know existed, a war between light and dark. They are trained to wield the elements of a previous force known as the Council of Elements, consisting of fire, water, earth, nature, and the most powerful of elements, magic. Before long, the enemy, Elliot, the master of darkness, defeats them in a battle they thought they could win and the master of fire Cody is captured, and their main conduits for power are destroyed. Cyfrin, the master of magic, works with the other members of the council to get their powers back, and in turn they figure out they can use their abilities without the crystals. With their powers back, they plan to save Cody and stop Elliot for good by taking his elemental abilities. The plan works with Cyfrin getting a power up from his ancestor, and Elliot is stripped of his powers, and apparently his memory. The group thinks they have won, until their celebration is cut short by a prophecy spoken by the real ancestor of Elliot, speaking of a grand evil looming over them.

<><><><><><><><><><><><><><><><><><>

The portal closed behind Cyfrin as he crossed the threshold of the courtyard, leaving the group with only one way to go. Around them, dead grass poked out from behind gravestones, and a dead tree loomed over the gate leading up to the ominous structure of the castle. Vines twisted up the walls that surrounded the courtyard, filling in cracks in the stones from years of weather and low-upkeep.

The sun's light seemed to dull as they advanced through the yard. Grass crunched beneath every step. The group was about half way into the court when a branch fell to the ground, and startled Maya to the point that she made her weapon materialize in her hands, the light blue outline of an arrow already notched and aimed at the fallen stick.

"Maya!" Cyfrin loudly whispered, "this is supposed to be an in-and-out mission. What if—"

"What if I heard you?" Cyfrin held out his hand, letting a spark grow into a bo staff and held it in defense to the unwanted guest in front of them. "Aw, not happy to see me?"

"Elliot."

The boy leaned on the gate, his legs dangling over the edge of the stone wall. His black suit shone in the midday light, the lines of silver detailing covering most of his inner chest with a line of silver fire on his left arm. He let out a bitter laugh, his scythe still strapped to his back. "I see the old man finally showed you your 'true potential.'" He hopped off the wall, the grass beneath him darkened when he made contact. "Or whatever he calls it."

Ashma took a step towards Elliot but was stopped by Cyfrin. "Just give us Cody back and we'll leave." He seemed to think about it but pulled his scythe out and sent a wave of energy towards the group. Cyfrin's staff spun in his hand and blocked the attack, then sent the pole backwards to raise his other hand in protest. "What do you even want with him?"

"I don't think that's any of your business," Elliot said as he prepared a second attack. Cyfrin rolled his eyes but raised his staff in defense.

He nodded to the rest of the group, then to the castle. "Go get Cody. I can handle this." The rest nodded back in reply, and ran for the castle, but were stopped by a wall of silver flames.

"What the hell?" Ashma said.

Puddles of tar appeared around Ashma and the group's feet, and rose to form bodies of pitch-black armor. Their eyes glowed with an envious silver as the group summoned their weapons. The armor glinted from the shine of the magic. A wicked smile grew on Elliot's face. "You thought I would take you alone?"

A spark flew from Elliot's hand and soon became a large silver flame. The area around Cyfrin's hands on the staff sparked as his grip tightened. "I was hoping it wasn't just you." Cyfrin charged at Elliot, his staff behind him, but when he swung, Elliot dodged with ease.

He tried again, but his staff only met air, while Elliot just blinked in and out of sight. "Wow, can't even get one hit in, can you?" The world seemed to grow red with anger as Cyfrin kept throwing himself into each swing. Only one thing raced through his head, defeating Elliot. His voice was muffled, but Cyfrin could make out another taunt from Elliot.

"Let Cody go!" Cyfrin yelled, his voice carrying energy through the courtyard. His ears rang, his body ached, but his heart still kept fighting. A fire he had never felt before raged inside him, and filled his body with more energy than he could ever think possible. But the energy, as soon as it appeared, dissipated, the world returning to normal as he slowed down.

Elliot teleported in front of him, then laughed. "You won't even be able to save yourself." Elliot swung the back of his scythe into Cyfrin's side, which sent a shockwave throughout his body, and dropped him to the floor. "What makes you think you could protect Cody?"

Those words rippled through him as the world went dark around Cyfrin, but a calm washed over him at the same time. "Now come on, what are you doing on the floor?"

The soothing voice pacified his nerves, and Cyfrin started to notice how much his head hurt. He slowly stood and faced a lady dressed in a white suit, intricate gold designs woven throughout the jacket. The designs were reminiscent of the golden flames on Lyphon's robe, as well as the silver flames on Elliot's jacket. "Who are you?"

"I am the one you call Life." She walked around the space that consumed Cyfrin's mind. "The first light elemental."

"But, that's impossible, you're not—"

"A human?"

"Yea." Cyfrin knew it was a stupid thing to say, but it confused him. How did Lyphon get the element if it was Life that had it first?

"As the source fell to earth and spread its gifts to the people of earth ..." A vision of the source swirled together in the mist, the roots spreading to the twelve civilizations of old. "Death and I came into contact with some of this raw energy, which fused our essences to create a physical connection to your world."

Two leaves on the tree fell, one gold, the other silver, but instead of falling to the ground, the leaves started to glow, brighter and brighter until two people replaced the leaves, one in a black suit, the other in a white robe. "That's how the elements got passed down?"

"Yes, death and I found mortal companions, and had children. But overtime, we realized that our descendants did not only carry light or dark. They carried one more element."

A boy ran into the vision, carrying a staff with a purple jewel. A shiver ran up Cyfrin's spine. The staff resembled his old one. "I'm—"

"You are a descendant of light, with the element of magic." Life looked down, her face solemn, as the boy disappeared in the mist. A second boy, also carrying a purple jewel, chased after him. "While Elliot is a descendant of darkness, with the same element."

"But—but Lyphon said it was impossible for two people to have the same element at the same time." Cyfrin's head spun. The thought of he and Elliot sharing a power made him want to puke.

"And for a while, that was true." Life kneeled down to be eye to eye with Cyfrin, and put her hands on his shoulders. "You are my most powerful descendant. That is why I chose you to carry the element of magic."

Tears filled his eyes, not because he didn't want his magic, but because Life gave him a chance, when no one else did. "Thank you."

"Now ..." She stood, and waved her hand across the mist, the scene before them showing Elliot's forces marching on the temple. "You must win this fight, for the fate of the world is decided on how this turns out."

"No pressure."

She smiled at Cyfrin, then returned to the mist. "I have one last thing before you go." Life's hand glowed gold, then produced a golden leaf. "This is the leaf that brought me into the physical world. It holds the power of transcendence, and when used by an elemental master of magic, will give them the power of the Golden Flame."

"What the hell is the Golden Flame?" Cyfrin took the leaf in his hand, and a wave of energy washed over him. "Woah."

Life stepped backwards and closed her eyes. "Remember, light will always triumph over darkness." As she finished her sentence, the light around them moved inward and exploded in a supernova that sent Cyfrin back to reality.

Cyfrin opened his eyes, Elliot still stood over him like he hadn't even been gone. But, instead of Elliot gloating, he looked horrified. As Cyfrin stood, he realized that he was now wearing a white suit with the golden flames wrapping around him, his staff now covered in gold. "How did—"

A surge of power fueled Cyfrin, the golden leaf reached his soul, his very essence now tied to life, to the source. He stretched his arm outwards, the flame on his suit swirling around his arm until a spark of gold appeared in his hand, which grew into a raging golden flame. Cyfrin looked at the flame, and a vision played in his mind.

Five people stood together, the middle holding a glowing sphere. Words played like a slow-motion video. Cyfrin repeated the words as they were said in the vision, and held the golden flame to the sky. "The ancient prophecy of the twin flames, broken by corruption."

The group, who were still fighting their way to the castle, stopped in their tracks. They looked at one another, their bodies giving off a hue that matched their elements. "What the—"

"Only the power of the council can reverse." The flame above Cyfrin burst outwards, and pulled the elemental energy from the group into itself. "Five elements as one." A single thread of red shot out of the castle and joined the other four energies. "Ancient power of the source, to bring light to the dark."

A final wave of energy was sent throughout the yard, and passed over the castle. Any tar warriors left dissipated, leaving Elliot to fight alone. Cyfrin's eyes glowed with the energy of the source, his body radiating power. When he spoke, his voice tripled and echoed inside their heads. "Go get Cody."

"You can't defeat me just because you got a little upgrade!" Elliot's arm's strained as he lifted a wall of solid silver flames from the ground, completely encasing the castle. He dropped to the floor, his breathing heavy. "And you left your friends powerless."

Hundreds of tar warriors rose from the ashes of the fallen, each one carrying a cutlass sword. The group had just gotten to the wall when they were surrounded by the army, swords pointed directly at them. "Cy! What do we do?" Maya screamed through the cries of the enemy.

Cyfrin's mind started to race again, but this time with more clarity. His eyes moved from one scene to the next, the beads of sweat on Elliot's forehead, the wall of flames blocking Cody, and the tar warriors surrounding the group. He could do this, he just needed to concentrate. He took a deep breath in, closed his eyes, and blocked the world out. He focused on the leaf, as well as the words of Life. "Light triumphs over Darkness."

His hand slowly rose to the sky, his veins popping outward with a glow of gold. The air around Cyfrin began to spark and formed a line of golden flames that swirled around him. Elliot stood there, his eyes following the fire as if he were in a trance. He shook his head and spun his scythe to block the light. "Come and fight me instead of hiding behind Life's gift!"

Cyfrin's eyes shot to where Elliot stood and were followed by Cyfrin. His staff was like a blur, a shot from the side, a jab from the front, and finally he swept Elliot's feet from under him, and Elliot fell to the floor in a flurry of gold and silver. "I was never hiding." With the butt of his staff, Cyfrin knocked out Elliot.

Cyfrin's arm rose to the tar warriors, and in a flash of gold, the army was obliterated. With Elliot out cold, the wall around the castle fell and allowed the group to enter. But before they could, Cody ran out of the building, with a worried look on his face, with good reason. Cyfrin's eyes closed, and the gold aura that had built up around him during the fight faded. He started to fall, but Cody ran up and slid down on the ground and caught him in his arms.

"Hey, hey, I've got you," Cody said, his tone light and airy, but his face solemn and full of worry.

Cyfrin's breathing steadied, and his eyes slowly opened. A smile grew on his face, and he put his hand up against Cody's cheek. "I thought I lost you." Cody laughed a bit, and his smile had come back.

"I'll always find my way back to you." Cody pulled Cyfrin upwards and braced his lips against Cyfrin's. The world around them slowly melted away as they embraced each other.

The group had gathered around Elliot, who was still passed out in the grass. Most of them looked away, but Maya smiled while Ashma handed her a twenty dollar bill. By the time the two pulled apart, little specks of gold had lined Cyfrin's eyes, as well as little streaks of gold in his hair. "Looks like someone had a makeover."

Cody stood, holding both of Cyfrin's hands and hoisted him to his feet. "I guess these are aftereffects of the leaf." He stumbled a bit, and fell into Cody's chest, but quickly stood straight again. "It might take a bit for my head to stop spinning."

A groan escaped Elliot's mouth as he pushed himself to his feet. "You will not defeat me." Cyfrin's hand glowed gold and balled into a fist at his side. A slight glow appeared around Elliot. The gold mixed with silver as Elliot started to scream.

A sliver of black tar exited out of Elliot, and the aura of gold followed it. The tar shifted and stretched, like putty in a child's hands, but formed a circle when enclosed in the aura that shrunk around it. Elliot, now as pale as a ghost, crumbled to the ground. His eyes went wide as his power, his elemental powers, were turned into a circular medallion. An etching of a snake eating its own tail shone in the light of the fading golden aura.

"I just did," Cyfrin exclaimed as he took hold of the medallion.

Elliot struggled but managed to sit up. "What did you just do?"

"I stripped you of your powers." Cyfrin dangled the amulet in front of Elliot, who did not look amused.

Elliot started to walk towards the castle, when he doubled over and clutched his head. He let out a shriek of pain, his eyes rolling back into his head. "No, no, no!" He started rambling in a language that was new to the group until he sat up, his eyes completely pitch black, and all emotion drained from his face. His voice was the same as Cyfrin's when he was using the leaf, but this one seemed darker. "In one month's time, the forged ones shall rise. Evil's power will be unleashed with the Seven, and the help of the dark one. Life and Death are two sides of the coin. One must control both to defeat the Grand Sin."

With that, Elliot fell to the ground, and his eyes rolled back into place. Cody looked at him but focused in on his eyes. "Guys, why are his eyes purple?"

Elliot's eyes went wide at Cody, and when he tried to run, he tripped over his feet. "Who—who are you people? Where am I?" He looked around, terror mixed with confusion as he took in the surroundings.

The group had formed a sort of semi-circle around Elliot as they shared a look of confusion as well. "You seriously don't remember?"

"What exactly am I supposed to remember?"

Blue Skies in Aden, 2031

JOSLYN SMITH

Grade 12, Elkhorn North High School, Omaha, NE. Honorable Mention.

The year was 2031, and the Houthi rebel attacks had evolved into a full-blown war. For being on a battlefield, however, Corporal Cilian was having a pretty good day, until a radio transmission reunited him with an all-too-familiar voice. With the help of a friendly medic, he ventured into the war-torn city of Aden, desperately searching for a girl who should never have been here in the first place. They found her considerably worse for wear on the beach where an oncoming drone strike threatened to bring a fate worse than death. Haunted by the mistakes of his past, the Corporal took matters into his own hands, setting to ensure his companion's death was absolute, even if it meant killing them himself.

She was lying in the rocks, sopping wet and burnt to a crisp, her body trembling. Her pilot's uniform had melted away to reveal some of the skin underneath, especially on the underside of her arms and the top of her shins. She was taking shallow, fast breaths, and her neck was developing a ring of purple bruises where the Houthi rebel had been choking her before. To Cilian's greatest horror, however, a triangle of blackened flesh covered her left eye. If she even still had a left eye.

But dammit, she was alive.

"Private."

Both the medic and the pilot looked up.

"Not you, Snatch. Her."

"Hey, Captain."

"Hey, Private. What ... the fuck happened?"

"I Star Wars'ed that shit ... Blew a hole straight to the ammo hold and sent my Raptor in it ... Whole ship went up, took my parachute with it ... you know how it be."

"Holy hell."

"Yeah, but I got the bastards."

"Lift your head please, Lieutenant," the medic said as he removed her helmet to treat her wounds. She complied, though with some effort.

NOVEL WRITING   191

"You have a lot of nerve damage. The fire exposed your flesh to the elements, and the freezing cold water didn't exactly help. I'm guessing you were in shock until the Houthi came by to finish the job."

"Yeah. Asshole really couldn't just leave me be to die in peace. Had to make a whole spectacle of it. Kinda embarrassing."

I was the one who was supposed to die, Cilian thought. The idea faded as quickly as it arrived, but it remained lurking in the back of his mind. It had for a long time.

There was a light crackle as the Corporal's radio came to life. He left Snatch and Private so as to not disturb them with what was likely some depressing military mumbo-jumbo.

"Viper-3, this is Viper-1. Do you copy? Over."

"Viper-1, Viper-3, hear ya loud and clear, Sarge. Over."

"Objective status? Over."

"We've located the target. Lost transport, in need of medical evac. Over."

"Multiple enemy bogeys spotted 4 km south of Aden coast. Second wave of drones on standby. Target unclear, break ... wrong, second wave inbound, target unclear, advancing to your position. Over."

Cilian gazed towards the south, over the dazzling Yemeni waters. Blue was never his favorite color, as he greatly preferred orange, but for a moment, the infinite sapphire of sky and sea was the most gorgeous thing he'd ever seen. Something in the distance darkened that brilliant blue, however, and it was getting closer.

"Correction, Viper-1. They're already here. Over."

"Cream ... we can't send anyone. There's too many of them ... You're on your own. Over."

Sarge was trying not to let on how unlikely his comrade's survival was, but Cilian knew. He could see the drones in the distance. A hand went to his forehead as the realization hit him.

"*Fuck.*"

He paced around for a moment watching the metal demons in the sky grow closer. He looked to his comrades, who were chatting on the beach, completely ignorant of the coming danger. He couldn't hear a word, but the conversation seemed weirdly chill for a guy giving first aid to a girl with half a face. Cilian wished he had done something differently. Anything that would have them safe right now. But the past had passed, and now, they wouldn't know what hit them.

They won't know what hit them.

<hr />

It's happening again.

The world around him began to spin. It was happening again. Someone would sift through the rubble, like he had all that time ago, and find them all, worst case scenario, alive.

No. Not again. Never again.

"Sarge, permission to call a Broken Arrow? Over."

"Negative, Corporal. What are you trying to do? That will look terrible on my record. You … you have to try to survive, Cream. That's an order. Over."

"Sir, those drones are coming for the city or the base. My life means nothing compared to all those people. Let me order the strike, over."

"Cream … you aren't seeing the transmissions HQ's been sending. This strike … it's a big one. It's not worth organizing another attack. Just … don't worry about anyone else. Get to safety, west if you can. We'll be there assisting in the evacuation. Out."

Cilian could have crushed the radio with his bare hands. He could hear in Sarge's anxious informality that there was no safety. Maybe if he had stayed with the squadron, if he had gotten here sooner, if, if …

If I had done everything right, would he still be …

The Corporal looked towards the soldiers on the beach. As he approached, he could hear their relaxed banter, still completely unaware.

"—I call the other one Mex, but sometimes I wonder if he's really Mexican. He's totally the kind of secretive asshole to lie about that. I bet he's really Colombian or something. Point is, I be catchin' him in Tex's tent sometimes, hence the ship name, TexMex."

The pilot chuckled, as much as she could with a crushed esophagus. "Any others I should know about?"

"I mean, I have written some colorful self-insert fanfics about Cream over there, but unfortunately none have come to fruition. Speak of the devil, what's the news from our intrepid leaders?"

"We're forecasted for blue skies in Aden in the year of our lord 2031, temperatures reaching highs of a whopping 97 degrees with lows around 80."

Snatch stood from his crouched position, admiring his work with the bandages before gazing at the heavens above. "Yeah. Not a cloud in the sky. Gotta love that infinite azure. It's my favorite color, y'know. Must've been good flying weather."

"You'd think," the pilot chimed. "Hardly clear up there, though. Drones by the thousands."

Maybe Snatch wouldn't have noticed had she not said that, but Cilian saw the change in the medic's face as he stared southward towards the incoming fleet.

"Johnny, can I talk to you for a moment? Privately?"

Cilian hoped for the moment that his comrade would respond with the typical. *Actually, you can talk to me corporally*, joke, but it never came. In its place was a grim nod and eyes wide with terror. The men started up the rocky beach towards some of the city buildings where they could speak freely.

"Hey, you guys aren't leaving me here, right?" the pilot coughed. Cilian could only see her right eye, the other being covered by bandages, but in it was enough worry for two. He wondered for a moment if she, too, had seen the oncoming attack.

"Don't worry, I'll be right back. And we won't go far, so we should be able to keep an eye on you. If you see anything, holler."

She nodded in agreement, as well as she could, and the soldiers walked in the direction of that nautical restaurant they had passed earlier. As soon as they were out of earshot, Snatch started to pace around the street, shell shock growing more and more prominent in his eyes.

"Okay, that's ... whoo, that's a big one."

"And headed straight for us, I'm sure."

"This whole town is a burning crater already. Look at these buildings. They'll topple like playing cards. And ... and we don't have a car ..."

The medic's breathing quickened as he panicked for ideas.

"What should we do? Should we commandeer a civilian vehicle? Find cover? Jesus, Cream, that's the biggest strike I've ever *seen*—"

"Could she see it?"

"The, *what*?"

"The strike, on the horizon. Did she make any indication that she saw it coming?"

"Uh, no, I mean, her eyes are too messed up anyways. One's full of seawater and the other boiled away in her skull when the blast hit, it's straight-up *gone* ..."

"So you and I are the only ones who know it's coming?"

"I, yeah, so we gotta think of something ... Jesus, man, I'm not ready to die. I'm only nineteen ... who will make my M*A*S*H spinoff?"

"Okay, relax, we'll think of something. Look at me, no, at me ... you aren't dying in a drone strike. You got that, Private? I promise."

Snatch's eyes were still wide with fear, but they narrowed slightly, and he nodded to his superior.

"Why don't you look that direction for a car or shelter, and I'll look this way?" The Corporal pointed in two opposite directions parallel to the shoreline. Snatch turned and took a couple steps away, eyes darting around for a functional vehicle or safe area.

"Anything over there?"

"No ... none of these buildings look like they could survive the attack, but maybe this blue one—"

He was cut off as his mouth was covered with a burnt, gloved hand. The other hand stuck a knife deep into the youth's neck. Snatch struggled for a moment, clawing at the perpetrator's arm and making muffled calls for help to Cilian, the pilot, anyone as he begged to be let go. Eyes rolling back and hands relaxing, he tasted something metallic in his mouth, and Aden began to fade to black.

The pilot watched the tide roll in and crash onto the rocky beach. She couldn't see very well, and had no idea of the time, but it seemed as though night was coming in, as the sky was darkening quickly. Usually the sunset was supplemented with a bright pink or purple (her favorite color) against soft orange, but this incoming night was desaturated and dark. She tried to turn her head to the West, where the sunset might be more vibrant, but her neck hurt far too much to move. She elected, then, to watch the waves as she waited for her companions to return.

"I promised I'd come back."

The pilot jumped a bit at the sudden voice behind her. "You scared me, Captain."

"Sorry. How are you doing?"

"Fine. It's not so cold anymore. The Yemeni heat wave dried off the seawater relatively fast."

Cilian crouched down next to her on the rocks, eying the incoming drone strike as she watched the waters.

"Peaceful, isn't it?"

"Eh. 'Bout as peaceful as the calm before a storm."

"I thought that meant that it was *super* calm."

"Calm until the storm breaks," the Corporal said as he sat fully on the beach, a little further back than his companion.

"Who cares that there's a storm coming? We can't control it. Might as well enjoy the calm while it lasts."

"You sound real wise for a 24-year-old, Private."

"That's why they call me Stoic."

"Is it really?"

"No. They call me that 'cuz the T.I. found *Meditations* by Marcus Aurelius in my personal effects after I forgot to lock my crate and *literally* threw the book at me."

"T.I.?"

"Training Instructor. Skyrat-talk for Drill Sergeant."

"Oh."

The soldiers sat a little longer. It was like old times, when they were just Private and Captain; they could talk about anything without disturbing solitude, or say nothing at all with no lack of camaraderie. There was nothing uncomfortable about the silence, save for the pilot's nagging feeling that the good medic had been gone a bit too long.

"Where's your friend?"

"Just looking for a vehicle. Ours was KIA."

"Oh. Okay."

They sat a little longer. The darkness on the horizon grew closer, so much so that the pilot could have sworn the darkness was more of a looming black cloud, a locust swarm of biblical proportion.

"Hey Captain, what time is it?"

"About 1500 hours or so. Why?"

"Only 1500? Sure is getting dark fast."

"Yeah. Weird how night is different on another part of the globe."

She wasn't an idiot. That made no sense.

The swarm grew nearer. The pilot shifted uncomfortably on the rocks. Behind her head, a pistol steadied.

"Can you go look for Snatch? He's been gone too long."

"Don't worry about him. He's infantry. He'll be okay. Just enjoy the ocean until he comes back, okay?"

"I'm just concerned, is all. There were more Houthi survivors. They could be anywhere, looking for a G.I. to shoot. And that cloud up there ... something's not right about it."

"He's a big boy. Just enjoy the ocean."

The pistol shook a bit in his hand, but the barrel remained pointed at her.

"Cilian?"

"Hmm?"

"You aren't gonna let the drones kill me, are you?"

He blinked back a tear. "No."

She shook a bit in the ocean breeze.

"Just ... make it quick."

The sob that had been held off escaped for only a moment, a tear or two trailing down the soldier's face.

"I ... I can't do it," he choked.

"Sure you can. You were going to already. Just ... finish it."

The gun shook violently. The Corporal was practically gasping for breath, trying to keep the despair in his throat. He dropped his hand and rested his forehead in the other.

"I can't. I don't want to hurt you."

"I was engulfed in the flame of an explosion I started. Then I fell into the ocean and washed up on the bank where a man strangled me. My eye is gone. My face is fucked. You couldn't hurt me more than I already have been."

The swarm grew closer now, close enough to hear the demonic whirring of the drone blades. He raised the gun once more.

"Remember way back ... when you were Captain, and I was Private, and all of this was just a game?"

"Yeah."

"I'm a Lieutenant now. Who would've thought me to be an officer back then?"

"Plenty of people. You always had something I didn't."

"Well, it doesn't matter now."

He held the gun more firmly to the back of her head.

"Read back."

"What?"

"Message is 'I love you.' Read back."

He took in a shaky breath, blinked back misty eyes, and steadied his weapon.

"I love you."

With a shake in his hand, his voice, and his very soul, the Corporal pulled the trigger.

He sat there with her, quietly crying, watching the waves lap up for just a couple minutes more.

The drones drew closer, and never before had he felt so accepting, no, grateful for an oncoming death. Cilian stood, arms wide, sure of everything except for which would get him first, the fire or the bullets.

"Come on ..."

They were practically right there, so close he could feel the breeze of the propellers on his face.

"Come on. Hit me."

The swarm suddenly froze in place, so uncomfortably still that he almost wondered if the world itself had frozen in time. He felt the eyes of a thousand cameras staring at him, and those eyes spelled *shame*.

Please. Just fucking kill me.

All at once, the drones started moving.

But not straight on.

They strayed to the right. No fire, no bullets, no advance. They lazily floated westward, not even bothering with the soldier on the beach.

"No ... No ... Where are you going? Where are you going? I'm right here, just come get me already!"

The drones paid no mind to the ravings of a madman and continued on.

"I'm right here! Just fucking ... FUCK!" He picked up his XM7 off the rocks, firing blindly into the sky.

"Look at me! Look at me and kill me you cowards! Just fucking kill me, please!"

Drone after drone fell to the shore, but for each gunned down, thirty filled its absence. And not a single one acknowledged him. They were leaving him. Leaving him there with Stoic and Snatch and the Yemeni man and his own twisted mind. He sank to his knees.

In a moment of clarity, he stopped screaming, stopped crying, stopped firing bullets into the blue sky that was destined to turn a hellish orange as Aden became a distant memory. Someone else's memory.

The last thing he saw was the sky. The last thing he heard was the lap of the ocean onto the shore. The last thing he felt was a cool breeze on his face that wafted in a last smell of the fresh sea air.

The last thing he tasted was the muzzle of a handgun nestled comfortably on his tongue.

POETRY

DIVORCE

ARMANDO ALVAREZ

Grade 8, Elkhorn Ridge Middle School, Omaha, NE. Honorable Mention.

Married forever
With the wind ever-changing
Free falling until the end

They could handle it all
Till death do they part
Love still kindling

In a snap
They're alone
The same in their ways

Loving another
Hate strong in their heart
Nothing can stop the detest

Nothing except a child
Before birth they're a part of their parents
Nothing can break the bond

This child is the savior
The beginning of the change
Lost and then found

If only it were so simple
Nothing can repair the damage
They stay apart leaving the child helpless

While the child has to face
This terrible, devastating reality
Of being alone forever

Dear Past Lover

Hannah Beckwith

Grade 11, Millard North High School, Omaha, NE. Honorable Mention.

Dear past lover,

Every day you cross my mind. Thinking maybe I could have done something
    different
If I had done things differently, could I have changed the outcome?
No, how would I have known what they did, how they hurt you?

How they pushed you down while you begged them to stop.
How you called my name over and over but I didn't hear.
How would I have known they had planned this for weeks?
How they wrote down all the horrible details and plans.

If only I knew, I could have been there to save you.
But I couldn't have known, you were on your way home when they stopped you.
They grabbed your phone first so you couldn't call for help.
They put you in their car and took you home.
They tried drugging you but you fought back, you were always so strong.

They took you to their room and tied you to the bed, god I wish I was there to
    help.
If I could have been there, I would be able to see you in person, not your
    headstone.
We would be able to laugh together again, you always had the prettiest laugh.
We could go to your favorite restaurant, god how you loved that place.
I would be able to hold you once again, you can't imagine how empty the
    house is without you
If I could have stopped them you would still be here with me, god how much I
    miss you.

Dear past lover, I will always love you.
If only I could have saved you.

DEMENTIA POEM

KELLEN BEES

Grade 12, Bellevue West Senior High School, Bellevue, NE. Honorable Mention.

Slow passer by,
Staring death in the eye.
No mind escapes its own decline.

So say goodbye
To the home of your youth.
"Son, my god, I think of my tomb,"
But soon, there'll be no fear.
A child, now gone to the past,
Knew not what it had,
'Till we blow out her wish,
And she says she wants youth.
At evening's crest my old woman
Smiles, "I've known you long
And I'll love you longer."

Tonight, it floats without fear,
For a wish has been received.
My loved ones, they say goodbye,
And forsake she'll say it too.
Now a rebirthed child,
Doesn't know who we are,
When we blow out her wish,
And she says she wants two.
Now a little child
Smiles, "I don't know who you are,
But I think I'd like to."

No mind escapes its own decline
Past the foggy breaches of time's
Slow passing by.

A Coward's Reverence

EVE BISHOP

Grade 11, UNL Independent Study High School, Lincoln, NE.

Will you forgive me when I drink from murky waters and taste you on my
  tongue?

A cruelest of indignities: to feel you, bitter and silvery,
clinging to my lips like rouge, clawing down my throat like a sickness.
My teeth gnash against the silty grime, desperate for drops of heaven-
  sent water,
only for me to uncover the guileless visage of you,
trembling and tepid on the roof of my mouth.
Your flavor dips into me the way a wide-eyed nymph lowers herself
into a blue spring of lilies and glass, and a sea of bile quivers at the notion.
Souring as you slip further into this desecration, you gnaw on my teeth
and eat away at me from the inside.

Rotted and deprived of a proper burial,
you looked up at me helplessly, desperate to hold fast to the precious life being
  taken from you.
"Tell me what it means to revere." You whispered it like a prayer, and I had no
  answer.
What is reverence, if not clinging to you as your weary body grows cold in my
  arms?
What does it mean to revere? The words died on my lips,
and when your breath stilled,
I left you there.
You watched me go with the hollow eyes of a lifeless barn owl,
obsidian and haunting like murky waters.

I keel over, and when the bile slips off my tongue and into the dirt, it tastes of
  you.
You wrench a sob from my aching throat, dry from days gone without water,

and I grovel on the ground with my face smeared in the soil.
I ache from the inside out, because I know that, at least for a brief moment, I
    revered you.
But this: this is not reverence. How could it be? You must know it,
by how you fester and decay, by how you churn in my stomach.
And you weep, because you know that I cannot yet join you.
I cannot yet release my hold on this precious life. How could you not know?

Still as the night, the water surely watches me.
My fingernails dig into the muck and I crawl onto my knees, sunk deep in the
    sludge.
Like wounded prey, weak and despairing, I drag myself forward.

What does it mean to revere? I beg of you, tell me.

Will you forgive me when I lap up another drink of these murky waters to
    quell my thirst?

SOMETHING PRECIOUS

EVE BISHOP

Grade 11, UNL Independent Study High School, Lincoln, NE.

Let the muffled stillness kiss my lips, this world washing over me in quiet
waves.
Bit by bit,
inching ever closer to the sky,
until this body of mine is no more.
Faintly tasting of yuzu and oolong, the wind dances from leaf to leaf, golden
and bleeding.
The feel of rewritten words on gentle parchment beneath my fingertips,
vague and once calloused,
the smeared ink translated by miragelike beings of envy and dark waters.

My mother holds my head in her lap: a sunlit moment, a blurred memory I
hold.
I have never seen her cry.
I wonder how well I really know her,
and when the time comes that the earth turns itself over in its slumber, will I
know her then?

Power lines tower over me,
rusting from the inside out and burrowing deep into the ephemeral rot of this
place.
The smell of rosemary and prickly summer grass of the first home I ever knew,
it all folds in on itself over and over again like a paper crane.
Mountain fold,
valley fold,
fold and fold and fold and fold until the paper wrinkles and tears
without resistance, without questioning, without longing for some greater
fate.
Fold until everything unfolds itself,

until there is nothing left but the shredded remains of something that was
    once beautiful,
inexplicably so.

Absolute zero fills this space so that we may drown in it (when did you come
    back for me?),
and, holding your hand,
I think of my mother and if I will ever see her again.
I wonder if she will cry.

The waterwheel grinds to a stop as the overhead torrents freeze across the thin
    chains of silver.
Pilgrims rise up from the ground like ghosts and offer to take us to the moth-
    erland.
You refuse for the both of us (when did your voice begin to sound like that?),
and the rawness of the world begins returning in quiet waves.
Soon, these bodies of ours will be no more, churning with the earth until we
    are stardust.
Empty, dead stardust.

But for now,
let me bask in the sweet gentleness that is so surely you
(when did you learn how to hide your fear so well?
When did you gain the calluses on your palms? When did you—),
and let me try to memorize every part, for when it is gone,
who can recall the softer aspects (the sunlit moments) of love?
Who can recall when I held your head in my lap?
Who can recall the first thing a mother says to her daughter?
Who can recall—
(Can *you* recall—)

You are silent. The wind, torn and faltering, halts with a gasping, frigid stutter.
Your hand squeezes mine, a reminder of something precious I had left in your
    palm
(or was it something I had promised to you and forgot about?).

You don't say a word (what did I forget to tell you? What did I promise to
    you?).
You don't say a word. (Why won't you—)

The ocean mutely falls away.
A paper crane lays unfolded beneath the receding stillness,
and something precious lolls back and forth, back and forth, back and forth.
(What did I leave behind? Why didn't you—)

(But in the end, I suppose it is better that way.
I would not want you to see me cry.)

FROM THE SHADOWS OF GIANTS

GABRIELLE BURNS

SILVER

Grade 11, Millard North High School, Omaha, NE.

I am small in so many ways,
If you measure my inches or number my days.
Compared to the Sequoia tree piercing the sky,
I am merely a blink in history's eye.

I have yet to reach a moon or star,
Or had "historical" not seem far.
I know tomorrow isn't a guarantee,
I know I won't last 'til eternity.

A sequoia second is my hour,
As it takes a long time to tower.
I don't have scars burned like doors to a sacred core,
Nor rings of time, but that's what memories are for.

I stand beneath a relic that will stretch to posterity,
And ponder how much this one sequoia could see.
Would it be better to live forever standing still,
Or to live a moment with freedom and free will?

FLIGHT 93 NATIONAL MEMORIAL

GABRIELLE BURNS

Grade 11, Millard North High School, Omaha, NE. Honorable Mention.

So much can happen in a place;
But the world won't notice or slow its pace.
Such a tragedy has happened here, don't they know?
But the clueless, colorful wildflowers still grow.

The fawns leap through heavy, solemn air;
They jump, and run, and frolic without a single care.
The caterpillar still prepares to be a butterfly;
Through so much sorrow, only weeping willows cry.

The birds still sing their sweet song;
Can't they tell something is wrong?
The clouds still catch gold and rose;
The sun, if anything, only brightens its glow.

Though this time, dark and sour;
Seems sweet in a golden hour.
Still, the wind will swing and sway;
Like any perfect summer day.

I expected rain; I expected dark;
But the world is far from dull and stark.
When people come dressed in black and grief,
The world adorns its brightest flower and most colorful leaf.

The Weeping Willow

GABRIELLE BURNS

Grade 11, Millard North High School, Omaha, NE. Honorable Mention.

I danced in a weeping willow—
As lacy leaves formed chandeliers.
A ballroom built from bark and woe;
As the leaves once were tears.

They call it a *weeping* willow—
As misty olive leaves cascade.
I don't know why she's been named so;
But my guesses have been made.

Does she weep for a broken heart—
Was it for a sad turn of fate?
Or when two roads came to a part;
Did she not choose and wait?

Standing with decisions to make—
Not knowing what each road could hold.
Needing a few moments to take;
Stole time 'til she grew old.

I dry her tears on denim gown—
And dab her cheeks with cotton sleeve.
At crossroads of country and town,
That I will one day leave.

Through the Eyes

ANA CARSON

Grade 12, Doniphan-Trumbull High School, Doniphan, NE. Stacey McCarty,
Educator. Honorable Mention.

The old saying is,
It's all in the eyes
It's a myth really
But the truth lies in it
Eyes say everything about someone
If they're
Happy
Damaged
Guilty
Scared
Lost
It's all in the eyes
Blue eyes are reminders to me
Of unrequited love
Of a specific laugh
A smile that made my day
Maybe that's why I always notice eyes first
Because the person I first felt love for
Left me the reminders of him in others' eyes
Love
Comfort
Lust
Risk
Heartbreak
Can all be seen in blue eyes
Maybe not to you
But to me
Perhaps for my neighbor
Blue eyes remind them of the first look at their precious infant

The look of pure innocence
And the feeling of needing to shield that sweet bundle of joy from all the harm
    that the big bad world brings
Green eyes remind me of myself
Of me as an innocent child
My piggy tails flying in the wind as I chase my older brother
Green eyes scream innocence, but they also scream for what I know ensues
How life can break you
But also for what the future holds
For what I am to become
For who I become
And maybe then
When I see green eyes I feel something different
Maybe to a dear friend
Green eyes remind them of their partner
Of how much you can truly love another human being that isn't your blood
Maybe they were taken back to their wedding day
When green eyes were pricked with tears
And looking at them while giving the vow to love them for a lifetime
Or maybe they are taken back to their first date
The nervousness that was evident in those same eyes
Right now
Nothing comes to mind when I think of brown eyes
And it makes me wonder how long that will stay that way
What the future will bring to make me cherish or despise seeing brown eyes
What memories will come with them
And maybe I will never associate brown eyes with anything more than the
    color
And I will be fine with that
Because maybe to a stranger on the street
Brown eyes remind them of grief
Of a life lost
Or a life lived
Maybe it reminds them of an old friend
That they haven't seen since their childhood
Who left such a mark on them

That those with dark eyes will always bring back memories
We all see different things
Get different reminders of our pasts
But yet we all see it in something as simple as someone's eyes
So maybe the myth isn't that unbelievable
It really is all in the eyes
You can see the whole world in one pair
And see nothing but a shade of a color in another
You will carry the reminders of life with you
And see them only for a brief second while glancing up at a stranger's eyes
Perhaps maybe for you, they are just eyes,
But to me
And to many others
They are memories
They are reminders
They are history
They are everything at once

I Am Not an Angry Person

Ana Carson

Grade 12, Doniphan-Trumbull High School, Doniphan, NE. Stacey McCarty,
Educator. Honorable Mention.

I am not an angry person.
Angry is not a word anyone would ever use to describe me.
But when I think of you, I get a little angry.
Actually not just a little.
You ignite a rage in me that burns me inside and out.
It's always there,
Lingering.
I've never felt anything as strong as it.
How am I supposed to heal,
When this rage is all I have left of you?
This is all you left me with,
Unimaginable anger.
I don't show my rage.
It boils on the inside,
Every time I see you,
Every time I hear you,
Every time I think of you.
I am not an angry person,
But I think internally,
You made me one.
You turned my tenderness into a seething anger.
Sometimes it seeps out.
And sometimes I want to let it all out.
I want to scream at you,
I want to yell until you feel what I've felt.
But I won't.
Because in my rage,
There is love.
And that love also lingers.

And sometimes,
It can extinguish the fire that burns in me.
Until it's only tiny embers that spark occasionally.
And I only want you to remember the love.
The compassion.
The warmth I showed you.
I won't let you know what you have done to me.
You will never know of the anger I have felt.
You will never see how short my temper is now.
You will never get burned by the fire you ignited.
This rage resides in me.
But it will pass.
I am not an angry person.

MAPLE

MADALYN CROTEAU

SILVER

Grade 11, Bellevue West Senior High School, Bellevue, NE.

from the time we got that pup,
scrawny and skinny with ears too-big,
we knew she was meant to be ours.
fur black and white covered in spilled syrup,
we deemed her "maple,"
and the second we got home,
she was running all around,
leaving trails of dust and
shrill barks in her path.
years went by and her whines were
never left unheard at the back door,
well before the rooster would crow.
she turned a blind eye at her kibble,
only to beg at the table for scraps
that my parents knew we kids would
wind up giving to her anyway.
her long and slender nose often found
our resting arms,
begging for belly rubs and
pats on her head.
even more time passed,
and her syrup-covered coat began
to turn white with her age.
she still tried to play sometimes,
and we did the best we could
to make it happen.
but no one could deny, that the
scrawny and skinny pup we once knew
was getting old.
after a sudden night of puke and blood,

we skipped school to lay with her on
the floor by the fireplace,
her favorite spot in the whole world.
we tried to feed her burgers and chocolate,
but she was simply too tired.
i held her paw as we waited for the vet
to give her the shot,
and i looked in her eyes
and realized i could still see
that pup in the shelter,
with too-long limbs and sticky
syrup on her fur.
i like to think that she's running around
in dreams, now.
leaving sweet syrupy trails in
wonderlands of kids' dreams,
making them as happy as
she made us.
forever scrawny and skinny,
and always covered in syrup,
our pup,
maple.

MY FUTURE SELF

MADALYN CROTEAU

Grade 11, Bellevue West Senior High School, Bellevue, NE.

SILVER

my future self is a 20-year-old girl
living in a strange city with no friends
and no clue how to make it through the day.
i hold her in my arms as she cries,
for not being brave enough to
talk to that boy in the coffee shop
or tell the kind girl in her class
that her hair was cute.
my future self is a 40-year-old woman
with no husband, partly because
she was never brave enough
to talk to another guy,
and partly because no one ever
found her as pretty as the blue eyed
brunette with a short but
slender figure and pretty laugh.
she doesn't have kids because
she's never wanted any,
but it would have been nice
to have the option.
my future self is a 70-year-old
woman with creaks in her
bones and cracks in her heart.
the only company she has are her
dogs and cats with their
powdered sugar faces
and big old paws.
she has lived alone
nearly her whole life
and she wishes she could go back

and change something, anything,
so that she wouldn't have to cry
herself to sleep at night
for being so lonely.
i hold my future self in my arms
as she cries, staining my shirt
with her tears.
i gently comb my fingers
through her hair,
still a comfort to me
after all these years,
and i find myself crying
with her, *for* her,
and all of the pain and hurt she feels
for facing life on her own.
but i wake up and she's gone.
she's nowhere to be found,
and the only memory
she's left behind are the
tear stains on my shirt.
or did i leave those stains,
from wiping my face free of
the salty tears and the heavy cries
that i couldn't help
but let out last night,
the tears i cried for my future self?
am i grieving for the person i've yet to become?

DECISIONS, DECISIONS

MADALYN CROTEAU

Grade 11, Bellevue West Senior High School, Bellevue, NE. Honorable Mention.

i am on an evening walk when
blazing red fur melts into white, and
a fox runs past, catching my vision.
he must be in a hurry to get home
to his wife and cubs.
the goose strung over his back
honks at me,
desperate to get my attention.
i'm quick to follow,
to ask what it needs.
in response, it tells me
to help it be set free.
the fox, still running,
tells me that the goose
is the only food he has
gotten all month.
i shake my head,
not knowing what to do.
the goose deserves to live,
but the fox has a family to feed.
my head is spinning,
fighting with itself on
what is morally good and what
is rightfully good.
i'm still standing there deciding
what to do when the fox is
cooking the goose into
soup and his cubs are gnawing on the bones.

Me and the Moon

Madalyn Croteau

Grade 11, Bellevue West Senior High School, Bellevue, NE. Honorable Mention.

it is late at night in the month of october when i am wearing my sister's old jacket from high school and a matching scarf and skirt, deep red pulled together by the black of my boots that fit perfectly. the fall air feels like the playing of an out of tune piano, just stale enough to send a shiver down your spine. walking quickly down an empty sidewalk surrounded by brick buildings, my footsteps are amplified by the lack of bodies surrounding me, and looking up to the sky, the glitter echoing off of my cheekbones shines with the illumination of the moon. her round body provides just enough light to give way for the whites and creams and that hint of purple to shine on our un-perfectly cracked concrete canvas of the sidewalk. i had put on the glitter earlier in the evening, taking careful note of the colorful shards covering pale skin and brown freckles that have faded with the lack of sun. my goal was to provide enough color for the celestial body in the sky to make a beautiful kind of art on the sidewalk that just the two of us could share. reflecting onto the floor, the specks that shine in the cracks of the floor seem more beautiful than the obvious ones on the flat slab of concrete somehow. a hidden beauty, in a dark way. a deer standing still in an unlit pine forest, poison hemlock growing silently by a deep black lake. i can't help the smile that creeps up my face, looking at our masterpiece just then. closed eyes and a sudden understanding of the night make the perfect equation for a minute of trust between the two of us, unbroken by the ticking of seconds from a grandfather clock in an apartment nearby, and just for a minute—i feel as though we are one and the same. no longer multiple beings, but one conscience inside of one body. tonight, i painted stars on my face to shine with the same intensity of the real stars that linger in the sky with the moon to mask my vision of the pain and misery in life. i was born to look like her, the ruler of the night sky and my very best friend in this whole world. it always was, and forever will be, *me and the moon*.

No-Caramel, No-Cream, Extra Sweetened Coffee

MADALYN CROTEAU

Grade 11, Bellevue West Senior High School, Bellevue, NE. Honorable Mention.

sometimes, i feel as though
i am cursed to be stuck in the middle.
i am the added sweetener in coffee,
mistaken for the creamer
and looked over for the
cold foam with caramel drizzle on top.
i am the deafening silence
that plays loudly in between songs
for only a few seconds;
always just enough to make
people shift uncomfortably as
they wait for drums and guitars to
be played again, to fill the
already too-full silence.
the lukewarm rain,
the not perfectly drawn hearts,
the bed sheets two or three days
after being cleaned;
all of it resonates in my heart,
the same heart that's stuck in the middle
of my very being, being caged-in
by my ribs made of stained glass
and weak bone, filled to the brim
with a no-caramel, no-cream, no-cold foam,
extra sweetened cup of coffee.

Steady under the Saddle

Madalyn Croteau

Grade 11, Bellevue West Senior High School, Bellevue, NE. Honorable Mention.

the kids are out screaming through the unlocked back door and the water spilling down my throat is lukewarm and leaves me feeling sickly in the heat of july. the sun beats down on my chestnut hairs and i bow my head in malevolence, as the rays leave me sweating and filled with a feeling of utter despair. there is no shade. i am tired but nowhere near sleep. i begin to feel a rope being put on my face for the third time in two days. two awfully hot days with nothing but warm water and what's left of the grass on the ground. i am led to a wooden pole in the dry dirt and tied around it. they don't even bother to brush me out anymore. i hear them utter a string of words resembling "it's so hot," all while they wear shorts and hide in the shadow of their hats, cracking open another one of those cans filled with some sort of cold liquid.

must be nice.

i feel the all too familiar weight thrown against my back, and my legs quiver under the unexpected mass as i try to remain steady. i no longer try to resist. i used to, before they left scars across my body and shame in my eyes. my head shoots up when they tighten the saddle too tightly, too quickly. it's uncomfortable and i cannot breath very well. i rock back and forth as they keep going tighter, and tighter, and tighter, and they walk in front of me now. they grasp my nose, not caring to be gentle, and try and force that bit of metal through my teeth and over my tongue. i won't let them. not this time. i flail and kick and scream but it's all for nothing because i feel the hot metal burn my tongue within a matter of seconds. i don't have any time to react or adjust because i feel an even heavier weight being thrown onto my already weak back and sharp heels being dug into my side. but something inside of me is too angry to ignore this time. so i do what i havent had the strength to do in a long time. i resist. after the third harsh kick in my side, i begin to buck and jump and rear up, not stopping until my back is freed of the extra weight. i want to run and feel the breeze through my hair and race the birds in the sky. i do not belong here, with the kids still screaming at the top of their lungs, and my only food being the spare grass growing out of the ground in clumps. i am wild. i am angry. and i am certainly not tame. i can practically taste the freedom, but it's soon replaced by the stinging of the metal bit and i am dragged back down to reality by dirty hands that can never be cleaned of their impurity. i am hit over and over with fists and boots until my thin demeanor cannot take it anymore. i collapse because it is all too much. i try to croak out a few sounds but they dissolve in my throat before my mouth can open. the last thing i see is the saddle that was once on my back laying on the floor in front of me, being carried off to the appaloosa a few feet away from the fence. she whinnies at me, a desperate sound, and i try to respond. to tell her to run, and get away before she meets the same fate as me. but i can only sigh for the last time, and feel the weight finally be lifted off of my back.

TODAY WILL BE DIFFERENT

MADALYN CROTEAU

Grade 11, Bellevue West Senior High School, Bellevue, NE. Honorable Mention.

for me, each and every morning is the same. even as the temperatures change and the leaves fall and grow back, i always rise with the rooster and the sun. i am met with the same view of the dirt covered barn floor every day as the sun illuminates the walls covered in grime and filth. when i open my eyes with the light, i hardly ever have time to drink from the dirty water trough in front of me before my back is met with the harsh weight of my saddle. after that, it isn't long until the sting of rusted metal is pressed onto my tongue. my legs don't shake as much as they used to when i feel another weight sink onto my back, and i don't have to imagine what will happen next. i wince to prepare myself for the sharp spurs that kick my ribs and re-open the scars that close every night. they've never had time to fully heal. i can feel the blood slowly trickle down my sides as the sound of a tongue clicking fills my ears and my legs begin to move on their own. i know what comes next; every morning is the same. i work and work and work until the hottest hours of the day leave me sweating and panting. i don't try and keep track of the time anymore. i am too dizzy when i run and prance around outside to think about anything. most of the time, i am not fully myself when they work me. it is as if i am a robot that simply fulfills its duties and is good for nothing but work. *i am good for nothing but work.* i soon snap back into reality as the second weight leaves my back. the squeaking of my saddle as i walk towards the nearest bucket for water is loud and leaves my ears ringing, as i am more awake than i usually am. something deep inside my chest leaves me feeling hot and burning with energy. *today is different.* i can feel it in my old and weary bones that used to be new and pillar-like. now, they are just twigs that hold up the weight of a house with too many occupants. i drink the lukewarm water that fills my burning throat and i can't help but shake the feeling. *today is different.* i'm just not sure why yet. i barely have any time to let the water meet my stomach before an even heavier weight meets my spine again. i have come to learn the difference of the people that ride me; in the morning, it is a girl who wears boots too big for her and hair the same color as mine. in the afternoon, it is a heavy and mean man who has a voice so loud that the birds cry in terror every time he speaks. this is the hardest part of the day. he shouts commands at me and he doesn't bother to be gentle with my reins. he yanks my head to the right and i walk towards the arena. i can see the barrels in front of me, and i already know what i need to do. as i prepare to carry my own weight and the weight of the man on top of me, the feeling in my chest slowly fills me from my ears to my hooves. *today will be different.* i am waiting for a miracle to happen. for the man to jump off of me allow me to run in the fields of the neighboring barns with full-bellied and happy appaloosas and chestnuts, to loose the weight of the leather on my back and the disgusting bit of my bridle. i wait and wait and wait. but nothing happens. i feel the spurs on me once again, and i take off, leaving my disappointment behind me at the starting gate. i'm so fast that nothing can catch me when i run, even my own thoughts. i beeline for the right barrel and turn until i am facing the left. it seems as thought my body is aligned with the ground before i am upright and facing the final barrel. i gallop as fast as i can to make my final turn, and once it's complete, i run even harder than before. i am almost past the finish line when the burning in my chest is too loud for me to hear the disgusting words that string out of the man's mouth. i cannot think about anything else. *today is different*, and before i know it, i am on the ground. *today is so very different.* i think i am finished with my run. im not too sure, but there's nothing on my back anymore. i spit out the metal and taste sweet grass and hay on my tongue. my eyes drift close as the burning in my chest turns to a sweet sting that echoes in my body. i'm hit with realization as i take a deep breath in. i know i am finished now. the last thing i see before my eyelids cover my eyes is the barn that is so clean and fresh on the outside; the red paint hides the disgusting stalls and dirty water within the barn doors. if only people knew what the inside looked like; maybe i could've been saved. but i don't need to worry about that anymore.

today was different.

Self-Reflection

Rebekah Daily

Grade 11, Home School. Honorable Mention.

You!—barbermonger!
Your face is not so stunning
That the world has stopped.

And your vanity
Is quite revolting enough
To disfigure you.

Though your hair is thick
Your mind has been thinning for
Some many years now.

The contour of lips
Cannot disguise the decay
And rot of falsehoods.

Eyes fringed by lashes
Are veiled by shame and disgrace
Borne of selfishness.

Your every virtue,
Each, oh! so superficial
Can have no real worth.

You!—barbermonger!
You, who stare across the world
At me through the glass.

MOTHER DEAR

CLAIRE DAVIS

Grade 12, Hastings Senior High School, Hastings, NE.

I often wonder,
If my mother had never known her father,
Would she be happier?
And if she was happier
Would she never have met my father?
And told him she loved him,
Or—
Would she have met a man
Kinder than him
That would take her to see the skyballoons
That only drank champagne, and
Only drank on Sunday
That could teach her that dust is not a reason to lose sleep
But, life—
Life is
Then maybe she would learn to dance
And her feet would find cobblestones in Italy
And her hair would know the wind of another state
And her smile would be enough for him
And she would be happy with herself
I might never have existed,
But, even if I did
Somehow—
I know deep within my soul
That I would never have thought she could be happier
In another life

MODESTO

CLAIRE DAVIS

Grade 12, Hastings Senior High School, Hastings, NE. Honorable Mention.

That glimmer in your eyes came from the scorching sun of Modesto, CA
They say that the streets are paved with magic
Destiny is an airborne illness
A drug you took in the middle seat, 17th row of your 'forever flight'
That's how your dreams stayed alive
Even with the beat of that old amusement park back home
Taunting your hippocampus—
Dum ba dum ba dum dum dum

Postcards of almond blossoms and palm trees caravaned, cluttering our mail-
      box back home
Collecting little red kisses at every bend of the road
You sent me little metal charms for my bracelet
My wrist sounds like little fairies laughing
Remembering the rhythm of the California breeze
You send pop caps, shoe laces, pretty rocks
—anything that you liked

You promised you'd stay in your new city
Addicted to the jolt of life

Even when you saw that boy
—Shot dead
Fireworks, like glass ornaments pinned on the clouds, making the stream of
      his blood glimmer
Like his soul was washing away in the busted-open hydrant's tears
The world forgot him when the groggy-eyed sun called roll on the city
But his dreams dried out on the pavement for weeks before you "forgot"
You "forgot" the gap between his two front teeth that made his s's drunk with
      joy

You "forgot" his blue Champion hoodie
The one that slept on the thin striped couch in your living room
You "forgot" the bubblegum machine ring he promised you

Even when you saw that boy
You said you never knew him
Even when you saw that boy
You said you never cried
—but you loved him

I see the scream California implanted in that starched smile—
Tears plastered behind your eyes

So time's frozen since you've come back home
Even that teacher you told to "screw it"
Came to say hello

You say you miss Modesto
But I think you miss life
You used to say that dreamers only stop breathing
—when their dreams die
No, I've never seen someone … not alive
And the California sun is still hung in your eyes
But you've been just a corpse
For a year's time …

Autumn

Claire Davis

Grade 12, Hastings Senior High School, Hastings, NE. Honorable Mention.

The leaves have dusted off with the migrant birds
Onward toward far off yesterdays
My tomorrow
How quick they learned to fly—
the leaves
Simply jumped and flew
While I sat stagnant, living the reruns I watch
Eyes glazed over
Decaying into age-old rock
Oh to be born of a youthful tree
To dream
To be amongst the stars—so close you can hear their weeping
And in the painting of the sky, you are brothers
Oh to be hung in elevation away from the horrors and the critters
Where flying is primal and innate
Where life is effortless and death is beautiful
Where do you sleep before spring's never-ending beauty is incarnate?
Whose hand do you hold?
Who gets to admire you as I once did?
It seems everything that is beautiful has died
Our sorrows hang in the sky
Heaven had a child,
Her name is Autumn
She is unfaithful and lecherous
She smokes in the company of death and betrayal

WINTER

CLAIRE DAVIS

Grade 12, Hastings Senior High School, Hastings, NE. Honorable Mention.

My hands are cold and broken
A film of Winter rests—
Heading the grass
December bore the breath in my lungs
(Now)
January has come and passed
The Evergreens know not of church bells
And Heaven owns no peace
The only home I've ever known
Is charitied by my grief
Soon Springtime will hunt for my spirit
But I, washed clean by the snow
Will rest in the shadows of darkness
Till Winter, I once again—

    know

GREAT ELM

CLAIRE DAVIS

Grade 12, Hastings Senior High School, Hastings, NE. Honorable Mention.

Husking roots that bound through the horizon of carpentered farewells
Knocking on the gilded doors of sleepers
The maggots and decay too afraid to answer
They wind onward and outward
With depth as their ministry
Oh how awful, the Great Elm
Preying on death
Praying on death
Knocking on pandemonium's searing iron gates
Laughing
In hallowed mockery
His wicked, mossy cloth he shrouds himself in
He cloaks his power in green, fuzzy linen
His limbs seize at the sky
Threatening to tear the heavens down
Trust not the tortuous one
Even as He masks in the change of the season
Remember the roots
That clutch weak ankles
And bind them to their own rock-bottom
For he is the master of all crooked things
Put your ear to the ground, Child
Listen to the vicious pulsing
Look up, at the paper snowflake branches—
His pounding on a highway to the sky
Catching a jetstream
Clouding the sky

STAR-CROSSED LOVERS

MIA DONOHUE

Grade 12, Daniel J Gross Catholic High School, Bellevue, NE. Honorable Mention.

She looms over her domain,
Sprinkling sand on the nocturnal souls,
To place them in their deep sleep.
She tenderly emits sweet dreams
And pacifies anxious minds.

Owls and bats alike rouse
With the familiar essence.
They are her soldiers,
Flying with the purpose
To ensure a haleness realm.

Fungus bask in her proximity,
Colonizing off her power.
Tidal waves swell beneath her gravity.
Vicious seas tamed, possessing travelers
Navigated by her luminosity.

Her functions are essential.
Yet she yearns for acceptance.
Starstruck by her polar opposite.
Her duties, overwhelmed
By a radiance she can never reach.

His brilliance engulfs the land,
Vanquishing the twilight.
He cradles each dreamer,
Warmth becoming a blanket.
Rays enact famous paintings.

He sends the mourning doves.
Each depart as alarms.
Awakening the drowsy
With their delicate hymns,
Achieving an irreplaceable melody.

Blades of grass collect dew,
Protecting the earth's soul.
He commands a gentle scent
To attack the noses of the eager,
Bringing tranquility to their prologue.

His functions are essential.
Although he worships another.
His polar opposite, but his beloved.
The embodiment of perfection.
An eternity, out of reach.

ENVY

AUTUMN HALL

Grade 12, Daniel J Gross Catholic High School, Bellevue, NE.

SILVER

We are pages bound together.
Your cover is tender and attractive
Eager to be opened.
Mine is solid and plain,
Protective and hesitant.

We are words on pages.
You are calculated prose
And flowery poetry. I
Am scribbled out phrases,
Ink bleeding through paper
And onto the floor.

We are lives in literature.
You are read over and over,
Creased and cherished.
My spine is pristine, never
Been cracked open.

We are books on shelves
You're sat on the one below
Me and we are miles apart.
Different genres, characters,
With vastly different stories.

We are humans
Desperate to be art.

Solitude

SOPHIA HEGARTY

Grade 10, Duchesne Academy of the Sacred Heart, Omaha, NE. Honorable Mention.

comfortable in solitude
stripped of definition
in the near future
it will be all of humanity

he makes gentle strokes
wispy trails across the canvas
only to create
an illegitimate joke

one that only he understands
one that can only be understood
by those who try

old, weak bones
stained and yellowing with age
clouded even more with smoke
emerging from the lit cigarette

rotting away
quietly
only to be forgotten
only to be ridiculed

premature loneliness
hanging low like smoke
suffocating those
who wish to be released from commotion

disintegrating flesh
slowly eaten away
to reveal the bones stained
with the smoke of solitude

LETTERS TO MY LOVED ONES

CONNOR HOLMSTEDT

Grade 10, Fort Calhoun Junior/Senior High School, Fort Calhoun, NE. Sara Gross, Educator. Honorable Mention.

To my Beloved,

I search for love like a camel searches for an oasis in the desert.
I am Orpheus and you are Eurydice.
Lost in the pits of hell, in shambles, in search of you.

    A Lover in Distress

Dear God,

God, please send me a sign.
Do I go with my heart and chase my dreams?
Should I be an artist and perform on the stage, or get a conventional job and
    make everyone but me happy?

God, please help me decide.

Do I get paid in love and affection, or in worthless heaps of a cotton blend
    fabric with no true value?
God, do I live on the stage for an audience, or watch in the box as the enjoyer?
Do I follow the joy in my life?

Please, God, respond.

    A Future Maestro

To my past friends,

Why do you hurt me knowing it is just me in the world trying to find myself
    and figure things out?
You were there during my lowest and still you make an ass out of me?
I clench my eyes tight and hide my face to hold back the tears.
Tears which you caused.

But why do I come back?
Do I miss the good times, or do I just crave friendship?
I'm not sure anymore.
I just want it to stop.
I just want a true friend.

    A Boy with a Mask on

CRAVING AND LIMITATION

JULIAN KRUSE

Grade 9, Bennington High School, Bennington, NE. Honorable Mention.

It is a month of some sort,
Probably September or April
When things seem to be their most poetic.
And I am lying on my bed
And you are lying on my floor.
The whole thing smells like apricots and tree bark.
"Hey, what do you think love is?"
You ask.
"Well isn't that the fun part,
Its inability to be defined?"
You frown.
"But I didn't ask that.
What do *you* think it is?"
And that hurts me because you are right.
I am a liar.
"I think it's a lot of things."
You nod.
"Name one."
I sigh.
"The bottomless plates of fries they serve you down the street.
We share them because there's no way we can do it all alone.
And we realize we can take whatever we can have and it'll be okay.
So we do ... but we find the cruel limit of the human stomach.
We want it all.
We are allowed it all.
But *we* only allow so much."
You lie silent for a while.
"So love is craving and limitation."
You were always better at being concise.
I fear I ramble more then you care.

"How about you then, what do you think love is?"
I asked, curious now.
You smiled slightly and traced patterns in the stucco ceiling with your eyes.
"If you must know, I think love is listening to a poet tell you about bottomless
    fries."
My heart jumped, bubble of carbonation in the Sprite we drink.
You looked at me,
"Love is letting you weave metaphors when all I can hear is 'you and me.'"

Seaweed and Sandcastles

JULIAN KRUSE

Grade 9, Bennington High School, Bennington, NE. Honorable Mention.

A sailor drops to his knees
At the altar of the sea
And the sea, in his cold beauty, sat and watched
Cleaning his bloodstained teeth with his tongue.
And the sailor wipes the dirt from his face and bows his head.

The surf crashes onto the shore.

The sailor says, "I am a shipwreck."
The sea hears, "I am a vessel."
The sailor says, "I have weathered the world."
The sea hears, "I can weather more."

The surf crashes onto the shore.
The rocks erode and become the sand.

The sea says, "Have you ever built a sandcastle?"
The sailor startles and grips the altar in fear.
The sea smiles, teeth still stained red.
"Forged a palace out of the broken parts of yourself?"
The sailor nods, voice in pieces against the Siren's song.
"I am a testament of sand."

The surf crashes onto the shore.
The fishermen breathe in the spray.

The sea regards the sailor,
"I will tear your castle down."
The sailor holds a harpoon in shaking hands,
"I'll kill you."

And the sea hears,
"My offering is your restitution."
The sea says,
"Do it."
The sailor hears,
"Consequence."

The surf crashes into the shore.

The sailor stands from the altar.
Knees bloodied and life restored.
The sea lounges back again
Licking the last morsel of flesh from his teeth,
Hand resting lazily on the harpoon lodged in his gut.

The sea said,
"You don't need to weather anymore."
The sailor heard,
"I'll see you again when you are nothing but pieces."

NATURE'S WONDERS

ADRISHYA KUMAR

Grade 9, Brownell Talbot School, Omaha, NE.

SILVER

A slow, loud cricket's song chirping in the night,
the loud trumpet of an elephant looking for water
a lonely bee drinking from a flower
a small deer grazing in the bright yellow plains
the growl of coyotes looking for food
Nature's wonders.

The song of birds in the morning dew
the howl of wolves at the days end
the stomping of bison in the late afternoon
the snarl of tigers on the savannah
the clicks of dolphins in the deep blue water
Nature's wonders.

Turtles slowly crawling to reach the ocean
dying because of humans
plastic choking the sea,
ripping its blueness away
confiscating the lives of these animals
Nature's wonders must be preserved
for our future to glow in the sunset.

IMMIGRATION

Grade 9, Brownell Talbot School, Omaha, NE. Honorable Mention.

My mother used to ride to school
On her father's scooter
Come home in the dark

My father used to go to school on a government scholarship
Saving money to get into medical school
His whole life dependent on his intelligence.

They used to live on diet coke and chips in America
The luxury of their poverty.
They stayed in a small condo
And just got by with what they had.

They struggled but climbed up the mountain
To allow their two precious kids
To be shielded from the dangers of the world

Since they never want their kids to face what they did.
My mother and father
Worked for their yellow brick road.

A STURDY DESK

SAMANTHA LADWIG

*Grade 12, Fort Calhoun Junior/Senior High School, Fort
Calhoun, NE. Sara Gross, Educator.*

A desk is a place where I go to work
Atop sits my papers, my pencils, my tests
A desk is a place where I sit and talk to my friends, passing notes
A Sturdy Desk can hold all my things,
It can hold the heavy weight of my books and pens

A **Sturdy** Desk is a place where I hide
Whispering to my friends, "Don't worry we will all be alright"
I sit undercover, hoping that my school is not next,
A place where I will text my mother for the last time.

A Sturdy Desk was made to hold all of my things
Atop sits my papers, my pencil, my tests
It holds the weight of my heavy books and all my pen
A Sturdy Desk will not stop a bullet
Because it is only a **Student's Desk**

DIFFERENT TYPES OF MONSTERS

SAMANTHA LADWIG

*Grade 12, Fort Calhoun Junior/Senior High School, Fort
Calhoun, NE. Sara Gross, Educator.*

I'm two years old and I'm scared of the Monster under my bed
He's big and scary
He's the one who gives me the bad dreams
and if I'm not careful he'll take me to his world where he can eat me
I don't know how to get rid of the Monster

I'm six years old and I'm afraid of the Monster in my closet
This Monster is worse
They're crueler than the last one
They have sharp pointy teeth and claws dipped in blood
The Monster whispers awful things to me, I scream for my mom
She turns on the light and he disappears
I wonder what will happen when my mother is not there to save me

I'm ten years old and I'm scared of the Monster in the mirror
She is different than the others
She's not scary, but she is mean
She's just different because she looks like me
I can't escape the things she says to me, the thoughts she plants in my mind
You are not good enough,
You aren't pretty, you aren't worth it.
If I break the mirror will she disappear?

I'm thirteen years old and I'm still scared of Monsters, not the fake ones but
    the real ones
I'm scared of the humankind, the real kind
I'm panicked of the ones that say "it will be our little secret, no one has to
    know"
I'm fearful of the ones that hide in dark places

I'm terrified of the ones that don't know the meaning of no
I don't understand how to deal with these types of Monsters

I'm eighteen years old and I'm still discovering Monsters
The type that is harder to understand
Like the bloody war that many soldiers will die in
Or the children left with no place to call home
I think about all of the trouble and sorrow the world is filled with,
The Monster lurking in the shadows
I am terrified of the Monster that is humanity
I feel two years old and afraid of the Monster under my bed
And I still don't know how to get rid of the Monsters.

THE BODY / THE DISEASE

MAGNOLIA MORIARTY

Grade 11, Millard South High School, Omaha, NE.

Now I lay me down to sleep, I pray the Lord my soul to keep.
Dear Lord lift me of this suffering, kill me now for my life I am not savoring.
Dear lord Thank you for waking me
Dear lord, why did you wake me?
I paint my face with creams and blushes
Smudged from tears, from sweat, from time.
I put on my most beautiful sundress
The one he took advantage of you in.
I shower, my burdens swimming down the drain with flowery soap
But you will never be clean from where he touched you.
Because my body is a temple
But you are no God.
Because my body is an endangered species
And I am no GoFundMe.
And I am lonely
So I will hold you on your worst nights, leave you hungover by morning.
And I fear this is all I will ever be
You cannot leave me.
I do not matter to anybody
And I still love you.
And I do not matter to anybody.
And I still love you.
Things will always be like this.
And I still love you.
And I still don't love you.
And I still love you.
And I still don't love you.
And I still trust you
So I will love you until my love becomes your only worth.

A Dead Dog Is a Happy Dog

Magnolia Moriarty

Grade 11, Millard South High School, Omaha, NE.
Tessa Adams, Educator.

I want Kasey to grow old and powdered-sugared.
Because I can never wear makeup to pick her up from doggy daycare
They always bring her to me running and jumping up to lick my face clean.
And I want that to last forever.

I want every dream Kasey has
To be fast-paced squirrel chases
Where she can't help but wiggle her legs
And let out little yips.

I want Max to grow old and powdered-sugared.
Every day he escapes from home, his paws muddied and his bark strong
And every morning I find him at mine and carry him back home.
I want to never wake up without him there.

I want every dog to grow old and powdered-sugared.
Reserve road kill on the side of the street for possums, skunks, and raccoons
Not someone's chihuahua,
Slipped out of his collar.

I want there to never be a day
When someone comes home
To find Max, Kasey, Nameless Chihuahuas, powdered sugar spilled onto the
    floor,
Not chasing any more squirrels.

"WELL, THE BIG RABBIT GETS F***ED, DOESN'T IT? PROPER F***ED?"

MAGNOLIA MORIARTY

Grade 11, Millard South High School, Omaha, NE.
Tessa Adams, Educator.

grey muzzle on his nose
grey hairs along his back
greyhounds weak and disposed
running for the attack

grey hairs along her back
born only for the kill
running from the attack
hare guts begin to spill

born only for the kill
greyhounds bred with boiling blood
hare guts begin to spill
greyhound paws push through the mud

greyhounds bred with boiling blood
a man gambles like blackjack
greyhound paws push through the mud
he pushes in another rack

a man gambles like blackjack
his yelps reek of rich booze
he pushes in another rack
he doesn't know how to lose

his yelps reek of rich booze
greyhounds weak and disposed
he doesn't know how to lose
grey muzzle on his nose

HOSPICE

Grade 11, Millard South High School, Omaha, NE. Honorable Mention.

The first thing that they notice is the sun.
Either too bright—blazing in your face—rendering you unable to think,
    breathe, she's raging too warm, too uncomfortably, or not powerful
    enough.
The first thing they always seem to notice is the sun.
Whether they find it in a memory of the park, or trying to find itself through
    the curtains,
They always mention the sun.
They ask for it gone.

And they always notice the sounds.
They tell me about their heart monitors,
the screams—
Amplified—
Blisteringly loud.
They always mention the ringing,
They ask me to turn it off.

They always talk to ghosts.
It's as if the rest of the room is gone,
It's only she and her father now.
As I scramble with her pager,
she laughs at his jokes—
And I have no choice but to draw the curtains,
Turn off the monitor—
The slowness is deafening—
hand her back to her father,
and move to the next room.

Sage Stems

MAGNOLIA MORIARTY

Grade 11, Millard South High School, Omaha, NE. Tessa Adams, Educator.
Honorable Mention.

You had a passion for houseplants.
Your heart was the color of fields of poppies, daisies, snapdragons, milkweed,
    and fireflies.
your veins were thick vines,
dancing through your skin.
Cactuses lined your window sill,
pothos wove itself across your cloudy wallpaper,
sage, rosemary, and thyme out on the back porch,
and a monstera in the corner near the fireplace.
It used to be taller than me,
and we both grew.

You said you had a black thumb,
that you couldn't keep a plant alive for the life of you.
But I've seen the things come into your home,
withered and yellowed, brown and black spots, drooping and slow,
that brightened by being in your warmth.
You say that you don't love deeply,
but I've seen you water your jades until they were drowning,
until their petals puffed up like a balloon,
because you just had too much to give.

You were once growing,
like the monstera in the living room.
A trail of flowers once followed you.
You were once strong and stiff,
your roots expanding across the world.
Alaska, Taiwan, Carolina, London
but now your roots don't extend past the edges of your bed.

You now are as weak as your sage stems back home,
without you, they have wilted.
You said that you had a black thumb,
but I knew your eyes didn't work well enough to know that.

Your vines grew thorns that stabbed your skin,
Your heart was so full of love that it puffed up like a balloon
until it was all too much to handle.

You said that you wanted to leave in fields of poppies, daisies, snapdragons,
    and milkweed,
but I hope your hospital bed is close enough.
I promise one day I will deliver you fireflies

WHILE THEY STAY

MAGNOLIA MORIARTY

Grade 11, Millard South High School, Omaha, NE. Honorable Mention.

Damp autumn leave line
the cracked cobblestone—
The path that leads to the church,
the paths that lead to the cemetery gates,
They line the ones through forests and through towns.

Damp autumn leaves line
the lawns and driveways of the neighbors.
They've been mown through too many times
by shirtless dads in green-stained tennis shoes
And yet they stay.
Damp autumn leaves meet in clusters by the gutters.
Damp autumn leaves are too heavy to be moved by the wind
And so they stay.

But the damp autumn leaves that hide in gutters never move.
They never dry.
They never leave for new sights,
new scenes,
new breezes to take them away.
And so they stay.

Damp autumn leaves huddle in heaps and piles
Until the cool breeze turning into snow and sleet
leaves the damp autumn leaves grey and buried—
until Damp Autumn Leaves
become Soggy Winter Forgottens.

THE WEIGHT OF A SOUL /
OF MOUSE AND MAN

ANTHONY MUSSER

Grade 12, Omaha South High Magnet School, Omaha, NE.

I just saved a mouse.

He was terrified,
and he bit me a few times,
but I saved him

and when I put him outside
covered in olive oil
he looked at me

he looked at me
with his big beautiful orbs
like he was saying
"You are fear
in godly form,
but you saved me.

"If I survive,
I will tell my children about you,
and my children
will tell their children,

"and generations
upon generations
will tell the story
of the white giant
who clumsily freed me
from captivity
even after i attacked.

"who tried to feed
my little body
even after i tried to flee,

"all out of the goodness of their soul."

I kneeled there in the damp rain,
hands covered in mud and oil
my knees scraped
by the harsh concrete
I had thrown myself down upon
staring at this mouse

yet it was almost like
I could hear him
in my mind.

He said to me,
"If there ever comes a day,
somehow,
in another life,
I will repay your goodness
tenfold,

"for you decided a life
so small
and unseeming
was worth saving."

I don't know how long
I sat there in the rain
staring down this creature

seconds, minutes, maybe.
but it felt brash in comparison
to how many more minutes

this mouse
may be allowed
to live.

I set my hand on the ground
a few inches away from him,
with cheerios and cheese
in my hand.

He looked at me.
My hand,
and then back at me.
questioningly.
He brushed his small paws
over his greasy face
as if in contemplation.

He trotted forward,
outstretched his paw,
and took a piece of cereal.
He kept staring at me
as he held it.
As if wondering
if now
was my time to strike.

And when he realized
that I came in peace,
he took another piece.
He shoved both in his mouth,
turned around,
and scampered away.

I hope he lives.
I hope he thrives.
And if he doesn't,

at least I will always carry
the weight of his soul
with my own.

How to Disable Parental Controls

Anthony Musser

Grade 12, Omaha South High Magnet School, Omaha, NE.

SILVER

sometimes i ponder
if my mom still loves me.
on the days when
i do nothing but inconvenience her,
where i lay in bed
pretending i was never born,
i wonder if she purports the same way.

now i know it's not true.
my mom finds pulchritude in me,
she's told me in
a million and one ways
how i preserved her life,
made her a better person
but lately, i can't remember
the last time she patently said
i love you.

what if the day i move out, she leaves.
packs up her things
and moves to colorado
to read her books in peace,

to not have to deal
with my presence,
where she can be present
and her descent into
madness
is no longer prevalent
indifferent, may she feel
about my precedent actions

passionate may she be
about how
pest free she can live,
on her own
and prominent she will be
without me.
without me there.
and maybe
she can live
peacefully ...
peacefully ...
peacefully ... !

peachy!
i feel peachy.
i'm just fine
of course, i'm
passive, i'm passive
don't mistake my pessimism
for something else like patrony
towards her
i am angry.
there is no p word for that.
believe me, i looked.

pause!
i yell into the crowd,
and in parenthesis, i wrote
(the crowd, of course, being my own parietal lobe).
perturbation is what i feel
because of her.
i am a pacifist, i swear
i throw no punches
with my fists,
only phrases with a pen
and paper

but my mind
is a perverse place
of constant penance
that is
persistent,
ever persistent.
my mind is a battlefield
the First Amendment not protected
the parasite that plagues me
fills me with
a blatant pestilence.
it is one that stings
my fragile paradigm
like a bitter poison
and it screams
i. am. unloved.

and maybe if i was a book
with a plethora of pages
maybe then
she would look at me
with a pinch
of indignity.

J.M.R.

ANTHONY MUSSER

SILVER

Grade 12, Omaha South High Magnet School, Omaha, NE.

old folklore tells us that the stars are everything.
they make up our directions,
our sciences and math,
the way we view ourselves
and the way we love

the shapes
in which stars stand
are labeled as
astronomical phenomenon,
and they all have meaning.

I believe he must be a star.
fallen from the heavens
on accident,
tripped over the cosmic rays
of oblivion,
because he is my every direction.
he is my hypothesis,
my tangent.

he runs his hands
over my most insecure areas
with a type of love
in his eyes,
only the stars
would ever know.

and deep down inside,
in the abyss of his eyes

I can see the constellation
he was meant to be a part of.
Orpheus.
Ad aeternum fidelis.

DOVE AND WAR

ANTHONY MUSSER

Grade 12, Omaha South High Magnet School, Omaha, NE. Honorable Mention.

i want you close,
i want to lay my head on you
i want you so close
that i may
press my temple
into your sternum
crack open your ribcage
and sleep next to your beating heart
a lullaby of rushing blood and love
like a mourning dove in its nest
singing a melancholic song
to itself

but my body yanks back
silencing me
with thoughts of malice.
"How detrimental
must it be
knowing he merely
tolerates you.
how can anyone love
something that
weighs them down?
quiet, little dove
no, not a sound
silence the coo
mute the song you sing
for how could any man
even him,
cherish something
so tiring?"

i am at constant
war with myself,
nothing a dove
and olive branch can fix,
with every emotion
i feel,
another song
i write
another song
i sing
another thought
i erase
but it just comes back.

or, does it ever leave?

this is pointless,
i sing to myself
as the sun rises.
not through words,
but in a mix of
whistles and tweets.
how *can* anybody admire
something so exhausting?
as the sun rises, though
i find my answer.

SHADOWBANE

ANTHONY MUSSER

Grade 12, Omaha South High Magnet School, Omaha, NE. Honorable Mention.

I can hear you
in the corner of my mind.
I know you.
You scratch at the walls
of a desolately empty space
fawning at the sight of freedom
though you etched the thought of it
into the floor.

You're everywhere.
In every person I see
In every tree and pathway I walk upon
I see your shadow behind
those I used to know
like a rabbit
mocking a hunting fox.

I can't escape you.
Though I can forget about you.
I've learned to wander
aimlessly through life
my peripheral vision
purposefully blocking you from view
until you need to be heard,
you say you live to serve
to protect me from what I can not see
but with you around, I can not see
anything.

I can hear you.
tapping at my window
knocking at my door,
I can feel you
in every broken bone in my body
not broken by physicality
but broken through undeserving
mental challenge

You interrupt my bloodstream
and control my joints
you roundhouse my system
my temporal lobe bracing for an impact
that though I cannot see, nor feel,
I'm told it is there.

You do not protect me.
You protect yourself.
You are locked inside of a cage
one of which where
you hold the key
inside a rage filled palm.
You do not want to be free.
You want to be in control.
And for the first time in my life,
I am letting you fight your own battle.

Maybe, Maybe, Maybe

L. M. NELSON

Grade 12, Logan View Junior/Senior High School, Hooper, NE. Emily Saylor, Educator. Honorable Mention.

The frustration of hating touch but craving it,
Is hard to emphasize with pretty words.
It's an ugly feeling with an ugly root,
That's partially torn from the ground.
As I've now shown it to you.

Maybe the frustration is caused by society,
And the standards that make humanity.
I can't be human if I don't operate like the majority.

Or maybe I do truly just want to be loved.
Maybe I want to be held like I never was.
Maybe I just want to feel safe with someone.

I'll never truly know, though.
The human mind is tricky,
And it's difficult to dissect my own,
So I'll let you alienate me, like that's what I want.
Because I truly don't know.

Then You Knew

*Grade 12, Logan View Junior/Senior High School, Hooper, NE. Emily Saylor,
Educator. Honorable Mention.*

Then you knew.

The air burns,
Everything hurts.
It's on my fingertips.
It's under my nails.
I'm bleeding on myself.

Layers of skin,
Scratched away again.
It's on my conscience.
It's under my eyes, embedded.
I'm bleeding myself.

You didn't see,
Because I didn't want you to.
You didn't know,
Because I didn't want you to.

I told myself it was miniscule.
To easily hide the truth.
But it ate me alive,
And then you knew.

I used my own brain against myself.
Because I thought the pain would help.
But the harm took the self.
And I had to get out.

You Can Call It a Poem

KATELYN OMER

Grade 10, Millard North High School, Omaha, NE.
Whitney Hansen, Educator.

SILVER

I get grief withdrawals
when I'm doing too well
when I get grief withdrawals
I go to the well
thirsty, but don't drink
I search for rock bottom

it sounds odd, ungrateful
maybe it's the poet in me
what am I to do
with this torn, taped paper
but tattoo it in tragedy?
I'll pen a promise—
you can call it a poem

I tried to make depression leave
its place at the heart
as it blew my fire out
but I believe too strongly
angels are just demons with broken wings
and demons need homes too
I don't want my depression to be homeless

I tried to be scared of suicide
but the preacher keeps teaching
death is not the end
my greatest temptation is to take God up on that
I would die, and I would get to
rest

be cleansed of my tearstains and polish
away the scuffs and stab wounds from the pain
of this old lifetime
three days, then I'd rise
ready to live
finally
ready to live,
and with wings too

but this is my promise—
you can call it a poem
oh, my God
my breath is resurrected every millisecond
cause hope is its own religion
and I have faith
that the sky, black and blue from the night before
will always heal and flame at dawn
I'll meet you there

my tears were never worth their weight in gold
my sorrow may be a thorn
in your side, but no longer will I wait
for you to throw roses on my gravestone
to sweeten our marbled loss

I swear I'll plant seeds
in the creases
of every tattered journal
the space between
the bloodied breastbone and still blooming heartbeat

I'll grow these flowers for you,
my sunlight
smiling and swirling in rain
I'll grow these flowers for the most beautiful souls
swirling in hurt worse than I'll ever know
to sweeten your marbled loss

but oh, my God
I swear I'm ready to live
even without wings

this is the promise I've penned
you can call it a tattooed tragedy if you don't believe me
and a poem if you do
and me, yours
to watch heal and flame at dawn
I'll meet you there

ONE MISSISSIPPI

Grade 10, Millard North High School, Omaha, NE. Whitney Hansen, Educator.
Honorable Mention.

you squirm in your prison cell
or your cells squirm in you
out of tune strings twisting caution till it's crippling
till panic ripples, rips apart currents
till every beach is strewn with scattered seaweed
like veins beating against hourglass sand
slipping as you slip,
beating against the bars
scarred you want the walls of your cell black and blue
but only your cells will scream of blossoming bruise
clouding the chipped mirror in the morning—
when light finally reaches the craters on your temple,
tempest torn and tempered to be bookshelves for grief
you will see
you were the one that scratched a deathmark by your birthmark
you were the monster all along—
for pounding your heart against too many bars
the bars
the club bars
composed bars
and bars of fool's gold

you knew they weren't real
but you could overthink yourself to overdose with the way
you let anxiety call the shots
and shoot the glass
you could give a masterclass on how to bandage
a cut from those shards of cut paper and broken heart
hurt from third degree burns cause

you always throw yourself into the fire first
there's just no time to cry
but a firefly is dark every other second
a phoenix is ashes every other second
and you will drag the loss of that one mississippi across the whole river
till you drown in the sound waves
of them calling your name with a compassion you call foreign
cause you've been treating yourself like an outsider
ever since the streetlight found you
slumped and smothered in saltwater against that chain link fence

that stethoscope finds your pulse slumped against your chain linked ribcage
you wonder why you can't breathe
you lean against a white picket fence
wishing for a yellow brick road
to roll against the flow of your downward spiral
and upside down to the sunset—
where you can't get claustrophobic in your own mind
cause you're just air and cloud and sky

uncurling like the silk crown folds of her gardenias
there is love in the crease
there are breaths of beauty for the beast
there are fireflies that glow half the time
and sunshine tomatoes growing along your ribcage
behind your white picket fence
because you refuse to pick yourself apart with chains
for a colorblind brain that doesn't want to color in between the lines
or at all sometimes
the blind don't bet on pink the depressed don't bet on affection
but I'd place all my foolish gold at the bottom of the pool
70 x 7 times that if you use the pennies at the bottom for seeds
you will see gardenias around all the bars
and your sound waves calling you from the stars
loved
those pennies

those seeds
ratting in your music box of a voice
nice things that no longer sound so foreign

DREAMS #1

ISABELLA PARMELEY

GOLD

Grade 11, LPS Arts & Humanities Focus Program, Lincoln, NE.

Take your dreams away
From the ones who lost theirs
To the ages and erosion.
Those who don't think you'll make it.

Take your dreams away
From those who don't understand.
Set yourself free of the
Haters who want you to drown in sand,

Trapped, a bird without the sky
Because that's how they lost
Their lives.

They are not you
You are not them
Everyone wants different things
So you need to cast them away.

Be the sailor who braves
New waters, the one who takes a
Chance, and takes a leap,
And maybe falls, but at least you didn't stay in the safety of your bay.

Constant as the Sea

Isabella Parmeley

SILVER

Grade 11, LPS Arts & Humanities Focus Program, Lincoln, NE.

The summer was young
But the days were already old
Sunsets came and went,
But we stayed the same.

Constant as the sea
Never changing, always the same
Insensibly, we never fluxed
(until we did)

I looked at you, and I said
"Why are we like this?"
You laughed, said
"Don't worry."

But I should have
Should have worried sooner
Because we didn't change for

So

Long

I didn't think it was possible.
The seasons came and went
But we were never spent
Or tired or anything except ...

Who

We

Were

Constant as the sea
Never changing, always the same
Insensibly, we never fluxed
(until we did)

I looked at you, and I said
"Why are we like this?"
You laughed, said
"Don't worry."

But I should have
Should have worried sooner
Because we didn't change for

So

Long

Now you are dark
And I am light
Different as day and night
How did it happen?

The spring has come
Great change that always comes
Outside ...
How did it happen?

(until we did)

Was is the boom and bust
The endless outer world

Wearing us down?
Was it this or that or that?
I wonder while I
Wander alone
Along our coast
Staring at the sea that

Maybe
Changed
Us

Never again as ...

Constant as the sea
Never changing, always the same
Insensibly, we never fluxed
(until we did)

But I should have
Should have worried sooner
Because we didn't change for

So

Long

(was it the unchanging sea
that changed us?)

(never say never)

POETRY, ACTION, FAITH, HOPE

ISABELLA PARMELEY

Grade 11, LPS Arts & Humanities Focus Program, Lincoln, NE.

SILVER

Poetry,
Faith,
Action and
Hope are
All that you can hold
On to, when the
World is
Balanced on
Knife
Edge,
Thin and
Precarious.

Do what
You
Can to make the
World as
Good as
Only
You can make it.

There is something more than
Fear.
I refuse to let fear
Dominate
Me.
Maybe, there is
Something to be afraid of.
But that is
Not

All
There
Is.

SEASON POEM

KATHLEEN PARMELEY

Grade 11, Lincoln Northwest High School, Lincoln, NE. Honorable Mention.

Winter means heavy coats, hats and mittens
the nipping cold on your bare nose
a howling north wind rattling the bare brown tree branches,
icicles hanging off the barn roof.
A layer of frost on a blanket of snow,
gray skies and gentle flakes
slick ice on the driveway.
Inside, cozy quilts, the hum of the heater and hot chocolate.

Spring means shoots of green grass
little tree buds
geese coming home, the smell of rain after a thunderstorm.
The *suck* sound that mud makes on boots,
that wonderful feeling of running without your coat for the first time in
    months
the gloriousness of being warm without a sweatshirt.
Dandelions,
great yellow fuzzy beds, so bright and vibrant.

Summer means no school, sweat, heat, bug bites, long days,
sunshine, sunflowers, physical labor.
Hours spent in trees, hidden by great masses of green leaves
the taste of homemade popsicles
dirt under your fingernails
goat milk waffles, goat milk cream cheese, goat milk everything.
The taste of homegrown strawberries, the flavor bursting on your tongue, so
    sweet and strong
walks to the mailbox, wind in your hair.

Fall means the end of something glorious, a chill returning to the air
trees aflame with red, orange, and yellow
coats and textbooks come back out.
Crickets chirping in the basement, and the smell of the bug spray used to kill
   them
withering weeds and grass.
The smell of the heater as it comes on again,
cold toes and wool socks
the flurries of a first snow, speckling the ground with white.

ROADKILL

JAY PETERS

Grade 12, Omaha South High Magnet School, Omaha, NE.

You set foot on the concrete,
And immediately recoil.
It is freezing from the cold night air.
Biting at your paw pads,
Well-worn as they are
From a lifetime of rough silt and brittle leaf litter.
Stings something terrible.
But you plant one paw down,
Then a second,
Swallowing any protesting sounds that might escape.

You see, there is something on the other side.
Salvation is a ditch next to the asphalt.
There is nothing left for you over here.
Nothing to eat that has enough meat to pull from the bone,
Nothing to drink that isn't bitter and smoke-soured.

The ones who laid this vast stone plane are the same who choked your
     streams,
Made barren your forests,
And named you an intruder in your own home.
But you do not fault them.
There is no hatred in your little mammal heart.
There is only hunger,
And so you walk on.

There is something bright blooming on the horizon as you go.
You remember a story like this,
Safe with your mother curled around you and your kin,

Telling you of a great ball of light cresting above the concrete crossing over the
    river,
Of a warmth, a comfort brought by the sunrise
The end of a short dark-sky winter with its rabid winds and howling barn
    owls.
The light is a protector of your kind.
It loves you, so you embrace it with nothing but gratitude.

Then pain.
Sharp, stinging, all-encompassing fire in every inch of you.
You're knocked to the side as the sun blazes past you without a second
    thought.
You hit the ground and something more splinters,
But your shrieks fall on deaf ears.
The light has vanished into the distance,
And you are left alone to suffer in agony.

No one is there to watch you die.

The real sun rises after your body has cooled.
It sets again once you have started to decompose.
Rises once more when the insects arrive.
It is on its way back to the western horizon when he comes to you.

He is one of *them*. The malevolent gods who trample underbrush on two legs.
His hair falls into his eyes as he crouches down next to you.
He has a sheet of white plastic in one gloved hand, and the other he lays gently
    on your side.
He is weeping.
His tears drip onto your fur as he lifts you up onto the plastic.
He murmurs to you the whole way down the hill.

"I am so sorry, sweetheart.
This world should have been yours too.
You were ripped from it too soon.
I'm sorry.

It is a cruel place here.
You deserved more.
I'm sorry.
I pray you have found peace.
I'm sorry.
I'm sorry,
Sweetheart,
I am so sorry."

He lays you down in the grassy ditch that you called heaven and kneels.
He does not speak anymore,
Just rests his hand over your cold paw for a minute longer.

He leaves you when the sun goes down,

To an afterlife he hopes is gentler than this one.

No. 15 Scalpel Blade

JAY PETERS

SILVER

Grade 12, Omaha South High Magnet School, Omaha, NE.

Dissection is a funny thing.
I find a clinical sort of comfort in it.
I think of the steel,
Cold, passionless blades,
Gliding through unfeeling skin that parts like the red sea,
And I breathe at ease.
There is a peace I am certain I will find nowhere but the mortician's table.
Maybe it's the knowledge that one day, someone will see me, (breath)
And they will see only meat and bone.
Silent and lax without the pulse of blood and the quiet stir of breath.
Piercing fluorescent lights cannot blind eyes that no longer see.
They are merely the haloes, as white coats are the wings,
That turn the surgeons of our world into the seraphim of the next.

They want to help you.

It will be messy and it will be ugly,
But it is for the best.

Purgatory is not a pretty thing.
It is not a clinic waiting room with ancient magazines and tinny stereo.
There is no way to excise sin from the chest cavity without breaking a few ribs.
There will be no anesthetic. For the dead.
And that is truly divine.
A clean y-cut down the torso is all it takes.
Their hands do not shake anymore.
They know how the procedure goes.
It is just monotone work.
Flatline.
They will not hesitate when they reach for the scalpel,

Or look down at the specimen on their operating table and think,
"*Oh, what a love this mind held.*
Thoughts like river rocks
And feather down."
They will not empathize with it.
They will look upon the creature,
And they will think only of where to cut.

MEMORIES

SILVER

Grade 11, Millard West High School, Omaha, NE.

In the endless maze of our minds,
The VCR playing the best or worst,
We try to unwind but our mind rewinds,
Memories unrehearsed, unreversed,

Regret of an earlier occasion,
Haunting my every future action,
Darkness in my mind like an invasion,
A flower can wilt in a tended garden,

A family can be torn apart,
Friendships can be broken beyond repair,
When we lose someone, it will break our heart,
Some may see life as a ball of despair,

Death is the reason for the word never,
Why does a memory last forever?

294   POETRY

Not That Simple

Grade 11, Millard West High School, Omaha, NE. Honorable Mention.

It's not as simple as some think,
There are no rules written in ink,
No tutorial this far in,
Can't even find where to begin,

"Everyone wants to get a drink,"
It's not as simple as some think,
No matter what I seem to try,
Rarely do I get a reply,

I'm not the person to go out,
"It's difficult to go that route,"
It's not as simple as some think,
A guy's voice makes my face go pink,

His eyes can make my heart go still,
Didn't occur to me until,
He started asking for a drink,
It's not as simple as some think.

THE RED STRING

CAMDYN PRUETT

Grade 11, Millard West High School, Omaha, NE. Honorable Mention.

A knot twists and turns,
Wrapping around the finger,
What the heart yearns,
Is to find the other.

The ends in a dance,
Boundless waltz with time,
Their lives governed by chance,
But became partners in crime.

A string that can't be severed,
A knot that can't be undone,
Unable to be weathered,
And destroyed by none.

Twin flame,
Destined soulmate,
All the same name,
The red string of fate.

A Dance to Forget

Dahlci Studley

Grade 12, Northwest High School, Grand Island, NE. Honorable Mention.

The shadows reveal that once, not so long ago, a dancer had danced upon the stage. The dancer pranced around and around the dull stage, a sight that held everyone's attention—not out of admiration, but humor at the poorly decorated scene. And yet, the dancer left a mesmerizing trail, one that remains so hauntingly beautiful.

When the dancer performs their tricks, sinking deep into the audience's minds, they are filled with awe and praise. But one must realize: this is not art, nor is it music. The symphonies you hear are too beautiful to be mere music. The red—a shade far too sweet to be paint—is something far better. This is a form of art that everyone should see, hear, and taste. Everyone should let the tiny dancer move across their own stage and feel the intoxicating sense of control—control over what they see, what they do, and what they create.

Because I am not an artist. I am a creator. One that all men should come to see, to try, to feel. It is an experience like no other.

When you see the first buds begin to bloom, you know the show has only just begun. The buds turn into little rivers, swaying and flowing in mesmerizing patterns that leave you breathless and wanting more. So much more that you force the little dancer to go harder into their routine, deeper into your stage—creating bodies of luscious red that even rubies cannot compare to. This newfound sea you've brought to life runs deeper than the blue oceans and shines brighter than a million burning stars.

THEIR AMERICA, NOT OURS

JUPITER STURM

*Grade 11, Boys Town High School, Boys Town, NE. Beth Sulley,
Educator.*

This is the nation
Built on the idea
Of freedom
The nation
Whose legs
Are brittle,
Built on tree bark
And broken treaties
This nation
Which encompasses
Gluttony
Greed
The grandeur of wealth
Which we flaunt facetiously
To those who possess less
Our entertainers are placed on
Pristine pedestals
While our working class wastes away
Watching the flickering fridge fluorescence
Fruitless.
Feel themselves fade
Forgotten
We place our politicians
In positions ideal for
Pressing us precisely against a precipice
Passing pointless precedents
Restricting our rights
Regulating our residency
Contaminating our presidency

Claiming to leave a legacy.
This America
Was built by
People seeking freedom from corruption
Only to find it fluttering
Frantically within themselves
Unfixable
Unfathomable
Unattainable
This may be American
But it was never made for us.

WAR FINDS WAR

PRISCILLA TON

Grade 12, North Star High School, Lincoln, NE.

I'm a grandchild of war
Which means i'm a product of pain
A generation of loss and bone-breaking violence
And within the midst of it all,
Two war-stricken families found their way to Nebraska
Cornstalks of safety and fields of futures on the horizon
Swaddling, each, a newborn child
One—the youngest of six
The other, the oldest of three

The Korean War divided Korea at the 38th parallel
The Vietnam War divided Vietnam at the 17th
And America divided my parents into Asian-made Americans
Poor, longing, and angry
With lost languages and forgotten fathers
Trouble seeking trouble seeking refuge
Finding love, finding the shrapnel remains in blood rivers
And gunpowder dusted fingers finding cradled hearts
English sews them together, two pieces of loose fabric
To be American was to be,
To be anything else was to not
To be alive was to fight
And my parents were so alive

Scars of wars that had birthed them
Were sharpened spears swept across their parents' honing steels
Love finds love finds love
Like thumbs pressing into purpled bruises
Freckles like a tombstone dotted hill with forgotten names
Ego, like pride, like patriotism

I am told to take cover in the trenches, cover my ears
Trauma triggers like pointed rifles
Silver stars like collared decorations
Love finds love finds love
And war finds war finds war
But sometimes love is not always worth fighting for

I Am So Sorry Dear

Daniel Yoo

Grade 10, Southwest High School, Lincoln, NE.

I'm so sorry dear my friend,
That I feel like I've let you down
I'm so sorry my dear Lord,
That you do all this work for me without anything in return
I'm so sorry dear my parents,
That my behavior does not reflect your thoughtful parenting
I'm so sorry dear myself,
That you have to pay for all my mistakes
And dear Ukraine, I'm so sorry that I'm not yours,
That bombs and fear rain down like a flood,
That only the pitch darkness is ahead
But today, forever,
Against violence and autocracy,
We're all Ukrainians,
Defending our home with a soaring democratic spirit.
God save Ukraine.

The Flaming Fire of Freedom

Daniel Yoo

Grade 10, Southwest High School, Lincoln, NE.

Today, February 24
the day that will go down in history, the day that is history,
Boom, Russia invaded Ukraine
Now Ukraine is on the frontlines of democracy
In a flaming fire of freedom … struggle
They are not fighting for so-called freedom to take off masks
They are not fighting for so-called freedom to be hurtful
Oh dear sons and daughters of the Revolution those things are not freedoms
Freedom is being able to read whatever newspaper you want
Freedom is not being subject to foreign intervention, to live in a safe, hospitable place,
To believe in what you want, to say what you want,
Freedom is Earth's greatest present
Will every four corners of the world be free?
No probably not,
But maybe in the future we open together, the world'll be like a paradise,
Maybe before we came, the world was a paradise.
Free Ukraine.

THE REMEDY

The Way to Fix a Dying Me

DANIEL YOO

Grade 10, Southwest High School, Lincoln, NE.

*Each spouse stares out at the shimmering night sky from the elevated balcony, both singing in a low, tired melancholic tone.

I am a normal wife, I am a normal husband,
Married to a spouse who does not love me.

(Echo)

I am a normal husband, I am a normal husband,
Married to a wife who does not love me.

(Echo)

I am a normal wife, I am a normal wife,
Married to a husband who does not love me.

(Echo)

I am a normal husband, I am a normal husband,
Married to a wife who I do not love

(Echo)

I am a normal wife, I am a normal wife,
Married to a husband who I do not love

(Echo)

I am a normal husband, I am a normal husband,
Married to a wife who once loved me

(Echo)

I am a normal wife, I am a normal wife,
Married to a husband who once loved me

(Echo)

I am a normal husband, I am a normal husband,
Married to a wife who I once loved

(Echo)

I am a normal wife, I am a normal wife,
Married to a husband who I once loved

◇◇◇◇◇◇◇◇◇◇◇◇◇◇◇◇◇◇◇◇◇◇◇◇◇◇◇

We are married,
But that does not mean we are happy
The only way to fix a dying me,
The only way to fix a dying us,
The only way to see the blossoming flowers,
The only way to see the green mountains of May,

is love.

ALMOST TO THE HORIZONS

DANIEL YOO

SILVER

Grade 10, Southwest High School, Lincoln, NE.

Dear my brother,

To this day, if there is one thing that I remember about my life in the United States, it is citing the pledge of allegiance on the first day of American school in August 2018.

I did not know the words and more importantly, I did not know the meaning, but as I murmured alongside my standing classmates that day, I knew that these words would change my life forever.

With every word and every sentence of the pledge of allegiance deeply committed to my memory and my heart, every day since then, I dreamed of our family receiving permanent residency. The arrival of the green cards would take many years after we arrived in the United States on our father's student visa, but indeed, in the fall of 2023, we were slowly getting closer.

Oh dear my brother,
I know that we both hugged each other and cried when we received our green cards,

Oh dear my brother,
I know that we believed that with a green card, only a brighter future lay ahead,

Oh dear my brother,
I know that my life feels like a tangle yarn—

And I know that yours does too.

I do not know where it has gone wrong.

I keep believing that things would turn out alright, putting all my eggs in the
true American value of hard work—but it is hard to believe so when our
parents' efforts and their quality of life are inversely related.

Oh dear my brother,
I hope you would understand why I gave up, for I know that if anyone asks me
what I did over my summer, I would say I dreamed.
Once I had dreamed of a better life, once I had planned for an improved
future, and once I had imagined a happier world.
But a great storm had washed over me, and instead of dreaming, I resorted to
surviving.

Full of ambitions and aspirations, I once looked to the ocean sky, ahead to the
bright horizons that laid in front me, but now I have no choice but to only
look down at my feet to make sure that I am not drowning.

I see our stressed father at his desk downstairs, our hardworking Doctor of
Philosophy dad, unable to find employment and worrying about family
24/7—Every week he applies to dozens of jobs, yet none of them calls him
back wanting to do an interview. Not a single corporation sought after our
father. Not a single company wanted our talented, hardworking, and kind
father.

I see my mother with her concerned face, pacing the living room, concerned
for our father's health and morale. She knows better than anyone that he
has worked hard all life long—yet she also knows that the forces beyond
our control have not been favorable to him.

I don't know where our lives have gone wrong,
And I may never know.
Today I write to you under the lonely moon in the night sky, breathing the
crisp fall air but wondering if it is truly free.
Today, I choose to take a course of action—to do something—that our society
has discouraged since its founding—give up.

I decided to give up all my future ambitions and ambitions in favor of living
    day-to-day, fighting the daily struggles as they rose by.
But giving up doesn't mean that I am rage quitting.

I am only giving up—laying down my hopes and future dreams—so I can no
    longer feel anxious and so I can persevere.

You must beoteuh (Persevere), I tell myself every day.

And I am going to persevere.

Today, I choose to take a course of action—to do something—that our society
    has discouraged since its founding—give up.
I decided to give up all my future ambitions and ambitions in favor of living
    day-to-day, fighting the daily struggles as they rose by.
But giving up doesn't mean that I am rage quitting.
I am only giving up—laying down my hopes and future dreams—
so I can no longer feel anxious and so I can persevere.

You must beoteuh (Persevere). I tell myself every day.

And I am going to persevere.
And I am going to persevere.

You must beoteuh (Persevere). I tell myself every day.

I will persevere.

DEAR MY LORD

DANIEL YOO

Grade 10, Southwest High School, Lincoln, NE. Honorable Mention.

Dear Lord,
Ever since I was young, I went to church with my mom,
Prayed every night under the cover of darkness,
And read the Bible.
And what did you ever do for me?
Then the sky flashed and realization rained and God answered,
I kept you fed,
I kept you housed,
I kept you educated, so you could be a brighter light in the sky
I kept you entertained, so you will never cry

And most importantly, I kept you happy
Isn't that enough?
Then I realized,
That God's love is different from my parents
In a way
That it is the basic foundation of my life,
As valuable as life itself,
As valuable as value itself

ACROSS THE SEA

DANIEL YOO

Grade 10, Southwest High School, Lincoln, NE. Honorable Mention.

People immigrate
seeking freedom
seeking safety
seeking opportunity

But I wonder,
why did my family?

Is it worth it to live in a country where
we have to worry about gun violence every day?

Did we lose
more than we gained?

No we did not,
I tell myself.

I am happy
and that is what matters

In 30 Minutes, I Die

Daniel Yoo

Grade 10, Southwest High School, Lincoln, NE. Honorable Mention.

In 30 minutes, I die.

In 30 minutes I depart,

In 30 minutes I leave,

In 30 minutes I go.

In 30 minutes I am going to die.

My brain wires bursting with greed,
my veins exploding with contempt,
my blood being pressurized by jealousy,
my blood pressure soaring with every ounce of responsibility that I cannot
    take anymore.

In 30 minutes I will die.

But who do I have to blame but me?

I chose this.

I chose this life.

And now,

I choose this death.

So who do I have to blame but me?

It is the life that I chose.

Only, I didn't know it would turn out like this.

This is the responsibility that I cannot bear to take anymore.

I depart.

My Piece of Heaven

Daniel Yoo

Grade 10, Southwest High School, Lincoln, NE. Honorable Mention.

Lying down after lunch on the mattress my brother dragged down
my mom tells me to stop, saying you shouldn't lay down after a meal
but inside I'm thinking,
maybe Heaven isn't much
it is just a place where you can truly be happy

MY WATCH

DANIEL YOO

Grade 10, Southwest High School, Lincoln, NE. Honorable Mention.

My watch
On top of the fireplace
A Swatch
Given by my aunt

Lingering in the past
Sometimes hours
Occasionally days

It moves me around
Shows me the past
Like the cracked screen
From when we played tag

Grew up with me
Moved with me
Cried with me
Laughed with me

Symbol of my maturity
Part of contemporary me

DRAMATIC SCRIPT

Sigurd the Monster Slayer

Miah Fox

Grade 12, Paxton Consolidated School, Paxton, NE. Honorable Mention.

CAST

HELDI	TORRIN
ERIK	ZIVA
KALIA	DEAD GUY
BO	KING
MAUVE	SIGURD
HERALD	MONSTER
VICE	

(Takes place in medieval times, with an evil lair on stage left, a throne room at stage right, and a town at center stage.)

Scene One
(HELDI is in CENTER STAGE, a cauldron in front of her is glowing as she is stirring it. OFFSTAGE, the cast makes a beat of stomping feet as RED LIGHT shines down on her.)

HELDI

Eye of Newt, dragon's tongue, wolf's nail, now he's done. Blood of a royal, heart of a slave, the debt of the betrayer will now be paid.

(The beat becomes louder and faster, and there is a roar offstage. LIGHTS BLACK-OUT as HELDI cackles. During this time she takes the cauldron and freezes at STAGE LEFT.)

Scene Two
(LIGHTS come on at STAGE RIGHT. ERIK is writing with a paper and quill and studying certain artifacts on his work table carefully. PRINCESS KALIA enters STAGE RIGHT, but ERIK is too focused on his work to notice. She walks up behind

him and lets out a sharp whistle. ERIK yells and jumps in his seat, whipping around to look at PRINCESS KALIA.)

ERIK

Your Highness! You scared me!

KALIA

You sure are preoccupied. What are you studying that's got you so focused?

ERIK

It's ... some old artifacts that were found recently. (*He lifts one up for her to see.*) See these marks on the surface? They look like normal scratches from being dropped or kicked, but they form a pattern that suggests that they were purposefully made. I actually think that these were made by a thick but sharp weapon of some kind ... (*He looks at KALIA, then shakes his head.*) But you didn't come for this. What can I do for you, Your Highness?

KALIA

Ah, well my mother wanted to talk to you, something about her medicine and stuff? I don't know. She said that you would understand.

ERIK

Oh, uh, yes of course. (*He looks at KALIA a bit confused.*) Why didn't one of the servants come to inform me?

KALIA

(*Nervously, scratching the back of her head.*) Uh—I figured if it involved the Queen it must be urgent, so I figured I'd just deliver the message myself. (*Nervously laughing*) Not like I just wanted an excuse to see you or anything.

ERIK

What was that?

KALIA

Nothing. I better leave you to it then.

(*KALIA rushes out STAGE RIGHT. ERIK packs a few mysterious items into his bag, walking STAGE LEFT where HELDI was frozen in place with her cauldron.*)

Scene Three

(*ERIK clears his throat, making HELDI look up from her work.*)

HELDI

Erik, my dear boy. Did you come with the ingredients I asked for?

ERIK

All right here, Your Majesty. They were ... difficult to find.

HELDI

Not too challenging I hope. I also hope that discretion was practiced as well?

ERIK

Of course, though with all due respect to Her Majesty, my discretion won't really matter when someone sees you stirring a pot as big as a dragon skull.

HELDI

(*Looks down at her cauldron, then back at him.*) I'm making soup.

ERIK

Right ...

HELDI

I'm glad you kept my secret Erik. Sorcery is often falsely advertised. I mean, it's not like I kill people.

ERIK

Of course, Your Majesty. I understand.

(*LIGHTS DIM. ERIK and HELDI exit STAGE LEFT as TOWNSPEOPLE group together at CENTER STAGE over DEAD GUY.*)

Scene Four

(*TOWNSPEOPLE are murmuring amongst themselves. MAUVE cries over DEAD GUY loudly. BO enters STAGE RIGHT.*)

BO

What's going on here?!

MAUVE

Oh, Bo! The beast got him!

HERALD

It's the third night this week!

VICE

It steals the crops!

TORRIN

Kills our herds!

MAUVE

Murders our husbands!

HERALD

We know it's a beast, Bo! Ziva done see it!

ZIVA

Oh it was awful, like a banshee with huge claws! And eyes as red as blood!

BO

Many of the other villages I went to trade with are having the same things happen to them. We need to find a way to deal with this.

HERALD

The king is doing nothing to help! How can we get rid of this monster?!

BO

Don't worry, I know someone from the castle. He works closely with the king. He'll convince His Majesty to help us.

MAUVE

Oh thank you, Bo! You're a hero!

(LIGHTS DIM and TRANSITION MUSIC plays as TOWNSPEOPLE exit off stage. ERIK enters, and he and BO talk silently at CENTER STAGE as the KING enters with the DUCHESS, who are hugging each other and silently flirting. ERIK turns to meet the KING before the LIGHTS BRIGHTEN.)

Scene Five
(ERIK sees KING and DUCHESS and freezes in shock as the MUSIC does a record scratch. KING sees ERIK and jumps away from the DUCHESS.)

KING

Erik! What a surprise! (*Looks at DUCHESS.*) Uh ... Yes, that trade agreement sounds quite alright with me. (*The DUCHESS timidly nods, rushing out STAGE RIGHT as ERIK watches her go.*)

ERIK

Your Majesty! What was that?!

KING

Well that was the Duchess of the Valley of course! We were just discussing some trade agreements.

ERIK

Are you certain? Because—

KING

(*Angrily.*) Are you questioning me, your king?

ERIK

No, of course not, Your Majesty.

KING

Good. What the public doesn't know won't hurt them. Now what was so urgent that you had to interrupt my business meeting?

ERIK

Uh ... right, well. (*He straightens up with professionalism.*) I've been getting many messages that are very concerning ... Have you heard of a beast that has been destroying villages in the kingdom?

KING

(*Annoyed.*) Oh. That foolish rumor. Yes, I've heard of it. It's just the peasants getting bored.

ERIK

I don't really think villages miles apart would just invent a monster at the same time ...

KING

Oh please, it's a made-up story. Once a few people say it, then everyone wants to join in. There's no beast.

ERIK

Right now, your majesty, your people are dying. I implore you to care!

KING

You have no right to advise me on how to run my kingdom.

ERIK

I am your advisor! Please, your majesty, I truly believe there is weight to these reports.

KING

Then you believe wrong. (*He pushes ERIK away.*) There have always been many false rumors and reports. It's part of running a kingdom.

ERIK

You have nothing to lose if you choose to act. In fact, if it is real, then you are a hero, and all of your people are in your debt.

KING

(*Pauses a moment, then waves a hand.*) Very well. I'll send soldiers.

ERIK

Actually, my king, I don't think a few soldiers are enough.

KING

So what would you have me do instead?

ERIK

A monster slayer, Your Majesty. I have heard that one of those types of men could handle something like this easily.

KING

Are you sure of this Erik?

ERIK

If there is a monster, then a monster slayer will handle it.

(*BLACK OUT.*)

Scene Six

(*SIGURD kneels at CENTER STAGE, studying something silently. He runs his hand over the ground and sniffs it before gagging and wiping it on his pants. BO, HERALD, and VICE enter STAGE RIGHT.*)

BO

Whoa, never seen you around these parts. Who are you?

SIGURD

(*Looking back, he stands up and places his hands on his hips and puffs out his chest.*) Sigurd the Monster Slayer—at your service.

HERALD

Sigarg?

SIGURD

Sigurd.

BO

Oh, Sinnard.

SIGURD

It's Sigurd.

HERALD

No, I get it. It's Snicker.

SIGURD

It's not— (*Throws his hands up in the air.*) Is this where the villager died?!

BO

Yes, you said you were a monster slayer?

ERIK

(*Entering STAGE LEFT.*) Yep, I was the one who hired him.

(*BO sees ERIK and smiles, running across the stage and wrapping him in a rough hug.*)

BO

Erik, my friend! You came through!

ERIK

Of course, this beast sounds like an awful problem. (*They part, and ERIK holds a hand up toward SIGURD.*) This is Sigurd.

BO

Yeah we talked to Sinner a bit. What have you found so far?

SIGURD

None of your concern. I don't need some sick puppy following me either.

ERIK

Apologies, but this is a very serious situation that I want to be sure is handled properly. I am quite skilled in tracking things—

SIGURD

Bah! If you want to stick around, then you can carry my bags. (*He drops his backpack into ERIK's arms. ERIK buckles underneath the weight. SIGURD addresses BO.*) You. What does the beast look like?

BO

It looks like some sort of reaper or banshee from what I've heard. One with huge claws and red eyes.

SIGURD

You ever see it?

BO

No, but I've heard from the people who have. Ziva's one of them, she lives here with Torrin.

VICE

Yeah, she says it's gray, with these really torn up clothes, and a hood over the most terrible face.

ERIK

Was it anything like a human?

BO

Ain't like any human I'd hear of. People've been hearing this most awful roar as well.

SIGURD

She ever tell you where this beast went?

HERALD

North, I think.

ERIK

(*Toward STAGE LEFT.*) Then we're going North.

SIGURD

Hold on. I'm the professional; I'll call the shots. (*A moment of silence before he points stage left.*) Let's go North.

(*BO, SIGURD, and ERIK hurry off STAGE LEFT. BLACK OUT.*)

Scene Seven

(*HELDI is reading a book on STAGE LEFT. KALIA enters STAGE RIGHT and politely clears her throat. HELDI looks up from her book.*)

HELDI

Sweetheart, how are you doing?

KALIA

I'm frightened, mother. What if the beast comes here?

HELDI

(*Grabs KALIA'S hand.*) If that happens—which I highly doubt—then I'll be here to protect you, Kalia.

KALIA

But how can you fight the beast?

HELDI

(*Points to a sword on the shelf.*) You see that? That sword can kill just about any-thing. I'm sure it can handle some simple beast. You won't get hurt by this monster.

(*KALIA nods, then looks at the book that HELDI was reading. She picks it up before HELDI can stop her.*)

KALIA

Mom ... what is this?

HELDI

Kalia, put that down.

KALIA

"Sorcery: How to Create and Command Wraiths?!" (*She backs away from HELDI with wide eyes.*) It was you! You created the beast!

HELDI

I really wish you hadn't seen that.

(*HELDI grabs the book and pushes KALIA through a door on STAGE LEFT. KALIA pounds on the wall OFFSTAGE.*)

KALIA

Mom! Mom, let me out!

HELDI

Don't worry, sweetheart. It'll be over soon.

(*BLACKOUT*)

Scene Eight

(*BO, ERIK, and SIGURD walk in from STAGE RIGHT. ERIK has the backpack on his shoulders. He bends over and puts his hands on his knees like he's tired. The cast OFFSTAGE begin to quietly make the beat from the first scene, growing louder.*)

ERIK

Please ... we've been walking for hours. Night's falling soon. Shouldn't we make camp?

SIGURD

If you can't handle it, then you can just stay behind. You are hindering my skills.

BO

By 'your skills' do you mean simply walking aimlessly toward the North?

SIGURD

It's worked for me in the past. Not anyone can earn the title of "Monster Slayer" like I can.

BO

Could've fooled me.

SIGURD

What'd you just say to me?!

(*There is a loud roar. Smoke rolls onto the stage. ERIK looks toward STAGE LEFT.*)

ERIK

Look! It's the beast!

(*The BEAST comes out STAGE LEFT, and knocks into SIGURD, causing him to drop his sword. BO runs forward and grabs the sword before the BEAST hits him back too.*)

ERIK

Bo! Sigurd! (*He falls back and scoots away as the BEAST comes closer. He looks on the ground, a little confused.*) You walk on the ground, but you leave no footprints. (*The BEAST stops. ERIK is breathing heavily.*) I know what you are.

(*The BEAST suddenly roars, rushing off STAGE LEFT.*)

BO

Erik! Are you okay?!

ERIK

Yeah! I know what that thing is! It's a wraith! They don't leave footprints, but they do leave behind a trail of sulfur. But they need to be created by someone.

SIGURD

(*Struggling off the ground.*) What?!

ERIK

It has a master!

BO

Who would be its master then?!

ERIK

Someone powerful. Someone who has to be really angry about something, angry with the entire kingdom! (*He straightens up.*) Like just finding out you've been cheated on. (*He gasped.*) That's why it didn't attack! She *recognized* me!

BO

Who're you talking about?

ERIK

The queen! She's the one doing this!

BO & SIGURD

The queen?!

ERIK

Yes, well … she's actually a sorceress.

SIGURD

You're saying all of this is caused by some woman? Impossible.

ERIK

The king is having an affair, and she has the power to create the beast. She must be attacking the kingdom as some sort of revenge! The castle isn't that far from here. She's going to try to kill the king! The princess might be in danger too!

SIGURD

I slay monsters, not girls!

ERIK

I'm sure about this!

BO

It's … kind of a stretch.

(*ERIK stares at both of them, who shake their heads, hesitant to trust ERIK'S word. He drops the backpack on the floor.*)

ERIK

Fine. I'm going to stop her. You go chase your tails! (*He angrily leaves STAGE LEFT.*)

SIGURD

(*Stares at the backpack, then shrugs and scoops it up.*) Looks like the squirrelly guy is gone. We can track it ourselves. Let's go.

(*SIGURD walks off STAGE LEFT. BO hesitantly follows. BLACK OUT.*)

Scene Nine
(*KALIA pounds on a wall OFFSTAGE.*)

KALIA

Help! Someone help me!

ERIK

(*Rushes in STAGE RIGHT. He looks at the door.*) Princess Kalia?

KALIA

Erik! I'm locked in here!

(*ERIK rushes to STAGE LEFT, kicking the door open. KALIA jumps through.*)

KALIA

Erik! It's my mother!

ERIK

I know, hide in your room until this is over.

KALIA

You don't plan to fight, do you?

ERIK

(*Pauses.*) I ... guess I do.

KALIA

(*Looks at the sword on the shelf, then grabs it.*) Then use this, you'll need a weapon.

(*ERIK nods, both exit STAGE LEFT.*)

Scene Ten
(*The scene is now cut in half. When things are happening on STAGE RIGHT, STAGE LEFT is frozen, and vice versa. A roar sounds as BO and SIGURD fall and roll across*

the ground from STAGE RIGHT. SIGURD stands as fast as he can and he points his sword as the BEAST enters STAGE RIGHT.)

SIGURD

My sword isn't working!

BO

Erik was right! It's heading for the castle!

SIGURD

Take this you monster! (*He swings his sword once more but is knocked down.*)

BO

Sigurd!

(*STAGE LEFT lights up. HELDI is standing and waiting with a smile as the KING enters STAGE LEFT.*)

KING

(*Slightly surprised.*) Oh, my dear. How thrilled am I to see your beautiful face.

HELDI

(*Bowing her head.*) And I yours, my king.

KING

Come on, Heldi. No need for titles when we are alone. (*The KING kisses the back of HELDI'S hand. She stares at him with a smile.*) You are my wife, after all.

HELDI

Very well, Jasce. (*Pauses for a moment.*) Does me being your wife actually mean anything to you? Or is that a pretty lie too?

KING

(*Hesitating, smiling nervously.*) ... What?

(*STAGE RIGHT. BO is now trying to fight the BEAST. SIGURD is trying to stand again.*)

BO

Get up! We need to fight it together!

(SIGURD lets out a battle cry, running at the BEAST with his sword. On STAGE LEFT, ERIK enters, breathing fast.)

ERIK

Your Majesty! Get away from her!

(HELDI looks at ERIK. Before the KING can turn away, she places a hand on his forehead. He drops to the ground.)

HELDI

Erik, you ruined all the fun.

ERIK

Stop this, Your Majesty! No more people need to die!

HELDI

He does! He broke my heart! I like you Erik. My daughter likes you. Don't make me kill you, too.

ERIK

(Raises his sword.) I get that you're angry, but think of Kalia! You're taking away her father!

HELDI

He is no longer her father! He is no longer my husband!

(STAGE RIGHT, the BEAST roars, clawing into BO and SIGURD. They drop.)

BO

(Pained) It's going to go straight through the castle wall!

Scene Eleven
(The two sides now combine as the BEAST jumps to STAGE LEFT. The beating begins once more.)

HELDI

He ruined my life, I ruined his kingdom. He broke my heart, and now I'll break him.

ERIK

No!

(*The BEAST roars again as it dives to attack the sleeping KING, and ERIK runs forward, swinging his sword. The sword makes contact and there is a hiss as the BEAST stumbles back. HELDI looks at ERIK in shock, then sees his sword.*)

HELDI

I recognize that sword.

ERIK

You should. It's yours.

(*As SIGURD runs toward STAGE LEFT with his sword, HELDI raises her arms up.*)

HELDI

Fine! I'll just kill you all myself!

(*At the same time, ERIK stabs the BEAST, and SIGURD stabs through HELDI from behind. The BEAST roars, and HELDI looks down at the sword. The BEAST and HELDI fall to the ground at the same time, and a moment of silence passes.*)

SIGURD

I ... I just slayed a woman!

(*BLACK OUT*)

CRITICAL ESSAY

A Conscientious Republic

BROOKE ADAM

Grade 12, North Star High School, Lincoln, NE.

The United States is a constitutional federal republic, guaranteeing that people vote to elect government representatives. In doing so, American citizens forsake their right to a direct democracy in order to be represented by elected citizens. I believe that members of Congress should vote their conscience, assuming that they are fueled by patriotism and justice.

Immediately, some may argue that elected leaders in a representative democracy must only be a voice for their constituents. On this topic, the recent effort to switch Nebraska to a winner-takes-all electoral system just before the 2024 presidential election comes to mind. Nebraska District 5 Senator Mike McDonnell, a Democrat turned Republican who represents part of the battleground Omaha area—a blue dot in a sea of Nebraska red—stood firm against other Republicans in the middle of a pressure campaign to make this shift before the presidential election. Because McDonnell was decisive in siding with his constituents—Omaha residents who likely petitioned him not to vote for this bill—Nebraska was able to uphold our distinct allocation of electoral college votes, maintaining the commitment to provide "all Nebraskans an equal voice in choosing our president" (Dunker). To me, this is a brave and exemplary act of representation which leaders do not always take. Voting against one's party is a choice that politicians hesitate to make, especially when faced with such pressure from out-of-state interests to influence a bill. McDonnell went with what he knew was right at the time, which is why I stand with elected representatives voting their conscience. I interpret this situation as McDonnell voting what he knew was the righteous decision—a surefire act of conscience. The will of the people rightfully informed his thought process, but the ultimate decision falls at the hands of our leaders. If we can't depend upon the judgment of those that we have entrusted so much as to elect into office, our entire representative democracy falls apart.

When our forefathers constructed this country as a republic rather than a pure democracy, they did so with purpose, ensuring that no citizen's voice may be left unheard. Elected representatives who pronounce the public voice are "more consonant to the public good" (Hamilton) than the public voice itself, because they achieve a more holistic representation of the people. We entrust our representatives because their established wisdom coupled with public opinion "may best discern the true interest of their country" (Hamilton), rather than strictly favor any majority, being that the will of the society and majority are made separate. Federalist 51 highlights the concern of the will of the majority being wielded over the entire country, so as to totally subvert the power of the minority, and proposes that the only solution will come by "introducing into the government a will independent of the society itself." That is, creating a set of principles that guide the nation and are not subject to ever-changing public opinion. I perceive this to be the principles of the Constitution and Declaration of Independence: a just and consensual limited government which maintains order and secures the unalienable rights of all people. While this cause, the founding force of a nation, stands true through time, public opinion is vulnerable to change. It was the Declaration of Independence that Martin Luther King Jr. cited in his "I Have a Dream" speech, not the words of the overwhelmingly white majority. These universal ideals, those that feel just right in our souls, are the ones that we must look to, even above the will of the people, which is precarious by nature.

We have a duty to our country, and it is to uphold these truly American principles that stand as a testimony to the foresight of strongly educated leaders who feel succumbed to benevolence and are brave enough to be it. Members of Congress must vote their conscience to follow in our forefathers' footsteps and sustain these values.

Works Cited

Dunker, Chris. "Daily Minute: Winner-Take-All Effort Stalls; Blomstedt to Lobby for NU; Gottula Impresses Rhule." *Journal Star*, 24 Sept. 2024, journalstar.com/news/state-regional/nebraska-winner-take-all-electoral-vote/article_cffd2ca2-79d5-11ef-a2f6-f34bfd559d44.html. Accessed 2 Dec. 2024.

Hamilton, Alexander. "No. 10 Madison." *Federalist Papers*, edited by Clinton Rossiter, New American Library, 1961, pp. 77–84.

CHILDREN SHOULD BE HEARD AND SEEN

A Student's Battle Cry for Agency in Education Amidst the Fight for Student Engagement

ARABELLA RICHLING

Grade 9, Grand Island Central Catholic School, Grand Island, NE. Honorable Mention.

In the classrooms of modern America, education is at war with its students, but it's neither the system's nor the students' fault. The story is much more complicated. If I were to open the door to a classroom, I might see rows of students sitting in chairs, backpacks propped up against their desks, and a teacher writing words or numbers across a whiteboard. Some things about this room may change, like the posters on the wall, the state of the teacher's desk, or the subject scrawled across the board. Some students may get sick and miss a day or extra students may fill in during study hall hours. The thoughts behind the students are similar, trained on the words of the teacher. Yet, lingering within the walls of their minds are thoughts that travel far beyond the formulas they are learning or the stories they are reading.

The education system is often treated as a solvent to fix the problems that many youth experience, but this is not its task. Sometimes, people may also see the system as an enemy, wishing to abandon it because it does not fit their ideals. However, the school system is neither a solvent nor an enemy. Its task is to serve students in their education, to provide them with standards to excel at, and to offer relief where it is possible through transportation or free lunch services. This imaginary classroom above is a microcosm of the contemporary system as many students are failing to engage in their studies. The words and formulas before them feel so much smaller than the problems they are facing: the near stress of a game later that day, the question of who will be picking them up from school, or something more serious like the thought of an illness their grandmother is facing. It is difficult to care when so much is on your mind.

Students need to understand not just that the education system cares for them but that they can care for their education system. Elevating student voices and concerns about their experiences in the classroom is vital for students. Providing students with agency is a difficult task. However, it is essential because students' focus is fading in and out, not just during class but also throughout school days. Their education runs second to their concerns, but, if we place students at the heart of the problem, they may find themselves at the pulse of what matters to them.

Students and teachers alike put an immense amount of effort into the work they do, as well as the policymakers and principals whose efforts place students at the forefront of their thoughts when they are making decisions. No one is at fault for not encompassing student voices. Yet, it is essential for students to feel included in the decisions that are being made. The focus of this essay is on the importance of connecting students to their learning through student agency and streamlined processes of advocacy.

Building a connection between learning in the classroom and the students who feel disengaged is crucial. Many students want to take ownership of their educational journey. Allowing students to have a say in how they learn or what they focus on makes students more likely to stay engaged and motivated. The 2024 Gallup and Walton Family Foundation Student Report Card shows that a student survey gave schools an average of a B ("Report Card 2024"). While this score is generally in line with standards, it reflects areas for growth.

About a quarter of students from this poll awarded the school system an A, but many more students gave it a C as well. This coincides with socioeconomic disparities where students in lower-income brackets tended to rank their educational experience lower. For students in these situations, school may be the last thing on their minds. If students cannot control their home situation, they may be able to have agency at school, giving them control over their world which may be the difference in that student's life.

During their formative years, students want to know that they are listened to by the people around them, but many students will not get this experience anywhere but the school system. Fostering not just a great education system but a great connection to this system is the bridge schools need to cross. Even for students in higher-income brackets, a connection to their education is something that may be difficult for them to manage. Whether they are handling personal issues or simply struggling to be passionate about learning, student agency provides students with the chance to be involved, forming a deeper connection between what they love and what they learn.

Additionally, a streamlined process of advocacy is critical. If students continue to feel as if their voices are ignored, it may also negatively affect personal well-being. In some school systems, the effects of a disengaged school population are being felt. Featured in *The New York Times*, the story of a school shutting down a newspaper following the publication of an LGBTQ issue became a discussion among many students in classrooms nationwide (Medina). In the wake of the incident, many students advocated for the reinstatement of their newspaper. They pleaded with the school administration, noting that the journalism team had earned the highest award it had ever earned only a few months before the paper was shut down. Former staff of the paper reached out to national newspapers to spread the story. Repeated contact with the administration showed an initially unresponsive team whose eventual answer did not satisfy the students.

While the administration was possibly handling many other situations and may not have had the proper resources to reinstate the paper, the fact remained that many students felt harmed by the situation. They expressed confusion as to whether this was a personal attack or whether the administration had proper reasons that were not expressed clearly to the staff. The continued advocacy for the paper to remain at the school was largely ignored. In this case, student voices and personal well-being were harmed, even if that was not the intention of the school. Providing students with a streamlined process of advocacy is essential to creating an environment that is not just academically rigorous but also inclusive, supportive, and adaptable.

To begin revolutionizing education, we must first listen to the students – the ones who sit in the classrooms, carry the weight of the rigorous standards, and experience the failures and successes of this system. As a product of the education system, I had to learn that school is so much more than tests and grades; school is about truly learning and how students feel in the environments they're supposed to thrive in. Students shouldn't feel like their voices have been muted. Students should be valued, heard, and motivated through feedback and open dialogue. Fostering a place for student voices and inclusivity is something I believe can truly impact the effectiveness of the education system. When I think of my educational journey, I think about the feeling of empowerment I received from the times when I was given a chance to vocalize my thoughts and opinions. Every student deserves this feeling. While providing an outlet for students' voices is the first step, making students feel like a priority in their education is the next.

References

Medina, Eduardo. "Nebraska School Shuts down Student Newspaper after L.G.B.T.Q. Publication." *The New York Times*, 29 Aug. 2022, www.nytimes.com/2022/08/29/us/nebraska-lgbt-school-newspaper-closed.html.

"Report Card 2024: America's Students Grade Their Schools." *Walton Family Foundation*, 25 June 2024, www.waltonfamilyfoundation.org/learning/report-card-2024-americas-students-grade-their-schools.

THE PREVALENCE OF RACISM
IN MODERN SOCIETY

LYDIA TURNER

Grade 11, Parkview Christian School, Lincoln, NE. Honorable Mention.

Modern society is based on and around racism. From slavery and segregation to the stereotypes and the families of poverty, all of it is connected through racism. For a long time even medical studies and procedures were based around racism. Many people claim to not be racist—they'll say they would never and have never acted in a racist way. They do—everyone does. Racism is something so deep-rooted in society at this point that many don't even realize that what they're doing is racist. Or rather, everything they do can be perceived as racist, no matter how innocent it really is. In our society we are constantly on a tightrope, watching our words and actions. Racism isn't going away anytime soon; it's embedded in our society from our history to the modern day.

Racism is relatively modern, not appearing in society until around the sixteenth century. Racism came hand in hand with "Racial Hierarchies" and went as far as "denying their humanity" (Walker and Meade). Slavery was the most prominent type of racism in the past—and the most cruel. In fact, people of color, especially black people, would have their souls "stolen" and then they would be sold off to white people (Walker and Meade). Paganism was also a key factor in much of racism's roots. As people in the ancient world were unaware of the large majority of the world's population, cultural and religious practices varied vastly—and many churches have been known to be corrupt. The Christian Bible says that a human has Spirit, Soul, and Body—without a soul it is believed you had no mental consciousness, and belief in more than one God— more than the God of Christianity—meant you worshipped the devil. That meant you had no connection to God the spirit and if you had no soul on top of that, back then that would be grounds for being treated as inhuman. On top of being judged and hated for their religion or religious practices, people of color were viewed as less developed and perceived to have the mentality of a child. Slave owners would use this idea to further their claims that black people could not support themselves financially.

Racism today looks vastly different than it did in the past, and this is due to the scientific advancements. Today we now know that all humans are the same species and that skin color is determined by the amount of melanin a person possesses. Race is not real, yet we continue to partake in racism. Rather than active racism, however, the most common type of racism in the modern world is passive racism. Passive racism is simply claiming to "not see race" or as some have put it "not see color." The people of today don't actively search to make racist comments or implications; however, they also choose to ignore or even promote harmful stereotypes and ideas. They continue to be indulged and when obviously racist incidents—such as police violence—occur, many often find another cause or explanation for what happened, which completely ignores and invalidates the trauma which comes along with those instances. People of color can't even call others out for being racist because then it all circles back. Racism has bled into every aspect of today's society, both obvious and hidden. TV shows often promote these stereotypes with utmost subtlety. These interactions and showcases of racism dictate your inner thoughts and emotions—they show you what they think people of color may act like and in turn you come to expect it. It is so deep-rooted in the world as a whole that racism may never go away. It will most likely be there, bubbling just under the surface of society, forever. Racism has evolved and become the norm for so long that it's impossible to not be racist.

Racism is ever evolving and ever present. In the past it was active—it was easy to see but now it's faded to the shadows. It's silent now, and everything you do can be taken as racism given the right circumstances. You can't be actively racist—people will see. So instead society has decided to let past stereotypes evolve into what they are today. In the past we saw black people as wild and uncontrollable. Then they were treated as stupid and inhuman. Then they were posed as violent criminals. Now we expect them to be self-sufficient. We expect them to be bold and brash, and not elegant; we don't expect them to need a shoulder to cry on. Society had turned its back on people of color in the past and now they have turned their backs on society. Slavery set the roots for racism in the modern day. When the United States Government ended slavery, people of color were still oppressed. They had the same rights as white people, in theory; however, segregation and new regulations on voting wouldn't give colored people a fair chance. On top of that, white people who had once been slave owners would pay the colored people to still work there. Many colored people didn't receive an education, so many couldn't read, and due to slavery almost none of them had much money. This lack of money and education as well as segregation has made it so that it was far harder for people of color to gain financial wealth. This lack of wealth, then, has still carried over to today as many black neighborhoods are considered low-end neighborhoods, compared to neighborhoods that are a majority white people. White people expect people of color to prefer being around their own race. Many expect others to be self-sufficient. People get angry if white people try to help, calling them racist. From being called racist, white people will stop trying to interact and that disconnection becomes fuel for stereotypes.

Racism has become a foundation of our society—it's in our past and still persists in our present society. Trying to extract it is possibly more dangerous than leaving it be. If we ignore the experiences of colored people, it invalidates them. If we fight these experiences, it draws attention to racism—and if we draw attention to it people try to find alternative explanations—excuses. Society has become dependent on racism. Racism can't be fought. It's a battle that can't be won—it's an eternal draw, forever stuck in a standstill against one another. If society tries to talk about racism, it gets brought up again, and then people get upset and turn on one another again. People will turn on each other and fight. If you're not careful with your actions or words, people will claim you're being racist. It is so prevalent in society that it has become a verbal weapon. They will use racism as a weapon and return the racism to white people—or even other nationalities. White people, black people, Asian people, Indian people, Native Americans, everyone experiences racism still today. Racism is, has always been, the seed of xenophobia—the fear of people different from oneself. The color of the skin was never the problem; it was the people wearing the skin who were the problem.

Works Cited

Pfeifer, Jeffrey E., and Daniel J. Bernstein. "Expressions of Modern Racism in Judgments of Others: The Role of Task and Target Specificity on Attributions of Guilt." *Social Behavior & Personality: An International Journal*, vol. 31, no. 8, Dec. 2003, pp. 749–66. *EBSCOhost*, doi.org/10.2224/sbp.2003.31.8.749.

Walker, Randolph Meade. "Racism: History of the Concept." *Salem Press Encyclopedia*, Oct. 2024. *EBSCOhost*, research.ebsco.com/linkprocessor/plink?id=98304ce2-6901-31e4-94ab-0230ff77bd15.

PERSONAL ESSAY & MEMOIR

SWEET DRIPS

Listen

BROOKE ADAM

Grade 12, North Star High School, Lincoln, NE.

SILVER

Dodging sticks and small crabs, I sprint barefoot to the shore. Once I reach that Goldilocks spot, close enough to let the brisk ocean waves greet the soles of my feet, and far enough that the water can't cascade up my legs, I ground my toes into the sand. Gazing upon the horizon before me, I inhale fresh salt and exhale gratitude with every breath; this is life. The sun beats a sting on my forehead, but the sweet California breeze equalizes its force.

My mom drags my sister and me to the Golden State every summer that she can find an excuse: a wedding, three graduations, maybe her uncle's wife's nephew returning from school in London. This never matters to me, because I already know what I'm there for: restaurants for every culture and cuisine, steadfast warmth filling the air, and unfortunate hours spent stagnant in traffic. Luckily, my uncle was a taxi driver in the city for 20 years, so he knows his way around.

It's impossible to be bored on a drive with my uncle. I'd say that he has a story for every street corner in Los Angeles, but his kids would just laugh. While my cousins see their father talking endlessly about some socioeconomic disaster that somehow personally impacts their lives, I see myself getting a sliver of quality time with the closest thing to a father figure that I ever had. My uncle, the person that made me love California, he who taught me the beautiful ins and outs of the most magical place I've ever known.

My uncle, Anteneh, is a generational learner, an *it takes one to know one* kind of guy. He's that kind of old person that possesses full-bodied, empirical knowledge that can't be learned inside any textbook. Real history, like how the avarice of big corporations led Uber lobbyists to run self-employed taxi drivers to the ground. Family heritage, including him receiving George H. W Bush's Diversity Visa, initiating my family's eventual migration to the U.S. Maybe even curious habits, like recognizing cars illegally driving without catalytic converters by paying close attention to the sounds of passerby engine sputters on the sardine-packed I-5. I love hearing little drips of my uncle's sweet wealth of knowledge, so I listen.

I listen to my calculus professor who thinks himself qualified to be an amateur electrician, just like my uncle. I share a smile with my substitute teacher from San Diego who insists that I'll go far in life, just like my uncle. I get to know the fellow food market volunteer that tells me about growing up in a small Nebraska town, building wealth the Warren Buffet way, and visiting the affluent California community of Walnut Creek. I seek to experience all of the "shades, tones, and variations of mental and physical experience possible in my life," yet "I am horribly limited" (Sylvia Plath). Truthfully, I cannot be everyone and everywhere that I wish. So I listen, and I leave Lincoln, Nebraska, to head out west every chance I get. And when I step out onto that damp sand, soaking in the breeze and the sounds of the sea spanning its song across thousands of miles and millions of years, I grow harmonious with the omniscient Earth that binds us all. While that blood orange sunset will always bring me to my knees, it is the people and the experiences rooted in an everlasting desire for discovery that drive me in this life.

Because It Is My Name

BROOKE ADAM

Grade 12. North Star High School, Lincoln, NE. Honorable Mention.

From tumultuous political events to rich cultural history, my six letters pack a punch. I was born as Brooke on October 1st, 2008. I like to say that I represent a kind of kairos, entering the world just one month before the monumental 2008 election. My mom's primary reason for naming me Brooke was that "Brooke is Barack. At the time we were so hopeful for the first ever black president. We weren't sure that Barack would win, but we put our faith in him, and glad we did." I'm proud to know that my birth was a mark of such a monumental time in American history, and I carry that legacy with me every time that I write my name down. My mom recalls, "There was such an uproar about his unique name, but Barack is Brooke in our language." Not only did she mean to recognize that Barack is so similar to Brooke in English, but Brooke holds significance in our home as well.

Both of my parents were born and raised in Ethiopia, a country nestled in the horn of Africa and home to a plethora of languages. In Amharic, the country's most commonly spoken language, the name "Brooke means blessed. You are blessed to be in the company of your mom," she jokes with me. Really, my mom believes the name Brooke means to be "blessed to have a life, blessed to be healthy." I am blessed to call Nebraska my home, a simple land of smiles and sandhills. I have belonged to the Lincoln Public Schools district since I started kindergarten at 4 years old, and I am forever grateful for my initial experiences here.

Just after dismissal on a fateful 2015 Tuesday, I was sent to wait in my elementary school's office until called into the conference room. Looking from the corporate-carpet floor to the sterile chairs that lined the office window-walls, to the secretaries typing away at eternity on their keyboards, I was completely unsuspecting. Just in time to ease my anxieties, the unsuspecting door at the end of the hallway glided open. Surprisingly, my eyes met with the Student Coordinator, and she welcomed me to the room with a smile on her face. Is this how they treat kids before suspending them? I had no idea how to state my case.

Stepping through the doorway, I was directed to the only empty seat at the head of an eerily long conference table. Around me, my past teachers and school admin lined the table, staring contentedly at my unsure expression. Straight across from me, Principal Jablonski peered into my soul before finally uttering my name.

"*Brooke*, you're moving to second grade."

Because of my academic capability, spotlighted by my incessant complaints over the ease of first grade, and through my mother's willful petition, I was formally recognized as highly gifted by my school district. By the next day, I left all of my friends behind for the second grade, and by the next year, I was taking accelerated math coursework separate from my peers. Much unlike the fate of other outstanding children that bear the same shades and tones as me, my divergence was honored. I was fortunate enough to possess such capability and be nurtured for it. I was favored with blessings that had been carried from the highlands of Ethiopia to the heartland of America by way of my name, an omnipresent reminder of the lengths that faith and good fortune can stretch.

Ethiopia, a country mentioned in all Abrahamic texts, serves as a melting pot of Christianity, Islam, and traditional spiritual beliefs, and boasts a deep-rooted religious history. There, Brooke, or rather Biruke, is a common name for its comprehensive meaning, yet it is entirely a boy's name. Much like other aspects of the patriarchy, excessive traditionalism saved the pinnacle of spirituality for men, barring women from being similarly blessed and instead allowing them to be Hana, graceful—the name of my older sister.

My mom wanted to teach us differently, both by pushing me to the top of my STEM classes and naming me Brooke. She liked to say that the name could be used for both girls and boys, but judging by the looks that many, many relatives gave me after I introduced myself to them as Brooke, however, she was definitely sugarcoating it. "We sure thought you would be a boy, but then we found out you were a girl. I was in love with the name, and I made a choice to keep it. Anyway, Brooke is a girl's name in America. We always wanted our children's names to work in both America and Ethiopia," she explains to me. I like to think that my name represents my mom's willingness for nonconformity. My sister and I were probably the first babies in our bloodline that attended sleepovers and didn't have their ears pierced as newborns. After coming to America, my mom made a distinctive choice to diverge from the conservatism that swallowed her lifestyle back home. Still, I was born Brooke Michael

Mengiste, Michael being my dad's first name and Mengiste sharing his surname, a common practice in African and Middle Eastern cultures.

My peers at my homogenous Nebraskan elementary school never understood this, though. Not just the silliness of sharing names with my dad, but my perplexing last name. Any time my friends asked me how to say it, a precocious smile spread across my face, and I relayed my preset reply: "You can guess all you want, but I'll only tell if someone gets it right." Meanwhile, I prayed and predicted, with good reason, that nobody would decrypt my last name, in hopes of saving myself from an inevitable interrogation after professing its correct pronunciation: Mung-ist-ay, a grotesque needle among a haystack of "Menjist?" "Men-geist?" "Menjistu?" Their native-born interpretation of English completely clashed with that of whoever designed my name, I thought. While my friends wasted away at the impossible task, I cursed whoever transcribed my last name into English. Luckily for him, my father hadn't stuck around to feel my wrath.

My parents divorced two years earlier, ultimately carving a dad-sized hole out of every aspect of my life. My father left our family to return to Ethiopia, and I was left baseless to defend my honor against my apparently vulgar last name. As soon as my mom could, which wound up being years later, she legally changed my last name to hers, revoking my dad's claim on the life that she built for me. While I was young and my mom was still going through this legal process, she eased my concerns by assuring me that my name was being changed to be seated together on airplanes as a family, as if cabin seats are organized in alphabetical order. I knew better than to believe that then, but nowadays I get the closure of her admitting that I was made to be Brooke Adam to help me succeed in school or my future career. My mom took the Adamu of her maiden name and etched off the "u" to make my last name Adam, a reformation fit for the refined western palate. She couldn't stand to pass onto me the struggle of being denied interviews due to the richness of her name. Because of my mom's foresight, I have never had to face the decision of altering myself to be more digestible for others. That agreeable person is who I am yet, a morphed silhouette of myself straddled between two worlds, belonging to everything but beholden to nothing.

My name doesn't match my face, nor anyone in my family. But art doesn't have to conform to a finite purpose to be perfect. I love my little name, the way that the o's are nestled between the tall towers formed by characters on either side, like each four digits of my birthday, 1001 2008. I adore the symmetry of it all, embodying the passion for math that rumbles inside of me. My reputation as a smart cookie gave me the childhood nickname Brooke Cookie, but I enjoy not having nicknames anymore. I'm just Brooke, who used to be Brooke Mengiste but now holds Adam as a last name and doesn't feel bound to claim what others say. I choose to enjoy it, because it is my name, because I cannot have another in my life.

I accept that my name is a one-syllable symphony, and its simple sound doesn't denounce me to insignificance. Upon further reflection, my name reveals that its development was a layered process with notable depth attached to it, and I should treat it as such. I want to be sure that once I'm reduced to references of my life's legacy, others understand that Brooke Adam was a spirited person filled with gratitude for the distinct experiences that shaped her. After I'm gone, I can't decide if I want my name to be retired like an extraordinary athlete's jersey or ubiquitous like the Jordan logo. Either way, my reputation is my own. I can only hope it won't be tainted by just any rookie.

My Heart Is Undecided

Emily Alison

SILVER

Grade 10, Millard North High School, Omaha, NE.

My name is Emily. My real name, Rawan. My blood is Iraqi, my accent, American. But when asked about my heart, undecided.

Growing up, I was the fortunate one. Among my extended family, my parents were the lucky pair who secured a future in America. The land of dreams, opportunity, and, as I was often reminded, the land of fitting in. But fitting in was the one thing that constantly eluded me.

As a child, the world around me was a blend of Arabic lullabies and English nursery rhymes. My parents would sing me to sleep with songs of a homeland I barely remembered, while my teacher would read me stories of American heroes and their grand adventures. At school, I was Emily. I played tag, shared my lunch, and laughed with my classmates. But at home, I was Rawan, a name that felt foreign on my own tongue, a name that carried the weight of a culture that sometimes felt as distant as the stars.

The hijab was my constant companion, which acted as my silent proclamation of faith and identity. Yet, it was also my biggest challenge. In the hallways of my fully white school, it was a beacon, drawing eyes and whispers. "Why do you wear that?" they'd ask, curiosity mingling with misunderstanding. I would smile, offer a rehearsed explanation, and move on, but inside, I felt the sting of being different. The fabric of my hijab felt heavy, not from its weight, but from the burden of the questions, the stares, and the whispers it invited.

Western media didn't help. Stories of hijabs were often laced with tales of oppression and exoticism. My hijab, a symbol of my faith and choice, was reduced to a headline, a stereotype. I would watch these portrayals and feel a mix of anger and sadness. They didn't see the beauty, the pride, the strength it took to wear it every day. Before I hadn't realized, but it was a barrier from the bad and a crown that I would wear as a constant reminder of my purpose in this world. There isn't any shame in holding such a title: a walking, visual representation of my beautiful religion.

Starting high school was a turning point. I remember a particular incident during my class discussion on the Middle East. An ignorant classmate approached

PERSONAL ESSAY & MEMOIR   353

me and said, "my grandfather fought and killed your people in Iraq." Feeling no sense of emotion, those words rolled off his tongue so easily. It felt like a punch to the gut. Did people really think like this? Were "my people" nothing more than faceless targets in a war, reduced to enemies in a conflict they never chose?

His words hung in the air, heavy and suffocating. The classroom fell silent, all eyes on me. I could feel the weight of their gazes, the curious stares, the unspoken questions. My hands trembled, and my throat tightened, as if the air itself had turned against me. It was a moment that seemed to stretch into eternity, a moment that threatened to break me.

Memories of my family flooded my mind—my grandparents who had lived through the war, my parents who had sacrificed everything to bring us to safety. I thought of the stories my father had told me, of friends lost and dreams shattered, of the resilience and strength it took to survive. I thought of my mother's tears, shed for a homeland she was forced to flee from. And now, here I was, faced with the casual cruelty of a classmate who had no understanding of the pain he had just inflicted.

I took a deep breath, trying to steady myself. I could have lashed out, let my anger consume me, but instead, I chose a different path. I stood up, my voice trembling but resolute. "Do you even know what you're saying?" I began, my words cutting through the silence like a blade. "What do you mean 'my people'? He obviously went there to fight the terrorists, which were harming the Iraqis, and those are not my people." I realized that this was the true reality of the Iraqis. People viewed them as harmful terrorists and targets in war. What they need to know is my people are not just numbers. They are fathers, mothers, children—human beings with dreams, hopes, and stories.

I looked around the room, meeting the eyes of my classmates. In that moment, I realized the power of my voice, the strength of my identity. I wasn't just defending myself; I was standing up for my heritage, my family, and everyone who had ever faced such ignorance.

That day marked a turning point for me, where I began to embrace my dual identity. I started a Muslim Student Association, where we celebrated diversity, shared stories, and learned about each other's backgrounds. It wasn't always easy. There were still whispers, still stares, but there were also moments of connection, of understanding.

Today, I wear my hijab with pride. It's a part of me, just as much as my American accent and my Iraqi blood. I've learned that fitting in doesn't mean losing myself. It means embracing every part of who I am, even the parts that seem contradictory. My name is Emily, but I am also Rawan. I am American, and I am Iraqi. My heart, once undecided, now embraces both worlds, finding strength in their union.

In a society that often demands conformity, I've found power in my uniqueness. My journey has taught me that identity is not a choice between two worlds but a beautiful blend of both. And that is something truly worth celebrating.

My Closure

TAYLOR DOUCHEY

Grade 11, Fort Calhoun Junior/Senior High School, Fort Calhoun, NE. Sara Gross, Educator. Honorable Mention.

Loss is defined as the state of feeling of grief when deprived of someone or something of value. Every person experiences a form of loss at some point in their life. Some people have this experience; young or old, prepared or unprepared. I had to experience this young and unsuspecting: this is my story.

From the earliest I could remember, I was a daddy's girl. We were constantly joined at the hip. I'd go to work with him; he was a construction worker. Running around the construction zone with him created so many laughs and smiles. He used to work at the zoo, constructing the new enclosures. It was well known in second grade that you got to go on a field trip to the zoo; it was the most anticipated field trip. All of the kids were so excited to go to the zoo, but as soon as we got there it was canceled because of the smoke in the air. Once my father learned this, he came and checked me out for the day. We spent all day exploring the zoo together. He showed me their construction sites, and I got to go wherever I wanted. One year for Christmas, I asked for my very own pink hard hat and work shirts. I got my baby pink hard hat and loved it. I placed stickers on it and gave it a special spot on my shelf. That was one of my most treasured gifts, until seeing that hard hat brought me the worst memories. I was nine years old when my father left us, and my life changed forever.

Since before I was born, my father had struggled with a drug addiction. After his children were born, he still continued to use drugs. As we got older many aspects changed, like when I was around 7 our grandparents had custody of us while our parents were in rehab. Our parents got custody of us again, after approximately six months. Many things changed around this time. We moved back in with our parents, my brother went to a different school, and we got our own rooms, but I never spent time in mine. Our parents did fight a lot, but we all had our own ways of ignoring it. Sometimes the fights were less prominent and sometimes they were more influential. After one specific time, my parents had us all sit in the living room, in front of my father. He apologized to us and told us that he would work on himself and become better. We were all promised something, mine was that he would teach me to ride a bike. That was something that I never learned how to do. After many scenarios like this one, my mother had noticed some differences in my father and discovered he was still using drugs. She made the best choice for her kids; she decided that if he couldn't get clean then he didn't need to be in our lives. I'm not sure how my father felt about this decision, but he didn't get clean. When my father didn't get clean, he chose drugs over his own family.

As a little kid, you don't understand what is happening very well. You get that your father isn't there, but you don't exactly know why. You understand that you miss him, but you can't really see him. The world around me kept evolving, but I was not ready for it; maybe I was never ready for it. There are so many conditions that change, but no explanation is given for them. There are also many circumstances you witness happen. I watched as my mother became a single mom and tried her hardest to take care of us. I watched as my sister had struggled with mental illness, but no one knew how to help her. I also sat there as I changed and slowly learned pieces to everything.

As the baby in the family, everyone wants to protect you. They don't realize how confused they leave you. You get left in the dark over and over again, never really knowing why. There are a lot of things I don't remember from my childhood; I have very few memories. Oftentimes I question if I just have a terrible memory or if this was my brain's response to trauma. It is something that I'll never be aware of. One notion I was told by my mother is that after my father left us I was mad at her because I thought it was her fault. Hearing this now, being older and understanding the situation, it breaks my heart. My mother was trying her hardest to do what was right for her babies, but I was mad at her for that.

My sister had developed a mental illness around this time. My mother and grandmother tried their hardest to be there for her, but they didn't know what to do. They didn't know exactly what was happening or how to help her. They were also confused and trying to navigate their way through this new, changed life. Sometimes they didn't handle the situations in the greatest way, and I always wish I could help my sister feel better. Over time my sister got the help she needed and many things changed. There was no arguing or crying; my sister was herself again. Even when my sister was struggling with her own problems, she never failed to be there for me. I remember crying to her when I missed our dad, or doing random things together when we couldn't sleep late at night. She was one of my greatest support systems at this time in my life. She was there for me through my pain, even though she was going through the same thing. She didn't have someone to help her through it like I did, but she still decided to be there for me. I love her so much for everything she did for me.

As you get older and time moves on, people stop caring about what happened. I felt as if we didn't talk about it or we acknowledged it less. My wound may have not been visible, but it still hurts like hell. I couldn't talk about the pain, though, because I felt like I couldn't. I thought it was weird if I still missed my father or thought about the good times with him. It also felt so weird to want him back when it felt like everyone else was mad at him. I felt as if I should've been enraged at him too, but I was still so sorrowful. When I felt like my emotions were so different from everyone else, I never shared my emotions. I basically isolated myself. I was so sad for so long, there were certain things I couldn't do. For the longest time, I couldn't listen to music because whenever I would, it would make me cry. And I could never cry because that would show emotion, and I never wanted to do that. Being open with my feelings was something that disappeared over time.

As I grew older, I learned that having emotions is okay. I had struggled over and over again, more and more. I felt so alone for so long until I finally realized I didn't have to be. I knew holding in all of my thoughts and feelings was a bad idea, so I slowly started opening up to the people around me. It was incredibly weird at first, bringing up myself and saying my emotions out loud. Every day it gets gradually easier. I still struggle from time to time. But, I know overall, no matter how I feel, it's okay to feel that way. I also learned that pondering the what-ifs wasn't bad. It's okay to be curious and wonder what your life would have been like. If he would've stayed, if he would've left earlier, what if I would have been different? I'll never know the answers to these questions, but they all float around my mind. Since I finally learned to feel comfortable with myself and my thoughts, I was able to be happier and build closer connections to the people around me.

Loss is such a weird thing to experience. Grief is even weirder and confusing to experience. At some point in everyone's life they are going to experience a loss that changes them, no matter what, or how, they want it to. It can change them for the better, or for the worse. This was my experience with loss, and over time I like to think it changed me for the better.

NO SOUL

MIAH FOX

SILVER

Grade 12, Paxton Consolidated School, Paxton, NE.

One, two, three, four ...

There was a time when I did not know myself. A time when I looked in the mirror and found nothing but someone borrowing a body in hopes of living on the Earth for just one more day.

Five ... six ... seven ... eight ...

I was an object just waiting for the next hour to pass by. I remember looking at myself and believing that it was impossible that I was real, that it was impossible that such a person would be conscious of this world we call our home.

One ... two ... three ... four ...

I would spend hours a day, counting each of the tiles in the ceiling of my room, forward and backward, across and diagonally. I always forgot the answer when I was done, and then I would need to start again.

Eight ... seven ... six ...

I hardly considered myself someone worthy of anyone's time, for I hardly considered myself worthy of my own. I felt like I was a computer without the feelings of mortals, a shell without any desires or wants.

One ... two ...

That wasn't quite true, I suppose. I did have one desire, something so ingrained in my bones that to deny it would be like trying to clench a hand tightly around a pile of sand, only for it to slip through my fingers and fall to the earth to expose itself to the world. It was a desire as clear as the number of tiles above my head, one I would forget, only to encounter its certainty once more.

It was those little questions. The little questions that your teachers would ask in attempts to make you think about your future, the questions a new friend would ask in an attempt to find common ground. The questions my parents would ask to try to understand the daughter that seemed to catch them off guard. I would always carry the same answer to all those little questions. Questions about my biggest passions, my biggest talents, my biggest values. It was an answer that came without thought, an answer that was so instinctual, that I believed I must've been born with it, perhaps even born *for* it.

Writing.

To write was to feel the small little bumps across the page made with the ink from your pen. To write was to graze your fingers across the keys of the computer and hear the sound of its letters splitting into the air. To write was to smell pencil lead until your palms were as gray as the storm outside the window. Writing was to immortalize the things of old and create things anew. Writing was to be able to remember the amount of tiles in the room even when the mind failed you.

Long before I learned how to be literate, before I even uttered the words of the ABC's, I had begun to write. I remember holding the closest pen in my clumsy, small hands and stealing away my mother's notebooks, just so I could do it. Page after page, I would write in a language only known to a toddler, chicken scratch that boggled the minds of my parents. I would scribble down so much that in an attempt to stop my thievery I received my own notebooks, simply because I loved the feeling of putting something down on blank paper. I remember wanting to write for real, wanting others to see the words that I saw within my foreign language. So I still remember the excitement of learning the alphabet, the fascination with the small letters and cursive font pasted onto my classroom walls. I remember being in awe of the small little details of words, particularly the sound a 'th' made.

When I became confident in my own skill, those little scribbles within my notebooks became real letters, and when that happened, I didn't dare stop. I looked around at my classmates, turning the girls into princesses that fought aliens and the boys into knights that slayed dragons. I carried small flip books around, carrying the small stories of spies and comics about cautionary tales. I wrote within pink journals and relished in the images of my own words written on a page. I even wrote within the books that I was supposed to read, although fortunately I was able to kick that habit. I became enveloped in the daydreams of my own characters, only to turn around and try to bring them to life in the form of words. There wasn't any part of writing that I could turn away from, for I was eager for any chance, even in the ways of writing essays and letters, going so far as to make my own crosswords just for others to solve.

It was towards the end of my elementary school life that I attempted my first novel. The writing was terrible, exactly how one would expect a fifth grader would write, but by the second attempt, I knew exactly what I would do for the rest of my life. The idea of writing for the purpose of reading was a concept so profound that I scarcely hope for anything more. Every inkling of knowledge became knowledge ready to be written down, every book became a teaching method to improve my own, every piece of myself ready to be memorialized into the pages of life itself. The ecstasy I found in writing what was known, and writing creations of the unknown, became the foundation of my soul. I have the voice of an inner monologue, and I can see images of things visualized in my mind, but some of my deepest thoughts form completely in the ways of words taking shape on a page before my eyes. There is nothing I think of more than writing, nothing I find more ecstasy within than to simply put words onto a page and hoping they elicit the emotions within souls like it does within mine.

There was a time when I did not know myself, a time when a mirror only showed empty eyes and a borrowed body. It was not there, because it was all written down. I had no desires, for they only belonged on a page. Even now, when I know that the eyes that I possess are mine, I find that I do not have a soul, not until a pen is in my hands, and paper is set before my eyes.

Ice Cream and the Fabric of the Universe

JULIAN KRUSE

Grade 9, Bennington High School, Bennington, NE.

SILVER

I tasted lightning once, and it feels like an addiction because now I look for the flavor in every new place. My grandpa tasted it too. He told me that I was a poet with a poet's mind, and that made everything I wanted crackle with electricity. We kept driving through the storm; I was looking out the window, rolling sparks around on my tongue and searching for another strike. Nothing came as close as the first one did. Nothing was near enough to reach out and hold. But it was enough to make the weatherman come on to tell us to get somewhere safe, that the wind was blowing airplanes out of the sky—enough for me to get the call that my best friend woke up from a nap to see a cornfield instead of a wall. My grandpa didn't listen to me when we went out in the impending storm, but he listened to the weatherman. He still needed that hint of rebellion, so we took shelter in a Dairy Queen because, "What's the point of a near-death experience if you don't get ice cream after?"

We pull in, and immediately I'm in a different headspace because there was an old run-down Dairy Queen sign in the yard of the house across from the building. For some reason it made me think of letting go, and the way we never really do. The air smelled like the storm, and the fluorescent lights of the building reflected off the damp asphalt of the desolate parking lot. And it is things like that make my insatiable need for poetry wake and cannibalize normal things. You'll have to excuse me. I was still high on the taste of lightning. Grandpa didn't mind. I think he could still taste it too.

Now there are five things you need to know about me and my grandfather. He's incredibly smart. We both love stars. He got me into writing. He knows how to pronounce everything. And we have never, in our entire lives, had a normal conversation.

So we sat and we talked, as we always do, about things that have no right being spoken of in an empty Dairy Queen in the middle of a storm. *But ah, maybe that is more right of a place for us anyway, in the unconventional and the blindingly bright and not so put together.* There I am. Cannibalizing normal things.

Grandpa then pointed out three things that were wrong while we were discussing photons and the fabric of the universe, *as the broken do in sticky booths with gum under the table*.

"Space and time are often seen as two separate things that have a space between them," he told me animatedly, through bites of a vanilla sundae with chocolate sauce. "But it's not space *and* time. It's space-time. It is all one entity. All one word. There is no *in-between*." I would nod and set down my Oreo Blizzard, smiling like I've just discovered the secret of the universe, which I suppose I had. *There are some things bound by their fabrics. You have the pleasure to live and love on one. A place where Oreo Blizzards can taste like lightning.*

As we ate, we observed, the tiles on the ceiling, the storm dying on the horizon, the employees speaking in hushed whispers, occasionally stopping to listen to whatever snippet of conversation would catch them off guard. And here is where we come upon the second thing that was wrong. My grandpa, in his carpenter's mind, was scrutinizing an art piece on the wall. I beat him to insulting it though, *my mind always worked a little like his*.

"There are no sesame seeds on the bun of the burger, and the fries don't have salt. I bet it would be flavorless," I commented. He nodded sagely, but his lips were quirked in an amused grin. It faded as he tilted his head to look at the mounting of the art. He sighed, "Muti-million-dollar company. Still can't hang something up." He looked almost sad. *Heartbroken?* I think he was just sad. *There is something deeper, I swear it.* He sighed again, "Look at it, off-center, scratched up the whole wall trying to put it on, a toddler could do better with their eyes closed." I nodded, suddenly feeling a little sad as well. *Heartbroken? Maybe a little.*

"People just don't care," I said quietly, scooping up another bite of ice cream, flipping the spoon in my mouth, as I always did. *But when people stop caring about things so little, what happens to the axis-tilting problems you ignore?*

My eyes wandered again. "That's a really interesting light," I commented after I swallowed. His eyes shifted. We studied it for a while.

"It kind of looks like a Möbius Strip."

"A what?" *This is my favorite part, where we see him become the nuclear reactor he is.* His eyes lit up, and a grin split his face. "So it's this trick you can do with paper, I'll show you when we get home, I used to do it with my students." *I wish in another life I could have been a student in one of those classes. I think I might have been.* "You draw a line on it, twist it and put it together. It curves in on itself in this mind-bending pattern. You cut it right down the middle and it stays in one piece." *He said something else here, I wish I remembered. It was so good.* We ate, and he tossed his empty cup into the trash. I had a few bites left so I took it with me. It sat in the freezer for two months after, but I didn't know that then. We headed out the door, the bell jingling weakly.

"Watch your step," I said quickly, noting the sudden drop in the dark concrete. He made a distressed noise and gestured at the unmarked step. He rubbed his temple as he found the third mistake he would point out that night. "Unmarked. I mean, if Grams was here and hadn't seen that she could've—" he sighed and kept walking. He stuttered for a moment, as if he couldn't quite figure out what he needed to say. I walked beside him.

He shoved his weathered hands in his coat pockets, his long stride carrying him across the damp parking light in the dying sun. I looked up at him. *There's that heartbreak in his eyes again.*

"It's a problem. It really is."

I nod. "Oh, one hundred percent, what if Grams tripped over that—"

He cut me off with a wave of his hand. "No, no, well yes, but I mean it's a problem how much I care about it." My heart twisted painfully in my chest. "I don't have enough time left to be stressing myself out over all of these little things, but I can't help it." The puddles on the asphalt reflected the shine in both our eyes. "I'm going to die, and all my complaining isn't going to have done anything."

Don't. Please don't talk about the day everything good in this world will turn like sour milk and become undrinkable.

"I'll have just been upset for nothing," he mumbled.

I sighed and blinked away hot and unbidden tears, shaking my head. "You're right, though. I don't know if it's any solace but you're really, *really* right."

He opened the car door and sat down. I slid into the passenger seat and shut us into our own little bubble. He turned to me. "We both do it." He smiled, eyes clouding up with a nostalgic fog. "You used to pick up pebbles on our walks and think they all had souls. Gosh, my pockets got so heavy carrying all the things you looked at for too long and couldn't bear to leave behind."

I almost broke down right then and there. "Didn't it rip one of your jackets?" I remembered softly.

He nodded.

We didn't even need to speak the words. The metaphor, the poetry, it wrote itself. So we pulled out of the parking lot in silence, the storm clearing just enough to see the sun setting, the clouds flashing a parting bolt for me to lick off my teeth. I closed my eyes to savor the last of it. The highway was empty and bathed in orange. I swear up and down I still taste it when we drive there, but maybe that's just me—cannibalizing normal things to feel lightning in the air again.

Unseen, Yet Noticed

Adrishya Kumar

Grade 9, Brownell Talbot School, Omaha, NE.

SILVER

As our substitute teacher calls out names in the class to take roll, they pause. For 1, 2, 3 seconds. They peer at the name on the attendance sheet, turning it from different angles as if that'll help them understand it better.

"Pardon me if I pronounce this wrong. O-dree-sha?" they ask, moving the paper back and forth as if trying to make sense of the word in front of them.

"Here," I pipe up from the very back of the room.

"Did I pronounce that right?" they ask, worried they've offended me.

"Yeah!"

No, they didn't. In fact, they weren't even close—they said a different name entirely. But who could pronounce *my name* right? The name of a divine Hindu goddess, one who cannot be seen, almost invisible. "Your parents named you INVISIBLE? Do they hate you?" my friends always ask incredulously. They think it's a joke, but for me, it's just another reminder that I'm neither fully one thing nor the other. I never correct them. I just laugh it off.

Ever since my first day of Kindergarten, I have been "codeswitching." I'm not a true Desi, but I'm not a true American either. So the same question lingers in my mind—*what am I?* I don't eat spicy food and I can't speak Tamil, but I still mispronounce words in English and I still worship Ganesh and Shiva. In India, I am constantly burdened with the thought of being too white-washed, but in America I'm considered too brown. I am constantly torn between two worlds.

I started showing signs of being too "American" as a kid. While most of the "normal" Indian kids would much rather spring for a savory plate of sambar rice, I would always jump at the chance to eat *yogurt*. Plain, bland, Greek yogurt with rice. I never made an attempt to learn Tamil. Not that I didn't want to— but what was the point? I would never need it anyways, right?

I learned early on that I'm too Indian to be considered American. I have learned to never bring up the fact that I dance, because when people ask me what kind of dance I do I'd have to say Bharatanatyam. The classic Indian dance, steeped in tradition, wasn't what most kids could relate to. What if it wasn't considered normal? What if my friends thought I was weird?

Rather than embracing my Indian roots, I spent years shunning them. When my teacher asked me what I know about Hinduism, I had to sit there in a pool of my own shame. What did I know about Hinduism? Nothing. I knew nothing about Hinduism, because I hadn't taken the time to learn, to understand. I didn't deserve to call it my own. Hinduism wasn't American, and I had to be American to fit in. My grandma has to make special dishes for me, because I'm the only one in my family who can't eat spicy food. It seems like I'm the only one in my family who struggles with the idea of being too "Desi."

I was still wrestling with the idea of performing my Arangetram, the culmination of all the Bharatanatyam techniques and skills that I had learned since I was five. How could I perform a cultural dance that I truly didn't feel connected to? How could I convince an audience that I *enjoyed* showing off my culture on a big stage, rather than being ashamed of it? Somehow, all of the negative thoughts I had about my culture and about my Arangetram shifted when I was invited to perform in the *Nutcracker* with the American Midwest Ballet as a part of their world dancing team. With the group of Bharatanatyam dancers, I was given an opportunity to share my heritage and showcase my culture. We danced alongside numerous ballet dancers, and I felt the most welcome that I had felt in years. It felt like a moment of pride rather than hesitation. Finally, it was my time to stand tall and show the world the beauty of what I had always tried to hide. There was a role for my Indian culture in the Western society.

This newfound experience brings with it the realization that my identity doesn't have to be a battle between two distinct worlds—it can be a blend of both. Being "too" anything is simply a matter of perspective, and I do not have to squeeze myself thin solely to fit into a box. I don't have to be defined by being too "Indian" or too "American," because in the end, I am both. I no longer feel out of place or am ashamed about the parts of myself that make me unique—such as the food I eat, the way I dress, or the dance I love. I don't have to choose one identity over another—I can simply be myself: unseen, by name, yet noticed for who I am. I am shaped by my experiences, my heritage, and my place in the world. And that's more than enough.

Leaving a Mark ... on My Chin

ADRISHYA KUMAR

Grade 9, Brownell Talbot School, Omaha, NE. Honorable Mention.

For most people, their first summer camp experience is a highlight of child-hood, a time filled with adventure and fun with friends. However, for me, my first summer camp experience was far more unforgettable than the rest—for all the wrong reasons.

In the summer of 2016, I wanted the same summer camp experience that every other five-year-old kid had—popsicles, scavenger hunts, maybe even a campfire story. I started off my first day by taking a tour of summer camp. I gazed at the grassy field, the sticks that had been laid down for the bonfire, and fell in love immediately. *This* was my summer camp, and I was going to own it.

That's when I laid my little brown eyes on the activity that made my heart race with anticipation. A slick waterslide, dark blue, with small ribbons of clear water cascading down it. I gazed at the screaming kids as they rode down the steep slope of the slide and promptly landed in the pristine blow-up pool that lay right below it. One thing about the slide struck me as odd, though—rather than being placed on the soft, cushiony goodness of the green grass, it lay directly on a plethora of jagged rocks. Yet, little five-year-old me wasn't focused on the clear safety hazards of the placement of the slide—she was only focused on the glory, the beauty, of cold water on a hot and sticky summer day. Only focused on *conquering* that slide.

With the help of a couple of counselors, I ran to the nearest changing room and put on my sleekest bathing suit. When I showed everyone my blue and fashionable suit, complete with an abundance of colorful flowers, I felt on top of the world. The only thing left for me to do was to conquer the beast.

After waiting in line for about 7 minutes, it was finally *my turn*. I practically jumped up the ladder, and positioned myself perfectly on the top of the slide. Behind me, a counselor quickly shouted some ground rules, but the only one that truly stuck with me was rule number one—DO NOT GO ON THE SLIDE WHEN THERE IS SOMEONE IN FRONT WHO HASN'T FINISHED THEIR TURN. I nodded in understanding and glanced in front of me. *No one.* With a scream of pure joy and delight, I pushed myself off the top of the slide and started cascading down. I'd say I felt like I was in heaven, for about 38 seconds. That was when I looked behind me and saw a kid who had violated rule number one. He had left his post before I had finished sliding.

In that moment, I had a decision to make: I could let him push me off, crashing who knows where, or I could take control of my own fate—by jumping off the slide before he could push me. Without thinking, I chose the latter. As soon as I pushed off the side of the slide, I realized my mistake... *the rocks*. But by then, it was too late. I felt the sharp impact of my body hitting the jagged stones. Pain exploded through my face, my knees, and my palms. But nothing could compare to the pain in my heart. *I had let the slide conquer me.*

The next thing I knew, I was being hoisted up by a counselor and taken to a small office where my parents were called. I held in my tears as long as I could—until I saw my mom. I could barely walk, and my chin was bloody, swollen, stiff, and painful.

The rest of the night was a blur. I remember lying on the cold marble countertop in a plastic surgeon's kitchen—an odd place for surgery, but since my dad is a surgeon and his friend was the one doing the stitching, it felt less unusual. With every stitch, the pain grew sharper as he patched up my chin. One of the counselors at the summer camp told me that rule number one would be more strictly enforced in the future, but I couldn't help but think that if that other kid had just followed the rules—or if the slide had been placed on grass—maybe I wouldn't have this scar, this constant reminder of my first camp experience.

Even today, at 15, when I look into the mirror or someone asks me why one side of my chin looks different from the other, I'm reminded of that little girl who faced a tough decision at her first summer camp. Contrary to what I thought back then, I did conquer that slide—because after my incident, the camp took more precautions. They moved the slide to a safer location, and the rules were enforced more strictly. Granted, I never went back to that camp, so I wouldn't know for sure, but what I do know is that my experience made a difference. The strength and resilience of that little girl still echoes in me, a reminder that even in the face of adversity, we all have the power to leave a mark—and sometimes, the marks we leave shape things for the better.

DECAY

ROMAN MAGLINGER

Grade 12, Elkhorn South High School, Omaha, NE. Honorable Mention.

I think it was the hair. Day after day it caught my eye. Everyone in that blasted class was brunette or blonde, but she was a dense auburn. These days it fairs more of a brown, but this is how I remember her most. I remember how she would walk past me every time she exited the room. If there was something else to pay attention to, it didn't matter. My eyes only wanted one person to focus on. I was dumbfounded to find that my new seat was located right behind her. There was always a desire to interfere with whatever she was doing, but for some reason, I could never muster up the courage to lift off of my seat and speak to her; she was unattainable from the start.

Sitting at that small desk, I observed her interactions with different people, never really hearing what she said, but always hypnotized by her smile. Many people, when casually talking about someone, will use the blank phrase: "Their smile could light up a room." For me, it was different. Seeing her face brighten meant more to me than any smile ever had before. So much so, that I developed a habit of looking to her smile for my own happiness. Such a desire came that if I didn't see that smile, tomorrow was not worth waking up for.

For a reason only God will know, we were to both be placed in a morning class the entire next year. This class consisted of few people, giving me a way to acquaint myself with her. Finally, I was able to see her personality through discussion, and not just distant observation. And what I found in her will stay with me for the rest of my years. I had discovered an individual even better than I could have imagined, with so many endearing and patient qualities that shone through even the drowsiest of mornings. Everything she touched simply radiated joy; a never-ending source of fortitude and warmth. There was always a certain sense of profound maturity within her when compared to the others in my grade. The type of maturity that will bring her unbound peace in her life. It is so hard for me to find the words to describe such a tender and affectionate being. Let any man a part of her future remind her of what she is. He must work extraordinarily harder than I did.

I had only one, simple goal with her. For me, the pinnacle of a relationship, before marriage, is a slow dance. I am a religious character who understands the full destruction that comes with fulfilling certain heavy-hearted actions at young ages. To me, a dance shows an unparalleled devotion where both sides prove themselves to one another. She was the only person so capable, complex, and worthy of sharing such an experience. I understand it sounds infantile, but if you would simply let me describe it. There is nothing more that I would have wanted than to take her hand and guide her through the night. Music surrounding us as time disappears. Swaying back and forth to the songs of old. To be held up by nothing but each other's adoration. How I longed for that sweet embrace, that moment of satisfaction. To know that she was mine. The world could have been ending around us, and it would be of no effect. Great and almighty God, I ask for nothing more.

During the last days of the school year, my heart begged for a relationship with her, but no matter how much I wanted or tried, nothing ever stuck with her. I was desperately trying to fulfill an action as basic as speaking with someone. I even offered flowers occasionally to try and prompt conversation, but I never gained any real response. The times I did receive a response, it was hollow, and without meaning. My approach was too strong and too fast for her liking. I was blocked. She had no interest. None. It was a brutal, yet simple reality. How on earth would a guy like me even begin to talk to someone of her caliber? I decided to never reveal what I felt. It is this decision that leaves me many nights without sleep but with much regret. She's better off without me. Though it hurts deeply to say it, it couldn't be truer. To be with her would be to stain an innocence the likes of an angel.

Her perfections and imperfections that made her so human were not replicated by anyone else, and how much time I've wasted looking for alternatives. She began to seem more like an idea rather than a person. She bled into every thought and action I had. I loved her so badly she wouldn't even have had to love me back. It was a poison that had spread, and I was decaying. In doing so, I ignored just about everything and everyone going on around me.

Time stretched further and further, and it became evident to me that I was never going to make a move. I was trying so hard to grab the ocean with my bare hands. Every last drop of passion slipped through my fingers and evaporated. I even had the opportunity to realize this was happening, in the moment, to reflect and evaluate, and it was here that I felt my greatest deal of failure. In that moment, I realized that no matter how much I try at something, I will never be able to attain something as beautiful as her. It was devastation in its purest form. Something that took so much thought, time, and love that I just *lost*.

We had to do a presentation; so simple, so easy. A task I had performed flawlessly millions of times before. I had to speak about a topic I had researched weeks on for only three minutes. I had an audience of just four. So they picked our groups and we sat down. I arranged my papers for business. As always, I was ready to rock and roll. And then I looked up. She sat in front of me. Why? Out of all the chairs around the table, why must she face me?

I was unaware of the others sharing around me, jotting down incomprehensible notes as they went on. My hands lost their grip, I was violently shaking. For once in my life I was afraid of my audience. I wasn't just scared, I was helplessly terrified.

She went through her presentation. My mind had separated so far from the plastic seat I was in. I just observed her, something I had not done for quite some time. Her innocent voice was still the same, the way it was trying to move in and out of words. Unparalleled grace. She touched her hair in all of the familiar ways. She looked down at her papers in discomfort. She just wanted to get it over with.

Another person went and then it was my turn. I was broken. I scrambled to get my mind right and then came the nail in the coffin; she was looking at me. Watching, waiting. Out of all these years, her attention was mine. Breathing became the most difficult of tasks. I saw her eyes; they decimated my capability of putting out any type of intellect. My words choked over one another, and then they ceased for an excruciating amount of time. I messed it up so badly, there is no mention of recovery. I can't stop failing in front of her. It's as if God is laughing at me just for having the will to try.

She sits there in all of her splendor and hasn't the slightest idea of what she means to me. I can look at her face the entire period and her eyes simply float past me over and over again. It's torture. It's as if I'm not even in the same world as her. I am translucent. To her, I am nothing, less than nothing.

It is unbearable to see her now, so full of joy and life that I am not a part of. I want just a crumb of what she has to fall from the table. A scent of her acknowledgment to be blown my way. I just wanted to make her laugh, to make her smile, to be with her, to talk to someone. How I want her voice to be at my side in the end!

My eyes will continue to jolt towards her smile when they detect it in the hallways out of old habit, but the happiness that used to come with it is destroyed. Oftentimes I wonder if I could have done things differently, even though I know it is wrong to dwell on things of the past. I dream if you ever knew; if you ever had a spark in her head. I just wanted you to know I was there.

THE CROWN

DANIELA MONZALVO TOLENTINO

Grade 11, Grand Island Senior High School, Grand Island, NE. Honorable
Mention.

"One who wears the crown, bears the crown" is a quote I heard from a TV
drama back when I was a kid. I really didn't think much of it. I mean, the whole
plot was about a rich guy who fell in love with a poor girl, and everyone was
against it. It was a really clichéd show, but I didn't care, since my mother and
I enjoyed watching those dramas. Even though we knew the characters would
fight against all odds to be together and end up together, we still got excited for
every new episode and couldn't wait for the next. I still cherish those nights,
with all the laughing and cuddling next to my mother. It was all a girl needed
to be happy.

Now, I am 17. I decided to rewatch that same drama. However, this time, it
was just me alone in my bed, with a blanket as the only thing to give me a sense
of warmth and comfort. And while watching it, that same quote came across:
"One who wears the crown, bears the crown."

However, this time, I paused my screen. Instead of dismissing it, I wrote the
quote on a ripped piece of paper and tucked it behind my phone case because,
at the time, I was planning on removing the crown. I couldn't bear it anymore.
The reason I believed that was because I was facing the reality of the regretful
decisions I made one night. I've told my story before—the one about a young
girl leaving the comfort of her home and family in Mexico to achieve greater
things on the other side and, hopefully, become something in life. That young
girl had no idea what she was getting into once she landed on American soil.

It's pretty stupid how I can relate a quote from a silly drama to the hardships
of life. I mean, all I wanted was to rewatch a romantic drama and forget about
the reality I'm living in. But I guess that no matter what you do or where you go,
your decisions will always catch up to you. It's just a matter of when you decide
to face them. At this point, you may be wondering what it is that I regret so
much in my life. Is it the fact that I regret moving alone to another country? Or
the fact that I can't watch dramatic TV shows with my mother anymore? Well,
if you said either of them, you are correct!

But I guess the only reason I took such a dramatic action in life was to prove to others that I wasn't the helpless girl they thought I was. I mean, my parents never let me do sports because they believed I was weak. They also gave me an extra vitamin gummy during the cold seasons because they knew I got sick the easiest. And it wasn't just my parents—my sisters too. They never invited me to play because they knew I'd just end up crying. My aunt also never let me go with my sisters and cousins on one-week trips because they knew I'd miss my parents the moment I left the house.

Even though growing up, I started changing my ways of doing things—like trying to work out or finally eating my veggies to avoid getting sick—my parents, my sisters, and my family still saw me as this vulnerable girl. The comments they made about how sensitive I was always left me with this feeling—a feeling of pity for myself. So, to prove everyone wrong, I moved far away from home and decided to start from scratch here in the U.S. It was all going well. I was getting straight A's, joined the swim team, made new friends, and had new experiences. However, even though I was doing all of this myself, I always felt this slight depression because I had no one to share these joyful moments with.

I would usually come home to my mother and tell her about my day, and we'd laugh about the things I did while she was cooking. It was such a beautiful moment, and I never realized how important those memories were until, every time I came back from school, I came back to an empty, silent, cold house with no scent of a freshly made soup from my mother. So, from a full table of laughter to a lonely dinner with just my shadow and me. And in that moment, I told myself, Was it really necessary? Was it necessary for you to do all of this just to prove others wrong? Was it necessary for you to live in silence and pretend everything is so great just so you could have an "Aha, in-your-face moment"?

Ever since then, I've never thought the same about myself. Those questions engraved themselves in my mind forever, and for the longest time, I had an existential crisis. At one point, I thought, maybe I am that vulnerable girl who is weak and needed her extra vitamin gummy. I believed that maybe I was pretending to wear this crown that I never had in the first place and that the weight I was carrying was ego and pride. Ego and pride were the reasons I ended up here—depressed and alone.

I'm not saying my parents' or family's words didn't mean anything, but I think there could have always been other ways to solve issues instead of taking grand decisions. It's like wanting to go from floor 1 to floor 10 in an elevator that got stuck on floor 1. You could have taken the stairs, but you chose not to because the feeling of instant accomplishment felt better than the feeling of trying.

Fast forward to now—here I am, lying on the floor, writing this essay and finding a way to end it. I almost wrote, "But eventually, I figured everything out and lived happily ever after." It would be nice to end it like that, but I still need to figure life out. And I think that's what this essay is about. This essay marks the start of my fight with ego and pride because destroying them would finally give me the peace I've always been looking for. It was never them but me and how I would react to situations—always looking for an escape.

But I officially want to stop running away. I want to stop regretting. I want to stop pretending.

In the end, "One who wears the crown, bears the crown."

Source: Korean drama *The Heirs*, starring Lee Min-ho.

BUTTERFLIES

MARYBELLE WARD

Grade 11, Valentine High School, Valentine, NE. Honorable Mention.

In the years of my childhood, I spent every waking moment outside. My backyard was always filled with playful, wild schemes. I loved learning from and exploring the natural world around me. One day I discovered little green worms behind an old shed. Naturally, I was curious, so I took the worms and leaves they were on and put them in a jar. Those worms turned into little green cocoons. Even though they were ugly, I loved my new worms. The jar fascinated me. I couldn't believe my eyes as I watched the butterflies emerge from the cocoons my caterpillars hid in. I still remember my amazement when butterflies replaced my ugly green worms. Despite my attachment, I had to let my former worms go. I had to set my beautiful butterflies free. I watched in awe as my butterflies flew away.

It was the summer of 2022. I had signed up to be a camp counselor for a few weeks at Camp Witness. Butterflies were rising in my stomach. I could feel my heart rate increasing as I arrived at Camp. My heart wouldn't stop fluttering. Camp was a new environment, and I didn't know anyone. I was worried about what everyone would think of me. Despite my worries, my nerves were quickly calmed when the rest of the staff welcomed me. Instantly I felt like I had known them my entire life. Somehow these newly made friends became my family. Even though strangers surrounded me, I was at home. Everything outside of Camp ceased to matter. Laughter, tears, joy, heartache, pots of coffee, and sleepless nights filled my summer. I finally felt at home. No matter what the next moment brought, I knew I was not alone. Camp showed me love, freedom, and most importantly Christ.

Sometimes caterpillars don't get to become butterflies. Before they can even realize their worth, birds fly down from the seemingly bright sky and snatch up the ugly worms. Even though I try to portray my life as beautifully perfect, I am far from it. Before I met Christ, I was alone and obsessed with finding everything that was wrong with me. Life had no meaning; it was only painful. The hurtful desires of our world stole any hope I once had. I told myself that I was not worthy of love or even life. The seemingly bright darkness of the world stole my purpose. I was blinded by decisions that brought me temporary joy. I was consumed by hate, constant worry, and anxiety. I lost sight of what I was made for. Fear controlled my life, and it stole everything I once found beautiful. Pain stole my identity. I lost everything I truly cared about.

Thankfully God had greater plans for my life. I was lost in this world when I first arrived at Camp. He used that summer to metamorphose my life. At the beginning of the summer, I felt like an ugly caterpillar, and my life transformed like a butterfly by the end. Camp showed me the true love of Christ. I realized that no worldly thing could ever love me, and I decided to accept Christ's salvation into my heart. I was suddenly wanted and cared for. Jesus Christ loved me so much that He not only died for me, but He defeated death. He suffered so that I could have an undeserved eternal life. I knew I would never be alone. I slowly became a different person. Love filled the world around me. Jesus' love fulfilled my life, and I no longer had to be perfect. Despite my sins and mistakes, Jesus saved my life.

Ever since I discovered butterflies, they have surrounded my life. Their beauty has always amazed me. The more I obsess over these fluttering insects, the more I realize my life is the life of a butterfly. Much like metamorphosis, I needed a miracle to change my life. Jesus is that miracle. The pain and hurt that once consumed my life no longer defined me. God's love made my life complete. He made my brokenness complete. God created in me a want to love others. He gave me joy and made me feel content. Jesus transformed my life. He gave me a reason to live. As a young girl playing in my backyard, I didn't know that I was prematurely observing the events of my life. I had no idea what little ugly green worms could mean to me. Christ took my broken life and transformed it. He alone set me free.

THE COLDEST, DARKEST NIGHT

What I Waited for at 6 AM

DANIEL YOO

 SILVER

Grade 10, Southwest High School, Lincoln, NE.

5 PM
Afternoon

The time when you mistakenly believe that the bright afternoon sun would never die out and the warm days of happiness and joy would last forever.

I cannot stop smiling as I squint into the bright late afternoon sun, unaware that it is going to set soon. The red and orange sunset continues to slowly illuminate our neighborhood, and its smile is warm and heartfelt. The radiance reflects against our joyous eyes, and the sun is as bright as the smile on our faces. Our family believes that with our newly obtained status as permanent residents, only the bright future lies ahead.

We look at each other.

We cannot help but smile as we fidget with the green cards in our hands.

7 PM
Sunset.

The time when you experience a strange, mysterious sensation that something bad is about to happen, but you cannot really tell where this unknown fear comes from.

I stare up into the darkening sky. My lips press together and my eyebrows curve in a frown. I can see the sun setting on our lives ... I can feel the long night approaching.

A life without ambition, a life without greed, a life without want ... I secretly wish that I led a life of simplicity and indifference. Nevertheless, our family continues to strive for many things. We dream of living in a secure home of our own, we envision a magnificent European vacation, we imagine the restoration of happiness and laughter in our household once again. However, our lives are like a tightrope, and any external force, no matter how minor it seems, is sufficient to knock us off.

And prevent us from ever bouncing back.

11 PM

Night

  The time when you realize that darkness is what you have to face, and nervousness fills your heart.

  Things are not working out as well as we expected. As usual, my father sits at his desk, searching for a job. The fruits of our lives are dangling on the edge, and the proud products of our efforts are pushed to the brink. All throughout, we have never really doubted the great American model of hard work, but now we begin to wonder if our efforts are sufficient to make a difference in this economic rat-race. We do not know whether the choices that we make are truly of our own, or if we are even in control of our lives.

3 AM

Eternal darkness

  The time when you think you can make the night go away by filling yourself with all sorts of inspirational messages about perseverance.

  Anxiety plagues every bit of our lives. My parents toss and turn even in the midst of deep sleep, troubled by numerous unsettled matters. Time is rapidly flying by, but life is not getting any better. Bills begin to pile up and there is no health insurance, but yet, we continue to march on. We still believe that there is good in the world and that soon enough, the night will terminate.

  Everything has an end, we tell ourselves.

  We continue to dream.

  We sit outside at night, looking up at the glowing stars in the cool autumn sky, and tell each other what we aspire to be. Together, we close our eyes and envision the future that we want to build. We see ourselves occupying a pleasant home of our own, laughing, being happy and free ... the bells and the chimes of our family's freedom ring amongst our laughter and our joy.

  And then we look down, and our faces darken: This is the moment that we realize how far away from our dreams we truly are.

6 AM

Dawn, the darkest

  The coldest hour of the day when all hopes vanish and you think that there is no way out.

Not long thereafter, we have come to accept that our lives are simply ruined, and there is no future. The sole remnants of our once-radiant dreams are its gray ashes. We—all of us here on Earth—live because we had been born, and I persevere because I have no choice but to. Because what else can we do? Everything is out of our control. We continue to work hard, but nothing is going well. Once we desperately wanted to figure out how our lives came to be like this ... but attempting to understand only brought forth pain.

It did not take long for our lives to generate from ambitious to hanging on the edge.

We don't talk. We don't think. Our lives have fallen apart, and they have been thoroughly burned down, inside and out. Trying our best to march on, we do not mention anything of the past, or the enthusiastic dreams that we once had.

Only an occasional sigh fills the air. Our eyes, once sparkling with aspiration, optimism, and determination, lost their focus.

I look at my face in the mirror. I stare at it for a long time, standing in shock of what it has become. Once radiant and beaming with smiles, it is now crumbling downward from disappointment and exhaustion. My eyes no longer sparkle with joy, my mouth has fallen in resignation, and I stare out at the world with fatigue and detachment.

Just when we think that life cannot slide any further,
It does slide further.

And further.

And further.

And further down.

But just as we stop fighting for a better life,

Just as we give up,

Just as we prepare to stop,

Just as we let go of all hopes,

"Look!"

"It's the sun!"

I stare at the majestic star, slowly rising and lighting up our world—and our lives.

My face gradually spreads into a small smile, yet I cry at what I have lost during the night.

So the 6 AM has come. The coldest and darkest hours of the night are behind us, and only the warmth and the bright lights of the morning await. The sun does not make a sudden appearance out of the stormy rainclouds … rather, it rises gradually, slowly making its way up through the darkness. Just when we think it is all over, just when we believe everything is destroyed, just when we give up and put down all of our desires, the morning presents its gift of lights.

<hr>

With that being said, I ask you, what time is *your* life at?

Is it at the worrying hour of 11 PM, the anxious hour of 3 AM, or the darkest, coldest hour of 6 AM when you think the sunrise would never come?

A long time ago, unemployment and poverty made their way to my family. My parents spent many nights in fear, worry, concern, and eventually lost all hope. We tried our best to uplift ourselves, but we continue to reside in poverty. My parents are still unemployed, and our financial struggles are ongoing. But as I came to realize, the sun does not emerge with success or the resolution of the difficult problems—it comes only when we let go of our anxiety. You see, the morning lies within ourselves and our mindset is key. Almost all things in life are out of control, but this power that we possess over the sun is impactful. The sun only rises when we learn to deal with the uncontrollable circumstances presented—the morning only comes when we learn to persevere and install true resilience in ourselves.

I ask you once again, what time are *your* lives at?

But in a day, we have to do this all over again. The sun will set on our lives once more, and there will be another long, dark night that we must endure through.

What is the point, you ask?

What is the point of persevering and holding on desperately through the night when we know that that darkness will come back?

I do not know the answer.

I just cannot hold on anymore, and I know that you cannot either.

One day, as I waited for the sun to arise, I knew there would come a time where I can hold on no more and now is the time ... My hand is beginning to slip out of control and I begin to wonder about the meaning of all of this. No one is going to remember the work we put into perseverance, *the work we put in for a better life*, and I am burnt thoroughly out ... I am about to let go, I am about to fall, I am about to forever slide down into the abyss of darkness ...

But the morning presents its radiance once again, and I march on, because that is what resilience is, and that is what I waited for at 6 AM.

Love from South Korea

I Don't Have the Right to Smile at Prom

Daniel Yoo

Grade 10, Southwest High School, Lincoln, NE. Honorable Mention.

I don't even know where to start.

I am sixteen.

I am drifting in the immense ocean of immeasurable depth and width, with a thunderstorm raging above me in the darkness of the night. I do not know where I am at and what time it is. *"It's the life you chose, deal with it,"* the winds quietly whisper to me. I recoil back in shock as I realize that these are my own words that have been ringing in my ears forever. But I wonder, is it really though? Is this really the life I chose? Or is my life just a facade of false choices?

Fatigued from thoughts and treading the water, *floating* is not even the right word to describe my state—I am merely suspended above the ocean, just a mere inch or two from drowning. My focus is solely on surviving—once I had dreamed of reaching an island of paradise full of picturesque beaches and towering palm trees, but I only look down at my feet, trying to stay afloat and beat the water. Then suddenly, I glance up and catch a glimpse of the faint orange sunrise in the distance. I am not sure whether I am hallucinating or if it is real, but a sliver of hope begins to overflow my heart. However, at that exact moment, the sky explodes and I jolt back in my bed, shaking.

I have been having similar dreams and thoughts since the first day of 2024. My life now—it feels like it is stuck behind a solid, unopenable door.

◇◇◇◇◇◇◇◇◇◇◇◇◇◇◇◇◇◇◇◇◇◇◇◇◇◇◇◇◇◇

Tomorrow I will be going to South Korea without my father. I look outside at the June evening sky, and instead of packing, I am thinking, lost in thought, stuck in the past, unable to move on. I close my eyes, and the past rolls on like a panorama.

◇◇◇◇◇◇◇◇◇◇◇◇◇◇◇◇◇◇◇◇◇◇◇◇◇◇◇◇◇◇

One nation, under God, indivisible, with liberty and justice for all.

To this day, I remember citing the pledge of allegiance on my first day of American school in August 2018. I did not know the words and more importantly, I did not know the meaning. But as I murmured alongside my standing classmates that day, I knew that these words would change my life forever. With every word of the pledge deeply committed to my memory and my heart, I was determined to stay in this country.

The powerful provider of choice and liberty, the lifeboat, the light… This is what permanent residency meant to me. It may be absurd to think that a small plastic card would carry such significant value, but when I was fifteen, this was my belief. I had incorrectly assumed that it would free our family from all our difficulties. Thinking that my family was closer than ever to the sweet air of freedom, back in the fall of my freshman year, *way back in the day*, I had written that I had the right to smile at homecoming as my family finally became eligible to embark on the final phase of the notoriously complex green card process that October. So that magical fall, I had dreamed more than anyone else, I was happier than anyone else, and mostly, to reflect this all, I smiled more than anyone else.

Smile.

Smile—The well-deserved fruit of our turbulent lives had left me a long time ago. I could not even remember the last time I smiled.

A tangled yarn.

That was what my life felt like in the spring of my freshman year.

The green cards made our way to us on February 12, 2024, just as my life began falling apart. I have imagined this moment for years, yet then, when we finally got them, when our family finally became proud American permanent residents like I desperately wished to be since my first day in this country, I didn't feel anything. The day after the green cards made their way to our family—it was a cloudy, rainy Tuesday. Battling the depressing ambiance all-around, I headed to the bathroom during my lunch break and caught a glimpse of my face in the mirror. I stared at it for a long time.

Now I could get a paid job like everyone else in my school.

Now I could permanently escape the sinking cruise ship that was my home country of South Korea.

Now our father can obtain a full-time job, and when I am an adult, I can get married, have children of my own, and live the American Life.

Now my mother would no longer feel lonely here in the rural Midwest.

Now we can finally move on in life, possibly buying a home of our own.

Now I could dream.

Most importantly, I could go back to South Korea in the summer to visit my long-lost relatives.

This was finally when the meaning of permanent residency struck me. All the things that I missed about my home country spiraled in front of me like a movie. I could sit next to the beautiful shore of the Han River, I could climb up the Namsan Tower to catch the panorama of Seoul ... I could watch the summer bloom on the Grand Park Road....

But not without my father.

Our dad, our hardworking dad whom our mother worried about every day, armed with a doctorate and years of industrial experience, was unable to get a job—every week he applied to dozens of positions, yet none of them called him back, wanting him. Not a single company sought after my father. Not a single hiring manager wanted his experience. Only the ill-intentioned took advantage of my desperate father.

Back in the day, *way back in the day*, in the magical fall of my freshman year filled with football games, turning leaves, pumpkin spices, and the crisp autumn air, I thought the future would hold only brightness...but, in reality, the road in front only held clouds and fogs and smoke and nothing else. I had once naively believed that the bluer skies and a freer life were awaiting us with a green card, but the thing that was in front of us was life without health insurance. Once I was the contender for a better life, a brighter horizon, a bluer sky ... now I don't know where my life has gone wrong. It wasn't supposed to be like this. After getting a green card, my life was supposed to change, my life was supposed to improve, and I was supposed to dream. After getting a green card, life was supposed to illuminate with radiance, life was supposed to shine more than the lone star in the clear, winter night sky.

Winter and spring blurred through the cracks of the thick tears in my eyes and the deep scars of my soul, and by now it was late April. It was time for prom. I didn't smile at prom. I didn't have the right to, with everything crashing and burning right next to me. How could I smile and enjoy myself when I knew what my parents were going through? I knew their sleepless nights, their silent but desperate appeals to greater forces to help them, *to liberate them*, their regret and their guilt. I knew their tears, and I knew their wounds, and I knew their pain. I really wanted to cry at prom, but I had shed too many tears for my parents already that night, none would come out. Between working the dance, I went into the bathroom and looked at my unraveled work suit in the mirror and come close to tearing up because I knew that our lives had come too far and too astray, and no one knew why.

◇◇◇◇◇◇◇◇◇◇◇◇◇◇◇◇◇◇◇◇◇◇◇

Then came the summer.

On June 3, *tomorrow*, I will be going to South Korea without my father.

My father's parents will be waiting for him at the gates of their house out in rural Jincheon County, but he will not be there.

He is forced to stay back in the United States, at a home that is not even ours, rising from ashes of painful rejection and trying his best to land a job ... once more, once again.

I will be in South Korea, missing my father, with jealousy, contempt, and excessive desires torturing me day and night ... Just as I am now. The blue summer sky reminded me of where my life was—others have better finances than me, others have better academics and extracurriculars than me, others have better summers than me, and simply put, everyone else around me has a simply far superior life than me. But for some reason, while these reminders should have served as the symbol of my unrealized potential and an unfortunate life, I felt calm and content.

I am happy where I am.

I look up to everyone else in the distant sky far above the clouds, leading the best life ever, from my hole in the ditch where I brainwash myself into a state of false satisfaction and find forced, inauthentic joy in little bits and pieces of things.

I am okay with where my unfortunate life was. I am alright. I want to think I am happy. But I know that I am not happy. I have never been in my life. Happiness and fulfillment ... those are two things that are essential to our lives but I have always lacked. Those are what I pray for every night ... those are the things that I want the most.

Because I still had *hope*.

Six weeks.

Six weeks of my industrious father's job search.

Six weeks of me rediscovering myself in my home country.

It felt like the perfect plan to emerge into the calm, sunny morning from the oppressive darkness.

∞∞∞∞∞∞∞∞∞∞∞∞∞∞∞∞∞∞∞∞

Six weeks later

Looking back, my freshman year was the frightening ocean with the stormy sky and the violent waves. It was the eye of the hurricane and the peak of the typhoon, and now, God was telling me that everything would be alright. I wasn't sure if I was ready to believe Him quite yet, but what could I do? I could not do anything but to trust him, and I could only continue to work hard in the situation that I was in and that was presented to me. But none of this explained why God continued to forbid my father from leading the "Good Life." I didn't understand why God could not grant my father a comfortable lifestyle that everyone else around us already had. Then I realized one thing. Religion is more than just belief. It should not be centered on understanding the belief systems, as it is us rather weak human beings' desperate way of trying to communicate with the greater forces of the universe that are in charge of our lives. Religion is the only thing we can cling on to when things are out of our control. It is the only lifeboat that we can cling on to in the turbulent ocean of life.

If anyone asks me what I did over the summer, I would say I dreamed.

Once I was the contender for a more satisfactory life, a brighter horizon, a bluer sky ... I had dreamed of many things, *far too many things*, in life. But a great storm had washed over me, and instead of dreaming, I resorted to surviving day to day. Full of ambition, I once looked to the ocean sky, ahead to the limited horizons full of possibilities that laid in front me, but now I only look down at my feet to make sure that I am not drowning.

I want more to life than this. This is not the life that I aspired to have. So instead, on our 10-hour flight from Seoul to Seattle, I chose to dream once again.

With the sentimental classics coming out of my earphones on the quiet, dark airplane that rapidly cruised through the night, I imagined my father being happy at his job, I saw my mother being happy at her job, I saw my brother and me doing well at our respective schools, I saw our house, full of laughter and happiness, *a home that my parents can now proudly call their own*, standing with a solid foundation in the ground. I could hear the children playing outside under the bright orange sunset ... I could hear the chimes and the bells of our family's liberation.

And most importantly, I saw our family finally being ... free.

Living the best life ever.

Nothing has been decided yet, our parents have said since the start of my freshman year.

So much of the future is up in the air—

...

And it still is.

So dear my brother Richard,

This is the rather dynamic and unfortunate story of my life, the life that has not found fulfillment or happiness yet in its sixteen years of existence. You can never really understand a person until you actually become trapped in their lives, but regardless, it is my hope that you can at least begin to accept my choices and decisions in the past year after reading my rather long explanation.

If justice prevails, the sun will rise in the morning and shine on our family's life. If justice prevails, better times will come to our family. Our hardworking parents will get a rewarding job, they will have a satisfactory career, and we will be a happy Korean-American family.

Dear my brother Richard, I understand your anxiety and nervousness, because every day, I feel the same way. Someday, the sunlight will shine on our lives ... but up until then, we must persevere. Maybe if we run hard enough, maybe if we run far enough, maybe if we run fast enough, we may be able to outrun the dark, gray storm clouds above us and powerfully pose under the warm, shining ray of the benevolent lights of the spring sun.

Until the day that hard work truly pays itself off and we can all be happy and free,

—Your brother, with love from South Korea.

P.S. I have the Right to Smile at Homecoming, but I don't have the Right to Smile at Prom.

HUMOR

Mindfulness Journal

Rebekah Daily

Grade 11, Home School.

What's the silver lining in a recent challenge you faced?

Her name was Lucy. The moment I laid eyes on her, my heart stopped. Not literally, of course. It wasn't until Van Helsing buried a stake in my chest that it *literally* stopped. They were both a challenge to me. Her beauty, his insatiable desire to end my life. Both an unexpected delight, in one way or another. I hadn't seen either for such a very long time—it kindled in me something. A fighting spirit? Not exactly. Will to exist and to bring others over to my way of doing it. Not that such passions did me much good. There is still, of course, that nasty wooden barb protruding from my sternum, a tangy smell of garlic in the air. Oh, yes. And the coffin. Cold and slick and silver-lined.

Write about a friendship that has evolved over the years.

I hardly remember a time before Benny. I take it back—I *don't* remember a time before Benny. But when I first started hanging around, all he could ever talk about was life without me. He was always trying to ditch me places. Friends' houses, school, his grandma's place, the park—even at a shrink once! Jerk. Soon enough he figured out that I wasn't going anywhere. Benny and me? We were made for each other. It took Benny a while, but what started as grudging tolerance became humorous acceptance. He liked to introduce me to people, since they always went all bug-eyed and pale. I kinda spooked them, I guess. We got real good at pranks and stuff. Benny tried to get me an airline ticket once, but they didn't let me on the plane. I didn't have the right ID or something, so I had to sneak through. Benny and I were pretty proud of that stunt. We couldn't talk the stewardess into giving us a spare packet of peanuts for me, though. It really messed with her, but Benny kept on asking—being a good friend, you know. Lady ended up kicking us off the plane entirely. She made up for it though, don't worry. Got us into this great place. Benny and me are sharing it now—roommates. And even though I'm pretty sure the neighbors are all a little crackers, it's a pretty good set up. All in all, I couldn't think of a better way for our friendship to work out.

Your favorite quote is ...

"The most valuable of talents is that of never using two words where one will do." —Thomas Jefferson

"The most valuable of talents is never using two words where one will do." —Thomas Jefferson

"The most valuable talent is never using two words where one will do." —Thomas Jefferson

"The most valuable talent is never using two words where one works." —Thomas Jefferson

"The most valuable talent is never using two words where one works." —Jefferson

"The valuable-est talent is never using two words where one works." —Jefferson

"Best talent: never use two words where one works." —Jefferson

"Best: never use two where one works." —Jefferson

"Best: one is better than two." —Jefferson

"Best: one, never two." —Jefferson

"One, never two." —Jefferson.

"Concision." —Jefferson.

How do you navigate the balance between giving and receiving?

You know, I was in a support group for this for a little while. My profession (mythological indentured servitude) has an unhealthily high burnout rate. When the guys and I aren't doing our nine-to-five with LAMP (Lazy Answers to My Problems), we get together and talk about it. And you know what? It turns out we're all pretty much dealing with the same garbage: on call—all the time, backbreaking workloads, NO benefits, and an appalling lack of reciprocal respect in the workplace. (My supervisor has called me Genie for the last three years, despite the fact that I've introduced myself as Jim, like, fifty times. But I have to call him "master" or some other overstated honorific.) Anyway, it's been good to get that all out in the open. But we decided, what the hey? We give until it hurts. But who says it has to hurt us? So we put together a little union and made this system. Think of it as indentured *self*-servitude. Let's say my supervisor gives me a command like, "Make me totally gorgeous." Then I would proceed to give him the flawless physique of a purebred Arabian Stallion. It falls within the parameters of the wish, gives me a day off—and a good show. My buddy was commanded to deliver his supervisor "the wealth of kings." And boy did he deliver: he gave that guy a king's wealth of enemies, of paperwork, of clothes (but not closet space), and of public disfavor. You want my advice? If things aren't balancing out quite right, consider putting your thumb on the scale.

What's something you wish people knew about you?

Oh. So many things. It's like the English language is totally lost on society. How about, for starters, that "you" is the *plural* and *formal* form of the second-person pronoun. Why on earth does my boyfriend use it to refer to me? I have assured him on multiple occasions that I am neither plural, nor especially superior (except in matters of grammatical clarity, obviously). And it's not even the subject pronoun! So why are ye using it at the end of your illiterate sentences?! (Or, where appropriate, Why art thou using it at the end of thine illiterate sentences?!) It's disgraceful, honestly. We've lost all verbal nuance. And for those who tell me that it cuts down on awkward social interactions (e.g. that necessary conversation one has with another when deciding if one ought to switch to "thee" over "ye") I say with all the conviction of a unanimous jury that those conversations would surely decrease the number of people who are ignorantly the intimate friend of someone-or-other! World peace would prosper, surely, if the world's languages were but a little better used.

Write about something you've been procrastinating.

How does the changing of seasons affect you emotionally and mentally?

I'm a modest sort of guy, really. It's why I love fall—so much coverage. Spring ain't bad either. Nice bushy flowers to help shield the nooks and crannies. Honestly? I don't even mind summer that much. But every year I dread November worse than the sound of chainsaws or the smell of camp fires. It's humiliating, all right? Sure, there are those who call it "free" and "natural" but to me, it's just plain indecent. Getting picked on for months before finally being stripped naked till April? I think I'd rather be one of those stupid evergreens that shed everywhere—leave my own little trail of bad hygiene wherever I go. It's better than quarterly nudity. Sheesh. Shameful, that's all I can say. It's shameful.

What is your personal philosophy in three sentences?

The only thing that we know—that is, that we know without not having no knowledge to the contrary—about life, which is to say existence (not non-death), is that not living—to whit, not non-existence but rather non-life, or death—is the knowledge (not accompanied by any additional knowledge only non-knowledge, which may be called theories) that we know, which knowledge is an absence of doubt, or non-surety. And if this death is inevitable—not to say inescapable, rather to say a fundamental end—end being result, not non-beginning—of existence excluding no one, then life (not non-death) is and ought to be for the purpose (not arbitrarily) of that inevitability, which is not inescapable. Thus we live, which is not to say not die, but rather to exist (to whit, not not-be) to do either of two things, which requires that not both of two things are done; which two are: (first) that one lives—one does not not-be—such that one's death is bad, or not good, for one's life having been (or not non-existed as) bad, or (second) that one's death is good for one's life having been bad, which badness is not good, and said goodness is not definable to anyone (which is to say excluding no one, which "every" excludes—or does not include—anyone), with badness being the opposite thereof.

JOURNALISM

THE GATE TO FREEDOM

MARIA-AGELIKI BERNITSAS

Grade 9, Duchesne Academy of the Sacred Heart, Omaha, NE. Honorable Mention.

The following is a first-person narrative of the escape of Kazimierz Piechowski and three friends from Auschwitz during World War II. It was constructed from published sources.

"Go fetch, you filthy Jew!"

The guard cackled as he threw the prisoner's hat into the air. James hurried to retrieve it; he knew better than to disobey a guard.

"BAM!"

I flinched at the sound of the gun. My eyes darted to James' lifeless body. For a second, I lost track of my work, but quickly forced myself to refocus. I couldn't keep up with the thoughts that sped into my mind. *If I keep slacking off, I will end up like James.*

It became progressively harder to hold the shovel as sweat flooded my palms. My hands, raw and itchy from the prolonged exposure to the sun, could barely keep a grip on it. I begged that the suffering would end soon.

"Kazik! It's over. It's all over," Eugeniusz cried.

I stared blankly at my friend.

"I'm going to be killed!"

"How do you know—no one knows when they will die!" I could not accept the thought of losing him.

"My friend told me! He works in the offices and has access to the documents!"

I felt the little bit of life left inside of me die.

"I can manage to get us a car! I can find a way to steal one and hijack it. We can't stay here!" His voice shook as he spoke. Eugeniusz was a car mechanic, and as talented as my friend was, an escape was just impossible. There were barbed wire fences surrounded by guards all around the camp.

The sound of glass doors shutting and guards yelling filled my ears. I had recently started working in the storage area. As I organized equipment, I noticed a room filled with the guard's uniforms and guns. Slowly, an idea formed in my head. I knew what to do. I knew how to escape.

Eugeniusz and I gathered two more people: Jozef, a priest, and Stanislaw, a scout. We formed a plan and made sure every detail was perfect. It was risky, but it was better than dying in Auschwitz. We all agreed to kill ourselves if the plan did not work out.

For the next couple days, we paid extra close attention to the space around us. I examined every part of the camp I came across, looking for any possible areas that would help us with our escape. I went through the plan several times in my head, scouting for any possible flaws.

The day was June 20, 1942. I had been at the camp for two years. Since it was a Saturday, work stopped at midday, when we would gather to review the plan one final time. Right after work, I was supposed to head to my housing block. Instead, I went to the attic of a half-built building. I waited till the guards were distracted and then dashed inside. I snuck down into the attic, where the three of them were already conversing.After reviewing the plan, we prayed for our families with tears in our eyes.

Eugeniusz, the other 2 prisoners, and I grabbed a wagon full of garbage. The unswallowable cotton ball in my throat made it too difficult to speak. I remained quiet on the way to the gate. My heart pounded as we talked to the guard and asked to be let through. We told him we were part of the group that was supposed to carry out the trash. I was relieved when he didn't check to confirm our story. We went through the gate and abandoned the wagon.

Could we really be free?

Next, we were faced with the task of finding and hijacking commander Rudolph Hoss' car, the fastest vehicle in all of Auschwitz. Eugeniusz worked on that, while Jozef, Stanislaw, and I carried out the rest of the plan. Our hearts pounded as we jumped into the coal hatch, which I had managed to open that morning at work. We rushed through the hallway. Our feet were quiet, but our hearts pounded like the footsteps of an elephant. My mind was frozen; I could not think.

As we scanned the area, we found the room that held the guard's uniforms and guns. We took out a crowbar and used it to pry the door open. As we stepped outside, we found Eugeniusz waiting for us in Hoss' car. I felt a bit of weight lift off of my shoulders.

Then I saw it—an SS officer standing in the distance. We had no choice but to pass by him as we drove. But his face didn't hint of suspicion. Instead, he raised his arms and said, "Heil Hitler!" To which we responded by reciprocating the movement.

We were almost free.

The last obstacle would be the most risky. I drove the commander's Steyr 220 towards the final gate. A series of guards stood around it. We hoped that they would notice our SS uniforms and open the gate as we approached.

The gate remained closed.

We kept driving.

Nothing.

We were almost there.

Heading straight for a closed gate.

"SCREECH."

I suddenly halted the car.

"Do something," Jozef whispered to me. I thought back to what we rehearsed; if this were to happen, I would scream at the guards in an attempt to scare them into letting us through the gate. Despite my feelings of helplessness, I put on a strong voice and shouted at them to open up the gate. To our relief, the guards listened and we proceeded out.

We were free.

After surviving a few nights in the forest, we all went our separate ways. Stanislaw went back to Warsaw, where he would be safe. Unfortunately for his parents, they were imprisoned in Auschwitz and were killed in revenge for Stanislaw's escape. Jozef got sick and stayed with a parish priest. Eugeniusz went to Ukraine. As for me, I went to Poland and fought in the war against the Nazis. I never saw Eugeniusz or anyone else I escaped with again. None of us were ever captured; however, I served 7 years in jail for my escape. This was because Poland became a communist state in 1947. When I was finally let out, I was 33 years old. The Nazis had taken away my youth, but more importantly, my peace. I was forced to relive the memories throughout my life, with flash-backs and nightmares that haunted me. Regardless, I tried to continue my life as I desired. I became an engineer and traveled the world with my wife. I felt it was my duty as a scout to live the rest of life with cheer.

References

Khaleeli, Homa. "I Escaped from Auschwitz." Interview. *The Guardian*, 11 Apr. 2011, www.theguardian.com/world/2011/apr/11/i-escaped-from-auschwitz. Accessed 15 Dec. 2024.

Stilwell, Blake. "This Holocaust Survivor Recounts His Daring Escape from Auschwitz." *We Are the Mighty*, 29 Jan. 2022, www.wearethemighty.com/mighty-history/this-holocaust-survivor-recounts-his-daring-escape-from-auschwitz/. Accessed 15 Dec. 2024.

ROE V. WADE

TAYLOR DOUCHEY

Grade 11, Fort Calhoun Junior/Senior High School, Fort Calhoun, NE. Sara Gross, Educator. Honorable Mention.

In June of 2022, a decision was made that would affect many people's lives. This decision changed the rules to our rights. The Supreme Court had ruled 5 to 4 to overturn the Roe v. Wade law. To understand what this means, first you need to understand the cases leading up to this.

The very first important case, from 1973, that started everything is the Roe v. Wade case. This case progressed when "Jane Roe," a pseudonym, sued Henry Wade. Roe stated that you should have absolute access to an abortion no matter what. The court had disagreed, but they considered it unconstitutional to leave the restrictions up to the states. So, the court put federal laws over abortions to maintain rights and privacy. During the first trimester, up to 12 weeks, no court could interfere with the abortion. The regulations put on the second trimester, 13 to 27 weeks, stated that the state can regulate abortions, but they are not allowed to prohibit them. During the last trimester, 28 to 40 weeks, the state could regulate and even prohibit abortions. Although, in the Roe v. Wade law, they stated that you cannot criminalize abortions if they are necessary to protect a life.

The second important case that gave women rights to abortions was Planned Parenthood of Southeastern Pennsylvania v. Casey. This was a Supreme Court case from 1992. This case held five important rules. The first being that when receiving an abortion, all doctors are required to inform the patient about any negative side effects. The second and third aspects of this law regarded consent. The second one said that you are required to tell your husband that you are getting an abortion before receiving one. The third part said that any teen seeking an abortion must get consent from a guardian before receiving it. In addition, in the fourth section, it stated you must wait 24 hours between deciding to have an abortion and getting the procedure. The fifth section of this law put requirements on the facilities providing abortions to report the procedure.

The last case contributing to abortion rights is the Dobbs v. Jackson Women's Health Organization. This case took place in Mississippi; they adopted the

HB1510 law, also known as the Gestational Age Act. This prohibited abortions after 15 weeks, which is before the viability point that occurs at 24 weeks. When the law took effect, the Women's Health Organization took it to federal court. They stated that the law was possibly unconstitutional. This federal case stated that states may not ban abortions prior to the point of viability. They also stated that all Mississippi residents must have access to abortions up until that point. The state of Mississippi did not like this ruling, so they took it further up.

The Dobbs v. Jackson Women's Health Organization is what led to Roe v. Wade being overturned. When the Mississippi case was sent to the Supreme Court, they said that laws banning abortions before viability are not unconstitutional. When they appealed this case, it led them to review Roe v. Wade and Planned Parenthood of Southeastern Pennsylvania v. Casey. They reviewed these cases in May of 2021.

In May of 2022, the decision about the case was leaked. The leak showed that the court was agreeing to uphold the Mississippi law and overturn Roe v. Wade; although, it couldn't be confirmed yet. In June of 2022, the final decision was issued. The Supreme Court ruled 5-4. Some people believe the Supreme Court ruled this way because the court has a majority of conservative members. They stated that there is no constitutional right to abortion. After this decision was made, the rights to abortions changed drastically.

Since these laws are overturned, it means that each state can place whatever restrictions or bans they want on abortions. They can also make abortions illegal, even if it is necessary for somebody's health. In some states, this is not a problem, but in other states it is more dangerous. For example, in California abortions are still completely legal. In other states, like Texas, abortions are completely illegal with criminal penalties. Taking away these laws completely changed the rights that people have to their own bodies and possibly our future.

Works Cited

Better Health Channel. "Pregnancy - Week by Week." *Vic.gov.au*, 2012, www. betterhealth.vic.gov.au/health/HealthyLiving/pregnancy-week-by-week.

Center for Reproductive Rights. "Abortion Laws by State." *Center for Reproductive Rights*, Center for Reproductive Rights, 2023, reproductiverights.org/maps/ abortion-laws-by-state/.

———. "Roe v. Wade." *Center for Reproductive Rights*, 2022, reproductiverights. org/roe-v-wade/.

Duignan, Brian. "Dobbs v. Jackson Women's Health Organization | Definition, Abortion, Background, Arguments, Roe v. Wade, & Planned Parenthood v. Casey | Britannica." *Encyclopædia Britannica*, Dec. 2021, www.britannica.com/topic/Dobbs-v-Jackson-Womens-Health-Organization.

"Planned Parenthood of Southeastern Pa. V. Casey, 505 U.S. 833 (1992)." *Justia Law*, 2019, supreme.justia.com/cases/federal/us/505/833/.

"Planned Parenthood of Southeastern Pennsylvania v. Casey." *Encyclopædia Britannica*, 2019, www.britannica.com/event/Planned-Parenthood-of-Southeastern-Pennsylvania-v-Casey.

———. "Roe v. Wade." *Encyclopedia Britannica*, 7 Dec. 2018, www.britannica.com/event/Roe-v-Wade.

THE HUMAN COST OF SUDAN'S CIVIL WAR

ASHMIZA SHAIK

Grade 10, Millard North High School, Omaha, NE.

In April of 2023, a new wave of fighting broke out in Sudan, a country already facing massive political instability. "I woke at 7 AM in the morning on April 24. While I was brushing my teeth I heard [rocket fire] very close to my house, around 500 meters away," 29-year-old Jamal explains. "It escalated quickly. Later we learned that clashes had erupted between the Sudanese Army Forces and the Rapid Support Forces," he told Human Rights Watch. As both of the military powers in Sudan continue the battle for power, chaos remains throughout the nation to this day.

Through persisting conflict, several human rights violations have been recorded by both of the military groups. "We were ethnically discriminated against in the schools. We were targeted based on our skin color. We used to be beaten up when we spoke our mother [tongue]," Jamal continues. The countless deaths occurring within Darfur have now been characterized as GENOCIDE.

Despite several international efforts, it seems progress is going backward for Sudan. After Sudan's military coup, the African Union, responsible for peacekeeping in Sudan, removed the nation from their union. Due to a lack of enough international pressure towards the issue, the civil war isn't showing any signs of stopping soon. "Sudan keeps getting forgotten by the international community," UN Aid Chief Martin Griffiths told diplomats in Geneva. The United Nations set a funding goal of about 2.7 billion dollars for the humanitarian crisis; however, as of April, only 5% of that sum has been collected. With over 12,000 deaths since the start of the conflict, the humanitarian crisis requires urgent attention. A study conducted by Foreign Affairs explains that by the end of this year, over 2.5 million deaths could occur due to hunger-related reasons.

But one of the primary reasons why the war isn't ending soon is because of the players funding the Rapid Support Forces' war effort. The ethnic cleansing is being fueled by the arms that the United Arab Emirates is sending to the RSF. Without the help and support of the UAE, the RSF would eventually run out of weapons to keep the war going, but also the power struggle would eventually come to a stop.

However, as the focus of most Western leaders including the United States rests on the crisis taking place in Gaza, all eyes haven't been on Sudan or to halt the UAE from fueling this war. With most of our international community actively working to bring a ceasefire agreement or peace to Palestine, Sudan isn't receiving enough attention or pressure. No incentive exists for both the RSF and the Sudanese Army Forces to stop the ethnic cleansing. There's absolutely nothing stopping this war from escalating.

Over 10 million people have been displaced throughout the nation. Because of the conflict, development is being pushed back and growth in the nation has been stunted.

What is most vital—the health of the population—is now at risk. With diseases such as cholera, malaria, and measles cn the rise, the crippled healthcare system facing massive resource shortages isn't able to restore the health of millions of citizens. As 2 in 3 people lack adequate access to healthcare in Sudan, it is more than clear that the civil war is making this much worse.

At the end of the day, to prevent stories like that of Jamal's, or to stop the ethnic cleansing and human rights violations taking place in Sudan, international action is crucial.

Works Cited

"Interview: 'I Didn't Think I Would Survive This' | Human Rights Watch." *Human Rights Watch*, 9 May 2024, www.hrw.org/news/2024/05/09/interview-i-didnt-think-i-would-survive. Accessed 31 July 2024.

Prendergast, John, and Anthony Lake. "The UAE's Secret War in Sudan." *Foreign Affairs*, 31 July 2024, www.foreignaffairs.com/sudan/uaes-secret-war-sudan. Accessed 31 July 2024.

"UN Calls for $4.1bn in Aid for Sudan, Says Crisis Needs World's Attention." *Al Jazeera*, www.aljazeera.com/news/2024/2/7/un-calls-for-4-1bn-in-aid-for-sudan-says-crisis-needs-worlds-attention. Accessed 31 July 2024.

AMERICAN POLARIZATION

The Rise, Causes, Implications on Society, and Solutions

ASHMIZA SHAIK

Grade 10, Millard North High School, Omaha, NE. Honorable Mention.

Americans are increasingly expressing concern about polarization: a divide caused between different ideological groups, spurring hate throughout our nation. As issues like immigration, abortion rights, and the economy become increasingly debated, especially with the 2024 US Presidential election, citizens are shifting more towards one political party or the other rather than collectively working on crucial issues. Polarization makes individuals stick to their own opinions and be more unwilling to listen to others who share different narratives than them. This is influencing our nation on a broad scale.

The Rise of Polarization Throughout the Years

Throughout the last 40 years, polarization has risen significantly in our nation compared with other democracies. Political parties have been taking opposite stances and viewpoints on all issues leading to opposing ideologies to be formed within US politics. Americans' attitudes against members of the other political party have worsened faster than those of Europeans and other significant democracies. Compared with nations like Canada, India, and the United Kingdom, polarization has increased faster than any of these nations. We are currently facing the largest amount of polarization in US history. This significant increase in polarization is unique to the USA.

Causes of Polarization within Society

Polarization in the USA has been provoked by several factors. The major cause of polarization—especially within politics—is an individual's political identity. Feeling strongly affiliated towards one political party or the other leads to a party vs. party mentality, creating a lack of agreement. This has not only enhanced the divide but created a system of hatred between those of different political parties. Leaders from these parties have been utilizing emotional appeals to mobilize citizens toward their party. This shapes opinions and makes citizens affiliate themselves with a political party rather than the issues that they'll solve for our nation. Instead of candidates focusing on major issues they wish to come to a consensus on, their major way of recent marketing has been to spread hate and highlight mistakes in the opposing candidate. This makes it difficult to compromise on key issues and bridge the divide in our nation.

Another cause of polarization is the media creating an echo chamber effect. An echo chamber means that algorithms on social media will filter videos directly to what the viewer resonates with and what they've been enjoying. They do this to create a curated feed for the viewers based on their preferences, yet this doesn't allow viewers to engage with opposing opinions, creating what's known as an echo chamber. People simply hit the follow button on creators they agree with, but unfollow or scroll past creators that share different views. This further contributes to the echo chamber generating polarization. Social media isn't just a way to spread opposing viewpoints; it influences polarization as a whole. On the contrary, people who engage with different forms of media, even those that differ from their values, tend to be more tolerant of other viewpoints.

America is one of the most diverse nations in the world as we receive large-scale immigration from around the world to achieve the American dream. This diversity is something we pride ourselves upon. However, in recent years, this diversity has caused us to divide rather than unite, as people are becoming more opposed to listening to those sharing different narratives. America's polarization is interwoven with racial identity. Subordinating minority identity to a common American identity makes minorities less interested in contributing over time. Racial or religious hate against minorities being spread throughout the media has further polarized our nation.

Modern Day Implications

Increasing polarization is causing a gridlocked Congress. Polarization is making it harder for Congress to pass bipartisan legislature causing a legislative gridlock and an inability to take action against key issues that plague our nation. Today, over 75% of unresolved issues in Congress are due to legislative gridlock and disagreement between parties to come to a compromise. This is making issues such as climate change, gun rights, and abortion to be commonly disagreed upon. It is instrumental in minimizing polarization to ensure that the gridlock is eliminated.

Misinformation has also been on the rise along with polarization. With citizens more likely to support ideas they support, this drives misinformation. People are becoming more susceptible to this, and more likely to believe and share false information just because it aligns with their views. This is setting a dangerous precedent as misinformation generates hatred for certain groups and furthers the divide in America. In fact, in the United Kingdom polarization has caused riots and protests caused by misinformation spread against the minority Muslim population within the UK. It has also caused the UK to see a fragmentation in politics. If polarization continues to go up in America, we could see even worse implications that diminish the status of our nation.

The Solutions to Polarization

One of the largest ways to reduce polarization throughout America is for all of us to take action. Polarization grows if we aren't willing to tolerate opposing groups. Civilians influence the increase or decrease of polarization within any nation. We must recognize that WE are the change. Being more open-minded and willing to interact with other groups that share opposing viewpoints can decrease prejudice among groups. Rather than collaborating with a homogenous group, highlighting diversity through cross-group interaction can reduce polarization and bridge the divides.

WE must also bridge our gaps by not strictly supporting one party or the other, but by having the willingness to listen to both ideas. By supporting bipartisan initiatives, we can ensure that our Congress becomes more effective in passing bills, but also ensure that we foster understanding in politics. Leaders must also adopt a more tolerable approach to opposing viewpoints to emphasize the common goal of bettering our nation rather than simply highlighting their narratives.

Polarization has only been on the rise and compromising the values of our nation. Therefore, to prevent this concept from deteriorating American progress, we must take action to fight it.

References

Kimball, Jill. "U.S. Is Polarizing Faster Than Other Democracies, Study Finds." *Brown University*, 21 Jan. 2020, www.brown.edu/news/2020-01-21/polarization.

Kleinfeld, Rachel. "Polarization, Democracy, and Political Violence in the United States: What the Research Says." *Carnegie Endowment for International Peace*, 5 Sept. 2023, carnegieendowment.org/research/2023/09/polarization-democracy-and-political-violence-in-united-states-what-research-says.

IMMIGRATION

The Climate Refugee Crisis

ASHMIZA SHAIK

Grade 10, Millard North High School, Omaha, NE. Honorable Mention.

As the world works to combat climate change's negative implications, immigration remains severe, affecting the most vulnerable developing nations, promoting a worldwide refugee crisis. Previously, immigration and asylum seekers have been known to apply for refugee status due to political instability or economic hardship. However, we're entering a new era as climate change is now leading to more climate refugees than ever, further worsening the refugee crisis.

Climate change has been increasing global temperatures, exacerbating natural disasters. It's also causing rising sea levels worldwide. As sea levels rise, coastal areas remain most prone to flooding, causing people to become climate refugees. The United Nations Refugee Agency explains that the worst flooding has occurred in Kenya, Burundi, Somalia, and Tanzania. In Kenya, 210 people have died and 20,000 refugees have been displaced. These vulnerable communities near coastal areas are disproportionately affected by the impacts of climate change compared to others. Yet, these countries actually lack funds to address the climate crisis and build infrastructure to prevent flood damage, leading to direct displacement.

But these natural disasters like floods all cause a broader issue: triggering economic instability. They damage billions of dollars' worth of infrastructure and food supply, crippling the economies of impacted nations. The World Health Organization explains how recent floods and storms in Nigeria have caused a loss of food for over 8.5 million people, destroying agricultural produce. This has caused farmers' profits to completely diminish throughout the nations, pushing them to the brink of poverty. The countries that are the most affected by climate change are the ones in the developing world that can't recover from natural disasters like these that cause rippling instability.

Climate change isn't an issue that is getting better over time. In fact, it's been known to be causing an increasing number of natural disasters worldwide, further exacerbating the refugee crisis. From wildfires in Wyoming to floods in

Nepal, every corner of the world is being impacted by this crisis. Natural disasters linked to climate change are becoming prevalent. The University of Virginia puts into perspective that we have over 30 million climate refugees now, but by 2050, over 1.2 BILLION are expected to be under the climate refugee category.

Despite the number of refugees expected to rise in the future, anti-immigration rhetoric has been gaining attention. Nationalist and xenophobic ideals are seeking to limit immigrants and refugees from gaining stability in foreign nations. Specifically, European nations have been taking an anti-immigrant stance over the years with the rise of the right wing.

Right wing parties such as Germany's AFD party have been experiencing passive political success due to their immigration reforms. These parties have portrayed immigrants and refugees, despite them facing challenges like climate change, as a threat to public services and safety throughout Europe. By using the refugee crisis as a tool to elevate their political image and gain citizen support, right wing parties are marginalizing refugees and preventing them from gaining asylum.

The United Kingdom has also been promoting its "Rwanda Policy." This policy seeks to send all refugees coming into the UK to Rwanda. Despite where they came from, sending refugees to Rwanda only worsens their security. Rwanda is already experiencing instability and isn't even ready to be a safe haven for millions of refugees from around the world. It's time for industrialized nations around the world to step up and provide safety for our society's increasing number of refugees. Immediate action must be taken for the sake of those fleeing from the disastrous impacts of climate change.

References

University of Virginia. (n.d.). *Millions move: Climate change, displacement, and migration*. Retrieved October 26, 2024, from global.virginia.edu/events/millions-move-climate-change-displacement-and-migration.

UN Refugee Agency. (2023, July 15). *Climate crisis fuels flooding and deepens displacement*. Retrieved October 26, 2024, from www.unrefugees.org/news/climate-crisis-fuels-flooding-and-deepens-displacement/.

World Health Organization. (2023, October 20). *Devastating West and Central Africa floods affect over 4 million people, raise health risks*. Retrieved October 26, 2024, from www.afro.who.int/news/devastating-west-and-central-africa-floods-affect-over-4-million-people-raise-health-risks.

A "Memoir" to the Past

DANIEL VANOURNEY

Grade 11, Westside High School, Omaha, NE.

SILVER

Chief operating officer and partial owner of Flagship Restaurant Group, Anthony Hitchcock, helped start the company 21 years ago when he got a call from his first cousin, Flagship Restaurant Group's now CEO, Nick Hogan.

"One day, my cousin called," Hitchcock said. "He'd just gotten his law degree and asked me if I wanted to move to Omaha to open a sushi restaurant. I told him he was crazy. I didn't wanna move to Omaha."

Eventually, Hogan offered to fly Hitchcock up to Omaha to learn more about the opportunity. Hitchcock had been listening to NPR and heard them say that the thing people aged 16 and older regret the most is not taking more risks, and it stuck with him.

"I decided to leave a really credible employer that I had at the time in Texas and move here," Hitchcock said.

Hitchcock went to college with Tony Gentile, another one of the owners of the Flagship Restaurant Group, and they were both pursuing degrees for hotel and restaurant management. After graduating, they eventually found themselves at the same job, and Hitchcock was able to convince Gentile to come with him to Omaha.

"I convinced Tony to come with me because Tony is a very talented chef," Hitchcock said. "We drove up here to Omaha, joined Nick, and Nick had a good friend at the time, Tom, who was an architect, or had just gotten his degree in architecture."

Thus, Flagship Restaurant Group was born with Hogan as CEO with his law degree and knowledge of finances, Allisma as the architect and Gentile and Hitchcock with their hotel and restaurant degrees.

Fast forward 21 years and Flagship has expanded to multiple states and now has 20 Blue Sushi locations with another slated to open later this year, and recently opened up their brand new concept Memoir, Feb. 5, at 930 Harney Street.

"It would be easy to just have stopped with the couple of concepts that we had and grow those, but we love food," Hitchcock said. "We love restaurants and we travel a lot. So, we're always out visiting different restaurants across the country and getting inspired to want to have a concept like that ourselves."

Fans of Flagship's other concepts such as Blue Sushi Saké Grill, Blatt Beer and Table, among others, will find a little bit of everything for everyone on the Memoir menu, including, but not limited to, steaks and sushi.

To help bring this concept to life and open it, they brought in John Frans, who is a Regional Operations Director for Flagship and has been with the company for 19 years.

"The cool thing that I like about Memoir is that we title ourselves an American grill, but what we also do is we bring some of our sushi items to our concept as well," Frans said. "It separates us from the normal American grill, and we're able to do something Flagship does so well as sushi, with having all the Blue concepts as we have, and we've got one of our corporate chefs that does all the sushi helping us create this menu."

In addition to sushi, Memoir will have three separate steaks on the menu, as well as other menu items associated with the traditional American grill.

"We've got a filet mignon, a ribeye and a flat iron steak and they're all made a little bit different," Frans said. "We have seafood dishes, we have chicken dishes, we have a great salad menu. Starters are stuff that everybody will like and then like I said, the sushi aspect of it brings it all together."

Frans is also excited as this is the first restaurant he will be personally responsible for opening.

"I'm excited to show people what I've got as far as how I open restaurants," Frans said. "It's important to me to show to the owners what I can do to help get one of their restaurants off the ground."

Heading the creation of the menu is head chef and part owner of Flagship Restaurant Group Tony Gentile and Flagship corporate chef Nestor Rebolledo, in addition to Ben Maides who has made a name for himself in the Omaha culinary scene, even becoming a semifinalist for the 2020 James Beard best chef, and is the owner of Au Courant. He is also one of Flagship's Culinary Directors.

While Memoir has a diverse menu, it is more than just a restaurant to Hitchcock. Memoir was not only conceptualized to recognize the journey of Flagship and its owners, but to be an immersive experience. He describes it as classic, timeless, lively and family as there is a big family element to Memoir.

"We love food and we're also very passionate about people," Hitchcock said. "It's really neat for us to create a space where we know we can host people within a city and create experiences where they're going to walk and have memories."

Frans and Hitchcock also say that if someone is interested in working in the restaurant industry they should not be afraid of issues arising, and they should be able to be able to address those challenges and be positive.

"Positive energy inside of a restaurant is critical because it translates across the whole restaurant," Hitchcock said. "Making sure that someone is high energy, positive all the time and willing to change and adapt to whatever comes your way and has a desire to create experiences for guests."

Frans adds that you shouldn't be afraid to give it a chance, echoing that he started at the bottom and worked his way up.

"I encourage everyone to give it a chance, be confident in yourself and what you're doing," Frans said. "There's always tough services and everybody's questioning whether they still want to do this, but those happen at any restaurant and don't get discouraged when you have those rough shifts."

"Memoir is part of a big project where it's part of a series of concepts opening there," Hitchcock said. "Right after memoir opens, Châm Pang Lanes opens, which is our duckpin bowling concept, and right next to that is Ghost Donkey," Hitchcock said. "Some of the food for those will come from Memoir's kitchen. So they all kind of work off of each other. When I say family, there's an experience part to it because my wife and two children could go down at 4 PM and bowl at Châm Pang Lanes and have a 6 PM dinner reservation at Memoir."

Flagship is also set to open their Mediterranean concept, Clio's, in the coming months.

For reservations at Memoir go to ourmemoir.com.

Originally published as: Vanourney, Daniel. "A 'Memoir' to the Past." *Westside Wired*, 6 Feb. 2024, westsidewired.net/57612/ae/a-memoir-to-the-past/.

Mootz Pizza Opens
in Countryside Village

Daniel Vanourney

Grade 11, Westside High School, Omaha, NE. Honorable Mention.

Westside alum Collin Adkisson started Mootz when he lost his job due to the COVID-19 pandemic. He recently opened up the brick and mortar pizza restaurant in Countryside Village. Adkisson started small and built Mootz up to what it is today.

"Me and my brother started making pizza out of our garage and we had a link in our Instagram bio where you could have pizzas delivered to your house," Adkisson said.

Eventually, this evolved into a food truck, and then a brick and mortar restaurant this August. They're open Tuesday through Saturday, 11 AM to 9 PM. Mootz still has the permits to take the food truck out to the public more, but it is usually for private events only.

"We're closed Sunday and Monday," Adkisson said. "We usually use [the food truck] for events only. We don't take it out to the public on the street as much."

Since Adkisson grew up in the Westside area, most of his friends live nearby. Westside itself is located near Mootz, which is one reason why Adkisson chose Countryside Village.

"I worked downtown most of my career and with pizza I always just wanted to be in the neighborhood and to have the families and neighborhood people [as customers]," Adkisson said.

An average pizza is fifteen dollars, a slice is about four dollars, and drinks are two dollars.

"You can call in, and we do pickup and to-go orders as well," Adkisson said. "We're currently not on Doordash or UberEats, but we're looking into it."

While Adkisson's favorite cheese is grana padano, a cheese similar to parmesan, he did not like cheese as a kid. He especially didn't like sharp cheeses and smelly cheeses.

Now, though, he doesn't want overly fancy toppings; he is branching out.

"The menu has fairly simple toppings," he said. "Pepperoni, sausage, hamburger, supreme, just cheese pizza, and we recently decided the Hawaiian pizza."

Mootz also has a crispier crust as they are a neo-neapolitan style pizza, which is similar to a neapolitan pizza. A neo-neapolitan pizza is more American, and is cooked at 700 degrees, which is what makes it crispier. It also has heavier dough, and can have a raised or flat rim unlike a traditional neapolitan pizza, which just has a raised rim.

"I'm not sure what Noli's or other places do, but as far as Mootz, what sets us apart is we use the best ingredients that we can get," Adkisson said. "We use traditional methods and traditional equipment, but we also make our own pizza. We follow guidelines, but we don't let them restrict us at all."

Adkisson is aware of the public's differing pizza opinions, so he offers a variety of options.

"I think whatever you want to put on pizza is okay," Adkisson said. "I know some people think pineapple on pizza is sacrilegious ... we put ranch on pizza here so, like, I know there's some people that would cringe at the sound of that."

Another thing that makes Mootz special is that they make their ranch, Italian dressing and blue cheese in house. They also offer a unique condiment for more adventurous people who like a kick of spice.

"One thing that we don't make in house but a condiment that I love is our Mike's Hot Honey," Adkisson said. "It's real big in Brooklyn and it was started by a guy who was a pizza maker and had a pizza shop in New York. He eventually branched off and started making hot honey."

Mootz also has a gluten free crust, and offers vegan options. They can make all of their pizzas without cheese, and have many veggie-only options, including their veggie pizza with mushrooms, green peppers, onions and black olives. As for vegetarian options, it isn't just pizzas to look forward to.

"We [also] have garlic confit here," Adkisson said. "We're considering doing garlic knots as an appetizer."

Adkisson is always thinking of new specials as well.

"We actually had a barbeque chicken pizza," Adkisson said. "We've done a buffalo chicken pizza before, too. We used to run them as specials on the food truck."

As far as dessert, Adkisson is still playing around with the options, but they do currently have a classic on their menu.

"We have chocolate chip cookies right now, and in the future, we'll have different cookies and possibly a chocolate cake here soon," Adkisson said.

Adkisson has always wanted to make pizza since he was a child.

"I remember one day I ate pizza for breakfast, lunch and dinner and I remember thinking, 'man I could eat pizza all day, everyday,'" Adkisson said.

Adkisson's favorite pizza he sells at Mootz is either the pepperoni or the margherita pizza.

"To me, I feel like pepperoni pizza resembles what pizza is," Adkisson said.

Since Adkisson doesn't eat much processed food the only pizza-flavored thing he has tried is the Pringles, which he thought were not bad.

"I think pizza is a good marketing strategy, if you want to sell something just put pizza on it," Adkisson said.

However, he doesn't just like pizza because it tastes good or has grana padano cheese on it.

"I'll say I like pizza specifically because there's a little bit of an art to it and a little bit that's out of your control," Adkisson said. "With pizza it's a living thing and you can go down a rabbit hole with it."

Roberto Garcia, an employee at Mootz, knew Adkisson's brother and was looking for a job after he moved back from Oregon. He was told he could work at Mootz, and help out.

"I think he knows a lot about his staff, he's knowledgeable, he researches a lot, he executes well and you know that's what I like," Garcia said. "The standard, the oven is beautiful, the place, you know more than anything this is a family business."

While Garcia has been a chef for almost four years, pizza is a new land for him and he invites everyone to come to Mootz.

"Invite everyone to come try the pizza, it's really good, it's a nice place, it's a family business and it's really close to the school," Garcia said.

Originally published as: Vanourney, Daniel. "Mootz Pizza Opens in Countryside Village." *Westside Wired*, 9 Sept. 2023, westsidewired.net/56070/feature/mootz-pizza-opens-in-countryside-village/.

Omaha Native Thankful to Work on Film in Nebraska, Freshman Has Supporting Role

Daniel Vanourney

Grade 11, Westside High School, Omaha, NE. Honorable Mention.

Nebraska native Justin Blecha never thought he'd find his way in the film industry, but over a decade later, he had the opportunity to work on Snack Shack, a film shot in Nebraska. Westside freshman June Gentry also played a supporting role in the movie.

"I was actually in California working on another project, a TV show called Blackish," Blecha said. "By word of mouth I heard one of the guys on my crew talking about how his wife was offered a job on a project in Nebraska. But she turned it down. I was just so happening to be heading back to Nebraska in two weeks, so I got the phone number of the production designer."

This led to him cold calling the production designer, explaining who he was, how he grew up in Nebraska and always wanted to work on a film there and how he was interested in working on the film.

"She said 'can you come today after you get back to town?' and I said 'yeah absolutely,' so I just jumped on it," Blecha said. "The next day I was down in Nebraska City working on the movie. It's just the right place at the right time."

Blecha worked on the set decorating department for Snack Shack, and as it was a period movie that took place in the 1990s in Nebraska, they had to think outside the box to get set decorations as they did not have access to the prop houses that Hollywood has. This also happens to be the same era Blecha grew up in.

"When you're trying to create 1990s Nebraska, you have to take a step back a bit further because you're going to have elements from the 70s and 80s that kind of creep their way in," Blecha said. "Everything that was in the movie, we had to source locally from antique shops or people's garages or basements, wherever we could find period-correct set dressing."

Nebraska memorabilia was easiest to find as they shopped around Nebraska and Iowa.

"It was cool to be able to go through people's prized possessions," Blecha said. "Some of it we rented and a lot of it we bought from folks."

Blecha also had fun sneaking in things like Dorothy Lynch salad dressing and yellow ribbons tied to the trees.

"Nebraska also during that time, there were conflicts that we as a country were involved in, so there were yellow ribbons tied on all the trees to show support for our troops," Blecha said.

Additionally, Westside freshman June Gentry had a supporting role in the film playing Chrissy, A.J.'s (Conor Sherry) sister.

"I heard about a casting call and decided to submit for fun," Gentry said.

Gentry enjoyed the experience a lot and loved working on the film.

"It was so fun going to the premiere and seeing the movie for the first time and telling funny stories about when we were filming," Gentry said.

Blecha also enjoyed working on the film as the director grew up in Nebraska City, and was an approachable director.

"It was awesome working with the director, who's a local guy born and raised in Nebraska City," Blecha said. "It's important to make sure everything is period correct, and a lot of the directors that you work with aren't as approachable as he was."

Blecha is also part of IATSE Local 44, a union based out of Hollywood.

"Our locals are craft specific," Blecha said. "Omaha is Local 42. That's a mixed local, so it's one union that encompasses everybody's job. But the California Local 44 is specific to my craft which falls under the property department. That's like your set decorators, your prop masters, your set dressers, anybody who's involved with handling any of the set dressing or props or set construction falls under local 44."

Another thing that makes being a part of a union make sense in Hollywood is that a lot of the work is gig work so people may not be employed or working on films or shows the whole year.

"It's a way to make sure that the way we're being paid is consistent and that we're earning wages that we should expect to earn on different projects," Blecha said. "So they negotiate our wages for us and through that we have a pension and health care, all the stuff you would get from a regular nine-to-five job."

Looking back on it, Blecha never expected to end up in Hollywood working on shows such as Blackish and Cupcake Wars as well as working on films with directors like Rob Zombie and Quentin Tarantino.

"My older brother moved to Los Angeles to go to art school," Blecha said. "And he kind of just fell into it and told me he was going to be focusing his efforts on building a career in film and TV."

Through this, his brother eventually convinced Blecha to come down to LA and give it a chance.

"One day it was like the middle of winter and I was sick and tired outside of the cold and snow and he convinced me to come out and work on one job," Blecha said. "So I went out and worked the one job and had a great time. I fell in love with it. And then I figured it would be over and I'd have to go back home into the real world, but then another job came up and then it just kept going and going and I kept getting more phone calls for more projects and the next thing you know, joining the union and the work keeps coming."

Blecha also says if people are interested in this line of work, they should 100% pursue it.

"The benefits are great," Blecha said. "I know it seems a little far-fetched for some people that this is really a line of work and they can pursue it and be successful, but there are hundreds and hundreds and hundreds of people across the country that it's a reality for them."

Originally published as: Vanourney, Daniel. "Omaha Native Thankful to Work on Film in Nebraska, Freshman Has Supporting Role." *Westside Wired*, 8 May 2024, westsidewired.net/58250/ae/omaha-native-thankful-to-work-on-film-in-nebraska-freshman-has-supporting-role/.

SENIOR PORTFOLIO

The Woes of Eternity

MIAH FOX

Grade 12, Paxton Consolidated School, Paxton, NE.

SILVER

I Shall Stare Back

I know what you think of me. I know of the whispers muttered alongside my name. I know you think of me as a monster rather than a human. The killer that is undeserving of the mercy granted to the lowest of miscreants. How ugly and gruesome I am—how evil my soul has become. I am a villain of the blackest of inks. Now, what if I told you that there was a time in which I was not only beautiful, but good? Innocent.

I never commented on my beauty. I never boasted, I never bragged, I never acknowledged their stares on my auburn curls, but I was beautiful, in a way that I was not even aware of back then. I was the light of the sun reflecting off stained glass, the flame of a single lit candle in a dark room, and yet, I did not heed their stares. I looked away, for I was a woman not meant for a man's touch. I was a priestess of the goddess Athena, only and always, and I would never break her law of celibacy.

I had believed that, anyway.

I still remember the stare of his deep, cobalt eyes, blues that clashed against each other, battling to find the purest shade. I still remember the way his hair waved in the wind, carrying the scent of the sea. I remember his old, cruel smile, and I remember when he had followed me, followed me to the temple of my goddess, and stood before me at the altar of my protector.

Here's the thing about the gods. A funny, terrible thing. It doesn't matter if you praise them, if you have devoted your life to them. It doesn't matter if you are the most innocent to walk the grass of Athens. For as long as you are human, you are no more than a toy to their wicked emotions, and the gods love beautiful toys.

I didn't want it. Just like any man that had cast their gaze on me, I did not desire this god, but Poseidon was angry with Athena, angry at my goddess, and he was not swayed by the will of a human.

It was beside that altar that he tore away my clothes from my shoulders, and it was beside that altar that I broke the laws of my goddess, and yet still, I had cried out for her, for the protection that I had faith that she would provide. I reached for the altar with both body and heart, but my goddess did not stop her enemy. Frozen with fear, her name was the only thing I could bring to my lips, and for as long as the god had his way, my prayer came upon deaf ears.

It was only hours later, when Poseidon had left me bleeding and humiliated by the altar, did she come by my side. Her touch was cold when she laid it upon my shoulder, her gray eyes belonging to those of a warrior. I begged her to forgive me, to lay mercy for the sin I had committed. She spoke with no warmth, no sympathy. She was not willing to fight against the god of the sea, but she gave me an offer.

I ask you, what would you give for protection? How cruel would you become to gain security? Would you choose to live in human shame, in human vulnerability? Or would you become something for the gods to fear? For all men to fear! I would pay any price, give away the last of my innocence so that I-I would no longer be the prey, but the predator!

Gone were my locks of auburn and copper. Gone was my smooth, glistening skin. The light in which I casted with my beauty was extinguished the day the sea laid their hands on me. It wasn't until I lost it did I realize how lovely I was, but lovely lay the gates to my downfall.

I now had a temple of my own, an altar in which I lay to sleep. My skin is the texture of gravel, thick and imposing. My teeth now bare fangs with which I eat, and my hair, my lovely gorgeous hair that was wrapped tightly in his fingers, now had the ability to bite back. Poseidon shall not be the only one to fear my gaze, for every man that dares to approach and stare, I shall stare back.

I was beautiful once, I possessed so much gorgeous light. I was beautiful, and innocent. Now I am neither.

The Shadows of the Past

"Down, down down
The little mockingbird comes around, 'round, 'round
Sing a song for me and I'll sing for you
The little mockingbird sang as he flew ..."

"It's always a tragedy for one so young to go so soon ..."

There was a frigid rain that morning, the cold foretelling the winter to come. It was almost as if God was crying with us, as if God took pity on me.

"But to go as a child means to live only as a child. For he knew no evil. He did not see tragedies such as this day, he held no sins or shadows. He lived happy, innocent, and pure. And forever he will remain this way in our memories."

It was strange to me, God's sympathy, because he is the one who first took my husband away, and now my son. Perhaps this was not the compassion of the lord, but instead his way to mock me. To fill my bones with the cold of grief.

"He was given the utmost care and compassion by a mother so caring and kind."

Yes, he was mocking me. Telling me he has doomed me to be alone.

"And while his life was short lived. It was one that was fulfilling."

I may have asked why God had chosen to curse me, but I was too busy cursing him.

> "The mockingbird danced around his head
> His voice calling out to him as if as a friend
> 'Little boy, from you I ask,
> Will you sing, sing till the sky turns black?'"

"Melinoe, please, hear me."

I turned away from the roaring flames of the fire, my fingers burning from being so close. Behind me stood Joane, holding a hand-woven basket in her hands.

"Yes?"

Joane's blue eyes scanned mine. I hated the pity I saw in them, the pure sadness. But she was my friend, and I knew she was only doing what she thought was natural.

"Melinoe. Are you alright?"

What do you think? But I responded softly. "I'm fine, Joane, what did you bring to my home?"

Joane lifted the basket. "My husband brought home extra meat from his hunt. I thought you could take it instead."

I kept silent. I knew how scarce game was in the forest. Joane's family had nothing to spare.

"Where do you want me to set it down?" She continued on after my silence grew too long for her. I nodded over to the table, putting a small smile on my face. "Thank you. But I must ask Joane, are you sure you can spare this for me?"

"Oh it's no issue. Honestly you'd be doing me a favor taking this off my hands." She set the basket on the warped wooden table. Three chairs sat around it; only one was pulled out for recent use.

I knew that I should've invited Joane to stay, to keep in her company so that I may build strength. But I lacked the foundation to build upon. Instead, more than anything, I just wanted her to leave.

"Thank you, Joane. I wish you well."

Joane turned back toward me, her face cast in a bright glow from the fireplace behind me. "Are you sure you'll be okay, Melinoe?"

I came closer to her, pushing her out the door. "Of course. I'm just tired at the moment."

Soon she had backed up toward the door, and reluctantly she turned the handle, her face filled with sadness. "Okay, I hope you get some rest. When should I come to visit again?"

"If I need anything I'll come to you."

Joane opened the door, and the frigid air of winter drifted into my home. "Okay, Melinoe."

Then she left, and my home was empty once more.

"For the deer love your song
And with it the flowers drift along.
Desire to hear you fills the fish
For it is all of the forest's only wish."

It was a few days later, when the first snow fell, that I was back at that fireplace. In my hands held a sock that was as big as my palm, and a needle and thread. I carefully sewed the hole I found in the toe, each flash of the needle in the fire light was another flash of thought that passed. Complete silence except for the crackling of flames. He's going to appreciate that I fixed these up for him. Who?

I looked down at my work, seeing that I was done. Confusion filled my mind for a moment, and my fingers drifted over the stitch work. It wasn't right, I'll need to redo it.

I dug my fingers back into the fabric, pulling and snapping the strings apart until I was back to where I began. Though I noticed that I had pulled the hole to be bigger now, the fabric was even more frayed than before.

It's okay, I can fix that. He's going to appreciate that I fixed them up for him.

> "The boy sang, his voice bringing joy
> For the forest loved the sweet boy
> A song of hope, a song of despair
> His voice was so fine, for the message no one cared."

Winter was arriving in waves, falling and receding over the course of many days. I was lucky enough to be able to gather enough snow to boil for my stew, made with the game given by Joane. With the river being frozen, it would be such a hassle to gather water from there.

I smelled the rich scent of my cooking, and a smile drifted across my face. Quickly, I set the table, spoons, bowls, and I made sure to let enough water cool down for some drinks.

Filling my bowl with the savory stew, I sat the warped table. My voice came out gentle, softly spoken.

"Jonathan, it's time to eat. Come out of your room."

There was no answer. I didn't worry, he was sick after all. He just needed more rest.

I continued eating my stew in silence.

> "The mocking bird looked and saw the smiles
> Just to see the boy he had traveled for miles
> But hearing his song he knew the truth,
> And so once more he sang to the youth."

Winter came strongly now. I looked up in the sky to see that storm clouds had built into what was surely going to be a blizzard. But I need not the fire to warm me. These days I don't feel so cold.

Still, I began to cover our home. Using old shirts and rags, I stuffed the fabric between windows so that the cold may not invade. This winter will be difficult. I only hoped that our food may last us.

> "Little boy, fly with me,
> I'll show you the sky
> Little boy, brave as thee
> Let's fly, fly, fly ..."

Snow fell onto my black hair as I dug into the ground. Falling so fast that with every scoop of my shovel more had replaced it. But I continued my task. For it had been a long time since Jonathan had been able to come outside, he was too sick to get out of bed these days. After I clear this spot he may have the strength to get up from his rest.

The wind howled, and the snow blinded me, but even though my fingers were numb and my lungs filled with thin air, I didn't quite feel cold. A strange feeling it was, but it empowered me. For perhaps God was giving me the strength to create this small gift.

I finally stopped my digging, straightening up my sore back and smiling at my work. The snow was falling faster with every moment, but perhaps for just a little while Jonathan may step outside.

I walked back into our home, going into my room and grabbing extra blankets for him to use. Slowly, I came to his door, and lifted my knuckles to knock. It had been a long while since I had seen him. He usually comes out while I sleep, grabbing whatever food I leave out on the table for him. So I could only smile to reunite with him again.

"Jonathan? I have a surprise for you."

There was no answer on the other side of the door; I called his name once more, and was only met with silence. My smile faded a little, saddened, though perhaps he was only asleep.

"Jonathan, I'm going to come in, okay?"

Slowly I turned the brass door knob, walking into the room that I knew as my son's.

He liked to collect rocks, and it was these rocks that you saw when you first entered the room, stacked on the shelves, piled on the edge of his writing desk. A couple books on geology were there too, ones that I spent too much on in order to get them for him. To the right corner of the door, his bed was nestled against the wall. His own bow, much smaller than his late father's, hung directly above his head board.

My eyes fell to that perfectly made blue bed, and I paused, confusion filling my mind like it always did these days.

Where was Jonathan?

"Jon?" I asked, my voice tinted with hesitance. I received no answer, silence filling my home.

No, *our* home. Why did I say *my* home?

"Jonathan, where are you?" Worry was now filling my heart, I bit my lip, looking around the small space with no luck. "Jonathan, come out, you're scaring mommy."

Where could he have gone?

Did he get up from his bed?

Did he sneak away when I was shoveling the snow?

My eyes fell on the window, sitting right across from my son's bed.

Of course, he must've gone outside. He saw me out there and wished to follow.

I dropped the blankets, leaving the room so hurriedly that I knocked into our kitchen table. Bowls of soup and plates of food fell to the floor. Confusion marked my mind on why they would be there in the first place. But that didn't quite matter. I made a note to clean it up when I got back, and rushed out the door.

I nearly was knocked off of my feet by the wind, unprepared for its onslaught. This snowfall was much heavier than usual. I wondered why.

It's not snowfall, it's a blizzard.

But I didn't feel cold.

"Jonathan?" I called out to the haze before me. "Jonathan, where are you?"

His disappearance was worrying to me. What if he had gotten lost? He always liked the forest too much, I always told him not to go alone.

Panic filled my lungs. I tried to calm myself down, but to no avail. The fear absorbed me so fast that I hardly had the urge to quell it. I felt the cold now, if only slightly.

God as my witness I would not leave my boy to die in this snow.

The snow crunched under my boots as I ran out into the haze. The cold invaded my throat as I tried to raise my voice over the wind. Calling for him, calling for my son. I ran past the buildings and past the covered streets. The snow came to my knees, and it was growing higher.

"Jonathan! Jonathan, where are you?!" I cried. The snow froze my tears before they could fall.

I was on the edge of my village before long. Turning my head frantically for any sign of him. It was here that Joane's house was placed. She must have heard my wailing, for I saw her door open. There my friend stood, her eyes wide with panic and concern.

"Melinoe, what are you doing out in the snow?!" she called, the wind making it so that her words were little more than an echo.

I was about to respond, about to ask for her help in searching for my lost son. But from the sides of my vision I saw a flicker of movement. A shadow, just the perfect size for a small boy.

I looked back at Joane. She was yelling something again, but the wind was growing stronger, too loud for me to hear. I could try to get her help, try to hear her frantic words,

Or I could save my boy.

I dove toward the woods, and that shadow, just at the edge of my vision, ran away from me.

Running, clambering over snow, digging my numb hands around whatever was available and pushing myself forward. It wasn't long before my sight was completely gone. When the snow bored itself so strongly within my bones that I wasn't sure if I was climbing over the snow or buried within it. How did I not feel the cold before? I had forgotten what warmth felt like.

"Jonathan—!" My voice cut short, my throat frozen so much I was sure it would shatter. If I couldn't call out, how would he be able to find me here? How could I just leave him like this? How could he leave *me* like this?

How could he leave me?

I paused, my limbs falling still as confusion marked my mind once more. Something, something was there, at the edge of my mind, what was it?

"Mom, I'm sorry."

I looked up, my head shaking, trembling with the icy fingers of the devil as he raked his hands down my spine.

"What could you ever be sorry for?"

"I just wanted to hunt like dad did, I didn't mean to get sick."

My lungs started to burn. The cold was so condemning.

"I just wanted to be outside like dad always was."

No, it wasn't the cold. It was my sobbing. Deep, racking sobs that rattled my ribcage.

No, no no no.

How could he leave me alone in our home?

How could I ever live there alone?

The wind howled in my ears. A deep, unending wail. Carrying my sorrow, my grief up to the heavens to a God that has abandoned me.

It was *my* wail. *My* son. *My* home. It wasn't supposed to just be *mine*. It was supposed to be ours.

The cold, the pain, the tears, my wail sent them away. Sent them all away until that sound went silent too.

Everything was gone after that.

The Painter and Her Flame

Kamaria

He was beautiful, his eyes a light blue with joy and warmth. His golden hair was a shining light to all of those around us. His smile came easy, and his voice was one that calls to the birds and the people. To imagine there being anyone brighter was blasphemy.

Where my voice falters, his voice grows bolder. Where he brings warmth, I bring a frigid cold. I am no more deserving of his love than that of an isolated mountain peak.

To think, he has been cursed with me.

Haru

She was beautiful. Her white hair was a soft light on the world, her eyes were as dark as obsidian and as deep as the lowest seas. She listened to those around her, an observant and wise eye on all.

While I speak with arrogance, she speaks softly. And when I burn those around me with my brutishness, she cools the very air that I breathe.

To think, I've been blessed with her.

<><><><><><><><><><><><><><><><><><>

"There he goes again."

"My, he burns as bright as fire, he need not the coals for a torch."

Haru walked along the village path, unaware of the conversations the townspeople had about him—unaware because he was too wrapped in the beauty of the one next to him.

"Ah, she travels with him today."

"Such a unique pair, why he chose her I don't know."

Kamaria, always observant, heard their words, though she was wise enough to keep her eyes on her brilliant fire.

"Are these the brushes you want, Kamaria?" Haru asked when they came to the vendor.

"Haru, we came to buy from Adamo. I don't need more brushes."

"Yours are getting old now."

"I only brought enough for Adamo's order."

Haru smiled, though he put the brushes back.

"If only my son could be blessed as Haru is." The townspeople continued as the couple walked away. "Perhaps we wouldn't need to fill our home with the constant smoke of fire."

"The Speaker is coming today. Perhaps she will choose to bless more than just him."

Cana, Speaker for the Gods, was worshiped and respected as if she was one of the very gods that she served. The human woman treated her role as emissary with utmost importance. And it was here on this day that she came into the small, impoverished town of Elouan.

The Speaker carried a staff that had an ornamental lantern atop it as she walked into the townsquare. Her rich robes of silk and satin gleamed in the low light of the flames. Onlookers stared in awe, and when she came to the well marking the center of Elouan, she raised the silver staff and called in a voice that was both light and firm.

"I am the Speaker for the Gods, come to hear the humans of Elouan's words. Ask, and may their generous blessings rain down on all of you."

The villagers came forward, one after another in a line carrying their offerings to Cana and the gods. Kamaria and Haru went home, for they had all the blessings they ever could desire.

"Speaker, I am Hitendra," the villager called out as he kneeled before Cana. "My prayer for the gods is for one wish alone. I wish for a strong light of my own."

"Speaker, I am Peregrine." She, too, bowed before the Speaker. "And I have but one desire, to see my way down the path without the use of fire."

"Speaker, I am Obi," the man declared as he was last in line and kneeled low before her. "My prayer to the gods is to be able to see without the harshness of a fire's glare—for seeing my wife without the distortion of smoke is rare."

Each one had given a similar wish; each one desiring the same blessing.

"What of the blessing of fire?" Cana asked them all, raising her flame-lit staff high. "Is that light not enough for you?"

All the townspeople gave her the same answer.

"Haru is blessed to light without fire, can't the gods bless us too?"

<><><><><><><><><><><><><><><><><><><><>

The home of Haru and Kamaria was unimpressive. It was made of stone with a hay roof, and only possessed two rooms: one, the bedroom and one, not. The latter was a small room with square windows that held no glass. They had very little—a fireplace to cook food, tools to prepare it, a pile of hay and blankets on which they slept, and the only luxury they could afford: Kamaria's art.

Paintings and brushes and canvases—her art was something valuable within Elouan. She sold her paintings every week, and it was with this money that she and Haru made their living.

"Haru, why did you ask to wed me?"

The question came suddenly, and Haru turned toward Kamaria, who sat on the floor with a canvas of golds and blues before her.

"What do you mean?"

She was bothered by what she heard the townspeople say. "You bring light to everyone, there is none that does not love you." She dragged the color of brilliant gold across the canvas with her brush, "And yet, I am the one who receives that love back. I haven't quite understood yet."

Haru got up from the fireplace by which he sat. He crossed the barren stone room to Kamaria, seeing her canvas in full view.

"It looks like something made by the gods."

Kamaria gave a secret smile, knowing that he did not see the same image she did. It was beautiful, indeed, with blues the same as Haru's eyes, and golds the same as his hair.

"You haven't answered me, Haru. Why am I the one blessed by your light?"

Haru paused, kneeling before the canvas in silence. When his light came close, the gold of the canvas glimmered, casting light across the entire room.

"You bring light, Kamaria. Like this," he said, gesturing to the painting. Haru looked up at their hay ceiling, the gold had shone on it like glitter. "It's as if the sky was dotted with fire."

"That light is coming from you, Haru. And it is not as strong."

"But when you reflect it, it reaches places that would be blind otherwise." He grabbed her pale hand, raising it to his lips. "I love you, Kamaria, because you make my light your own, and you make it beautiful."

A knock came at their flimsy straw door then, and both the painter and the flame looked up. Kamaria walked lightly to the door, opening it only to pause in surprise.

"Speaker," Kamaria said softly, as it was Cana, Speaker for the Gods, that stood before her.

Haru appeared at his wife's side, his blue eyes alight with curiosity. "Speaker, why are you visiting us?"

Cana did not need to ask to know that the glowing fire before her was the Haru that Elouan spoke of. He was truly as bright as they said he was, and one of the most beautiful men she had ever seen. She could hardly look him in his burning eyes.

Kamaria opened their door further, wise enough to know to bow her head. "Come inside, Speaker. It is an honor to have you here."

Cana hardly noticed the woman with white hair. She was small and quiet, someone she hardly found worth noticing. As she walked inside, she held her eyes on the warm fire that was Haru.

"Why have you come, Speaker?" Haru asked, snapping Cana's mind back to the present so that she could once again bring herself to use words.

"I've come to speak with Haru," she told the pair. She glanced around the room, feeling suddenly nervous around the man in front of her.

Haru smiled hesitantly, unsure of himself. "Why is that, Speaker?"

"Please, call me Cana."

"Okay. Cana, why have you come to our home?"

Cana remained silent not because she was unsure of herself, but for another reason. "How is it that you burn, Haru?"

Haru's smile came easy then. "Isn't it obvious?" He asked. "The gods have blessed me."

"The gods have given no such blessing," Cana declared.

Kamaria stepped next to her husband. "What do you mean, Speaker? How can you say that Haru is not blessed by the gods?"

Cana, for once, noticed the small, soft-spoken woman, and grew curt. "This is not a conversation for you."

Haru's light intensified in response, anger seeping into his expression. "Speaker, I ask you not to speak to Kamaria in that—"

"I shall fetch some water from the town well." Kamaria placed a cool hand on Haru's burning arm, and his anger was gone in only a moment. Kamaria bowed low before Cana. "It was an honor to see you, Speaker." And with that, she silently slipped from the house.

Standing alone, Cana found herself once again lost in the eyes of Haru. The girl had made her attitude brusque, and for a moment, Cana was not so cardinal in her role of Speaker, for she was wrapped within the warmth of Haru, and a jealousy that she did not possess that warmth for herself.

"Why do you live here with her?" Cana asked with a clipped voice.

Haru did not hesitate in his answer, "I could live no other way."

"This place, it is not deserving of someone such as you. You have no windows, no possessions, no wealth. I can give you a much better life."

The flame looked around his home—the place he lived with the woman that he loved—and he felt sure of the words he said next. "No windows, so that the breeze that passes cools the heat that I bring. No possessions, so that our home can be filled with more of my Kamaria's art. But you're wrong about our wealth, for she is my silver."

"And you are gold. She is not your match." Cana turned her back on Haru, viewing the surroundings as nothing more than a poor, impoverished home filled with the drawings of petty children. Little did she know of Kamaria's talent for reflection even as she stared within the very paintings that created it. "You will leave Elouan with me, Haru."

His voice was firm. "I will not."

She turned around. "You dare to defy the Speaker for the Gods?"

Haru was unafraid, standing boldly before Cana. "I do. You cannot ask me to leave my home and my wife."

"Do you truly love her that much? To live in such poverty when you can exist among the gods?"

His words were simple, "She is my perfect match. I will have you and your contempt in my home no longer. Leave, Cana."

Cana lifted her chin, an arrogance entered her eyes. "It is Speaker to you, Haru."

Her rich robes dragged across the barren floor as she walked out of the flame's home. Facing, for the first time, the feeling of rejection.

Kamaria watched with her wise eyes as Cana left Elouan, and hurried home to her husband. "What have you done, Haru?"

"She was speaking nonsense. I told her to leave." His light was still bright from anger, clearly emphasizing the worry in Kamaria's gaze.

"She holds great sway with the gods, Haru. Offending her is unwise."

Haru wrapped his arms around his wife, and he saw as her white hair gleamed in his glow.

"For what she was saying, I would offend her again."

The land of the gods was a beautiful place made of marble, gold, and diamonds, but today, Cana could not see that beauty. The Speaker was lost, staring at the flames of torches and lanterns that were lit both near and far. If only Haru was here, she would be able to see the true beauty that was this land. For his light is strong and persistent, nothing like the distortion of flames.

It was this thought that continued to pound within her mind, and when she opened the doors to the hall of the gods, it was this thought that she first spoke of.

"The humans wish for light," she called out to the dozen members seated in chairs at the round marble table.

Sunniva, Goddess of Flame, was the first to speak about this outrageous claim. "Do they not have the light in which I gave them? The fires that I have blessed them with?"

"This light is different—one that is constant and unchanging." Cana stepped closer to the gods. "I have found a man, a man that has such light. That is the light the humans wish for."

Beathan, God of Life, leaned forward. "A man that has flames?" He looked down the table at his fellow gods. "Has anyone given such a blessing to any man?"

Silence reigned, one that Cana had expected. "So, you had no knowledge of this man?"

"None," replied the god of wisdom, Aakil. "How can this be? A man that is blessed without the gods having blessed him?"

"There is still an issue of the light," Cana added carefully. "I have seen the light of Haru, and I believe that the humans may be correct in their desires."

Sunniva raised her chin in indignation. "My flame is enough! It is not worth the use of my power to give such strong, continuous light."

"You may not have to, Goddess Sunniva," replied Cana. She leaned forward on the marble table, the only human allowed to come so close to her gods. "I have a solution for both issues. Why not use Haru to light the humans' way? You will not need to use your power so often if you use his."

The gods looked at one another carefully, but Aakil was firm. "We do not even know where this Haru's light comes from."

"I agree, God Aakil," Cana said. "If you do not know how his blessing was received, then he may be dangerous. He cannot be left to walk among humans. But it would be a waste not to use his light, no?"

Abheek, God of War, shook his head. "There is no way in which this human can cast light across the entire land. Using his light will result in very little."

Cana paused at that, but then, her smile grew. "I have a solution for that, God Abheek. A second person."

"His perfect pair."

Kamaria

I was not able to say goodbye to him the day the gods cursed us. In one moment, his light, his warmth, his eyes, became so distant that my heart was wrapped in the coldness of his absence, cold with grief.

Haru

My Kamaria was right. I should not have offended Cana. For she was more childish than I ever imagined. For now, I am absent from her calm words, of her cooling hands. For now, I am absent from my Kamaria. And I burn—I burn without her to cool my heart. I burn with anger.

Kamaria

But I still sense you, Haru. In the distance, I see your light, and I reach out for it—reach out so much that the sea begins to churn. For when I do not face you, I am dark. For I hear the humans below speak of you and your warmth. They speak of how you grow life with your fire, and I feel nothing but pride for you. And pride that I can still sense you even here.

Haru

And I hear them speak of you. How beautiful you are, and how you paint the sky with dots of fire. How wonderful that your art can still be seen even now. If only I could see the silver hair they speak of one more time, and feel the cool breeze that carries your voice.

Kamaria

The gods fear you, Haru. They are not the creators of your flame. One day, that who has blessed you will come. And I will watch those below, and I will wait every day for the time in which we are reunited. For your light has always been stronger than the gods.

Haru
The gods will pay for what they have done to you, and I will make them pay. I will burn them with the flame that has been given to me. I will turn my curse into theirs. For Kamaria, my moon ...

Kamaria
My dear Haru, my sun ...
Even if it were to end like this again, I would still choose to love you.

The Cabin

The fog was like a physical person. Blanketing all of the barren land. The older woman could only see a few feet ahead of her. Could only hear her feet crunch into the cracked dirt. She wore the clothes of a traveler, and had the face of a war-torn soldier. Her black hair was cut only to jaw length, and even though the fog kept her blind, her blue eyes constantly scanned ahead of her. Her ears alert for anything.

She had no name, she had no need for one. Those who traveled with her knew her face, and that was enough. But it was there in that fog that she traveled alone. She needed to find her group again, needed to find shelter to wait out this fog. But the barren land gave nothing except sandy dirt and dead weeds.

It was when night started to fall, only known through the hazy light slowly falling down behind her, that she heard the familiar sounds of their call. Like guttural chirps, a bark cut short. The woman knew these sounds, knew that they were close. But just as the fog made her blind, it did the same for them. She kept utterly silent, listening to them slowly come closer and farther away as she walked. They had no reason for fear as she did, their footsteps were loud, their calls like a broken bell of death.

She nearly could scream at the sight of the cabin when she had found it. A small, shabby hunting cabin. It was the first building she could make out in this void of mist. Its dirty windows were unbroken, and its rotten door closed. They never opened and closed doors. They smashed their way in. She knew none of them could be inside.

She maneuvered her way up the crooked porch. She tried the door, but it was locked; fearing that breaking it open would cause too much noise, she lowered herself down, grabbing the lock picking tools from her bag as she slowly fiddled with the lock. It was stubborn, but with a faint click, the door squeaked open. She stood, laying her palm against the pistol at her side just in case.

The cabin was small, a main room, with only a short hallway at the back wall leading into a bedroom and bathroom. The main room only had a coat hanger in the back corner, and a raggedy couch placed in the direct middle. The woman sighed. Clicking the door shut behind her.

It was then that three girls came out of hiding from behind the couch.

The woman pointed her gun. They were very young girls. Pale and stick-like from lack of food. Each of them wore a thin white dress that looked almost pleasant with their black hair.

"Who are you?" the woman asked in a hiss. The three girls looked very alike, only differing in age as if they were sisters. The one that seemed to be the oldest held her hands up. Her eyes wide with fear toward the gun.

"We have no weapons. We mean you no harm."

"Why're you here?"

"Why are you?" challenged the second oldest. Her older sister elbowed her in the side.

"Please, put the gun down," the eldest said. The woman looked over the three girls. They truly didn't seem to carry any weapons. She clenched her teeth, and lowered her pistol.

The girls explained to her quietly their experiences. They had hardly any food or water, down to their last rations. They had stayed in the cabin for months, the fog was almost always around. It would stay for days, the oldest said, only leaving for a few hours and instantly rolling back in. They never were able to get out in time before they were left completely blind and had to track their footsteps back to the cabin.

It was during this time that the woman noticed the youngest girl of the sisters. She didn't speak at all, holding her head down and taking up as little space as possible. A scared, traumatized child. One of three who were starving and weak.

"I can help you out of here. I have food and supplies, we can make a run for it the next time the fog rolls out. I have a group too, they can take care of you."

"You'd really do that?" asked the middle child. Her eyes were hopeful.

"Yes, when do you think is the next time it'll be clear?"

The oldest girl shook her head. "A day at least. It was clear this morning."

The woman nodded. That's how she got stuck here; one second it was clear, the next, she was blind.

"Okay. Then we stay the night here. I have some canned food you can eat for now."

The girls nodded, eagerly biting into the food the woman sat out. The youngest barely touched any of it though. Hardly willing to look anyone in the eyes.

"How did you guys end up here anyway?" the woman asked the eldest quietly. "You aren't dressed for travel, and you don't have any supplies."

The girl swallowed. "Some men were taking us places. They had the clothes and food. We just were supposed to do what we were told." She glanced over at her sisters. "We got attacked by one of those ... things. We escaped, the men did not."

The woman glanced at the youngest. Those thin dresses ... prisoners to a band of men. No wonder she wouldn't look up to meet anyone's eyes.

They set up for the night. The oldest and middle child went into the bedroom, while the woman stayed in the main room behind the couch. The youngest, though, she didn't seem to bother to sleep at all. She sat in the back corner of the room next to the coat rack, her knees to her chest and her head down.

The woman didn't know how to handle kids. She was forty-three years old. Never married or became a mother. She didn't know how to comfort the girl so haunted before her. So the woman lay down behind the couch so that she could use it as cover in case something did come through the door.

She woke up to a scream. Loud and piercing. The woman sat up and grabbed her gun, looking around the main cabin room. The youngest girl was no longer in the corner, and as the woman backed away from the couch and pointed her gun toward the door, she saw the hand of a young girl fall from the other side of the couch, blood pooling from it. One of them got in. They killed the youngest.

If she wasn't so horrified by the sight, she might have been able to process the fact that the door was not smashed open. The windows weren't broken. They never opened and closed doors. They smashed their way in.

The woman stumbled into a standing position, waiting for it to rise from behind the couch. The oldest sister ran out of the room, just as the youngest sister stood.

Her eyes were red, as if they were entirely bloodshot, even her pupils. Her mouth was covered in blood.

"W-What ...?" The eldest could hardly speak. The woman froze in her spot. The youngest stared at them silently. The youngest had killed her sister.

"Go," the woman finally said. "Go—Run!"

The eldest didn't need to be told twice. She ran back into the bedroom, slamming the door shut. The woman dashed for the bathroom.

But not before she saw the hand move from behind the couch.

The bathroom was small and grimy. A small toilet next to a narrow sink and a hanging mirror was on the left side. There was a laundry basket placed next to the bathtub at the back wall. She grabbed the laundry basket and pushed it against the door. She shoved her back against the tub and her feet against the basket to barricade it, pointing her gun toward the door.

She heard pounding. Loud and steady, like drums beating slowly. She didn't feel the vibrations, the youngest was pounding on the bedroom door.

Then she heard the second pair of hands.

Pounding.

Pounding.

Pounding.

Silence.

She heard a plea, a cry of mercy before an earth-shattering scream came from the other side of the woman's door. She could hear her own heart beating in the silence that followed. But her hand stayed steady. Even as she heard the two pairs of fists pounding against her door. Her legs feeling the hit every time. Even as she heard the third pair of fists join in. She held it there, would she shoot these girls? Could she? Taking the life of someone on a battlefield, or something not even human was one thing. Could she kill children?

She saw, *felt* the door splinter and crash. Until it finally gave out. The laundry basket's weak plastic broke into pieces as it was thrown to the side. The door swung open violently, and the woman caught sight of the three young girls.

They all had the same bloodshot eyes. The two oldest had their dresses torn to pieces, their necks ripped out. The two youngest had reddened hands and faces. The woman shook in her spot. She needed to kill them. Needed to. How could she kill children?

Then they began to speak.

It was not a language known to man. Not one that could be spoken by one, either. They spoke in layers, together as one in eerie harmony. Then they said a name. One she recognized deep in her heart. She knew it was hers, but it felt wrong, dark.

"No ... no, get away."

She couldn't move her hand. She never froze like this. Never. They came forward, and she couldn't pull the trigger. They smiled, eerie and perfect.

"Get away!"

Eve's Temptation

My hands were cold, fingers shaking against the rough fabric of my coat pocket as the winter breeze hunted them down. I had spent my entire life for this day, my entire life to come upon this choice. I never believed I'd actually succeed, and when I did, I wasn't expecting the confliction that I felt. The power to change science for the rest of eternity, sitting within my freezing hands.

It was a place called the Apples Tavern: a small place, filled with the soft scents of fruit and liquor. Its doors were accented with gold handles, and a warm light filtered from its windows. If only to escape the biting cold outside, I walked through the doors, and found myself sitting at one of the seats next to the counter. Its surface was made of a deep brown oak, smooth to the touch, and worn away with the passage of hundreds of drinks and elbows being laid onto its surface.

"What can I get you?" the one behind the counter asked. He didn't look at me, but I knew it was me he spoke to, because there was no one else inside.

"What do you have?"

"Anything you want, I'll find a way to make it."

Anything I want. If I had the choice, what would I do? I found myself silent before him, but he said nothing. He only waited for my answer.

"I'll take a Bloody Mary."

I did not hear his entrance, nor did I see him sit beside me on my left. I wondered for a moment if he was there all along, and I just didn't notice until that moment. He was gorgeous, with dark eyes and combed black hair. His black suit shined in the light of the tavern, giving him the glow of someone with an inner brightness. He looked away from the bartender, and gave me a smile that formed dimples on his closely shaven jaw.

"I can get you one too. A beautiful lady such as yourself shouldn't have to pay for her own drinks."

His eyes sparked with intelligence and cleverness. I found myself without words, something that did not make the stranger's smile falter.

"You look ... upset," the stranger said, his eyebrows softening with sympathy. His words were like milk, smooth and sweet. "Is there something wrong?"

"I ... probably shouldn't say." Even his beauty before me was not enough to draw my mind fully away from the quandary that I faced that night. His face shifted with understanding, and he nodded just a little.

"I always believed that strangers are the best ones to tell your secrets to. They are the ones that can hold your sins without there ever being any price to pay, right?" He smiled easily, just as he set a Bloody Mary in a pristine glass before me.

Perhaps it was his expression of total empathy, or his easy demeanor, but I took a sip of the drink, and told him of my troubles. It was strange to put it into words for the first time. It was a conflict that built over the many years of my life, and yet I could explain it all in only a few sentences. The stranger leaned his head on his solid hands, listening with eyes that never left me, but when I finished, he was silent, as if waiting for me to continue. When I didn't, he scoffed softly.

"I apologize, I suppose I don't quite know the issue."

"What do you mean?"

"If what you say is true, then all that you accomplished is just your intelligence shining above all the rest. You are a scientist, why not continue your duty to science?"

"It seems so dangerous."

"Anything that is powerful is dangerous. If you spent your entire life for this, you deserve to use that power, no?"

I looked down at the red liquid of my drink. I suppose it's because I was looking down that I did not see her come in, for I only heard the shuffling of the stool to my right, and the worn voice that seemed to carry the millennia on its shoulders.

"A White Lady, please."

I looked at her, just as she looked at me. She wore a gray cloak that was ragged and torn, the edges frayed with time. Underneath that cloak, her face was no different. It was a face of deep, cavernous lines, ones placed in the forehead and nose, with smooth skin at the corners of the mouth and eyes, depicting a lifetime of agony and absence of smiles. The few strands of hair left visible were white and greasy, trailing down her face toward her haunted brown eyes. She held the warmth of the winter outside, absent of kindness as her mouth was twisted in a frown, the saggy skin contorting to follow her command.

"What a foolish girl you are," she said to me; it sounded as though her vocal cords were ripped to shreds, and she was simply trying to use what was left.

"What?"

"To claim intelligence, when you have no idea what you are doing."

It occurred that perhaps the old woman had heard what I said, and that she too was aware of what I faced.

"I ... never said I was smart. I just ..."

"No, but you believe it, don't you?"

The Handsome One let out a soft sigh, turning away from me and the woman to gaze up at the lights. "Not the most polite, are you, Ms.?" He tapped gently against the counter. "Placing such harsh judgment like that, it's unbecoming."

The woman coughed a little, she didn't even look at him, which seemed unusual considering that I hardly could look away from him. "It's best, girl, if you allow what shouldn't be to die in the unknown."

"Oh yes, and leave the world to waste away in ignorance, right? I don't see the point." The Handsome One casted his clever eyes back on me. "You could have the power of God, you know. You could give everyone the power of God. Why would you hide that away?"

He spoke as if he had as many years under him as the woman did, perhaps more so. He had such wisdom in his gaze, cunning like nothing I've ever seen before.

"It's because we are not God," the woman argued; she was looking only at me, even as the bartender sat her drink down on the counter. "We have no right."

The Handsome One laughed softly. "Is it because we cannot compare to God that we cannot make use of godly things? Or is it because we forbid godly things that we are unable to compare to God?"

"What? I ... I don't—" What exactly did God have to do with this?

"Everything, girl, everything."

I looked back at the woman, but I was certain that I did not voice my question aloud. She stared at me with those wise, haunted eyes. The look within them was enough to send bugs skittering up my arms. It was like I was looking into the agony of eternity, like I was seeing guilt in its original form.

"Who are you?"

The woman smiled, it looked unnatural on her face, like it took more effort than it did the frown. She laid a wrinkly hand on mine, and slowly, she passed me a glass with a white liquid inside, the White Lady that she ordered, completely untouched.

"I am a mother, girl."

The White Lady and Bloody Mary sat before my eyes now, but I don't believe I could handle drinking either one. When I looked to my left, the Handsome One still had one of those easy smiles, but it was the woman who continued to speak.

"The better it seems, child, the more humans will want to take it. They will take it, and then they will corrupt it, just as they've always done. As I've always done."

The saccharine voice of the first stranger was tinted in something else, now. Something that lacked that seed of empathy. "So much beauty was born from things that humans feared. Fear only ever held them back."

"Fear is what breeds our wisdom." Her voice lulled me to look at her once more, at her face filled with pain and that unfamiliar smile. "It is what allows us to learn, to adapt. Without fear, we would all die from the foolish choices we made."

I opened my mouth, perhaps once, then twice, but I couldn't find much to put onto my lips. I looked back at the drinks: one in red, one in white.

The Handsome One reached out to me then, reaching for my shoulder with such gentle hands I stopped breathing. "My Little Scientist, don't you believe yourself to already be wise? Why depend on fear for such a thing—"

His hand stopped a mere inch away from my coat, just as his words stopped. The bartender was there, reaching over the counter and clutching his wrist so tightly it would not budge even slightly. His eyes were pinned on the stranger, who didn't so much as blink.

"I think it's time for you to leave," he said.

"It's not as though I'm causing a fuss, am I?" The Handsome One withdrew his hand away from me, and the bartender let him. "The scientist doesn't mind."

"I want you gone." The bartender spoke with no aggression in his voice, only a simple fact.

"That's her choice, isn't it? That's what you said."

The bartender looked at me, then, his darker skin almost the color of the oak on the counter. Confusion entered my mind, but, looking at him, there was only one question I could think to ask.

"What should I do?"

The bartender looked down at the counter before me, he waited a beat, then two, and then he spoke.

"The choice is yours. You know the right one."

A red drink on the left, and a white one on the right. I scoffed to myself.

"That hardly helps, can't you just tell me ..."

I looked away from the drinks. The time I took to glance at them was only a moment, a single moment, but when I looked up, they were gone. The two strangers, the bartender, all vanished without a sound.

I was back in the lab, the winter breeze hitting the windows next to my office desk with enough force to sound like a pack of howling wolves. Apples Tavern was gone, and so was the oak counter. All that was left was my own desk, with a stack of papers before me. Papers that had the power to change everything.

My desk was always kept clear and clean, but not that night. No, there were two other things on top of the flat surface, besides the papers. On the left, it was a phone, with a small light blinking red, and on my right, it was a white candle, burning brightly in the dark room.

The choice was mine.

Burning Flowers

Velcro.

My tongue was made of velcro and my mouth was made of fur. My lips were made of Elmer's glue and the cords in my throat were stitched together with ribbon in my mother's sewing cabinet. I did not speak. Words stumbled out of my mouth like food I didn't chew being thrown up. They melt into the fur of my mouth like blood soaking into a carpet.

"The fuck is wrong with her?"

My neck would snap. My head would snap off and roll away from my body, carrying the words trapped within my esophagus. I want to tell him to get off my head, that his elbows are digging craters in my hair like the ones on the moon. He leans on me, I can see his fingers dangling at the top of my eyesight.

"She's fine, just a little retarded, right?" he said, his breath heated my forehead, he must be looking down at me. The blood in the fur of my mouth dries, permanently stuck. I don't speak.

"She's creepy, is what she is. Why the fuck is she staring like that?"

"Yeah dude, you wanna be that close? She might bite your fingers off."

Two, two standing in front of my desk. I do not know them. I do not look at them. They do not know me, they only know him, the one who will surely snap my neck.

"She's harmless," he said. He tapped fingers against my eyebrow. I blinked. "She doesn't do anything, see?"

A bored voice, one coated with chalk and beige. "Mr. Gersh, can you please sit down?" A moment, a sigh made of gray. "And please, you two, this isn't your class."

"It's a free period," said the first voice. "Our teacher said it was okay."

"Did I say it was okay?"

The elbows dug greater craters, weight multiplied as he pushed himself off my scalp. "Sorry Mrs. J, we'll keep quiet."

The shadows on my desk disappear. The heat of bodies is replaced by the cold of my skin. I do not move, the cold turns me to stone.

"She always like that?" said the second in a mutter. They went to the corner of the room. No one interrupts them, no one comes up to me.

"Told you man, she has a few screws loose." Gabe's voice carried a smile in the air. "You should've seen her yesterday though, this is nothing."

"Oh yeah? You were talking about that earlier, right? That's her?"

"Who else, man?"

Moments are memories left to die in the past. The present is an illusion, a time we can never attain because our brains will never catch up and process the now, they will forever be in the before. In the world, there are no occurrences that are sudden, only our limited perceptions that create an illusion of abruptness. We live in the past, and so we can never foretell the future.

I knew that when I heard the sounds, they had already happened. Their abruptness was only due to the fact I could not see the building of events. I could not expect the future, and nobody else could either.

A firecracker under a bucket, that's what it sounded like. A distant sound, distant, but loud. People looked up, I looked up, Mrs. Josti looked up.

Then the alarms went off.

Attention, a fire emergency has been reported in the building, please find the nearest exit ...

A fire alarm, one with flashing lights that spun in the little red box in our room. We stared at it, I stared at it, no one moved.

"What was that?" asked one of the strangers, one of Gabe's friends. No one answered him, he spoke louder, over the intercom. "What was that?"

"Was that a gun?"

What weird things words were. One word, one word so short, it carried only one syllable, and three letters. One word to turn kids into possums.

"What do we do?"

I don't even know who was saying what anymore. I don't think it mattered.

"Mrs. J, what do we do?"

"It's saying there's a fire, should we leave?"

"We should hide!"

"Mrs. J! What do we do?!"

Mrs. Josti wasn't much for critical thought. Ideas pinged against her head and glanced to the side. Every word of hers was a boiled carrot left unseasoned. She stared, and then she stood from her desk. We watched, watched her heels click against the floor as she reached the door. Neither panic nor certainty tainted her hands, hands that grabbed the lock and turned it, hands that pulled a sheet of paper down to cover the door's window.

Another firecracker went off.

A girl began to cry in gasps.

Everyone was standing now, standing and moving away from the door. My limbs were stone, my eyes pinned in by thumb tacks. We heard yelling outside the door. Yelling and screaming and crying. I was the only one left to be sitting, but I was not to be paralytic alone. With crying and whimpers and mutters and whispers, those of my class and the two strangers within realized a reality.

We did not know if the firecrackers were inside or outside.

We did not know if a fire was truly set.

We did not know if we should hide or run.

"Break the window. We can go out that way."

"Won't they hear it?"

"We'll just run."

"We should hide. The police will get here."

The girl with the tears now had a friend to hold her. Arms clenched around her shoulders, I wonder if the girl believed her friend to be comforting her, or if she knew her companion was stuffing her face into her chest if only to keep her hysterics quiet. Mrs. Josti stood with eyes wide, and a face that had become as white as the chalk coating her voice.

"Are you stupid—"

"Shh! Be quiet—"

"We need to—"

"But what if—"

I was the one to see it first, swirling its way in like rats scurrying through the cracks in the walls, its gray bodies falling over each other in hordes.

"Smoke," said a boy behind me. "Guys, it's smoke!"

"So there's a real fire?"

"I'm not gonna die in a fire," Gabe said. "We go out the window. Harry, grab a chair."

One of the strangers grabbed the chair beside mine, the one who suggested I might bite Gabe's fingers, and brought it over to him with his head ducked down like a turtle slipping only slightly out of its shell to check the time of day.

"Wait, wait, wait!"

Gabe had the chair above his head by the time the girl's protests slipped through the air. The girl pointed outside, her shoulders shaking.

"Look!"

I was a tree, an old tree with many roots. I was a tree and my chair was the dirt. But my classmates were flower petals, for they had no roots tying them down, and they drifted freely to the window.

More firecrackers, the girl in tears now screamed.

"Get back, get back!" Josti was yelling now. The flower petals flew away from the window with deep fear for the next wind.

"Think he saw us?"

"We can't go out that way! We need to go through the door!"

"There's a fire through the door!"

"He might've seen us!"

It is fall now, the tree loses its leaves in the fall. I shrugged off my leaves, my jacket falling off my shoulders to expose them to the cold.

"Mrs. J, what are we supposed to do?"

"Well, class, we just—We just need to stop panicking—".

A tree needs water, that is what a tree needs. A water bottle sat on the desk to my left. I grabbed the plastic cup and held it in my hands, just before pouring the water on my leaves.

"Wait, what's *she* doing?"

Soak the leaves, and soak my jacket. The bottle was empty quite quickly.

"Hey, what are you doing with my water?" A petal came to my side, a girl with hair that of the sun, wearing braids down her shoulders. She grabbed my shoulders, and as though a chainsaw cut through my roots, she pulled me like a weed from my chair. "Jeez, what is wrong with you? Can't you take this seriously?"

"Hold on, I've heard of that! It's supposed to help with the smoke!" The friend of the hysterical girl let go of her then, grabbing a jacket. "Come on, grab something and put it under the sink, we'll be able to breathe better."

The one with sun hair let go, looking back at the girl. Already the petals were scrambling, flowing toward the stream of water. My wooden limbs found a path toward light. I walked toward the growing number of rats beneath the door.

"Hurry hurry hurry! He's checking the other windows, you guys!"

"Close the shades then!"

Firecrackers, many firecrackers.

"We're gonna die!"

I touched the handle of the door. Hot, very hot. That was not good.

The window exploded behind us.

The glass was the knives of the devil, and the firecrackers were the words of his past victims. Screams were heard as the heat of hell revealed itself in its true form.

"Move!"

A boulder came between my shoulder blades, and a hand reached around me for the door handle. A yell sounded loudly in my ear like the roar of a lion being branded with a hot iron. Still the hand continued in its journey to open the door.

I was shoved forward.

My feet were made of cement, my eyes blinded by the lights of the underworld. I fell. I rolled. I burned. Hot flame surrounded us, catching onto the tiles that had fallen from the sky. The flames of Satan grabbed hold of my hair, my clothes. He licked my arms and back, and he sunk his teeth into my face. It melted the glue in my mouth, burning my throat with every breath, and I began to scream. Scream louder and louder, hoping to deafen the roars of death. I clawed out at the devil, rolled out of his grip hoping that I would escape his claws enwrapping my dress. I found myself gripping the edge of a cliff. No, it was a stairwell, one that would lead into the level below, going deeper than hell itself, and perhaps escaping its reach.

"No! No please!"

It was one of the petals. It was Gabe.

A firecracker was lit somewhere behind me.

Electricity found itself in my soul, thundering through my veins. I clawed my way to the cliff, and then I fell, I fell off and I rolled. One step then two, my shoulder, and then my back, and then my knee, rhythmically hitting the stone like a slinky being cast down. I was electricity and pain, I was flame and brokenness, I was the tree that was chopped and used as firewood.

The petals continued to burn.

Gabe.

He was the boulder that grabbed the door, the one who threw me into the arms of Satan, and he was the one who fell into the arms of Satan's partner. If I listened through the brokenness of air coming from my lungs, I could listen to hell torturing its victims.

This is what I have earned, for trying to escape hell yesterday. It has come back in new forms to devour us all, petals and trees alike.

"Honeybug?"

Last Tuesday, North Oakley High School had been brutally attacked by James Cormac and Reagan Brown, who planned and acted out a school shooting at the time that they had lit fires within the halls. Eleven were killed, and seven now remain in Saint Francis Hospital in the hopes of recovery.

I could not move, I would not move. I was a puzzle that had been put together wrong, all the pieces forced to fit; if I moved, I would only break once more.

Brown, 28, was seen entering the school grounds in the outfit of a janitor. Reports say that he was responsible for the fire, while his close friend and coworker went into the school with a gun. While Brown had walked out of the school and was later arrested, Cormac, 34, had ended up killing himself during the incident.

"Oh no ... Please no ..."

According to Brown's testimony, the motivation behind this attack was due to the fact that Cormac's daughter was attending the school, and was being severely bullied by her classmates.

I recognized that voice, the voice of warm oak and candle wax.

"Oh no, sweetheart ... I am so sorry ..."

After a particularly bad incident involving herself and six other students, Cormac had planned the attack in order to target these six students. He fatally wounded four of the names mentioned, while many more were caught in the crossfire.

A darkness was finding me now, wrapping itself around my mind, around my brokenness like a wound that promised that it would bring an end. It was cold, a relief from the heat brought down on my heart. This darkness enveloped my sight, obstructing it from seeing the world, and I was certain it covered my ears too, because I found a sound absent in the air.

Reports say that he might've continued on until the arrival of police, but he had stopped due to the fact that he had found his daughter, who had died after being caught within the fire and had fallen down a stairwell. It was most likely then that Cormac shot himself with his own weapon.

I realized that the firecrackers had stopped.

A Case for Mother Earth

Grade 12, Creighton Preparatory School, Omaha, NE.

SILVER

Recycling in Omaha

Pitted against my subversive desire to simply toss the breakfast burrito packaging in the trash, I scanned the back of the package for recycling information. A recycling symbol enveloped a number "6," prompting me, at the time, to automatically assume the packaging could be recycled. Throwing it in, I walked away with a sense of accomplishment and pride; I was doing good for our world, I was recycling. I discovered much to my chagrin later that the number "6" was indicative of the plastic not being able to be recycled, and that the funny little recycling symbol on the back doesn't necessarily mean that the product is recyclable. As with this case, it was quite the opposite. This experience, unfortunately, has been replayed many ways throughout the lives of many Americans. In fact, according to the 2021 Consumer Recycling Habits survey, despite ninety-five percent of Americans saying that they know how to recycle, less than fifty percent of them don't know the basics of recycling (New Survey Reveals Gaps in Consumer Recycling). The issue of whether or not our waste is recycled is predominantly attributed to the fact that the general public is ill-informed about how to best recycle, but the blame can also be brought upon large corporations in the manufacturing of their products, and on the city itself for its often inadequate system of handling the waste (Bowker; d'Ambrières; Badger). The City of Omaha needs major improvement to its process of how waste is recycled through pressuring large corporations to take responsibility for their role they have in the process of recycling, educating its people, and implementing an all-encompassing system of waste collection.

Ever since its conception, plastic has been molded and engineered in hundreds of different ways in order to best suit its purpose. Whereas the increasing complexity of plastic has led to the development of lifesaving devices such as vaccines and innumerable luxuries such as the smartphone, this in turn increases the difficulty of recycling plastics (What Is the Material of Your Phone Body?; Plastics Play a Critical Role in Immunizing the World). Plastic's versatility is abused by virtually every industry, from aerospace to food packaging to the machines that manufacture airplanes and food packaging (Plastics Applications). Many people, including myself, fall under the category of being "busy people [who] are asked to make split-second decisions about which bin something belongs in," and we often do what is referred to as "wishful recycling" (Wohlfeil). For me, this usually includes a frantic scanning of the back packaging to tell if I can recycle it, and if I am unsure I toss it in the recycling anyway—ignoring the mobile device in my pocket that could give me an answer in seconds. This hopeful spirit creates issues down the line and, with machines and humans working at "breakneck speed," the material is bound to be sorted incorrectly (Wohlfeil). But is this really all our fault? Many countries have asked similar questions and have begun to pass what is called an Extended Producer Responsibility law, or EPR, to combat this problem. An EPR is effective in that it forces companies that sell products within your region to make sure their product is either recycled, reused or composted. The company wishing to sell in that region pays into a producer responsibility organization (PRO), which manages all the finances and sale of recycled waste. This law functions by penalizing companies who promote hard-to-recycle products and using that money to ensure citizens have access to recycling facilities (Wohlfeil). Oregon is the nation's leader in EPR laws, with some EPR laws dating back to 2009 establishing guidelines around the recycling of paint (Oregon Becomes Second State to Pass Packaging EPR Law). As of today there are thirty-three states with EPR laws, yet Nebraska remains one of the few without these laws in any form (EPR Laws Map). The implementation of these laws in the City of Omaha could cause a cascading effect on the rest of the state. Given Omaha's leverage in terms of population, passing a law within the city could dissuade the selling of products in the rest of the state without their participation in the PRO. Within possibility, too, is that the law could influence smaller cities to pass similar laws, bypassing the often long debate among parties within a higher level of government. Passage of these laws is not entirely out of the question and the potential benefits are numerous. In speaking with members of the Omaha City Council, the passage of this type of law is unlikely, and can be best summed up by Mr. Pete Festersen's quote that the law "could be a challenge to get passed at the current moment." Mr. Festersen also included in his email a time in which he proposed the ban of single-use plastic bags in the city, only to be vetoed by the Mayor. He detailed this account to give me an idea of the "political climate"

(Festersen). Plastics, paints, and polymers are not going away anytime soon, and neither is the harm they cause if not recycled properly. EPR laws will create confidence in the citizens of Omaha, knowing that the products they hold in their hands are either recyclable or contribute to a better-encompassing system of recycling in the city. Although a large challenge at the moment, the city of Omaha still must work to pass EPR laws, in order to protect the health and beauty of our city and the surrounding area.

It is no secret that our world is in a climate crisis. Deforestation, plastic pollution, and rising global temperatures all top the list among the worst environmental problems of the year (Robinson). Stories of pollution's putrid burdens on the poor and plastic's poisoning of marine life are popular in the news. Where can we even begin to lend a hand? According to the National Ocean Service, the number one thing we can do is to "reduce, reuse, and recycle" (Protecting Our Planet Starts With You). Throwing items in the trash or recycling bin is a daily action for Americans that, when added up across the country, quantifies hundreds of millions of tons of waste (National Overview: Facts and Figures on Materials, Wastes and Recycling). Each individual in the state of Nebraska contributes roughly 6.2 pounds of waste per day (*Nebraska Department of Environmental Quality*). Given Omaha's estimated population of 485,153, the city of Omaha would be generating roughly 3,007,948 pounds of waste, or roughly 1504 tons of waste, every day (U.S. Census Bureau Quickfacts: Omaha City, Nebraska). Omaha has a significant responsibility to effectively manage and recycle this enormous amount of waste. What's more, despite seventy-five percent of American waste being recyclable, only thirty percent of it is actually being recycled (G. Alabaster). In speaking with a former employee of FCC, Lindsey Bowker, who worked closely with Firstar, a company that sorts and recycles all of Omaha's recycling waste, she emphasized the point repeatedly that education of how to recycle is the biggest area of improvement. She mentioned that breaking down boxes could "greatly affect the recycling process" and that there are incredible programs such as the Hefty ReNew program (aimed to collect hard-to-recycle plastics) that many people either don't know about or don't fully understand. She didn't touch on any radical solutions such as a machine to recycle plastic assisted by Artificial Intelligence or an electric recycling truck that could cut the fleet of trucks in Omaha by half in her argument. Instead, she highlighted the importance of one of the most protected rights in America—education (Bowker). We make the difficult decision of throwing an item in the trash or recycling every day, making the knowledge of what to do with the waste intrinsic to an effective system of recycling. Education of the citizens of Omaha can be in the form of social media posts, emails, mailing flyers, or even through direct dialogue. As stated above, Omaha's responsibility for effectively managing its waste is enormous, given the incredible amount of waste generated by the city every day. Omaha must work to educate its citizens on the basics of recycling so that we can be effective in keeping recyclable items out of landfills, contributing to a cleaner environment for all.

Furthering the issue of whether or not waste is recycled, the way Omaha handles the waste it receives can have a great impact on recycling as a process. The City of Omaha has a responsibility to both collect and to sort the waste it receives. Recently, as of 2021, the City of Omaha was granted $825,000 by The Recycling Partnership to replace recycling bins with over 135,000 new carts. Being given the opportunity to collect more recycling every week, citizens of Omaha recycled more and the city at large saw a sharp 68% increase in tonnage of recycling, far beyond what was predicted (Solving for Circularity). Yet, despite a much larger capacity for recycling, recycling carts are still being filled up. A few times a year my family will have to borrow space in a neighbor's recycling bin, after our bin fills up. An obvious solution to this issue could be a weekly pickup of recycling, giving less time for the bin to fill up. However, after speaking with Mrs. Bowker on this topic, she argued that more carts would be a better solution. She argued against switching to a weekly pickup, as it would require a large increase in budget due to more drivers, trucks, and more routes (Bowker). Carts, unfortunately, do come at the cost of $50.95 per year to the person buying (Current Pricing). This price has the potential to dissuade large amounts of the population of Omaha who don't have fifty dollars to give every year. This especially applies to families who have many kids but a low income; families who produce large amounts of waste but wouldn't be able to recycle much of it. Donations and subsidies from more affluent zip codes could help reduce this burden and increase recycling in poor neighborhoods. If the City Council agreed that the collection of recycling should be prioritized, the City of Omaha should prioritize time and efforts to the collection of money for the purpose of providing families with additional recycling carts. The availability of specialty recycling locations/drop-offs has a profound effect on whether or not someone recycles. A study done in China showed that people who had a willingness to recycle were twenty-five percent more likely to if they had easy access to recycling facilities (Zhang). On a similar note, Mrs. Bowker argues that there is not much work to be done in the sorting and recycling of the waste. She told me that the machines are "top-notch," but the biggest area of improvement is the collection of the waste in the first place—making sure every house has the opportunity to recycle (Bowker). With so many families unable to afford the cost of an extra recycling bin, the City of Omaha must help. Having space to place recycling during the week for families greatly increases the likelihood of them recycling. By providing extra carts to families who cannot afford carts but are in need of them, we will increase the percentage of waste being recycled. Omaha must fundraise money through subsidies and donations in order to increase the availability of carts throughout the city, especially to provide the opportunity to recycle for those who cannot afford to do so.

The City of Omaha, given its large population and therefore, responsibility, must deploy a new and effective system of recycling for the purpose of protecting its people, wildlife, and future generations from the horrors of pollution. This system can only be effective if it strives to put pressure on the manufacturers of goods sold in the city, educate its citizens, and implement an all-encompassing system of collection.

References

Badger, Emily, and Larry Buchanan. "The Absurd Problem of New York City Trash." *The New York Times*, 2 Mar. 2024, www.nytimes.com/interactive/2024/03/02/upshot/nyc-trash-rules.html. Accessed 3 March 2024.

Bowker, Lindsey. "Re: Problems with Recycling in the City of Omaha," 16 Feb. 2024.

"Current Pricing." *Wasteline Omaha*, City of Omaha, 21 June 2023, www.wasteline.org/current_pricing/. Accessed 24 March 2024.

d'Ambrières, Woldemar. "Plastics Recycling Worldwide: Current Overview and Desirable Changes." *Field Actions Science Reports*, Special Issue 19, 2019, journals.openedition.org/factsreports/5102. Accessed 24 March 2024.

"EPR Laws Map." *Product Stewardship Institute*, 29 Jan. 2024, productstewardship.us/epr-laws-map/. Accessed 24 March 2024.

Festersen, Pete. "Re: The Passing of EPR Laws," 30 Mar. 2024.

Gill Alabaster, Pamela. "America Recycles Day." *Personal Care Products Council*, 20 Apr. 2020, www.personalcarecouncil.org/perspectives/america-recycles-day/. Accessed 24 March 2024.

"National Overview: Facts and Figures on Materials, Wastes and Recycling." *EPA*, Environmental Protection Agency, www.epa.gov/facts-and-figures-about-materials-waste-and-recycling/national-overview-facts-and-figures-materials. Accessed 24 Mar. 2024.

Nebraska Department of Environmental Quality, nrcne.org/wp-content/uploads/2019/12/Measuring_and_Tracking_Recyclables_and_Organics.pdf. Accessed 24 Mar. 2024.

"New Survey Reveals Gaps in Consumer Recycling ..." *Paper and Packaging*, www.paperandpackaging.org/sites/default/files/2021-09/New Survey Reveals Gaps in Consumer Recycling Behavior and Knowledge - For Immediate Release_0.pdf. Accessed 24 Mar. 2024.

"Oregon Becomes Second State to Pass Packaging EPR Law." *Recycling Today*, www.recyclingtoday.com/news/oregon-signs-extended-producer-responsibility-law-packaging/. Accessed 24 Mar. 2024.

"Plastics Applications." *British Plastics Federation*, www.bpf.co.uk/plastipedia/applications/Default.aspx. Accessed 24 Mar. 2024.

"Plastics Play a Critical Role in Immunizing the World." *This Is Plastics*, Plastics Industry Association, 25 Apr. 2022, thisisplastics.com/safety/plastics-play-a-critical-role-in-immunizing-the-world/. Accessed 24 March 2024.

"Protecting Our Planet Starts with You." *NOAA's National Ocean Service*, 10 Aug. 2009, oceanservice.noaa.gov/ocean/earthday.html. Accessed 24 March 2024.

Robinson, Deena. "The Biggest Environmental Problems of 2021." *Earth*, 4 Mar. 2024, earth.org/the-biggest-environmental-problems-of-our-lifetime/. Accessed 24 March 2024.

"Solving for Circularity." *The Recycling Partnership*, 21 Feb. 2024, recyclingpartnership.org/wp-content/uploads/dlm_uploads/2024/01/Recycling-Partnership-State-of-Recycling-Report-1.12.24.pdf/. Accessed 3 March 2024.

"U.S. Census Bureau Quickfacts: Omaha City, Nebraska." *United States Census Bureau*, www.census.gov/quickfacts/fact/table/omahacitynebraskaPST045223. Accessed 24 Mar. 2024.

"What Is the Material of Your Phone Body?" *Global Supplier of Fabricated Products & Machining Parts*, www.samaterials.com/content/what-is-the-material-of-your-phone-b ody.html. Accessed 24 Mar. 2024.

Wohlfeil, Samantha. "How to Make Manufacturers More Responsible for Plastics Recycling." *InvestigateWest*, 15 Apr. 2022, www.invw.org/2022/04/21/

how-to-make-manufacturers-more-responsible-for-plastics-recycling/.
Accessed 24 March 2024.

Zhang, Suopeng, et al. "What Keeps Chinese from Recycling: Accessibility of
Recycling Facilities and the Behavior." *Resources, Conservation and Recycling*,
Elsevier, 19 Mar. 2016, www.sciencedirect.com/science/article/abs/pii/
S0921344916300283. Accessed 24 March 2024.

The Environmental Impacts of Solar Power

While commonly portrayed as the golden solution to the inevitable danger of
climate change, solar-farmed energy does come at a cost. In many ways, solar
power can be revolutionary in our fight against climate change. However,
numerous drawbacks are often overlooked. Too often, they are presented as if
they have none.

Fossil fuels, such as gas and oil, are used constantly in the world we live in.
Ever since the industrial revolution, we have abused fossil fuels to our advantage as humans (Shultz, sec. 1). In 2019, fossil fuels contributed to eighty-one
percent of the world's energy (sec. 1). Dependence on this form of energy, as
well as other forms, can have adverse effects (sec. 1). The burning of fossil fuels
releases greenhouse gases (GHG), which, in turn, cause changes in rainfall and
water levels, as well as many other detrimental effects (sec. 1). Thus, for all the
reasons listed above, solar power and other green energy solutions are highly
incentivized.

However, once invested into solar, many people are constantly desiring to
upgrade their panels. Lower prices and a higher conversion efficiency rate compared to the panels they originally bought ensure that they will get the most
out of the land they've dedicated to the purpose of solar power (Atasu, sec.
1). With arguments as convincing as these, consumers would be foolish not to
empty their wallets into the new technology for their property. With solar farms
being "competitive with all other forms of" energy generation, this desire to
continuously upgrade carries on to a much grander scale, solar farms (sec. 4;
sec. 2). The United States alone has more than 2500 solar farms (Mey, par. 1).
After the solar panels have been in use for an extended period of time, a huge
need for recycling these panels is presented. With panels endlessly going in and
out of use, recycling efforts are made seemingly futile. A company, First Solar,
has made efforts to recycle the panels. However, incentives to recycle through
them are very low (Atasu, sec. 3). It costs between twenty and thirty dollars to

recycle through them, as opposed to the one to two dollars if you were to just throw the panels in a landfill (sec. 3). About seventy-eight million tons of waste from the endless cycle of upgrading to the newest solar panels is predicted by the year 2050 (sec. 2). It is important to note that solar panels are not the only green solutions with the issue of recycling; wind turbines and others lack sufficient methods of recycling (sec. 5). "The science is indisputable: Continuing to rely on fossil fuels to the extent we currently do will bequeath a damaged if not dying planet to future generations," remarks Atalay Atasu (sec. 5). Whilst solar panels may appear innocuous, the growing demand to keep upgrading them leaves room for negative environmental impacts to seep through.

As you may have learned in chemistry class, the element lithium has an atomic number of three, is highly reactive with water, and sits directly below hydrogen and to the left of beryllium on the periodic table. What may not have been directly taught, but can be inferred, is that lithium plays a key role in lithium-ion batteries. Solar farms are commonly coupled with lithium-ion batteries in order to store excess electricity and provide a constant flow of electricity when needed ("Solar Integration: Solar Energy and Storage Basics," sec. 1). The process of mining lithium from the earth is quite the strenuous process ("The Environmental Impact of Lithium Batteries," sec. 2). Approximately 500,000 gallons of water are needed to mine one metric ton of lithium (sec. 2). As may be expected, this necessity for such a large amount of water affects farmers near the site of mining (sec. 2). In places such as Chile's Salar de Atacama, farmers are forced to get water from other locations besides the area they currently reside, which is extraordinarily unfair to the people trying to feed a population (sec. 2). Additionally, during the process of mining lithium, hydrochloric acid is released (sec. 2). In places such as Nevada, hydrochloric acid has been found to have impacts on fish in surrounding rivers up to one-hundred fifty miles downstream (sec. 2). Cobalt too, another element in lithium-ion batteries, carries its weight in downsides. Cobalt mines in Africa use child labor without the use of protective equipment (sec. 3). "This isn't a green solution—it's not a solution at all," states a lithium battery expert from the University of Chile (sec. 2). The process of mining lithium, as well as cobalt, is a grueling and arguably downright deplorable task.

As the process of mining essential elements in lithium-ion batteries is deplorable in its own right, we haven't begun to scratch the surface of issues with the batteries themselves. Unfortunately, lithium-ion batteries have been historically difficult to recycle, and continue to be, with even the best efforts being made inadequate. In Australia, about two percent of 3,300 metric tons of lithium in general is recycled (sec. 3). This is simply just staggering. One of the many reasons why lithium is so incredibly difficult to recycle is due to the secrecy of what exactly goes into the batteries (sec. 3). As may be inferred, companies are constantly looking for ways to get the highest value out of every millimeter of their electronics. Batteries are a component entailed in this never-ending conquest. Thus, companies are very secretive about what goes into their batteries, always attempting to thwart their competitors from gaining access to new methods they've invented. While this may bode well for upfront profit, the environmental effects don't prove to be so great. Oftentimes, lithium-ion batteries are disguised as lead-acid batteries and are sent through a crusher. In other cases, there have been fires at recycling plants where lithium-ion batteries were not stored properly (sec. 3). Thus, for all the reasons listed above, the recycling of lithium-ion batteries proves to be a risky and simply difficult task that is unfortunately very much a necessity.

Solar panels are oftentimes thought to produce no greenhouse gas (GHG) emissions whatsoever. To a certain extent, this thought is true, as they don't expel any greenhouse gases while running properly. However, the process of installation and maintenance brings about many hidden emissions (Shultz, sec. 4). Of these emissions, roughly ninety percent is attributed to manufacturing and materials that go into the panels (sec. 4). A study was done called the Life Cycle Assessment (LCA) in which a theoretical 16.4 megawatt solar farm was compared to the existing Brazilian electrical system (sec. 1). The Brazilian electricity system consisted of "66.67% hydro, 9.28% natural gas, 9.15% wind, 8.25% sugarcane bagasse, 2.79% nuclear, 1.62% coal, 1.55% oil, and 0.69% solar" (sec. 2.3). They studied both of these systems over their lifetime of about twenty-five years (sec. 0). An important factor in the study was that they assessed the equivalence of the systems beforehand, which many studies had failed to do prior (sec. 1). It was concluded that the theoretical solar system would emit about 0.044 kg of CO_2 per kWh it produced (sec. 3.2). On the other hand, the Brazilian electricity system emitted 0.277 kg of CO_2 per kWh it produced (sec. 4). Additionally, the solar system "yielded an environmental payback of five years, eight months," and one day, which is ten times lower than that of a thermoelectric natural gas power plant of equal measure (sec. 3) (sec. 1). This means that it would take roughly five and a half years to produce enough electricity to make up for the greenhouse gas emissions it produced in the processes of maintenance and installation. "Thus, it can be concluded that solar panels are crucial in the search for emissions mitigation... with demonstrated environmental benefits (sec. 0)." We cannot fail to remember the vast environmental benefits solar panels offer, providing, overall, much cleaner energy than fossil fuels, an energy source which we are so heavily dependent on.

Often, solar farms occupy land that could otherwise be used for farming, ranching and other essential services. There is an alternate solution to this problem called agrivoltaics ("How 'Agrivoltaics' Can Provide More Benefits Than Agriculture and Solar Photovoltaics Separately," sec. 1). This is, quite literally, the combination of agriculture and a photovoltaic system ("Agrivoltaics at Jack's Solar Garden." 0:40-0:45). A study was conducted in Arizona, in which chiltepin pepper, jalapeño and cherry tomato plants were paired with a solar farm ("How 'Agrivoltaics' Can Provide More Benefits Than Agriculture and Solar Photovoltaics Separately," sec. 2). The plants were located both under and behind solar panels, and by design would receive less sunlight per day (fig. 2; sec. 2). It was found that the production of "fruit" these plants yielded doubled in this particular agrivoltaic system (sec. 2). It was also found that both "carbon dioxide uptake (how much the plants absorb carbon dioxide) and water use efficiency" increased by about sixty-five percent (sec. 2). What's more is that, due to the transpiration of the plants, the solar system produced roughly one percent more electricity on an annual basis (sec. 2). Agrivoltaics is nevertheless an incredible solution for sharing land both agriculture and solar farms need, issues with agricultural production itself, and a growing demand for clean energy.

Agrivoltaics is not simply a theoretical idea, but a reality we live in. A twenty-four-acre hay and wheat farm in Boulder County, Colorado, was converted to an agrivoltaics farm after it was determined less "economically viable" to keep the existing farm (Byron, "Our Story (so far)," par.1). The panels are "relatively self sufficient," with frequent checkups needed to make sure they are functioning properly, and only one panel has been replaced in the span of about two years (Jackson). One thing very important to their mission is that they do not rely on battery storage, and instead pump the electricity right out to their local grid (Jackson). The panels are situated higher, so that the plants don't cover them, and enough space is provided between rows of panels to allow for tractors to gain access ("Agrivoltaics at Jack's Solar Garden," 0:47-0:56). As mentioned earlier, agrivoltaics cut back on water needs, sometimes cutting needs to about half ("Agrivoltaics at Jack's Solar Garden," 1:21-1:42). Furthermore, normally a plant shuts down its photosynthetic processes during the day, due to the intensity of the sun ("Agrivoltaics at Jack's Solar Garden," 1:08-1:13). However, the shade of the solar panels allows them to continue this process during the day, attributing to greater plant growth and production ("Agrivoltaics at Jack's Solar Garden," 1:13-1:18). Additionally, farmers get to work in the shade of the panels for the majority of the day ("Agrivoltaics at Jack's Solar Garden," 2:42-2:47). This change from hay and wheat to agrivoltaics brought about numerous community benefits as well. The owners of this farm work to educate members of the community about agrivoltaics, they donate two percent of the electricity they produce to low-income community members (about ten homes), and they also actively work to put food back into the community that they produce at the farm (Byron, "Our Vision," sec. 1; sec. 3). This is a tremendous example of the implications and positive effects that an agrivoltaic solar system can have, and it is truly a win for all.

Peeling back the cover a bit reveals that solar panels aren't all sunshine and rainbows, but quite the contrary. They can have many abominable downsides coupled with their incredible benefits. Although the lithium-ion batteries used in solar panels can be toxic to the environment in many ways, agrivoltaics can help to heal that wound and show forth a brighter future. Green energy is absolutely necessary in our fight against climate change, but its downsides shouldn't be overlooked.

References

"Agrivoltaics at Jack's Solar Garden." *YouTube*, uploaded by Byron Kominek, 11 October 2022, www.youtube.com/watch?v=FGMNFPC-9fk.

Atasu, Atalay, et al. "The Dark Side of Solar Power." *Harvard Business Review*, 18 June 2021, hbr.org/2021/06/the-dark-side-of -solar-power. Accessed 29 September 2022.

Byron. "Our Story (so far)." *Jack's Solar Garden*, www.jackssolargarden.com/our-story, Accessed 2 October 2022.

———. "Our Vision." *Jack's Solar Garden*, www.jackssolargarden.com/the-vision, Accessed 2 October 2022.

"The Environmental Impact of Lithium Batteries." *Institute for Energy Research*, 12 November 2020, www.institutefcrenergyresearch.org/renewable/the-environmental-impact-of-lithium-batteries/. Accessed 27 September 2022.

"How 'Agrivoltaics' Can Provide More Benefits Than Agriculture and Solar Photovoltaics Separately." *Energy Innovation Policy & Technology LLC*, 1 November 2021, energyinnovation.org/2021/11/01/how-agrivoltaics-can-provide-more-benefits-than-agriculture-and-solar-photovoltaics-separately/. Accessed 29 September 2022.

Jackson, Allison. "Re: Contact from Jack's Solar Garden." Received by Seamus Haney, 21 October 2022.

Mey, Alex. "Most U.S. utility-scale solar photovoltaic power plants are 5 megawatts or smaller." *U.S. Energy Information Administration*, p.1. www.eia.gov/todayinenergy/detail.php?id=38272. Accessed 26 September 2022.

Planas, Oriol. "Solar Photovoltaic Power Plants, How It Works?" *Solar Energy*, Ezoic, 13 May 2015, solar-energy.technology/photovoltaics/photovoltaic-power-plant, Accessed 3 October 2022.

Schultz, Herwin Saito, and Monica Carvalho. "Design, Greenhouse Emissions, and Environmental Payback of a Photovoltaic Solar Energy System." *Energies*, vol. 15, no. 16, Aug. 2022, p. 6098–N.PAG. EBSCOhost, doi.org/10.3390/en15166098. Accessed 24 September 2022.

"Solar Integration: Solar Energy and Storage Basics." *Office of Energy Efficiency & Renewable Resources*, U.S. Department of Energy, www.energy.gov / eere/solar/solar-integration-solar-energy-and-storage-basics. Accessed 24 September 2022.

Left on Red

Left on Red

Election day happened nearly a month ago.

Since then, the Republican Party has secured a trifecta. The Republican Party will regain control of the Senate and the Executive Branch, under President-elect Donald Trump, in January. They will remain in control of the House.

Previously, I detailed what a second Trump Administration could mean for the environment. Among Mr. Trump's Day 1 Policies are his commitments to "Drill, Baby, Drill," in reference to oil, and to roll back environmental protections and government regulations for companies to become more environmentally friendly. He's also vowed to pull the United States out of the Paris Climate Accord, undo parts of the Inflation Reduction Act and to dismantle the EPA.

In recent events, the nomination of Matt Gaetz to the position of Attorney General by Mr. Trump looked to be a loyalty test of the Republican members of the Senate. After his withdrawal from the nomination amidst allegations of sexual assault, the loyalty of many Republican senators of the 118th Congress to Mr. Trump (that Mr. Trump needs in order to pursue his policies) remains untested. It is unclear exactly what policies from Mr. Trump's agenda will be accomplished. What is clear, however, is that Mr. Trump intends to pursue these policies, and he never accepts "no" for an answer.

The future of environmental progress will be left in the hands of the red— the Republican Party. Donald Trump may leave the world bleeding, he may open wounds barely taped shut by the Biden Administration, or he could use his red, Republican, trifecta to advance progress towards environmental justice and stability.

Mr. Trump, the power is in your hands (as you very well know).

We, as citizens, still must do our part to preserve the health of our planet.

Plant-Based Meat: A Three-Part Analysis

Over the course of the next couple of weeks, The Leaflet will be examining three impacts of the choice to switch to plant-based meat. The issue of whether to switch to a plant-based meat diet is a contemporary one. The correct decision is not always clear, often offering a different conclusion depending on who you are. Over the course of the next couple of issues, The Leaflet will examine three major impacts of the choice to switch to plant-based meat—the impact on the planet's health, animal health, and your health. We will ultimately discuss drawbacks to the switch as well. We want to inform you of the impacts of switching to a plant-based meat diet, so that you can make the best decision for who you are.

Land

The land-efficiency of plant-based protein cannot go unmentioned. A shift entirely to plant-based proteins could free up as much as two times as much land as India and China combined (Ritchie). Yes, you heard that correctly. This land could go towards efforts of increasing biodiversity or mitigating the effects of deforestation in other parts of the world. The possibilities with all this land are truly endless.

Air

At the forefront of arguments for plant-based meat is its ability to lower greenhouse gases (GHG). This argument holds absolute validity. Meat and dairy production currently accounts for 14.5% of global GHG emissions (CarbonBrief). To put this figure into perspective, cutting just 11% of this 14.5% by 2035 (meat and dairy production now representing 12.9% of global GHG emissions) is the equivalent of decarbonizing the entire aviation industry ("Combating").

Switching to plant-based meat helps lower this figure substantially. If the world were to substitute half of the global protein market with alternative proteins (plant-based meat), "agriculture and land-use GHG emissions would decline by 31 percent by 2050" (Clark et al.).

What's more, shifting to plant-based meat could prevent up to 12,000 deaths related to air pollution in the United States alone (Tilman and Clark).

Sea
Roughly two billion people live in countries with inadequate water supply (UNICEF). Simply put, an individual switching to a plant-based diet can cut his/her water consumption by 50% ("Plant-Based Diets"). Plant protein requires far less water than animal protein to cultivate, leading to this drastic decrease in water consumption ("How Plant-Based").

A shift to plant-based proteins can also significantly reduce high levels of nitrogen and phosphorus in our waterways that ultimately impairs water quality by stimulating the growth of algae (FAO).

These are some of the impacts to the health of the planet of the switch to plant-based meat. As seen, there are no negatives to the health of the planet with the switch, compared to the production of animal-based meat. Of course, the farming of the plants used for plant-based meat still requires resources (water, energy, land, etc.), but compared with methods used to procure its animal equivalent, the resources that plant-based meat requires are significantly less.

We look forward to providing you with a further analysis of the decision to switch to plant-based meat in further issues.

Donating Blood as a Metaphor for Caring for the Environment
A random act of service I find myself repeatedly drawn to is donating blood. There's something about the cleanliness, order, and efficiency of the experience that draws me to donating. Much greater is the feeling I get knowing that I helped someone upon completing a donation. Admittedly, receiving a $30 gift card has been a great incentive for me to donate as well.

Only recently have I begun to compare my passion for caring for the environment with my habit of donating blood. I would like to explore this connection I've made in this article.

We are all connected. By donating blood, we are recognizing and working to preserve the sanctity of another human life. By caring for the environment, we are working for the good of all people, regardless of any race or religion. Solidarity is a theme underlying this point.

Communication & Collaboration.
We cannot complete a blood donation alone, and we most certainly cannot save our planet by our own individual efforts. We have to work together to make a difference, once again regardless of race or religion.

Life-giving elixir. Blood serves a similar function to our bodies as water does to our planet. Both flow through their respective systems and serve to give life to each individual component working to uphold the stability of its system.

Setting a precedent. Donating blood and working to save our planet both are not easy. They require a level of sacrifice not everyone has the time nor will to make. By doing these hard things, however, we are setting a precedent for others to work in similar ways to uphold the sanctity of life.

A single blood donation can save up to three lives.

Some ideas behind this article were guided by the Earth Charter.

Originally published as: Seamus Haney, "Left on Red," *The Leaflet*, 4 Dec. 2024.

References
CarbonBrief. "What Is the Climate Impact of Eating Meat and Dairy?" *CarbonBrief*, interactive.carbonbrief.org/what-is-the-climate-impact-of-eating-meat-and-dairy/index.html.
Clark, Michael A., et al. "Multiple Health and Environmental Impacts of Foods." *Nature Communications*, vol. 14, no. 1, 2023, www.nature.com/articles/s41467-023-40899-2.
"Combating the Climate Crisis with Alternative Proteins." *Boston Consulting Group*, www.bcg.com/publications/2022/combating-climate-crisis-with-alternative-protein.

Earth Charter International. "Blood Donation and Its Close Relationship with Caring for the Planet." *Earth Charter*, earthcharter.org/blood-donation-and-its-close-relationship-with-caring-for-the-planet/.

Food and Agriculture Organization of the United Nations (FAO). "Open Knowledge Repository." *FAO*, openknowledge.fao.org/home.

"How Plant-Based Eating Impacts Your Water Footprint." *Kibo Foods*, kibofoods.us/blogs/news/how-plant-based-eating-impacts-your-water-footprint.

PBS NewsHour. "What Trump Has Said He Will Do on Day 1." *PBS NewsHour*, PBS, www.pbs.org/newshour/politics/what-trump-has-said-he-will-do-on-day-1.

"Plant-Based Diets: Be Healthier While Reducing Your Water Footprint." *Clean Water Action*, cleanwater.org/2020/11/19/plant-based-diets-be-healthier-while-reducing-your-water-footprint.

Strickler, Laura. "Matt Gaetz Says He Doesn't Plan to Rejoin Congress after Withdrawing Name from Attorney General Race." *NBC News*, www.nbcnews.com/politics/congress/matt-gaetz-says-doesnt-plan-rejoin-congress-withdrawing-name-attorney-rcna181378.

Ritchie, Hannah. "Land Use and Diets." *Our World in Data*, Global Change Data Lab, ourworldindata.org/land-use-diets.

Tilman, David, and Michael Clark. "Environmental Impacts of Dietary Choices." *Proceedings of the National Academy of Sciences*, vol. 117, no. 51, 2020, www.pnas.org/doi/full/10.1073/pnas.2013637118.

UNICEF. "Water Scarcity." *UNICEF*, www.unicef.org/wash/water-scarcity.

A Grinch Who Won't Steal Christmas

A Grinch Who Won't Steal Christmas

Climate change is all your fault.

At least, that's what 'Big Oil' wants you to think.

If everyone were to minimize their individual "carbon footprint" (the total amount of greenhouse gases an individual has contributed to producing) and their environmental impact, then we'll stop climate change. This, too, is what Big Oil wants you to think.

In truth, these claims hold some veracity. It's true that we all hold some level of responsibility for climate change, no matter when you were born, or what car you drive. If you've ever breathed, you're a contributor to climate change. We each have a carbon footprint.

But isn't it strange that the idea of a carbon footprint was popularized by British Petroleum, an oil company? In 2004, the company released its Carbon Footprint Calculator, in order to show that *your* normal daily life is largely responsible for "heating the globe."

Their plan was two-fold. They wanted to shovel the blame to someone else, and they wanted to isolate efforts against climate change. If they keep us focused on what we're doing wrong, they position the blame somewhere else and they keep us occupied figuring out how we can reduce our individual impact. They know that there is no way that we can effectively fight climate change by worrying about individual efforts alone. We have to work together.

We, at The Leaflet, are working to do just that. Starting today, we will be releasing a series titled "Wrapped in Hope," highlighting efforts all across Omaha from various high schools and grade schools against climate change. Our goal with this series is to bring light to their efforts, and by doing this, strengthen communication between schools so that each individual effort is no longer isolated. This series will come out once a day over the next six days. We hope you enjoy this series.

The Costco Phobio Program

Ever since the invention of the computer, our lives have sped up drastically. Technology has led us to sophisticate our calendars to the absolute maximum. Not only have our lives sped up, but so has the demand to recycle these technologies. Roughly 5.52 billion people logged on to the internet in the month of October (Kemp). Even if every two people shared a computer, there are still 2.26 billion computers in the world. Like all things, these computers don't last forever. Eventually, we'll have to do away with our outdated machines. So, what do we do with an old computer when we no longer have any use for it?

Costco's Phobio Program answers that question—and more. Not only does this program offer to recycle your overworked, dilapidated, often lethargically slow device, but they also offer to pay you for it. Even with outdated devices, many components can be stripped down and reused again. Metals, plastics, silicone, are all found abundantly in these devices. It takes a significant amount of energy to harvest and manufacture these materials. It makes much more sense financially for these companies to take advantage of the materials in these existing products—thus why they offer to pay you for them.

The program is fairly straightforward. On the Costco Phobio Program website, get a quote for your device, download and print a printing label Costco provides, and send the device along its way. Phobio will inspect your device for its worth, and provide you with a Costco Shop Card loaded with the trade-in value.

Even if your device doesn't have any trade-in value, this program is a great way to ensure your device does go to some good. At the very least, the components are being recycled.

This holiday season, consider selling your old electronics to this program or donate them to a similar program to recycle your electronics. Companies such as Call2Recycle, Earth911, and Greener Gadgets all offer donation programs suggested by the EPA. You are not compensated for the value of your device through these programs, but the process can often be simpler. And you are also given the peace of mind knowing that these precious materials are being reused and recycled—which is something I personally find incomparable to money.

Originally published as: "A Grinch Who Won't Steal Christmas," *The Leaflet*, 18 Dec. 2024.

References

"Electronics Donation and Recycling." *United States Environmental Protection Agency*, www.epa.gov/recycle/electronics-donation-and-recycling.

"Greener Gadgets." *Consumer Technology Association*, www.cta.tech/Landing-Pages/Greener-Gadgets.

Heglar, Mary Annáise. "Big Oil Coined 'Carbon Footprints' to Blame Us for Their Greed. Keep Them on the Hook."

"How to Recycle Electronics." *Call2Recycle*, www.call2recycle.org/locator/.

Kemp, Simon. "Global Digital Overview." *DataReportal*, datareportal.com/global-digital-overview.

Kristof, Nicholas. "Will This Be the Decade When We Finally Tackle Climate Change?" *The New York Times*, 31 Aug. 2021, www.nytimes.com/2021/08/31/opinion/climate-change-carbon-neutral.html.

"Search Recycling Locations." *Earth911*, search.earth911.com/.

Solnit, Rebecca, "Big Oil Coined 'Carbon Footprints' to Blame Us for Their Greed. Keep Them on the Hook." *The Guardian*, 23 Aug. 2021, www.

theguardian.com/commentisfree/2021/aug/23/big-oil-coined-carbon-footprints-to-blame-us-for-their-greed-keep-them-on-the-hook.

"Trade-In Program." *Costco*, www.costco.com/trade-in-program-phobio.html.

Synthetic vs. Natural

Synthetic Leaves

The popularity of solar technology and photovoltaics (electricity derived from light) has waned and waxed since its creation. Advances in the motorsport industry and renewable energy in homes have shed a kind light on the potential for solar power. Even with the potential of solar, there is a considerable backlash for the technology. Perhaps the biggest argument against solar is that it takes up space. City-dwellers don't have room for it in their bustling urban landscapes; country-dwellers don't want their land to be taken away from them.

Space, especially in our rapidly growing world, is at a premium. But, new methods of implementing solar alongside existing industries have sprung up and, suddenly, if you own a plot of land, you may not have to pick between solar or not solar. It may not be so black *or* white.

Speaking of black and white, an example dealing with cows is a prime demonstration of this type of implementation. Matt Wilson is a professor of animal sciences at West Virginia University and has been experimenting with agrivoltaics and cows. Agrivoltaics is simply using solar for a dual purpose—as in this article, this is with cows and their grazing grounds. The goal of his study is to determine how the cows behave around the solar panels. Wilson hopes that there will be a balance in grazing grounds between the cows and the panels. He hopes that this will be a significant source of income for farmers without any deficit to their current income.

Although results from this study have not been published, the idea sheds kind light again on the use of solar power in our world—working towards a compromise that benefits the environment without any inconvenience to the landowner. With this compromise, the future for solar holds even more potential than before.

Ambition to Counteract Ambition

The phrase "It Takes Two to Make the World Go Round" implies collaboration. It implies that we cannot work alone to accomplish something big; we have to work together. When we fail to work together, we not only inhibit progress and development, but oftentimes our own ambition counters others' ambitions.

When the ambitions of humanity counter the ambitions of wildlife, humanity often wins, at least in the short term.

If there is anything that is stronger than man, it is nature itself. Examples of nature's power are everywhere. But in a more literal sense, gorillas are much stronger than humans. Gorillas are about 10 times stronger than the average human ("Gorilla Strength and Habits"). For the gym-goers out there, that means an adult male Silverback Gorilla can bench about 4,000 pounds ("Gorilla Strength").

Gorillas, like all larger mammals, play a key role in their ecosystem, dispersing seeds and making way for new foliage ("How Helping"). Bringing this article full circle, Gorillas are an endangered species because of humanity's selfish ambition impacting their environments; *all* Gorilla species are classified as endangered.

While there is no enlightening story that this article leads to, I would like to use this article to present this website (www.iucnredlist.org) as a tool for any research you wish to conduct on your own about wildlife conservation. The International Union for Conservation of Nature is responsible for the website "Red List." This website is a powerful tool in which you can find out the status, region it inhabits, and taxonomy of any animal. I highly recommend you spend a few short minutes searching around this website. There is so much to learn.

Originally published as: Seamus Haney, "Synthetic Leaves," *The Leaflet*, 20 Nov. 2024 and Seamus Haney, "Ambition to Counteract Ambition," *The Leaflet*, 6 Nov. 2024.

References

"Gorilla Strength." *Kabira Gorilla Safaris*, kabiragorillasafaris.com/gorilla-strength.

"Gorilla Strength and Habits." *International Fund for Animal Welfare (IFAW)* , www.ifaw.org/animals/gorillas.

"How Helping Gorillas Helps Forests." *World Wildlife Fund Magazine*, Winter 2023, www.worldwildlife.org/magazine/issues/winter-2023/articles/how-helping-gorillas-helps-forests.

"IUCN Red List of Threatened Species." *International Union for Conservation of Nature*, www.iucnredlist.org/.

"Solar Panels and Cattle Grazing Lands." *West Virginia University*, wvutoday.wvu.edu/stories/2024/06/11/wvu-animal-scientists-say-solar-panels-could-make-cattle-grazing-lands-more-profitable.

A Failure of Leadership: U.S. and Abroad

Insufficient Aid to Developing Countries

Our world is thriving. Our world is falling apart. Both are true.

Your perception of the world's state may be dramatically different from someone else's depending on where you live. Living in a developing country, your perception is probably grim—your life overshadowed by the realities of climate change.

This difference in perception was seen evidently in the 29th Conference of the Parties concluding yesterday. The conference ended with a deal for developed countries to pay poorer, often still developing, countries $300 billion annually to combat the catastrophic impacts of climate change.

This sounds like a lot. It's not. Many of the "rich countries" representatives were "amazed" by the discontent over this deal from developing countries ("EPA Staff React"). For good reason—this number would need to be 4.3 times higher in order to effectively help these countries.

India's representative, Chandni Raina, referred to the deal as "abysmally poor," and called the deal "nothing more than an optical illusion." China and Saudi Arabia are still classified as developing countries, raising the question of their responsibility in advancing environmental justice efforts of which developed countries cannot currently.

"We have arrived at the boundary between what is politically achievable today in developed countries and what would make a difference in developing countries," said Avinash Persaud, special advisor on climate change to the President of the Inter-American Development Bank.

This story brings into light once more the importance of our *individual* efforts against climate change. We, at The Leaflet, want to remind you that by subscribing to this newsletter, you are making a difference. But don't stop there; don't stop recycling, don't stop composting, don't stop being mindful of your practices, don't stop educating yourself about what you can do.

Don't stop changing the world for the betterment of others and our planet.

What a Trump Administration Could Mean for Climate Change

As Election Day shrinks further in the rearview mirror, many Americans are scrambling to piece together what a second Trump Presidency will look like.

Among Mr. Trump's claims preceding the election were his plans for environmental policy. We have compiled a list of his claims to summarize:

1. Mr. Trump will replace the EPA's staff with his own, seeking to undermine any progress the administration has made, most recently in the protection of clean drinking water (The Guardian). Russel Vought, Mr. Trump's director of the Office of Management and Budget, said recently, "We want to put them in trauma," when referring to shutting down the EPA's funding (The Guardian).
2. Lee Zeldin was selected to lead the EPA (D. Smith). Zeldin has voted against several measures the EPA has led, including replacing lead service lines across the country ("Trump's Strategy"). "Our lives, our livelihoods, and our collective future cannot afford Lee Zeldin," says Ben Jealous, Executive Director of the Sierra Club (D. Smith).
3. Mr. Trump still dismisses climate change as a "hoax" ("The Stakes"). In the wake of Hurricane Helene, he referred to global warming as "one of the greatest scams."
4. Mr. Trump has vowed to undo parts of the Inflation Reduction Act ("The Stakes").
5. Mr. Trump says he will pull the U.S. out of the Paris climate accord. ("The Stakes").
6. Mr. Trump will "expedite federal drilling permits, speed up approvals for fracked gas pipelines, and open up 'vast stores' of oil and gas for extraction on public lands" (M. Smith). "Drill, baby, drill," says Mr. Trump, when referring to oil (E&E News).
7. Mr. Trump has pledged to enforce a 60% tariff on China ("Trump's Strategy"). Who produces the most solar panels? China ("Largest").

The biggest impact of Trump's environmental policies? Wasted time ("The Most Consequential").

Republican or Democrat, Liberal or Conservative, we all have a responsibility to preserve the world around us. In the wake of an administration so determined to reverse any environmental progress, we cannot give up hope.

A Trump Administration will not be the worst thing that will happen for environmental progress, because there will be a reaction to his policies, stronger than any hindrances he's made. But a reaction cannot happen without action. We have to act—now.

Keep recycling, keep composting, keep learning. Keep sharing this newsletter with everyone you know. When we have an informed citizenry, environmental policies under Mr. Trump cannot win.

Orignally published as Seamus Haney, "Insufficient Aid to Developing Countries," *The Leaflet*, 25 Nov. 2024 and Seamus Haney, "What a Trump Administration Could Mean for Climate Change," *The Leaflet*, 13 Nov. 2024.

References

"EPA Staff React to Trump's Second Term." *BBC News*, www.bbc.com/news/articles/cp35rrvv2dpo.

"Largest Solar Panel Manufacturers." *SunSave Energy*, www.sunsave.energy/solar-panels-advice/solar-energy/largest-manufacturers#.

"The Most Consequential Impact of Trump's Climate Policies Was Wasted Time." *National Geographic*, www.nationalgeographic.com/environment/article/most-consequential-impact-of-trumps-climate-policies-wasted-time.

"The Paris Agreement." *UNFCCC*, unfccc.int/process-and-meetings/the-paris-agreement.

Smith, David. "Lee Zeldin Appointed EPA Administrator." *NBC News*, 11 Nov. 2024, www.nbcnews.com/politics/donald-trump/trump-taps-lee-zeldin-lead-environmental-protection-agency-rcna179658.

Smith, Michael. "Inside Trump's Plan to Bulldoze American Climate Policy." *Sierra Club*, 2024, www.sierraclub.org/sierra/inside-trump-s-plan-bulldoze-american-climate-policy.

"The Stakes on Climate." *The New York Times*, 11 Oct. 2024, www.nytimes.com/2024/10/11/briefing/the-stakes-on-climate.html.

"Trump's Strategy for Tariffs and Trade." *CNN*, 8 Nov. 2024, www.cnn.com/2024/11/08/politics/tariffs-donald-trump-strategy/index.html.

WHY HASTINGS?

Go Confidently
Your transition from college to a career begins your first semester. Every class, internship, research study and extracurricular activity adds to your experience. You'll **become your best** self, ready to go somewhere.

Your Experience Matters
Athletics. Band. Theatre. Art. Choir. Speech. Esports. Media. Experience all the things you love right here—with a scholarship to help you pay for college. Go Eroncos!

Engaged Learning
Our block schedule. It's a difference maker that lets you take just one or two classes at a time. The result? Students report less stress. And professors? They see improved performance.

SCAN HERE

Want to learn more? Schedule your personalized visit today!

HASTINGS COLLEGE

HASTINGS.EDU/VISIT